George McT. Kahin

THE PHILIPPINES:

Public Policy and National
Economic Development

THE PHILIPPINES:

Public Policy and National

Economic Development

✦

By Frank H. Golay

CORNELL UNIVERSITY

CORNELL UNIVERSITY PRESS

Ithaca, New York

This work has been brought to
publication with the assistance of
a grant from the Ford Foundation.

CORNELL UNIVERSITY PRESS

First published 1961

Library of Congress Catalog Card Number: 61-7869

PRINTED IN THE UNITED STATES OF AMERICA
BY VAIL-BALLOU PRESS, INC.

To My Mother

ALICE HINDMAN GOLAY

Foreword

THIS foreword will be helpful to the extent that awareness of the objectives of the author is communicated to the reader. Basically this study is an attempt to examine the role of public policy in postwar Philippine *national* economic development. An essential component of *national* economic development in the Philippines, as in all modern societies, is economic growth, i.e., increasing per capita real income. The concept of *national* economic development is, however, poorly approximated by economic growth, as the former must include such values as economic nationalism, industrialization, economic sovereignty, and external stability, which may involve substantial conflict with the pursuit of economic growth.

The purpose of the work is primarily descriptive rather than prescriptive. This is not to exclude appraisal and prescription in terms of appropriate economic criteria, but these are not the basic goals of the study. For example, industrialization is a major objective of Philippine economic policy. Yet there is little objective content in economics which would support assignment of a high priority to Philippine industrialization. However, merely to deplore industrialization as high cost and irrational is sterile if Filipino society is determined to industrialize and major aspects of policy are intelligible only in terms of such a goal.

The Philippine economy is essentially an enterprise type of economy with liberal rewards for entrepreneurial initiative. This is not to say that competition is the dominant characteristic of the economy but, rather, to emphasize the role of entrepreneurial initiative in organizing resources. The profit motive is the goad, but competition is not the regulator. Instead, the state by dispensing the largess inherent in its powers to tax and to spend—and in its equally important power, not to tax—tends to regulate the intensity of the profit motive. The Philippines has maintained a broad spectrum of legislative controls ostensibly designed to regulate private economic activity. Understanding of Philippine public economic policy turns, however, on an awareness that regulation results primarily from manipulation by the state of the intensity of economic incentives to individual action.

A word of apology is in order at this point. Following an introduction to the Philippine economy, including a brief survey of postwar economic history, the analysis is organized functionally by areas of public policy. Unfortunately, such an organization is repetitive. Economic policies are intimately related and do not lend themselves to compartmentalization. For example, in the Philippines, as in less-developed countries generally, monetary policy is preoccupied by management of the external disequilibrium and is therefore inextricably involved with exchange rate and commercial policy.

There is in the Philippines, as in all societies, an essential unity of public policy reflecting the goals and values of the society and circumscribed by the realities of integration into the world community. Functional organization of an analysis of public economic policy detracts from the unitary conception of policy. Therefore, there devolves upon the reader the additional task of striving to conceive the unity of policy.

The statistical analysis terminates with 1958. This reflects the availability of data. Otherwise the analysis has been extended through mid-1959, with some references to later events or conditions, although there may be significant gaps in information concerning developments following 1958. There is no particular logic to the terminal period of the study: the year 1959 was not a significant watershed in Philippine economic policy, as the years 1950–51 and 1954 were.

This study is the product of many influences. It reflects the contagious enthusiasm and inquisitiveness of the staff and students of the Cornell Southeast Asia Program. A comparable contribution has been made by the abrasive and illuminating give-and-take among the staff and students of the Department of Economics at Cornell. The analysis borrows blatantly from the ideas of many students of economic growth. The influence of W. Arthur Lewis, J. S. Furnivall, Ragnar Nurkse, and Joseph Schumpeter will be apparent. Mention should be made of Benjamin Higgins, whose analysis of Philippine economic development is consistently provocative. Reed J. Irvine read and criticized the manuscript. He will be aware of the magnitude of his contribution as well as of the stubbornness of the author.

The study originated in a year of field research in the Philippines during 1955–1956, supported by a Fulbright postdoctoral research scholarship as well as a Cornell Southeast Asia Program travel grant. Work in the Philippines benefited from the kindness of many people. Mr. Sixto K. Roxas, manager, Department of Economics, Research and Statistics, Philippine National Bank, was a sympathetic listener and perceptive critic. Particularly generous with time and research resources were Mrs. Fanny Garcia, director, and the staff of the Department of Research, Central Bank of the Philippines, and Dr. Gabriel Bernardo, director, and the staff of the University Library, University of the Philippines. Dr. Alfredo Morales, secretary, United States Educational (Fulbright) Foundation in the Philippines, made a major contribution to the productivity of all Fulbright grantees. The student of contemporary Philippine economic problems must also acknowledge a debt to Mr. A. V. H. Hartendorp, editor, *American Chamber of Commerce Journal,* for his comprehensive and discriminating reporting of postwar economic developments. The study has also benefited from the insights of Henry Brodie, Thomas R. McHale, Horst von Oppenfeld, David Wurfel, and Russell Moran, all competent students of the Philippine economy. The map on page 33 was prepared by Dr. Frederick L. Wermstedt. I acknowledge my substantial indebtedness to Tazu Warner, who typed the various versions of this study. Last, but not least, Clara, Frank, John, David, and Jane were patient and understanding.

FRANK H. GOLAY

Cornell University
August 1960

Contents

Tables

Notes and Abbreviations

The Philippine monetary unit is the peso (₱) and the official exchange parity is two pesos per dollar. Malacañan is the residence of the Philippine President and also refers to the Executive Office. The date of Philippine public laws is the date they are signed by the President. The Philippine fiscal year ends June 30. When reference is made to a period of more than one fiscal year, the years given are the years in which the beginning and the ending fiscal years terminate. For example, "fiscal years 1953–1957" refers to the five-year period from July 1, 1952, to June 30, 1957. Complete notation is provided in the initial reference to a source. When the publisher is not given in the first reference, this information does not appear on the publication.

The following abbreviations will be unfamiliar to a number of readers:

R.P., Republic of the Philippines
FAO, Food and Agricultural Organization
ECAFE, Economic Commission for Asia and the Far East
A.C.C. *Journal, American Chamber of Commerce* (Philippines) *Journal*
NEC, National Economic Council (Philippines)

DANR, Department of Agriculture and Natural Resources (Philippines)

The following abbreviations are used in the tables:

n.a. = not available
n.r. = not reported
N.A. = not applicable
—   = negligible amount

THE PHILIPPINES:

*Public Policy and National
Economic Development*

· I ·

The Role of the State

THIS is a case study of Philippine economic policy as it relates to the maintenance of accelerated *national* economic development.

As a first approximation, *national* economic development is considered to be measured by economic growth, i.e., increasing output per head of population or increasing per capita real income. While such a definition is subject to grievous shortcomings, it has two advantages.[1] First, it is relatively objective and subject to quantification, which facilitates communication. Second, such a definition is widely used and reflects the fact that economic growth is a universal goal in all modern societies. This is not to say that economic growth is at all times the dominant or overriding goal of social organization but to claim less strongly that it is an important goal which competes with other widely (or strongly) held goals. The goals of society may be complementary in the sense of being joint products or, at another extreme, they may be mutually exclusive. The structure of priorities assigned to policy goals is unstable over time, and material progress may be subordinated at different times to different goals.

[1] For the purposes of this study the terms economic growth and economic development are synonymous. For a discussion of the issues involved in defining economic development, see Jacob Viner, *International Trade and Economic Development* (Glencoe, Ill.: Free Press, 1952), pp. 120–150.

1

Economic growth may be derived from a number of sources—some fortuitous and some the result of deliberate action, either individual or communal. For example, fortuitous changes in demand conditions may sharply change relative prices and produce significant changes in per capita real income.[2]

If we abstract from such fortuitous changes, economic growth depends, in the first instance, on the availability of natural resources and on human behavior. It is obvious that poverty in, or inaccessibility of, natural resources can limit growth of output per head, and that a considerable part of the differences in economic growth of various countries may be explained by different resource endowments. It is also clear that there are great differences in growth between countries with comparable resources. Students of the Philippines are in agreement that the islands' endowment of climate, soil fertility, configuration, topography, minerals, and forestry and fisheries resources is not illiberal and will support a rewarding rate of economic growth.

If fortuitous changes are assumed away and if adequate supplies of natural resources exist, it is appropriate to consider economic growth as resulting from two types of human behavior. First is the will to economize, i.e., to modify human behavior in ways productive of goods and services. Changing human behavior may increase the availability of labor as a resource or it may increase the yield from a given input of resources. The will to economize is manifested in intensity of effort, innovation, specialization, risk taking, occupational and geographic mobility, and so forth. Needless to say, the intensity of the effort to economize varies widely between countries and over time for any country. The intensity and the diversity of the effort to economize reflect the accumulation of experience embedded in custom and tradition, the impact of technological progress, and, within narrow limits, the institutions and incentives created by social organization to promote social and economic progress.

Second is the accumulation of producible economic resources—tangible and intangible. Producible resources accumulate as the result of the allocation of labor and other economic resources to this purpose. At this level of abstraction, the principal producible economic resources are capital resources, human resources, and knowledge. Capital resources are accumulated by the application of existing economic re-

---

[2] Such a development is illustrated by the movement of prices of primary products in the last half of 1950 and the first half of 1951.

sources to natural resources to create physical capital in the form of improvements to land, plant and equipment, housing, stocks of commodities, and so forth. Similarly, intangible human resources and knowledge are produced by the allocation of existing labor and capital resources to this purpose. Such activity would include expenditures on education, public health services, experimentation, and research.

It is obvious that this is only one among a number of alternative ways to organize analysis of accelerated economic growth. Current discussion of this problem is handicapped by an arbitrary definition of "investment" (capital) inherited from social accounting. For example, expenditures on housing, construction of a movie theatre, or the accumulation of surplus agricultural commodities under a price support program are included in the accepted concept of investment, which tends to serve as the measure of capital accumulation. On the other hand, expenditures on agricultural experimentation and extension services, provision of teaching services, public health services, and the like are included in consumption. There can be little question that the intangible producible resources created by the latter activities may be more durable and more productive of income than the categories of investment cited above.[3]

While accelerated economic growth requires the allocation of existing producible resources to the accumulation of additional resources, economic growth and expanding welfare always occur together. The fundamental problem of accelerating economic growth is not to reduce consumption out of a given level of income but to organize the society to ensure that a relatively large portion of increments of output (income) is allocated to accumulation of producible resources. The "cost" of accelerated economic growth is a willingness to devise institutions and policies and to change existing institutions and policies in ways that are productive of more intensive economic activity. This is not to say that the task of accelerating economic growth is easy; it is extremely difficult. The point is that there is no material cost of accelerated economic growth. The "cost" of growth is social change— the disintegration of traditional societies, the harshness of industrial or bureaucratic regimentation, the rapid growth of population and

[3] Analysis of economic growth is also handicapped by an intellectual tradition within which economists have frequently attempted to use the methodology of a trinity of productive factors—land, labor, and capital—to handle problems inappropriate to such organization.

urbanization, the decline of institutions which contribute to individual security, and a lag in the creation of substitute institutions.

Producible economic resources accumulate as the result of two types of decisions: individual decisions to allocate existing resources to production of such resources and communal decisions to do so. The importance of public policies to such decisions is obvious. With regard to the individual decisions, the role of public policy can be critically important in establishing the relationship between economic activity and the rewards for such activity. With regard to the communal decisions, governments are devised to make such decisions while the agencies of government at various levels give effect to them.

There are a number of roads to economic development. Alternative types of social organization have demonstrated capacity to promote material progress. Similarly, accelerated economic growth has been achieved by a number of alternative types of economic organization. At still another level, economic development has resulted from diverse combinations and permutations of industrialization, agricultural development, international specialization, and the like. Finally, it is important to remember that there are an infinite number of alternative rates of economic growth. The point at which economic growth is assessed as accelerated is essentially arbitrary.

What is the proper role of the state in accelerating economic development? The answer to this question is circumscribed by a more basic decision: How shall the resources of the society be organized? The choice of economic organization—capitalism, mixed economy, democratic socialism, authoritarian socialism—will be made by the society through some process of communal decision making, i.e., government.[4] The Philippine society, for better or for worse, has made an unambiguous decision to organize its economy on the basis of private initiative. Central to analysis of public policy in the Philippines is the fact that the Philippine economy is essentially an enterprise economy in which economic activity by the individual is rewarded liberally. This enterprise type of economic organization is a legacy of American colonial rule, but during the past decade and a half of Philippine independence the indications have been strong that Philippine society does not intend to make substantial changes in the present enterprise economy.

[4] It is quite evident that, if interpreted strictly, all economies are mixed economies. Mixed economies can be predominantly capitalist or predominantly socialist.

Given the choice of an enterprise type of organization, economic growth will be critically dependent upon the quality and quantity of entrepreneurship. A significant number of individuals must emerge in response to strong incentives to initiative and enterprise—individuals motivated to produce rather than consume. Only if entrepreneurship adequate in quantity and quality appears is such an economy likely to produce economic growth sufficiently rapid to submerge the social tensions inherent in the gross inequalities on which such a system is based.

Within the basic framework of capitalism, what is the proper role of the state in accelerating economic growth? First, the state should participate directly in the accumulation of producible economic resources, tangible and intangible. The state is responsible for maintaining a high and expanding level of governmental services and social investment.

In an economy in which private net investment accounts for less than 5 per cent of national income and in which population is growing 2 to 3 per cent annually, economic growth will tend to be slow, if it occurs. In such an economy the government clearly has a role to play in accumulating capital through public saving and investment. No competent observer would contend that the Philippines has enough schools, roads, harbor facilities, irrigation works, power facilities, waterworks, good housing, and so forth.

Similarly, the production of many categories of intangible producible resources such as education, agricultural research and extension services, and public health services, as well as pure research, should result primarily from governmental activity and expenditures.

While economic institutions—migration of people, private foreign investment, economic aid in the form of grants, loans, and technical assistance—exist to transfer producible resources from one country to another, accelerated economic growth is essentially a national responsibility. It is unlikely that transfers of producible resources from the outside world will account for more than a marginal part of future Philippine economic growth.[5] First, Philippine nationalism will almost certainly be a continuing obstacle to private foreign in-

---

[5] Savings of foreigners transferred to the Philippines through the current account of the balance of payments have accounted for the principal part of Philippine net investment in the postwar period. As the Philippine economy has expanded, this outside contribution has decreased, both relatively and absolutely.

vestment. Second, the motivation of unrequited resource transfers
in the form of economic aid, reparations, and the like is relatively
weak and subject to rapid change. Finally, with possibly a few exceptions—Canada and Israel are prominent—international transfers of
producible resources do not account for more than a minor part of
the accumulation of producible resources accompanying sustained,
accelerated economic growth.[6]

Accelerated economic growth has been accomplished by national
efforts in the past, and few grounds exist for believing that such will
not be true of the Philippines. In any case the Philippines must seek
a national solution and should consider resource transfers from the
outside as windfalls which lighten the task but do not dispose of
the problem.

Second, the state is responsible for the maintenance of a structure
of institutions and incentives which will tend to maintain a high and
expanding level of private accumulation of producible resources. Inherent in government is the power to influence economic activity—by
"carrot or stick." Public power includes considerable capacity to
coerce citizens to perform, or not to perform, economic activities.
The Philippines has acquired considerable experience with exchange,
import and price controls, minimum wage legislation, and regulation
of tenancy in attempting to coerce private economic activity in
accordance with economic policy goals.

More important is the capacity of the state to use its command over
resources to establish incentives to private enterprise. Government
revenues are used to subsidize private economic activity both directly
and through functionally specialized credit institutions. Indirect subsidization through protection has traditionally been a dominant motivation of private enterprise. In the Philippines the state, by remitting
taxes and by forgoing its claim to the windfall arising out of import
restriction, has established powerful incentives for private enterprise.

Third, in a less-developed country the state has a limited responsibility to engage in directly productive activity, which in an industrialized, enterprise economy would be allocated to individual initiative.
The appropriate levels and techniques of government participation

[6] The 38 million immigrants received by the United States to 1920 represented
much more than a minor contribution to the resource accumulation which accounted
for economic growth in the United States. This institution is irrelevant to the
solution of the problem of resource accumulation in the Philippines.

in directly productive activity in the Philippines are indeterminate. Suffice it to say that the Philippines has acquired considerable experience with government participation in directly productive activity, and as a result of such experiences there is currently a tendency to shift from direct participation through government enterprise to indirect participation by providing capital through specialized, subsidized credit institutions.

Fourth, the state is responsible for establishing and maintaining a consistent body of policy priorities appropriate to the pursuit of the economic goals of the society. This is not to say that public policy should be inflexible, but rather to call attention to the fact that the success with which government participates in accelerated economic growth is highly dependent upon the will to see policies carried through to fruition. There are so many things to be done in less-developed societies that will obviously contribute to economic progress that the selection of a productive set of investment alternatives is not difficult. Within the framework of the type of economic organization selected by the society, the choice of particular activities—investment decisions—is less important than the maintenance of the particular hierarchy of consistent policy priorities initially selected.

The maintenance of policy priorities can be facilitated by partial economic planning. Philippine economic planning as that of other nonauthoritarian societies is essentially a function of the extent to which the government directly disposes of economic resources. In the case of the Philippines, the public sector presently accounts for approximately 10 per cent of economic activity, and there are few indications that this ratio is expanding. Under such circumstances planning will tend to remain partial and will be circumscribed by the level of public economic activity. The principal value of partial economic planning on such a scale is to maintain pressure on public resource allocation to achieve a succession of rationally determined economic goals. Although policies are needed to ensure that public expenditures are as productive as possible, more pressing is the need to expand governmental economic activities, which presently include little margin for resource accumulation over and above current consumption of goods and services through the budget.

Public policies are means to ends—the goals or values of the society. Material progress is only one among a number of competing goals, all of which generate more or less clamorous priorities. Social goals are rarely mutually exclusive. The pursuit of diverse goals, however, will invariably involve policy conflicts of greater or less severity. Among the goals or values of Philippine society the pursuit of which may involve conflict with the pursuit of economic growth, the following are assigned high priority.

The goal of national economic development envisaged by the Filipino elite is dominated by industrialization. Filipinos believe that their colonial economic development was not in the national interest. They believe that the nature of their economic specialization is attributable either to the exploitative nature of colonialism or to their late entry into the main stream of material progress. Filipinos are convinced that colonial specialization has resulted in instability of prices and incomes and that the prices received for their exports of primary commodities must inevitably decline relative to the prices they must pay for imports. They are aware that colonial economic development has denied them the very real external economies attending industrialization—the specialization at the level of the firm which must await growth in the size of the market, the diffusion of technical skills and attitudes, and the full utilization of social investment. Filipinos are very much aware that the colonial type of economy is weak in the face of external aggression and that the sovereignty to which they aspire is dependent upon industrialization.

The present character of Philippine specialization—dominated by primary production for export and by commercial activity and food production in the domestic sector—is a function of the markets to which the owners of Philippine resources have access. There is widespread belief that rapid Philippine industrialization can be sustained by policies which reserve the domestic market to national producers. Although the argument will be explored more fully later, it will have to suffice for the present to suggest that protection may be a necessary condition for economic development (industrialization) but it is probably not a sufficient condition.

The goals of accelerated economic growth and industrialization do not necessarily coincide. Bypassing the existing structure of comparative advantage will tend to sacrifice real income in the short run and may do so over the longer haul.

A social goal assigned relatively high priority reflects economic nationalism narrowly conceived, i.e., a determination to Filipinize the economy. Colonial economic development resulted in a dual economy in which a relatively modern commerce-oriented sector grew along-side a traditional, technologically backward, subsistence agricultural sector. Not only were these sectors economically isolated, but the ownership of the modern sector tended to be vested in the economically rational Chinese minority as well as in the dominant Western minority. Business acumen and a high marginal propensity to save and invest productively were richly rewarded by the laissez-faire economy exported to the Philippines in the latter part of the colonial period. Such qualities were slow to appear in the tradition-dominated Philippine society, and Filipinos tended to stand by and watch the alieniza-tion of their economy.

Filipinos have displayed great energy and initiative in devising policies to contribute to the Filipinization of their economy. Such policies range from nationalization of directly productive activity through social investment, to direct and indirect subsidization of Filipino entrepreneurial activity, to direct prohibition of alien partic-ipation in particular economic activities. The potential conflict be-tween pursuit of de-alienization and increasing per capita real income is obvious. Filipinos may now be more interested in nationalizing the current pie than in maximizing the size of the pie.

Still another value assigned high priority by Philippine society is maintenance of a tolerable equilibrium in economic relations with the outside world. Such an equilibrium is conceived to involve main-tenance of the pre-World War II exchange parity through stringent exchange and import controls. These policies will be examined in detail later, but here it may be suggested that the pursuit of such an ex-ternal equilibrium may conflict with achievement of accelerated eco-nomic growth. For example, the adverse consequences of such policies for private foreign investment are well known. More important may be the impact of such policies on the availability of foreign exchange. The Philippines has been bypassed by the rapid postwar expansion in world trade, and it is quite possible that the exchange rate policy is primarily responsible.

Another value widely desired in the Philippines is greater economic and political equality. Wealth and income in the Philippines are highly concentrated, and the numerically dominant peasantry exist on minimum requirements of food, shelter, medical services, educa-tion, and so forth. Democratic political institutions in the Philippines are not unfavorable to the appearance of policies which promote

welfare objectives, although in the past the politically dominant
agricultural aristocracy has been able to minimize change in this
direction. It is not clear that the pursuit of greater equality will
promote accelerated Philippine economic growth.[7] Alternatively, material progress sustained in the past has not been sufficient to submerge
social tensions attributable to economic and political inequality.
The priority assigned welfare objectives will tend to be magnified
with continued improvement in the functioning of democratic political
institutions.

Other values are capable of generating priorities which compete
with the priority assigned to accelerated economic growth. For
example, political and economic stability are important concerns of
the politically dominant elements in the society. Inasmuch as economic development involves socially disturbing change, there may
be substantial areas of conflict between these goals. Economic interests with a stake in the *status quo* are diffused throughout the
society and presently represent a formidable obstacle to change.

We are now in a position to refine the concept of *national* economic
development, which in the opening paragraphs was tentatively defined
in purely material terms. *National* economic development as conceived
by Filipino society is now defined as *relatively and absolutely increasing per capita real income accruing to Filipinos, with an increasing relative share of aggregate income generated by manufacturing and
a diminishing relative share of aggregate income generated by specialization and external trade in primary products and, equally important,
both an absolute and relative increase in the share of Filipinos in the
ownership and management of the productive assets of the economy.*

The role of the state in accelerating economic growth can, of
course, be assessed in terms of diverse criteria. A persistent effort has
been made to relate the policy description and appraisal of this study
to the Filipino concept of national economic development. The study
attempts to answer the following questions: What are the motivations
of Philippine public policies? What are the economic consequences of
public policies? Unfortunately, such a frame of reference will not be

---

[7] An important factor in the economic growth of capitalist societies is the concentration of increments of income in the form of profits, which are diverted to
the entrepreneurs or, through the institution of the corporation, to the managers
of large enterprises. These classes in a developing capitalist society are strongly
motivated both to innovate and to accumulate resources.

communicated to all readers. Some will be impatient for description
and appraisal conforming to a particular image of underdevelopment,
or a particular policy prescription for accelerated economic growth,
or both.

The theory (or theories) of accelerated economic growth encom-
passes many controversial issues and questions of relative emphasis.
An attempt to appraise public policy can rarely hope to produce categorical answers. However, an appraisal of policy can be useful if it
does no more than identify policy and indicate the nature of policy
relationships. Economic policy formulation, in the Philippines as
elsewhere, is confused by controversy. Protagonists of a policy change
are prone to exaggerate the alleged beneficial consequences, and opponents are equally energetic in pointing out the disastrous consequences of a change in policy. The student of Philippine economic
policy must penetrate the protective coloring of slogans before he
can hope to identify a particular policy and ultimately to appraise
it.

The analysis of the contribution of public policy to Philippine
economic development is essentially critical in this study. To a considerable extent the critical nature of the analysis is attributable to
the present state of the theory of economic development. Speculation regarding the processes of economic growth has been essentially
normative and *a priori*. Such "theorizing" has involved an abstraction
—a stereotype of the average underdeveloped country—which is more
or less related to any particular country. The Philippine economy departs from the stereotype of the underdeveloped country in many
substantive aspects.

A second source of criticism is the basic harshness of the emerging
economic organization. Corollary to Philippine reliance on private
enterprise is the conclusion that the Philippines is not a welfare state.
Income and wealth are concentrated, political power is highly correlated with wealth, and welfare goals are assigned low priority.
Western observers respond uniformly with compassion for the submerged mass of Filipinos who have been bypassed by postwar material progress but who are subject to increasing insecurity and dislocation.

The foregoing comments anticipating the critical character of this
work lead to a final observation. If qualitative changes in the
human factor which support economic growth occur, such growth

will take place in extremes of policy environments. This is not to say that public policy cannot influence economic growth; it obviously can. Rather, it is to propose that the nonauthoritarian state probably cannot initiate and sustain economic growth in the absence of intensification of the will to economize and accumulate producible resources. The organization of this study is felt to be an appropriate framework within which the Philippine economy can be examined and reflects the author's intrinsic interest in understanding the motivations and consequences of Philippine public policy.

· II ·

The Social Environment

of Economic Policy

AN attempt to describe the social environment of Philippine economic policy must be prefaced by the warning that the inevitable generalizations attending such an attempt are of varying validity. There is widespread agreement among observers that Philippine society is undergoing rapid social change. The processes of change are not uniformly distributed and presently contribute to diversity rather than unity of the society. Uneven social change is superimposed on wide regional differences in culture and economic organization. The Philippines has vital frontiers which contrast sharply with the traditional areas of high population density and subsistence agriculture. Still more striking is the distinctiveness of Manila, which tends to be the dominant source of impressions of Philippine society.

Manila is a dynamic, cosmopolitan façade to the Philippines. It is the domicile of an articulate legislature and an extensive bureaucracy staffed by relatively well-educated, competent civil servants. Diplomatic missions, military activities, and functionally specialized alien populations contribute to the flavor of Manila. Manila has the highest proportion of college and university students of any large city in the world, and it is well served by news media and other cultural amenities.[1] It is surrounded by burgeoning industrial and residential suburbs, and the visitor cannot but be impressed by the pervasive evidences of an emerging middle class. Philippine manufacturing activity is highly concentrated in Manila, which is also the principal entrepôt for the lucrative import trade.

But Manila is not the Philippines. Although it dominates important economic, cultural, and political activities, it includes no more than 6 to 8 per cent of the Philippine population. The economic activity of Manila, including government, commerce, finance, and limited industrialization to supply the domestic market, is, in an important respect, parasitic. The Manila economy is dependent upon economic development of Philippine resources and upon continuation of public policies which favor the functional specialization of Manila.

The description that follows is an attempt to identify dominant elements in the environment of Philippine economic policy. It is not a description of Manila—or of the rural Philippines. It is hoped that it is related to a more useful, composite image of Philippine society.

Philippine economic progress is conditioned by dominant elements in the cultural heritage of the Filipinos. Economic institutions derive their substance, if not their form, from the interplay of diverse Malayan, Spanish, and American elements in the Philippine culture. Similarly, such motive forces of social change as nationalism, religion, co-operation, and individualism are shaped by the heterogeneous influences in Philippine history.

As elsewhere in Southeast Asia, the social organization is familial. The basic units or building blocks of Philippine social organization are the elementary family, which includes the father, mother, and children, and the bilateral extended family, which embraces all relatives of the father and mother. This cultural factor has great economic significance and is the principal feature distinguishing the social environment from that found in the West. Spanish colonization in the Philippines, motivated by proselytizing zeal and highly dependent upon the church for administration, found the extended family with its matriarchal overtones a suitable vehicle for religious disci-

---

[1] In 1953–54 there were 93,488 students enrolled in colleges in Manila plus 15,140 students in special vocational courses. The population of Manila in 1948 was 983,900.

pline and political organization. Under the Spanish this institution flourished, and individualism remained relatively submerged.

The intense family loyalties of Filipinos result in minimum identification of individual welfare with activities of a group larger than the family. Security and status are attributable to family membership, and basic loyalties are to the family. Universal recognition of the loyalties and responsibilities of family membership has handicapped the development of co-operative business organization and the expansion of governmental functions and responsibilities. While co-operative effort within the extended family and within the barrio is widespread and thoroughly developed, it remains based on family relationships and has seen limited transfer to the corporation, co-operative, or local government level.

A second significant consequence of the bilateral extended family is the conservatism of economic decisions. Status and security in the Philippine society are primarily dependent upon wealth. At the same time the system of bilateral and equal inheritance would normally tend to dissipate wealth. As a result, there have developed distinct concepts of personal wealth and family wealth. Family wealth—the communal estate managed under the informal trusteeship of the family head—is managed conservatively, and the trusteeship is basically a responsibility to preserve wealth intact. Such responsibility limits the freedom to use family wealth as venture capital. The preferred form of investment has been rural and urban real estate, which has historically tended to maintain its relative value and has endowed the family with status not to be derived from other forms of wealth.

Also contributing to the economic conservatism of the extended family system is the extensive participation of Filipinas in economic decisions. Inheritance in the Philippines is bilateral and equal, and in their status as equal heirs women tend to exercise an important voice in decisions affecting family wealth. Feminine participation is reinforced by the Spanish common law principle of individual control of property under which conjugal property is strictly limited. The Filipina at all levels of society tends to "hold the purse strings." [2]

[2] Filipino custom requires that the head of the family turn over the earnings of the family to be managed by the wife and mother. To some extent the status of the male in the community and in the church has depended upon his observance of this practice.

Women whose economic functions and roles have been relatively circumscribed by the culture and by maternal responsibilities tend to be less willing to venture resources in new directions and to risk money to earn money.

A third economic consequence of the intense family loyalties and responsibilities is widespread nepotism. Employment and advancement in business and government are dependent upon family loyalties to an extent unknown in the West. Such a system is not only inefficient in the allocation of human resources, but is a significant deterrent to individualism. Important family loyalties and responsibilities are extended by the custom of sponsorship at baptism by nonfamily members. The padrino system in which the sponsor seeks economic and political preference for his godchild augments the abuses of nepotism.

Fourth, as is well known, the extended family system tends to stifle individual initiative. The extension of conjugal family responsibilities to remote relatives means that individual economic success may be followed by an increasing burden of dependency. The weakened relationship between individual enterprise and the material welfare of the individual has retarded the evolution of entrepreneurial qualities essential to economic development.

The system of family loyalties and responsibilities has also shaped Philippine political institutions. The two principal institutions of administration during the Spanish period were the mutually reinforcing clergy and the agricultural aristocracy or cacique class. The cacique class was the institution of indirect rule in both Spanish and American colonial practice. Minimum formal organization of local government characterized the colonial period and persists to the present. An extensive system of feudalistic rights and duties arising out of the organization of the rural economy substituted for more formal institutions of local government.[3]

Local government tended to be highly personal and was based upon a close-knit hierarchy of families within an ethnic or physical division. The physical and ethnic fragmentation of the Philippines has tended to reinforce the status structure derived from the extended family system. During the Spanish period the absence of transport and communications facilities minimized economic incen-

[3] It would be a mistake to minimize the role of the clergy, who, during the Spanish period, provided a network of communications as well as more direct functions of local rule.

tives to migrate. Moreover, insecurity due to Moro depredations, as well as the clerical policy of bringing the Filipino population "under the bells" to facilitate clerical discipline, contributed to the demographic stability. Local political leadership was strongly correlated with family leadership, a pattern which persists today. The dominance of personal leadership has meant the subordination of issues in political controversy. Finally, the regionalism inherent in such a political system has increased the difficulty of organizing the Philippines to pursue broader national interests.[4]

As elsewhere in Southeast Asia, the Philippine nation-state based upon the political unification of diverse ethnic and regional groups is primarily a colonial legacy. The colonial period produced a minimum of geographic and political integration to serve as the basis of Philippine nationalism. For years to come the sovereign Philippines must confront extreme language diversity, which hampers communication, complicates economic activity, and distorts political processes and institutions.[5] Although the major accomplishment of Spanish colonial rule was the conversion of the Philippine population to Christianity, this contribution to cultural integration has tended to dilute rather than intensify Philippine nationalism.[6]

The national political system follows the American system of the separation of powers. As in the American system the independence of the executive, legislative, and judicial branches leads to considerable fluidity in the distribution of political power over time. It has become a commonplace to comment on the power of the Philippine Presidency as compared to that of chief executives in other political systems. The formal powers of the President are quite impressive, and during the Quezon regime the omnipotence of the executive was a

[4] Under the existing system the "national interest" tends to coincide with the interests of the politically dominant agricultural aristocracy.

[5] A recent survey enumerated seventy-five main linguistic groups. When subgroups of the main linguistic groups are distinguished, there are more than 150 languages and dialects. No language is the mother tongue for more than 25 per cent of the Philippine population. See Harold C. Conklin, *Outline Gazetteer of Native Philippine Ethnic and Linguistic Groups* (Chicago: University of Chicago, Philippine Studies Program, 1952), mimeograph.

[6] The universal Roman Catholic Church inevitably found Filipino nationalism uncongenial. The Philippines remained a missionary province throughout the colonial period, and the clerical apparatus, dominated by aliens, overtly and covertly resisted Filipino nationalism as a threat to the prerogatives and power of the missionary orders.

striking characteristic of the Philippine political scene. To a considerable extent the impression of power derived from the homogeneity of government and the conjunction of the national interest as recognized by the executive and the interests of the dominant agricultural aristocracy. So long as government of the sovereign Philippines remained the minimum government of the colonial period, the executive exercised relatively great power, i.e., discretionary authority. The postwar period has witnessed a substantial rearrangement of relative power and authority and increasing competition among the political elites. This healthy development has tended to disperse the illusion of executive omnipotence which the political scientists have found impressive. Attempts on the part of Presidents Quirino and Magsaysay to bring executive power to bear on national economic objectives were increasingly frustrated by the legislature, in which resides the ultimate power to tax and spend.[7]

More relevant to the pursuit of economic policy objectives is, not the exercise of the executive power, but executive initiative or leadership. The importance of executive leadership is based not only on legal and constitutional prerogatives and upon patterns of administrative control, but on the President's position as a national leader.

The Filipino concept of national leadership is a distinctive one, rooted deeply in Philippine history and culture. It embodies the personification of government to a degree not found in the West. Three centuries of authoritarian Spanish civil rule, the extensive governmental functions performed by the priest administering to the needs of his parishioners, as well as the feudalistic system of mutual rights and obligations characteristic of the Spanish system of land tenure reinforced the Malayan concept of paternalistic political leadership. Four decades of American political tutelage produced little change in this basic relationship. The increasing isolation of the American Governor-General as the Philippine independence movement gathered momentum contributed to maintenance of the Filipino tradition of paternalistic, personal, national political leadership.

The importance of executive initiative is exemplified in the re-

[7] The economic power of the chief executive of a society which takes some pride in its claim to "being the least taxed people in the world" is not impressive and is not to be compared with the power of the American executive, which each year disburses considerably more than the Philippine gross national product in economic aid.

lationship of the executive to the legislative process. A major portion of all economic legislation originates with the executive either directly or through cabinet secretaries and agency chiefs who draft legislation which is sponsored in Congress by appropriate committee chairmen or members who are personal friends.

The Philippine Congress is only slowly accepting political responsibility commensurate with its power. At present, despite a small Legislative Reference Service in the House and a few well-trained assistants to the appropriations committees of both houses, Congress is so understaffed that it can draft little important legislation. The regular session of Congress is constitutionally limited to 100 days. Little legislative activity occurs until the closing days of the session, and few major policy questions are permitted to come to a vote until the closing sessions.[8] The near bedlam which has tended to characterize the final hours of a congressional session is not conducive to constructive debate but has frequently contributed to concealment of legislative chicanery and ineptness.[9]

The second avenue for executive initiative lies in the extensive power of the President to "legislate" through executive and administrative orders. This power, largely derived from the Emergency Powers Act (Commonwealth Act No. 671 of December 16, 1941), was sharply circumscribed by the Supreme Court, which nullified a number of executive and administrative orders.[10]

Finally, executive leadership is embodied in the strong veto power. A veto can only be overridden by a two-thirds vote of the total membership of each house.[11] In addition, the President has an item veto over revenue, appropriation, and tariff bills. The veto can be, and has been, used to kill measures not in accord with executive policy. During the first six years of independence approximately 10 to 12 per cent of the bills passed were vetoed. During the latter years of

[8] Legislation enacted in the first 90 days of the legislative session tends to be limited to privately sponsored bills creating barrios and municipalities and granting public utility franchises.

[9] In the First National Assembly two-thirds of the bills passed were passed on the last day. By 1954 the situation had improved so that the House passed less than 25 per cent of its bills in the last three session days. This 25 per cent still included the most important, and consequently the more controversial, measures.

[10] Republic of the Philippines, *Official Gazette,* 45 (1952), 4411–4478. See also Jorge R. Coquia, *The Philippine Presidential Election of 1953* (Manila: University Publishing Co., 1955), pp. 136–147.

[11] No law has ever been passed over a presidential veto.

both the Quirino and Magsaysay administrations these executives were vetoing almost one-fifth of the bills enacted by Congress.

Economic policies are evolved by a complex structure of institutions which react with each other in diverse ways. Broad policy decisions tend to result from executive initiative and Congressional conservatism. Congress has a tradition of making broad grants of authority over economic policy to executive agencies. The latter are expected to refine and adapt policies to short-run exigencies.

A dominant economic-policy-making institution in the postwar period has been the Monetary Board of the Central Bank. This results from both an extremely broad grant of authority from Congress and circumstances that have enhanced the economic consequences of exchange rate, commercial, and monetary policy. Monetary Board influence is also due to continuity of tenure and the strong leadership of the Central Bank governor, Miguel Cuaderno.

A second dominant policy-making body in the executive is the cabinet.[12] Important economic policy decisions frequently result from the interplay of personalities at cabinet meetings. Close liaison between the Monetary Board and the cabinet has been maintained through the personal influence of Governor Cuaderno with Presidents Quirino, Magsaysay, and Garcia. There exists a supracabinet Council of State which meets infrequently and serves to endorse and thereby give prestige to major executive decisions.

A third executive agency influencing economic policy which has grown in importance in recent years is the Budget Commission, consisting of a Budget Commissioner of cabinet rank and a Deputy Budget Commissioner. The Budget Commission has broad power to "assemble, correlate, revise, reduce or increase the requests for appropriations of the different departments and agencies of the Government." [13] Because of the weak congressional and executive commitment to economic planning, the fiscal planning of government receipts and expenditures by the Budget Commission has become an increasingly important guide to public policy. The liaison role of

[12] The cabinet includes the Secretaries of Foreign Affairs, Finance, Justice, Agriculture and Natural Resources, Public Works and Communications, Education, Labor, National Defense, Health, and Commerce and Industry plus the Budget Commissioner, the Social Welfare Administrator, the Executive Secretary, and the President's Press Secretary.
[13] Republic Act No. 992 of June 4, 1954.

the Budget Commission between the executive and Congress in recent years has enhanced the influence of this agency.

Finally, there is the National Economic Council. The NEC is responsible for the preparation of economic plans but in fact is isolated from most major aspects of policy making. An important exception to such a generalization is the Office of Foreign Aid Co-ordination within the NEC. This office, in conjunction with the United States economic aid agency, plans and supervises the use of United States aid and Philippine counterpart appropriations.

A "fact of life" which circumscribes the formulation and implementation of economic policy is the difficulty of organizing public opinion. The political strength of Filipino conservatism is enhanced by the low threshold of political discrimination of Philippine society. The appearance of genuine political alternatives will be slow because of the low levels of literacy and political sophistication of the average Filipino.

The appearance of alternative political and economic leadership is handicapped by the weakness of abstract ideas. Political controversy tends to be conducted on a personal level and is distinguished by the absence of issues. Demagoguery is rampant. No politician in the Philippines is on record as opposed to land reform, free public education, or "social justice," yet progress toward achievement of these goals remains frustratingly slow.[14]

Economic issues in the Philippines are also obscured by a relatively nondiscriminating press. As might be expected, the press is economically conservative in its editorial and news policy. The difficulties of thinking intelligently about economic issues are compounded by the persistent failure of news media to distinguish between the blatant pursuit of self-interest and responsible statesmanship.

The appearance of political leadership outside the dominant cacique class is retarded by the relative absence of a Filipino middle class. In the past middle-class economic functions have been performed

[14] The capacity of Filipino political reactionaries blandly to profess support for abstract goals requiring far-reaching social change is, I suspect, a manifestation of "face." In political controversy as in social intercourse, you avoid direct confrontation of an opponent. Little attempt is made to marshal facts with which to refute an argument advanced by opponents in political controversy. Political controversy is characterized by personal contests for power in which opponents are undermined by the subversion of local loyalties and the manipulation of political alliances.

by aliens, who can hardly be expected to provide national economic leadership. The relative absence of Filipino middle-class elements is particularly striking outside Manila. In provincial cities commercial economic activity is dominated by the Chinese. Professional groups are predominantly Filipino and are substantial in terms of numbers. However, the independence of thought of this class is presently limited by the tendency for new class loyalties to be assimilated with individual economic success. Equally important is the persistence of traditional values and attitudes associated with the extended family. As a result, the emergence of a socially stable, politically independent middle class has been slow, but offers great promise for the future.

Finally, mobilization of economic opinion is handicapped by the party system. Political party organization is formally democratic, but owing to the electoral system it is highly centralized. Political parties are dominated by officials, and all the party's senators, representatives, governors, city mayors, and cabinet members, if any, are ex-officio delegates. Other delegates, mostly municipal mayors, are supposedly chosen by the party's provincial conventions; but it is customary for these conventions simply to give a vote of confidence to the recognized political leader, be he governor, congressman, or senator, who hand-picks the delegates.[15]

Like American party conventions, few important decisions are made by the delegates. The national directorate of the party, dominated by officials, is the true locus of decision making. Within the national directorate the executive committee—composed of senators, representatives, governors, and nonofficials in roughly equal proportions—runs the party.[16] Centralization of power and the ideological homogeneity of the party leadership limit the emergence of alternative policy positions within the party system. The dominant political parties are neither interest nor leadership groups, but complex coalitions of both. There is no persistent ideological differentiation which would make a two-party system more effective.[17] Both parties rely

[15] For a concise description of the Philippine political process, see David O. Wurfel, "The Philippines," in George M. Kahin (ed.), *Governments and Politics of Southeast Asia* (Ithaca, N.Y.: Cornell University Press, 1959), pp. 462–487.

[16] Wurfel states that "the executive committee of the majority party to a considerable extent can be said to run the country" (*ibid.*, p. 483).

[17] Frequent transfers of party membership by political leaders—even at the level of presidential candidacy—are characteristic of Philippine politics.

on provincial and municipal leaders to deliver the vote, and issues are virtually nonexistent. Appearance of effective leadership in the interest of social change prerequisite to accelerated economic growth has been frustratingly slow.[18]

Perhaps the most useful conceptual tool for analysis of the Philippine economy is the "plural society." It is a society of relatively compartmentalized racial and economic groups characterized by weak demand for communal or national objectives. Economic pluralism in the Philippines—a heritage of colonial economic development—is characterized by minimum government and an uneasy equilibrium of suspicious, competing racial and economic interest groups.

Dominant political power is vested in the caciques—the Philippine land-based aristocracy. The political resiliency of the agricultural aristocracy has been remarkable. For example, the Philippine nationalist movement in the late nineteenth century involved two independent developments: a liberal movement of intellectuals originating in, but emotionally estranged from, their cacique heritage and a proletarian movement emerging from a long history of agricultural dissidence. The cacique classes captured the nationalist movement as early as 1898, and their hold was not subsequently weakened. The dominance of the agricultural aristocracy in the Philippine nationalist movement and the rapid expansion in Philippine political autonomy during the American period gave Philippine nationalism a character unique in Southeast Asia.

The power of the cacique class is firmly based on land ownership. While land ownership is concentrated, this has not led to mechanization or plantation agriculture. Large estates are rented or worked by hired labor in small parcels, and there is minimum application of capital. The economic base of the cacique class has been maintained by mounting population pressure, which has upheld a distribution of product highly favorable to the owners of land and at the same time has tended to support steady appreciation in land values. The cacique class has little awareness of innovation in the entrepreneurial sense, and its members remain content with the static technology of the last three centuries.

[18] Ramon Magsaysay gave considerable promise of new economic policy leadership. He clearly embodied a potential for leadership alternative to the entrenched oligarchy. However, during his partial term in office he chose to work within the Nacionalista party and in the process found his attempts to furnish progressive national leadership increasingly frustrated by his party.

As might be expected, the cacique class is strongly motivated to maintain the economic and political *status quo*. Its members generally equate an expansion of governmental functions to a redistribution of income at their expense. In the past they have tended to utilize political power to frustrate changes in the economic organization of agriculture, to minimize government revenues, and to prevent change in the composition and functions of local government. Cacique loyalties are primarily class and family loyalties, with little consciousness of the possibility of using public policy to promote the national interest.

Numerically dominant are the Philippine peasantry. This class is characterized by rapid growth, relative immobility, and extensive poverty. The peasantry are unsophisticated and relatively leaderless, although there has been a persistent pattern of agrarian violence. Within the peasantry there is a majority group of small holders who own all or the major portion of the land they cultivate. The economic status of peasant small holders varies widely over different regions, and in general higher incomes prevail in areas where a cash export crop is produced. Most depressed among the peasantry are the landless tenants, the agriculural proletariat. This element tends to be concentrated in the rice-producing provinces of central Luzon and in the densely populated Visayan provinces. The ranks of tenant farmers are steadily augmented by population growth and the foreclosure of debt incurred by small landholders.

A wide gulf separates the peasantry from other elements in the Philippine society. Peasant values are traditional values. Peasant agriculture is largely subsistence and static. The agricultural sector includes some seven-tenths of the population but produces only two-fifths of the national product. Because of the disproportionate part of the agricultural output transferred as rent to the owners of land, poverty and economic insecurity for the peasantry are inevitable. The long history of agrarian dissidence among Philippine tenants does not reflect an aptitude for revolution so much as it does the chronic desperation of this element of the population. Up to the present the entrenched power of the caciques, reinforced by institutions of public order, have frustrated the appearance of democratic peasant leadership. The poverty and privations which are currently the lot of this element of the population are a powerful force for either evolutionary or revolutionary social change. Political institutions and processes appropriate to evolutionary change exist, and the outside observer can hope that leadership will appear to mobilize the political power of this element of the population. The immediate objective of this group is relief from depressing poverty and removal of insecurity arising out of existing tenancy arrangements.

Pluralness also arises out of the functional specialization and social exclusiveness of alien elements in the Philippine population. The definition of alien in the Philippines is fluid and controversial, and the dimensions of the non-Filipino element in the population are indistinct. Aliens registered with the Bureau of Immigration as of December 31, 1955, numbered 143,000, including 133,000 Chinese, 5,000 Americans, 1,500 Spaniards, and some 3,500 of other nationalities.[19] Estimates of the size of the ethnic Chinese population with and without Philippine citizenship vary widely depending upon the concept of "Chineseness" employed. It seems clear that the population which identifies itself as Chinese is of the order of half a million.[20]

An influential element in the plural Philippine society is the Western minority. The existence of this group in the Philippines is explained by colonial economic development and the resulting economic specialization in primary production for foreign markets. As might be expected, Western enterprise in the Philippines is American led and dominated. The American business community far outnumbers any other group, although there is substantial British, Spanish, Swiss, and Danish enterprise in the Philippines. The objectives of Western enterprise are common to those of colonial enterprise elsewhere. Western businessmen correctly recognize that the burden of direct taxation falls disproportionally on them. Therefore, because of their limited participation in the welfare benefits, they tend to resist expansion in governmental functions and services. This group is politically active in the battle to limit nationalist encroachments on their entrepreneurial freedom.

The power of the American business community is derived ultimately from the substantial United States economic concessions to the Philippines. The principal item of United States largess is the sugar quota, which allocates to Philippine sugar producers a guaranteed annual sugar market of almost one million tons at prices which

[19] *Facts about the Philippines* (Manila: Philippine Association, 1957), p. 56. This does not include official personnel in diplomatic missions, economic aid agencies, and military establishments.

[20] See Sheldon Appleton, "Communism and the Chinese in the Philippines," *Pacific Affairs,* 32 (Dec. 1959), 377.

in recent years have tended to average almost double the prices in world markets.[21] Second are the large-scale military expenditures in the Philippines, which not only contribute substantial foreign exchange earnings but, more important, provide the Philippines with a relatively cheap guarantee of continued national existence. Finally, there is the proliferation of economic aid activities, Veterans Administration benefits, and other programs which have materially aided postwar Philippine rehabilitation and economic expansion. United States policy toward the Philippines tends to fall into two distinct patterns. First is the wide variety of institutions and programs through which the United States contributes to Philippine economic development. Second are the diverse concessions negotiated in the interests of the American business community. Western enterprise has, in general, followed United States leadership and has been sheltered by the militancy of the United States Embassy in serving American economic interests.

The Spanish business community has several distinctive features. First, this element has proved to be relatively assimilable, and the Spanish community in the Philippines occupies a unique social position of high status. Another distinctive feature of the Spanish community is the number of ethnic Spanish families who have acquired Filipino or United States citizenship and who provide a substantial part of Philippine entrepreneurial initiative. Among these the Soriano, Elizalde, Ayala-Zobel, Aboitez, and Ossorio families tend to be outstanding.

A fourth element in the plural society is the Chinese community. As in all other cultures, the Chinese community in the Philippines is highly resistant to assimilation. The Chinese community is functionally specialized and tends to dominate retail trade and the financing and marketing of small-holders' crops, particularly rice and coconuts. The Chinese community is cohesive, and the individual Chinese is industrious and frugal.

The Chinese community is the object of deep Filipino animosity, which has roots far back in Philippine history. There is a long history of Filipino-Spanish violence directed at the Chinese arising out of insecurity in the face of potential Chinese aggression, clerical frustration over Chinese resistance to conversion, and resentment of Chinese economic success.

[21] *New York Times*, Feb. 21, 1960, p. 1F.

The economic position of the Chinese has been subject to rapid erosion in the postwar period. Philippine economic nationalism has been focused on the Chinese community, and exchange and import controls as well as a succession of government measures designed to subsidize Filipino entrepreneurs have been used to drive the Chinese out of traditional lines of economic activity. Up to the present the Chinese business community has displayed considerable resourcefulness in meeting this threat.

The future position of the Chinese community will be affected by two developments. First will be the political developments in the Far East and the future role of mainland China in Southeast Asia. It is not inconceivable that future developments in the political power structure in the Far East will provide the Philippine Chinese community with the security that it does not now possess. Second, the economic and political pressure on the Chinese community may sharply accelerate the assimilation of this group to the Philippine community.

A distinction should be made between the economic nationalism of Manila, and the changing position of the Chinese community in Manila, and the position of the Chinese community elsewhere in the Philippines. Manila is the stronghold of Philippine economic nationalism largely because of the impetus given this movement by import trade nationalization and because of the migration to Manila of a considerable part of the potential Filipino entrepreneurial resources. Outside Manila, Chinese dominance of commerce and retail business tends to be complete. In the absence of Filipinos anxious to usurp the economic role of the Chinese, the pressures on this community outside Manila are of a different order of intensity.

The Chinese community, like other alien communities, maintains its own schools, its own institutions for public welfare, and the like. Chinese interest in *national* economic development is weak, and less government rather than more suits this community. Chinese businessmen, under the pressures of economic nationalism, have learned to mobilize economic power in the only way available to them—to purchase influence from corruptible politicians. Chinese business practices are believed to be sharp, and Filipinos with few exceptions believe Chinese businessmen keep two sets of books to avoid taxes.

Superimposed on the racial pluralism is a further structure of divergent economic interests. Although exports and imports in recent years have averaged only 10 per cent and 12 per cent, respectively, of national income, economic policy controversy tends to be concentrated on problems of external economic relations. Economic interests involved in foreign trade are organized into vocal interest groups and tend to maintain effective lobbies.

An economic pressure group of growing strength is the importing business community. This activity was traditionally dominated by Western and Chinese business firms, but since 1949 exchange and import controls have been utilized to expand Filipino participation rapidly. While Filipinos have been aggressive in expanding their share of this activity at the expense of other participants, the importing business community presents a common front with respect to major economic policy issues. The influence of this group is reinforced by the spatial concentration of importing activity. Philippine import trade is concentrated in Manila, with provincial distribution in the hands of Chinese wholesale and retail merchants. Importers are organized nationally into chambers of commerce along racial lines. The basic power of this group is derived from growing Filipino participation and from extensive American participation, which can mobilize effective support through the American Embassy. Up to the present little overt conflict of interest has been manifest between these two elements in the importing community.

A second well-organized pressure group is the export community. During the colonial period, in the Philippines as elsewhere in Southeast Asia, this group tended to dominate economic policy formation. This influence was due to extensive participation in export production and trade by nationals of the metropolitan power and to the extent of Philippine specialization in primary production for the industrial market in the colonizing country.

In the Philippines the most powerful export pressure group is the sugar industry. Sugar interests have exercised great power through political parties as well as through ownership of newspapers and other communication media.[22] Other exporting interests are organized along functional lines, with strong export associations in gold mining and lumbering.

The political influence of the exporting community has declined over the past two decades. First, the withdrawal of American sovereignty was followed by the evolution of national as opposed to

---

[22] The sugar bloc is divided internally over the distribution of the product between planters and the mills, or sugar centrals.

colonial economic policy. As elsewhere in Southeast Asia, there has been a national rejection of colonial specialization and trade. Second, the important small holders' export crops—coconuts and abacá—have been difficult to organize because of the spatial diversification of production, the political passiveness of peasant producers, and the political weakness of the Chinese, who are important in the assembly of the copra crop. Finally, the political influence of the dominant sugar industry has waned in the major political parties. The pursuit of its own interests by the sugar industry arouses little sympathy in the rest of the society, and envy and resentment of the sugar barons, who have been addicted to ostentation and arrogance, are widespread.

The cohesiveness of the export sector is adversely affected by the regional nature of specialization. Sugar production is concentrated in the western Visayas, gold in northern Luzon, pineapples in northern Mindanao, chromite in Zambales Province, and lumbering in Mindanao. Export unity has also been handicapped by the success of particular interests in making favorable arrangements outside the structure of governmental regulation and trade control. For example, the gold industry has shown considerable aptitude in obtaining special concessions.

A third economic pressure group is the heavily protected, rapidly expanding industrial sector. Levels of protection in the Philippines were moderate until the imposition of exchange and import controls in 1949. Increasing stringency of controls was followed by increases in the prices of imports, and this established high levels of protection. Protected industries represent a mixture of Filipino, Western, and Chinese investment. In addition to the shelter afforded by protection, material concessions have been extended to potential industrial interests by various policies. For example, industries classified as "new and necessary" are exempted from all taxation for a limited number of years and are also guaranteed exchange allocations for imports of raw materials. Such policies have encouraged industries that package or perform some minor processing of imported materials. For example, suburban Manila is cluttered with pharmaceutical plants which initially minimized their foreign exchange difficulties by importing pharmaceuticals in bulk and doing the packaging in the Philippines.[23]

All societies are plural, and Philippine society is perhaps less plural

[23] Filipinos sometimes joke of the "new and necessary" instant (powdered) coffee industry, which originally packaged bulk imports of powdered coffee.

than other societies only recently removed from colonialism. The significant distinction between the plural Philippine economy and the plural American economy, for example, is the relative weakness of the middle class and the size, apathy, and estrangement of the peasantry.

In the plural society the competing racial and economic pressure groups are relatively unwilling to expand governmental revenues and functions because of basic fears that social services will redistribute income in favor of some other element within the society. The dominant economic groups compete for subsidies and concessions, but they present a common front of opposition to economic leadership that proposes to utilize government to promote social progress. The capacity of these interests to dominate public economic policy is rapidly eroding under the growing pressures for national economic progress. The current balance must still, however, be assessed as favoring conservative economic policies.

It is a truism that those groups in society with a vested interest in the existing state of affairs are rarely the vehicles of social change in the national interest. The initiators of nonrevolutionary change have traditionally been the *bourgeoisie,* the middle class. Middle classes have tended to be politically and intellectually independent and to recognize the possibility of social progress through national efforts. The present Philippine middle class is numerically small and holds values compromised by traditional values inimicable to rapid social change. The middle-class elements are concentrated in Manila and consist of the bureaucracy, teachers, the new Filipino commercial and industrial interests, and professional elements.

Conditions are favorable for rapid growth of the middle class. The society is fluid, and mobility, both social and spatial, is relatively uninhibited. Social position is intimately related to wealth, and distinctions among sources of wealth have declined to minor significance. Entrepreneurial or bureaucratic accomplishments are rewarded by enhanced status. Concentration of communications media, industrialization, and government in Manila has accelerated the decline in the strength of traditional values. Middle-class status is also enhanced by Filipino identification with the West, which is manifested in adoption of the middle-class trappings of American society.

Rapid urbanization in the Philippines and the growth in the numbers of secondary and college graduates contribute to the reservoir of political power receptive to change. The emergence of independent political leadership in the growing Filipino middle class is the most promising alternative to resumption of class warfare between the dispossessed peasantry and the agricultural aristocracy. The future role of the Filipino middle class is attested by the political objectivity and sophistication of the Manila electorate.

· III ·

Structure of the Economy

THE Philippines consists of 7,000 islands, of which about 800 are inhabited. Twenty-six major islands constitute 96 per cent of the area and account for 97 per cent of the population. Its combined land area of 115,600 square miles and population of 22.3 million (as of mid-1956) compares with Pennsylvania, Ohio, and Indiana, which comprise an area of 122,800 square miles and population of 22.4 million (as of 1950).

Although areas and total populations are comparable, few other similarities are found. Normally, rural Filipinos do not live in isolated homesteads, but in clusters of dwellings called sitios, with one or more adjacent sitios comprising a barrio or village. According to the 1948 census, three-quarters of the Filipinos lived in 17,403 barrios, and agriculture provided a livelihood for at least 70 per cent of the Philippine population.[1] In contrast, the population of Pennsylvania,

[1] In the 1948 census 69 per cent of the population was classified as agricultural population, i.e., "persons who depend upon agriculture for a livelihood, that is to say, persons actively engaged in agriculture and their non-working dependents." See United Nations, Food and Agricultural Organization, *Yearbook of Food and Agricultural Statistics, 1956*, vol. X, pt. 1, "Production" (Rome, 1957), p. 16, table 4A. The population of chartered cities and administrative centers of municipalities accounted for only 24.1 per cent of the total population in 1948 (UN, Statistical Office, *Demographic Yearbook, 1958*, 7th issue (New York, 1955), p.

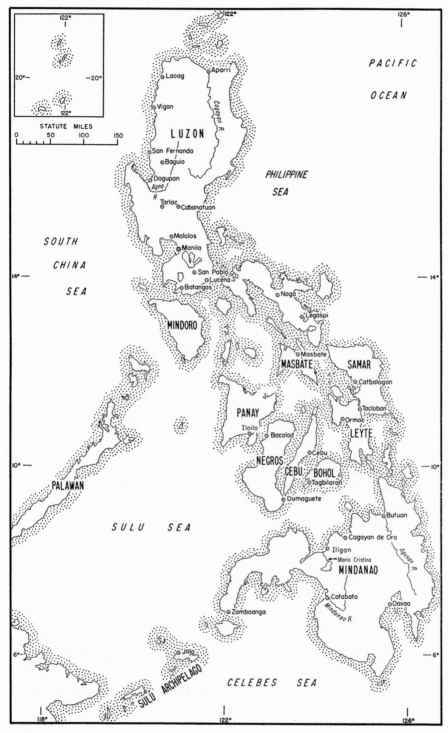

STATUTE MILES
0   50   100   150

20° —   — 20°
122°

122°   126°

PACIFIC

OCEAN

Laoag   Aparri

Vigan

LUZON

SOUTH   San Fernando
                         Baguio
CHINA
                    Dagupan
SEA   Agno   Tarlac
                 R.   Cabanatuan

PHILIPPINE

SEA

                    Malolos
                    Manila

14° —   San Pablo   — 14°
                    Lucena
                Batangas   Naga

                                            Legaspi
        MINDORO

                                        Masbate
                            MASBATE   SAMAR
                                                Catbalogan

                        PANAY   Tacloban
                                            Ormoc
                        Iloilo   LEYTE
                            Bacolod

                                    Cebu
10° —   NEGROS   — 10°
            PALAWAN   CEBU BOHOL
                                Tagbilaran
        SULU   SEA   Dumaguete

                                                Butuan

                                        Cagayan de Oro
                                    Iligan
                                    Maria Cristina
                                    MINDANAO

                                    Catabato   Davao
                        Zamboanga   Mindanao R.

6° —   — 6°
                Jolo
        SULU ARCHIPELAGO   CELEBES   SEA

118°   122°   126°

Republic of the Philippines

Ohio, and Indiana was reported as 69 per cent urban in the census of 1950. The dominance of agriculture in the Philippine economy suggests that a larger proportion of the land area in the Philippines should be under cultivation than in the three states just cited; in fact, the reverse is true. In the three American states, the area under crops has averaged one-third of the total land area in recent years, whereas in the Philippines it has averaged only one-fifth of the total land area. The size of the average farm in Pennsylvania, Ohio, and Indiana is 107 acres as compared to 8.6 acres in the Philippines (in 1948).

Western observers tend to interpret the low ratio of Philippine land under cultivation as evidence of an absence of population pressure on agricultural resources. Similarly, they are optimistic regarding the potentialities of tropical agriculture because of the acceptance of stereotypes of the vitality of jungle plant life and the steadiness of tropical rainfall and sunshine. Such appraisals of the potentialities of Philippine agriculture must be qualified. The Philippine Islands lie between 6° and 20° N. latitude in a climatic belt influenced by the Asian land mass and the northeast trade winds in such a fashion as to produce a monsoonal type of climate with distinct hot-dry (March–May), hot-wet (June–October), and cool-dry (November–February) seasons. Rainfall is relatively heavy and is ample during the wet season to provide for wet rice culture without supplementary irrigation. Rainfall is intermittent during the dry seasons and is inadequate to permit the cultivation of a second crop of rice in the absence of irrigation.

In common with much of Southeast Asia, the Philippines has suffered from the poor land use involved in shifting cultivation under expanding population pressure.[2] The heavy rainfall makes such cultivation extremely destructive because of mechanical erosion. A considerable part of the land area is covered by a coarse grass (cogon) which is a formidable obstacle to peasant colonization as well as a positive indicator of soil depletion. Philippine soils in upland areas are shallow, and in the heavily cultivated alluvial areas they tend to be clays suitable for the cultivation of paddy rice but not so good for other crops.

193, table 7). The Philippine Statistical Survey of Households of May 1956 reported that agriculture accounted for 69.8 per cent of male employment (*Statistical Reporter*, 1 [Jan. 1957], 31–32).

[2] Joseph E. Spencer, *Land and People in the Philippines* (Berkeley: University of California Press, 1954), pp. 49–58.

The major part of the Philippines has a rough topography and is unsuitable for cultivation under the techniques now employed in Philippine agriculture. As of 1953, of the total Philippine land area of 29.7 million hectares, 6.1 million hectares were under cultivation in land and tree crops and an additional 5.7 million hectares were

Table 1. Area under cultivation for principal crops [a]
(000 hectares)

	Annual average 1934–38	1938 [b]	Annual average 1948–52	1953 [b]	1955 [b]	1957 [b]
Crops consumed domestically						
Rice	1,963	2,080	2,350	2,655	2,656	2,768
Corn	695	913	969	1,101	1,394	1,787
Tobacco	67	58	44	39	53	81
Beans and vegetables	n.a.	109	n.a.	151	166	175
Fruits and nuts	n.a.	235	n.a.	333	378	395
Root crops	n.a.	178	n.a.	260	273	292
Other	n.a.	13	n.a.	24	28	31
Total		3,586		4,563	4,948	5,529
Export crops						
Abacá	292	292	285	272	217	232
Coconuts	n.a.	1,051	n.a.	990	990	992
Sugar	235	230	171	225	268	235
Other [c]	n.a.	14	n.a.	14	16	15
Total		1,587		1,501	1,491	1,474

[a] UN, FAO, *Yearbook of Food and Agricultural Statistics, 1957*, vol. XI, pt. 1, "Production" (Rome, 1958).

[b] R.P., Central Bank of the Philippines, *Tenth Annual Report, 1958* (Manila, 1959), p. 27.

[c] Includes kapok, maguey, ramie, rubber, and cotton. Information on acreage planted to pineapple is not available.

classified as "unused but potentially productive."[3] Caution must be observed before interpreting this estimate of the unused cultivable land as evidence of a lack of population pressure. The principal areas of land suitable for wet rice cultivation have been occupied, and the only large remaining area is in northeastern Mindanao in the Agusan Valley.

[3] UN, FAO, *op. cit.*, p. 5, table 1.

Philippine agriculture is bifurcated into two distinct sectors. First
is the food crop sector producing the subsistence needs of the cultivator plus a margin of production necessary to supply the domestic
market. During recent years crops consumed domestically have accounted for 80 per cent of the land under cultivation (see Tables 1, 2).
The principal crop of this sector is rice, which in 1957 was planted
on 2.8 million hectares or 40 per cent of the total area planted to crops.

Table 2. Production of selected agricultural commodities [a]
(000 metric tons)

	Annual average 1934–38	Annual average 1948–52	Annual average 1953–57	1958 [b]
Crops consumed domestically				
Rice, palay	2,179	2,767	3,230	3,203
Corn	427	696	812	852
Tobacco	35	23	34	50
Coffee and cacao	3	5	8	n.a.
Beans and vegetables	39 [c]	n.a.	221	242
Fruits and nuts	256 [c]	n.a.	621	715
Root crops	615	n.a.	1,214	1,330
Export crops				
Abacá	183	105	115	125
Copra	583	831	1,072	1,293
Sugar, centrifugal	960	827	1,114	1,250
Pineapple [d]	13	55	38	21

[a] UN, FAO, *Yearbook of Food and Agricultural Statistics, 1957,* vol. XI, pt. 1,
"Production." Root crops are primarily sweet potatoes.
[b] Central Bank, *Tenth Annual Report, 1958.*
[c] Central Bank, *Fourth Annual Report, 1952.* Production in 1938.
[d] Average annual exports.

Next to rice in importance as a food crop is corn, which accounted
for 1.8 million hectares in 1957. The principal remaining food crops
for domestic consumption during 1957 included root crops (principally *camotes,* a variety of sweet potato), 0.4 million hectares; fruits
and nuts, 0.3 million hectares; and beans and vegetables, 0.2 million
hectares.

Subsistence agriculture is organized into small units and is characterized by widespread tenancy. The 1948 Census of Agriculture re-

ported that the average size of all rice farms was 3.09 hectares, with 2.10 hectares under cultivation, while for corn farms the average size was 2.16 hectares, with 1.46 under cultivation.[4] Forty per cent of the rice farmers owned the land they operated, 14 per cent were

Table 3. Comparative statistics on yields of principal crops [a]
(100 kg per hectare)

	1934–38	1948–52	1954	1955	1956
Rice					
Philippines	10.9	11.9	12.1	11.9	12.1
Burma	14.1	14.1	14.8	14.8	16.0
Thailand	12.9	13.1	12.6	13.7	14.3
Asia, average	15.2	15.8	17.3	18.5	18.5
Corn					
Philippines	6.1	7.2	5.5	5.4	5.0
Java and Madura	9.7	6.8	10.8	n.a.	8.4
India	7.4	6.5	7.9	7.0	8.2
Asia, average	9.1	10.2	11.9	11.7	11.8
Sweet potatoes					
Philippines	24	41	41	44	42
Java and Madura	65	57	61	56	67
Taiwan	102	91	103	99	112
Asia, average	79	90	101	105	103
Tobacco					
Philippines	5.2	6.1	5.7	5.2	n.a.
India	9.4	7.5	7.4	7.3	7.1
Thailand	8.7	8.3	9.7	10.0	10.3
Asia, average	9.7	9.0	8.4	8.9	9.3
Sugar, centrifugal [b]					
Philippines	38.2	48.4	46.4	37.5	37.5
Mauritius	48.0	64.2	66.5	67.5	75.4
Puerto Rico	71.9	71.8	70.0	70.5	n.a.

[a] UN, FAO, *Yearbook of Food and Agricultural Statistics, 1957,* vol. XI, pt. 1, "Production."

[b] Computed from reported production of raw sugar and the area planted to sugar cane.

part owners, and 46 per cent were tenants. With corn farmers, the ratios were 47 per cent, 8 per cent, and 45 per cent, respectively. The average size of owner-operated farms (all types) was 4.09 hectares,

[4] A hectare equals 2.47 acres.

with 2.26 hectares under cultivation, whereas for tenant-operated farms the average size was 2.54 hectares, with 2.06 hectares under cultivation.[5]

In spite of the small size of farms and intensive cultivation, Philippine crop yields are among the lowest in the world (see Table 3). Philippine food crop agriculture is capital starved and therefore bound to a primitive technology which precludes rapid improvements in yields. The high incidence of tenancy has tended to maintain a crop distribution favorable to the landowner and to provide the tenant cultivator with a minimum subsistence level of living. The Philippine peasant proprietor who is entitled to the entire product of his small farm is in an enviable position when compared with the landless peasant who can lay claim only to the product attributable to his labor.

Filipinos obtain animal protein primarily from fish, fowl, and limited amounts of pork, sheep, and beef. In 1953 fish production was estimated to total 305 million kilograms valued at ₱294 million. This was equivalent to approximately 38 pounds per capita. As with Philippine soil resources, there is a widespread tendency toward optimism regarding fishery resources. The shallow inland waters around the Philippines are of limited productiveness when compared with shallow waters of higher latitudes.[6] The principal part of Philippine fish production is now derived from commercial cropping of fish ponds. The prospects for further expansion of fish farming are favorable. Information is not available concerning the quantity of meat produced in the Philippines.

In recent years the Philippine index of per capita agricultural production has recovered to prewar (1934–1938) levels (see Table 4). At these levels the average diet is short of preventive food, particularly animal proteins and milk, although substantial amounts of calcium are obtained from marine sources.

It has become an article of faith in the theory of economic develop-

[5] Summary tables from the 1948 Census of Agriculture are available in R.P., Department of Agriculture and Natural Resources, *Philippine Agricultural Statistics* (Manila: Bureau of Printing, 1955), vol. I.

[6] For an authoritative survey of the Philippine fishing industry see H. E. Warfel, "The Prospect for Philippine Fisheries," *American Chamber of Commerce Journal*, 26 (May 1950), 179–180. Warfel, an official of the Fish and Wildlife Service, U.S. Department of the Interior, was detailed to the Philippines to assist in the postwar rehabilitation of the Philippine fishing industry.

ment to attribute underemployment (disguised unemployment) to agriculture in less-developed countries. Underemployment means many things to many people, and there can be little question that the abysmally low yields of Philippine agriculture measure the opportunity for capital investment and technological change. However, underemployment in the rigorous sense of zero or below subsistence marginal product is not a characteristic of Philippine agriculture.

Table 4. Indexes of agricultural production [a]
(1934–1938 = 100)

Crop year	All commodities	Food	Cereals	Agricultural exports [b] (1937–1939 = 100)	Per capita indexes	
					Food	Cereals
1948–49	93	99	118	68	78	83
1949–50	103	110	124	84	85	96
1950–51	125	131	132	95	100	101
1951–52	130	139	136	106	104	102
1952–53	133	142	147	102	104	108
1953–54	137	146	151	109	105	108
1954–55	138	148	151	117	104	107
1955–56	143	152	158	118	105	109
1956–57	155	162	161	n.a.	110	109
1957–58	156	165	154	n.a.	110	103

[a] UN, Economic Commission for Asia and the Far East, *Economic Survey of Asia and the Far East, 1955, 1956,* and *1958* (Bangkok, 1956, 1957, and 1959). Hereafter referred to as UN, ECAFE, *Economic Survey.*
[b] Volume index computed for exports of copra, coconut oil, desiccated coconut, sugar (centrifugal, refined, and raw), molasses, abacá, leaf tobacco, and canned pineapple. See notes to Tables 8 and 9.

During the past six decades the increases in agricultural population (agricultural working force) and in area under cultivation have been closely correlated (see Table 5). Moreover, yields per unit of land have remained quite stable. While these facts do not establish, they do support, the conclusion that the marginal product of additions to the agricultural population may be close to the average product of the existing agricultural population.

Philippine agriculture, particularly the subsistence and cereal-producing sector, is traditional and static. It would be a mistake, however, to equate these characteristics to disguised unemployment.

Removal of a significant part of the agricultural population, in the absence of changes other than the resulting changes in factor proportions, probably would result in a roughly proportionate decline in agricultural output.[7]

Observers of the Philippines, with few exceptions, have deplored the colonial-type specialization in primary production for export. It has become commonplace to equate such specialization to technological dualism. Dualism is usually described in terms of a capital-intensive, progressive, productive, plantation-dominated, export sector existing alongside, but economically isolated from, a capital-starved, backward, unproductive domestic sector dominated by subsistence production. Such generalizations have limited validity in the Philippine case. The Philippine economy is not dominated by the export sector. The share of national income generated by exports has declined rapidly in the postwar period, until at present export earnings

Table 5. Land colonization in the twentieth century [a]

	Population		Farm area		Cultivated area	
	000	Index	000 hectares	Index	000 hectares	Index
1903	7,640	100	2,828	100	1,299	100
1918	10,151	133	4,564	161	2,416	186
1939	16,152	211	6,691	237	3,954	304
1948	19,144	250	5,727	203	3,712	286

[a] R.P., DANR, *Philippine Agricultural Statistics*, I, 13–14.

amount to less than 10 per cent of national income. Similarly, specialization in export crop production accounts for a minor part of Philippine agricultural resources. For example, in 1957 the acreage planted to export crops accounted for only 20 per cent of the area under cultivation. Moreover, approximately one-third of the Philippine sugar

[7] Although the average Filipino cultivator is not fully employed by his agricultural chores during a substantial part of the year, labor scarcity is intense during periods of soil preparation, planting, and harvesting. Unemployment arising out of seasonality is a major Philippine agrarian problem, but it is not to be equated to the concept of absolute overpopulation in agriculture, which is frequently attributed to less-developed economies. For an excellent survey and analysis of Philippine agriculture, see Horst von Oppenfeld, Judith von Oppenfeld, J. C. Santa Iglesia, and P. R. Sandoval, *Farm Management, Land Use and Tenancy in the Philippines* (Central Experiment Station Bull. No. 1; College, Laguna: University of the Philippines, College of Agriculture, 1957).

and copra production is consumed domestically, which means that no more than 14 to 15 per cent of the area under cultivation is devoted to export production.[8]

Philippine agricultural export specialization has been an efficient way to produce needed imports, and only to a very limited extent has it utilized resources which otherwise would have been used to produce commodities presently imported. Philippine food and fiber imports are not commodities which might be produced internally if acreage presently diverted to sugar, abacá, coconut, and pineapple production were made available. Philippine history is replete with experimental attempts to grow cotton and to produce breeds of dairy and beef cattle which will thrive in the Philippines—experiments not attended by conspicuous success.

Plantation and industrial production does not characterize the export sector.[9] Small-holder agriculture dominates the export production of coconuts, abacá, and tobacco and is widespread in sugar growing. The average farm size tends to be somewhat larger in these crops and the tenancy ratio to be substantially lower. This arises primarily out of the fact that these crops are produced in less densely populated "frontier" areas—tobacco in the Cagayan Valley, abacá in a belt extending from southern Mindanao to southern Luzon, and coconuts in widely distributed areas marginal to other agricultural production.

In the production of sugar a large number of small planters are organized into a mill district serviced by a sugar mill or central. The average size of farms planted to sugar is somewhat less than three times the average size of all Philippine farms (in 1948 the average amount of land under cultivation per farm was 7.1 hectares), mechanization is limited, and cultivation is largely through heavy use of landless labor. Philippine sugar is presently marketed almost exclusively in the United States and in the domestic market, which is reserved for domestic producers.

Coconut production is essentially small-holder production and is distributed widely. The average size of coconut farms in 1948 was 4.64 hectares, with 3.24 hectares under cultivation. Similarly, small-

[8] In 1957 the area planted to sugar and abacá, which accounted for 36 per cent of Philippine export proceeds, was only 4.6 per cent of the area under cultivation.
[9] For a contrary view, see Benjamin Higgins, *Economic Development* (New York: W. W. Norton Co., 1959), p. 59.

holder production has dominated abacá production since World War II. The average-sized farm in 1948 was 8.36 hectares, with 4.45 hectares under cultivation.[10]

Philippine pineapple production for export, which in recent years accounted for 2 per cent of export earnings, is limited to a single highly mechanized plantation of 6,000 hectares in northern Mindanao. This plantation is a subsidiary of the California Packing Company. Philippine pineapples are marketed exclusively in the Philippines and the United States. Rubber and ramie are produced on a handful of medium-sized plantations but presently make an insignificant contribution to Philippine export earnings.

The impression of economic dualism reported by observers in the Philippines is probably due to large-scale investment in the processing of Philippine export crops and is certainly not characteristic of the predominantly small-holder production of such crops. Sugar centrals, coconut oil mills, and desiccated coconut factories are probably the source of much confusion regarding the economic organization of export crop production.

Expansion of Philippine agricultural production for export is confronted by formidable obstacles. First, the unrealistic exchange parity has narrowed the range of Philippine comparative advantage, and minor products that were exported in significant amounts in the interwar period have virtually disappeared from the export lists. In the case of abacá, inability to solve complex disease problems will make substantial recovery of this export crop difficult. In the case of sugar, expansion over the past 25 years has been limited to the growth in the domestic market. United States sugar policy has not included increases in the Philippine quota, and Filipinos have been reluctant to explore other export markets. In the case of coconuts, few obstacles are apparent to further expansion in production and trade. Production of a number of minor crops to supply the protected domestic market has expanded rapidly in recent years, but the present exchange rate policy makes it seem unlikely that the Philippines will become a significant exporter of these commodities.

The agricultural resources of the Philippines are extensive and widely distributed. Agricultural colonization in the Philippines has slightly more than kept abreast of population growth over the past sixty years. Population pressure has led to the steady settlement of

[10] R.P., DANR, *Philippine Agricultural Statistics*, I, 4.

the Cagayan Valley in northern Luzon and in the filling up of the Cotabato Valley in Mindanao. The process of colonization can be expected to keep abreast of population growth over the next decade or two. Beyond this time further colonization will tend to await the development of techniques appropriate to the cultivation of upland areas. Probably more significant for future Philippine economic

Table 6. Production of minerals and metals [a]

	1938–40 [b]	1947	1949	1951	1953	1955	1957	1958
Gold (000 fine ounces)	1,012	65	288	394	481	419	380	423
Chromite ore (000 MT)	133	195	247	335	557	598	726	416
Copper, metal (000 MT)	6.9	3.2	6.0	12.7	12.7	17.5	40.4	47.0
Iron ore (000 MT)	1,118	—	370	903	1,218	1,433	1,346	1,099
Manganese ore (000 MT)	44	3	26	22	22	12	30	22.3
Mercury (000 flasks [c])	n.r.	n.r.	n.r.	n.r.	n.r.	.6	3.4	3.3
Lead, metal (000 MT)	1,221	3	380	571	2,434	2,318	814	1,284
Coal (000 MT)	41 [d]	74 [d]	123 [d]	151 [d]	155 [d]	130	191	108

[a] Central Bank, *Annual Reports.*

[b] Commonwealth of the Philippines, Bur. of Census and Statistics, *Yearbook of Philippine Statistics, 1940* (Manila: Bureau of Printing, 1941).

[c] Flasks of 76 pounds.

[d] UN, Statistical Office, *Statistical Yearbook, 1955,* 7th issue (New York, 1955), p. 139, table 39.

growth will be the productiveness of agricultural development expenditures. Current community development, agricultural extension, and agricultural experimentation plans are likely to bring about steady improvement in the productivity of Philippine agricultural resources. Filipinos are apprehensive of colonial-type specialization and are currently implementing policies that discourage further specialization of primary agricultural production for export. Future agricultural expansion will tend to be production for the domestic market and hence is unlikely to expand at rates substantially in excess of population growth.

The Philippines is richly endowed with mineral wealth and currently produces substantial amounts of gold, copper, chromite, iron ore, manganese, and mercury (see Table 6). The principal mineral shortage is in fuels, and at present the Philippines produces only sufficient coal to manufacture, at relatively high cost, a minor part of domestic requirements of cement. At present Philippine imports of petroleum and its products account for 10 to 12 per cent of the value of imports, and such imports have tended to increase during

Table 7. Trends in volume, unit value, and terms of foreign trade [a]

	Foreign trade (₱ 000,000)		Quantum		Unit value	
	Imports	Exports	Imports 1937 = 100	Exports 1937–40 = 100	Imports [b] 1937 = 100	Exports 1937–40 = 100
1937	218	334	100	89	100	132
1938	265	294	n.a.	95	n.a.	97
1939	245	316	n.a.	106	n.a.	90
1940	265	312	n.a.	109	n.a.	82
1946	592	128	117	19	209	223
1947	1,023	529	188	61	226	302
1948	1,172	638	212	62	228	360
1949	1,137	508	236	66	204	280
1950	712	653	140	85	204	296
1951	959	820	172	96	230	317
1952	852	696	155	107	228	250
1953	879	796	172	100	217	305
1954	903	824	191	111	209	271
1955	1,069	827	216	121	209	247
1956	1,019	931	210	138	213	253
1957	1,249	863	252	127	219	257

[a] UN, Statistical Office, *Yearbook of International Trade Statistics, 1957*, vol. I (New York, 1958). Series are converted to bases as indicated. The figures do not include trade in gold. Unless otherwise indicated, trade statistics refer to f.o.b. value.

[b] Unit value indexes are not available for 1938, 1939, and 1940. However, the unit value index for U.S. exports in 1937–1940 can be utilized to obtain an impression of the postwar Philippine terms of trade inasmuch as the United States provided almost 69 per cent of Philippine imports during 1937–1940. The unit value of U.S. exports (1937 = 100) was 100 in 1938, 105 in 1939, and 121 in 1940.

the postwar period. Limited oil exploration is being conducted, and geologists are optimistic regarding potential supplies. The Philippine gold-mining industry, which prior to World War II accounted for approximately one-fifth of the value of Philippine exports, has made only a partial recovery. The failure of gold production to recover is due to the overvalued peso exchange rate and the fixed price of gold.

Table 8. Commodity distribution of export trade [a]
(percentage of total value of exports)

	1937–40 [b]	1947–49	1950–52	1953–55	1956–58 [c]
Coconut products	25.3	68.2	46.2	39.4	41.2
Copra	10.0	54.0	34.9	30.6	29.4
Coconut oil, edible and inedible	9.9	5.7	5.6	4.2	5.0
Desiccated coconut	3.6	7.4	4.5	3.6	5.6
Copra meal	1.8	1.1	1.2	1.0	1.2
Sugar, raw, refined, and molasses	40.3	9.0	20.9	27.3	23.1
Abacá and cordage	12.2	12.3	15.4	9.0	8.3
Tobacco and mfrs.	4.3	.7	.8	1.1	1.4
Embroideries	3.6	1.8	1.8	1.7	n.a.
Metals, ores, and concentrates	4.4	1.7	6.3	9.0	11.9
Logs, timber, and lumber	3.4	0.8	4.3	8.8	11.9
Canned pineapple	1.4	0.7	2.6	1.8	1.1
Other exports	5.1	4.8	1.7	1.8	1.1
	100.0	100.0	100.0	100.0	100.0

[a] R.P., Bureau of Customs, *Annual Reports of the Collector of Customs.*

[b] Commonwealth of the Philippines, Bureau of Customs, *Annual Reports of the Collector of Customs.*

[c] Central Bank, *Statistical Bulletin,* vol. 10 (Dec. 1958).

Still another Philippine resource of considerable importance is the forest cover of much of the land. Philippine production and exports of logs, timber, and lumber have expanded rapidly in the postwar period until in recent years exports of these commodities have accounted for approximately 12 per cent of export proceeds. Technological dualism is not a prominent characteristic of the production of forest products. For example, in 1957 exports of logs and timber were reported by 180 firms. Inasmuch as the total value of such exports was ₱90 million, the average size of each firm was relatively small.[11] Exports of forestry products together with base metals, which have expanded rapidly since World War II, have offset the otherwise lagging growth of Philippine export production and trade.

Philippine foreign trade is characterized by excessive dependence upon a limited number of commodities and markets, a pattern which has persisted over the last sixty years (see Tables 7–9). Although there have been important shifts in the commodity composition of trade, the dependence upon primary production for foreign exchange earn-

Table 9. Trends in the volume of export trade [a]
(annual average, 000 metric tons)

Commodity	1937–40 [b]	1947–49	1950–52	1953–55	1956–58 [c]
Copra	330	708	717	718	904
Coconut oil, edible and inedible	171	42	76	66	94
Desiccated coconut	39	47	53	48	51
Sugar, centrifugal, refined, raw	893	217	634	868	867
Abacá	166	75	111	108	110
Logs, timber, lumber	201	24	246	554	1,034
Iron ore	911	124	892	1,305	1,277
Chromite ore	107	164	348	594	688
Canned pineapple	13	19	65	47	22

[a] R.P., Bur. of Customs, *Annual Reports.*
[b] Commonwealth of the Philippines, Bur. of Customs, *Annual Reports.*
[c] Central Bank, *Annual Reports.*

ings has remained at high levels. During the three-year period 1956–1958 exports of coconut products (copra, coconut oil, desiccated coconut, and copra meal) accounted for 41 per cent of Philippine exports, with sugar and molasses accounting for an additional 23 per cent. Exports of abacá, metals and ores, and logs, timber, and lumber accounted for a further 32 per cent.

As might be expected, Philippine imports include a wide range of manufactures, fuels, and foodstuffs (see Table 10). In recent years import controls have produced substantial shifts in the commodity

[11] Monthly exports of forest products by firm are reported in the *A.C.C. Journal.* In 1957 log and timber exports were widely distributed, the four largest firms accounting for only one-fifth of the licensed exports.

composition of imports, with imports of machinery and transport equipment and mineral fuels and lubricants tending to gain at the expense of textile yarns, fabrics and manufactures, and footwear and clothing. Food imports remain fairly substantial and in recent years have averaged almost one-fifth of total imports.

The colonial relationship with the United States and the so-called mutual free-trade policy tended to concentrate Philippine trade with

Table 10. Commodity distribution of import trade [a]
(percentage of total value of imports)

Import category	1937–40 [b]	1947–49	1950–52	1953–55	1956–58 [c]
Food	18.5	24.8	18.9	17.4	18.7
Beverages and tobacco	5.9	4.8	3.8	2.9	.7
Textile yarns, fabrics, and mfrs.	18.0	19.9	18.2	16.8	11.6
Footwear and clothing	2.8	3.1	1.1	1.4	.4
Mineral fuels and lubricants	8.3	5.5	9.8	10.6	10.2
Chemicals	7.6	5.6	8.5	8.1	8.7
Rubber manufactures	2.0	1.7	3.4	3.2	1.7
Paper and paper board manufactures	3.0	2.9	4.0	3.4	3.3
Base metals and manufactures of metal	12.0	8.7	10.8	10.4	12.6
Machinery and transport equipment	14.4	12.1	13.8	18.0	23.4
Other imports	7.7	10.9	7.7	8.1	8.7
	100.0	100.0	100.0	100.0	100.0

[a] R.P., Bur. of Customs, *Annual Reports.*
[b] Commonwealth of the Philippines, Bur. of Customs, *Annual Reports.*
[c] Central Bank, *Statistical Bulletin,* vol. 10 (Dec. 1958).

the United States (see Tables 11, 12). By the late interwar period the Philippines was sending three-quarters of its exports (by value) to the United States and obtaining two-thirds of its imports from the metropolitan country. This relationship continued during the first postwar decade, although the ratios for exports and imports tended to be reversed. The Revised United States–Philippine Trade Agreement of 1955 has resulted in a radical change in the commercial relationships between the two countries. Scheduled acceleration in the collection of Philippine duties on imports from the United States is rapidly reducing the concentration of Philippine trade with the United States. By 1958 the ratio for both imports and exports had declined to 50 per cent. This trend can be expected to continue and will result in a desirable market diversification of Philippine foreign trade.

Because the Philippines is made up of islands, the rivers are relatively short and drain small basins. Therefore, the opportunities to develop hydroelectric power and storage reservoirs for irrigation purposes are limited. The development of hydroelectric potential is

Table 11. Geographic composition of export trade
(percentage of total value of exports)

Trading partner	1937–40 [a]	1947–49 [b]	1950–52 [b]	1953–55 [c]	1956–58 [c]
United States	78.4	65.3	67.2	62.1	53.9
Asia	10.2	9.4	10.8	15.3	21.7
Japan	6.7	3.4	7.2	13.2	18.5
Western Europe	9.5	19.6	16.8	17.2	20.2
United Kingdom	3.2	1.8	2.4	1.4	1.5
Germany	.8	1.7	.8	2.1	2.5
Netherlands	1.4	.8	3.4	6.5	9.4
Belgium-Luxembourg	.4	1.1	3.0	1.4	1.9
France	1.1	4.6	.9	.6	.4
Spain	.6	.5	.6	.7	.5
Rest of world	1.9	5.7	5.2	5.4	4.2
	100.0	100.0	100.0	100.0	100.0

[a] Commonwealth of the Philippines, Bur. of Census and Statistics, *Yearbook of Philippine Statistics, 1940.*
[b] UN, Statistical Office, *Yearbook of International Trade Statistics.*
[c] Central Bank, *Annual Reports.*

also limited by the absence of markets at or near the available sites. For example, the outlet of Lake Lanao in Mindanao drops 2,500 feet to the sea in the course of about 25 miles and has a potential power output of 700,000 kilowatts of relatively cheap power. Only 50,000 kilowatts are in use at present, and further development of this power source must await the development of markets for additional power supplies. A second major hydroelectric project has been the development of the Agno River in Mountain Province. The power developed has a ready market in the Manila area, but must be transmitted 200 miles to this market. Philippine hydroelectric power resources are adequate for a market industrialization, and in view of the encouraging reports from oil exploration power resources will probably materialize at a rate which will not restrain Philippine economic development.

Table 12. Geographic composition of import trade
(percentage of total value of imports)

Trading partner	1937–40 [a]	1947–49 [b]	1950–52 [b]	1953–55 [c]	1956–58 [c]
United States	68.8	83.2	73.1	69.4	55.2
Asia	*17.8*	*8.8*	*17.8*	*18.4*	*25.3*
Japan	8.5	1.2	6.3	6.3	12.2
Indonesia	2.4	2.0	3.0	2.8	5.4
Malaya and Singapore	1.8	.9	1.1	1.7	2.4
Hong Kong	1.7	.2	1.7	1.5	1.5
Western Europe	*9.9*	*3.2*	*5.8*	*7.8*	*13.8*
United Kingdom	2.0	.8	1.4	1.9	3.4
Germany	2.5	.1	.8	1.7	4.2
Netherlands	1.9	.2	.8	1.7	2.1
Belgium-Luxembourg	.9	.8	.9	1.1	.7
France	.6	.2	.2	.6	.1
Spain	.1	.2	.3	.2	
Canada	1.2	2.1	3.1	3.1	2.6
Australia	1.7	.3	.3	.6	1.5
Rest of world	.6	2.4	—	.7	1.6
	100.0	100.0	100.0	100.0	100.0

[a] Commonwealth of the Philippines, Bur. of Census and Statistics, *Yearbook of Philippine Statistics, 1940.*
[b] UN, Statistical Office, *Yearbook of International Trade Statistics.*
[c] Central Bank, *Annual Reports.*

The most rapidly growing sector of the Philippine economy is manufacturing, which accounted for one-sixth of the national income in 1958 as compared to one-twelfth ten years earlier. Industrialization has been aggressively promoted by public policies including subsidization of capital market institutions and protection.

Philippine manufacturing is dominated by production for the domestic market and has been concentrated in nondurable manufactures

(Table 13). In 1956 manufactures of food, beverages, and tobacco accounted for more than two-fifths of the value added by manufacturing. Manufactures of textiles, clothing, and footwear, encouraged by high levels of protection, account for approximately 10 per cent. Durable manufactures have expanded at a rapid rate in recent years. Assembly of automobiles and trucks and construction of truck and bus bodies account for approximately one-quarter of such output, with plywood, glass containers, steel bars and rods, and light manufactures of metal accounting for approximately two-fifths. The principal part of the output of electrical machinery in recent years has been automobile storage batteries, light bulbs and fluorescent tubes, and air conditioners.[12]

The 1948 census tabulated 29,463 "manufacturing establishments" employing 77,500 wage earners and 12,600 salaried employees. More recently the *1956 Annual Survey of Manufactures* enumerated 7,208 establishments (five or more workers) employing 205,800 people. Manufacturing establishments employing more than 20 workers numbered 1,766 and accounted for 89 per cent of the value added by manufacturing and 71 per cent of manufacturing employment. Manufacturing employment of 205,800 was approximately 4 per cent of the estimated Philippine labor force.

The denominator of the index of economic growth, per capita real income, is population. Population is a means of production as well as the end of production, and qualitative changes in human resources will continue to be important determinants of the growth in real income. Philippine population, 7 million at the beginning of the American occupation in 1898, increased to 15.4 million in mid-1937 and in the following twenty years increased another 50 per cent to 22.7 million. A threefold population increase occurred in 60 years, and current rates of growth indicate a further doubling of population in not more than 30 years.

Demographic statistics from the Philippines, as elsewhere in Southeast Asia, leave much to be desired. The irregular censuses do, however, establish the outlines of population growth with considerable reliability. Intercensual rates of population increase have averaged 2.1 per cent annually during the period covered by reliable censuses. Moreover, during the past three years there have been a number

---

[12] See the detailed sample survey of manufacturing production, 1953–1956, in Central Bank, *Eighth Annual Report, 1956*, pp. 55–62.

of attempts to refine Philippine demographic estimates by use of the Philippine Statistical Survey of Households (PSSH).[13]

The age structure revealed by the PSSH suggests a crude birth rate in the high 40's per thousand people per year. The May 1956 PSSH survey round indicated that the "average number of children ever born" to married women in the sample who have completed their childbearing years is 7.1; this indicates a crude annual birth rate in the low 50's per thousand. A study of the number of children in the 0–4 and 5–9 year age groups according to the March 1957 PSSH survey round points to an annual birth rate between 46 and 53 per thousand for the period 1947–1957. At the same time studies of the age distribution of registered deaths show the death rate dropping from about 30 during the war to about 20 at present.[14]

Other studies independent of the PSSH data point in the same direction. A study of underregistration of births in one province indicated that only about 65 per cent of the births in that province were registered; if this is true of the nation generally, the birth rate must be about 53.[15] An attempt to estimate the birth rate and death rate for the country as a whole from the average of those regions with "relatively complete" reported rates indicates a national annual birth rate of 44.8 and a death rate of 11.5 per thousand.[16]

The various studies of Philippine demographic statistics are all subject to error of one kind or another; yet the convergence of independent research is impressive. Final word on the size and rate of growth of Philippine population must await the 1960 census. In the meantime it seems reasonably clear that the current birth rate is

[13] The Philippine Statistical Survey of Households, a joint project of the National Economic Council (Philippines) and the International Co-operation Administration (U.S.), was initiated in 1955. The PSSH drew up a sample design directed toward a stratified sample of Philippine households: 6,500 households in 300 barrios, 150 poblaciones, 58 provincial capitals and cities and metropolitan Manila. Between May 1956 and May 1958 six survey rounds were completed. In April 1958 an Inter-Agency Committee on Demography was established for reviewing the evidence on population growth.

[14] Recent Philippine demographic studies are surveyed in John J. Carroll, S.J., "Population Increase and Geographical Distribution in the Philippines," *Philippine Statistician*, 8 (Sept. 1959), 154–175.

[15] B. Aromin Basilio, "The Demographic Situation in the Philippines," *Statistical Reporter*, 2 (July 1958), 1.

[16] Frank S. Morrison, *A Study of Vital Statistics in the Philippines: Their Relation to the Annual Population Increase* (Manila: International Co-operation Administration, 1957).

Table 13. Survey of manufacturing establishments employing five or more workers [a]
(₱ million)

	Number of establishments	Value of product sold	Value added by mfr.	Book value of fixed assets	Employment [c] 000	Payroll
Food, manufactured	2,685	599	257	251	56.6	79.0
Beverages	118	149	98	49	8.4	20.2
Tobacco products	81	151	70	19	11.6	16.8
Textiles	186	118	43	38	10.1	17.4
Clothing and shoes	1,725	167	61	39	33.9	30.8
	4,795	1,184	529	396	120.6	164.2
Wood and cork products except furniture	344	123	50	55	19.6	31.7
Furniture and fixtures	340	26	12	7	6.5	7.8
Paper and paper products	75	47	19	17	3.2	5.5
Printed and published materials and allied products	299	64	34	32	9.8	23.2
Leather products except footwear and apparel	29	7	3	2	.7	.9
Rubber products	20	18	9	8	2.6	3.8
Chemicals and chemical products	252	252	92	76	9.6	25.1

	Number of establishments	Value of product sold	Value added by mfr.	Book value of fixed assets	Employment [c] 000	Payroll
Nonmetallic mineral products except those of petroleum & coal	168	75	43	53	6.0	11.9
Basic metal products	36	n.a.	n.a.	16	1.3	2.8
Metal products except machinery and transp. equipment	251	83	35	30	7.8	15.8
Machinery except electrical mach.	89	28	13	19	4.1	7.7
Electrical machinery, apparatus, appliances, and supplies	58	17	8	6	1.5	2.8
Transportation equipment	141	66	22	35	6.0	14.5
Miscellaneous manufacture [b]	311	163	102	84	6.4	13.4
	7,208	2,181	979	834	205.8	331.1
Including: Large establishments with more than 20 employees	1,766	1,858	874	720	147.3	272.7

[a] R.P., National Economic Council, *1956 Annual Survey of Manufactures*, vol. I, ser. 2 (Manila: Bureau of Printing, 1958).
[b] Including products of petroleum and coal which were combined with miscellaneous manufactures to avoid disclosure of information.
[c] Including working owners, production and related workers, and salaried employees.

close to 50 and the rate of natural increase is probably no lower than 3 per cent per year.[17]

Although the rate of Philippine population growth is a formidable obstacle to accelerated economic development, qualitative aspects of the demographic situation are quite favorable. The Philippines currently has a college population approaching 200,000 students. While the quality of education is low by Western standards, the system produces an impressive flow of graduates with minimum technical and professional skills. Filipinos have traditionally assigned prestige to training in law, medicine, accountancy, and so forth, but this value hierarchy is subject to rapid change and enrollment in technical and agricultural courses is increasing rapidly. In addition, the Philippines has a large and rapidly accumulating reservoir of individuals trained in the United States. It has been a long-standing Philippine tradition to seek higher education in the United States, and such students have been supported by private means as well as government subsidy—both Philippine and United States. The Philippine urban labor force is energetic, mechanically inclined, and receptive to training. Internal migration to the cities steadily augments the industrial labor force, contributes to industrial discipline, and limits the economic gains from rapid postwar unionization.

A dominant characteristic of the Philippine economic environment is the physical fragmentation. Not only does the Philippines comprise some 800 inhabited islands, but the physical features of the large islands tend to break them up into spatially distinct areas. Development of the internal market is restrained by the high cost of transportation and inadequate services.[18]

Rail transport has experienced limited development on Luzon, with a line extending from La Union Province through Manila to Legaspi in the extreme south, a distance of 550 miles.[19] Preliminary work is under way which will extend this system into the large and fertile Cagayan Valley in northeastern Luzon.

[17] Preliminary results of the census taken in 1960 and released in mid-1960 indicate that the official estimates of Philippine population, the estimates used in this study, were approximately 9 per cent too low. This error in the population estimates has been accumulating since the last reliable census of 1939 and does not substantially affect the statistical analysis of this study, although estimated growth rates will have to be adjusted downward.

[18] Spencer, *op. cit.*, pp. 74–85.

[19] There is a 72-mile railroad on Panay connecting Roxas City to Iloilo. This railroad has lost money for years, and operations are maintained at minimum levels.

Highway transport, also handicapped by island configuration, is the principal means of intraisland communication. Road construction and maintenance are centered in the Bureau of Public Highways and provincial Bureaus of Public Works and are supported by the proceeds of excise taxation on motor fuels and lubricants and proceeds from vehicle registration fees. The road system consists of approximately 18,500 miles of roads to service 60,000 passenger cars and 65,000 commercial vehicles, of which one-third are registered in Manila.

Interisland shipping compensates to a limited extent for the inadequacies of land transport, and all ports of economic significance receive regular service. About 4,000 vessels aggregating 350,000 tons are engaged in interisland shipping. Only about 100 are vessels of more than 150 tons. Although present facilities may be considered fairly adequate, the interisland fleet is rapidly becoming obsolete and many vessels are uneconomical.[20]

Internal air transportation has expanded rapidly since World War II, and all important islands and population centers receive efficient domestic air service. Domestic air transport revenues have been adequate to maintain a steady equipment modernization program as well as extension of services.

Philippine transportation facilities of all kinds are scheduled to receive substantial amounts of Japanese reparations, and the next ten years should see considerable modernization. In addition, the United States economic aid program has attached a high priority to road construction, particularly in the frontier areas. Considering the formidable obstacles arising out of the island nature of the country, the transportation facilities must presently be assessed as no more than adequate.

Philippine economic institutions are adaptations of the familiar framework of Western institutions. The monetary system is a managed currency system with a central bank. The central bank legislation specifies the customary techniques of central bank control, including the discount rate, open market operations, manipulation of reserve requirements, and the management of the international currency reserves. While legislation provides for the techniques of control which have been developed in industrialized economies, the operations of the Central Bank are restricted by the embryonic institutional framework

[20] Frederick L. Wernstedt, *The Role and Importance of Philippine Interisland Shipping and Trade* (Cornell Southeast Asia Program Data Paper No. 26; Ithaca, N.Y., 1957), pp. 130–132.

within which the bank must operate. Monetary policy is circumscribed by the disequilibrium in external payments, and the bank's principal function has been to manage the international reserve. Commercial banking traditionally concentrated on servicing foreign trade, including the provision of credit for producers of export crops. Branches of foreign banks were predominant, and limited resources were available to finance domestic trade, agriculture, and manufacturing. These functions were performed in large part by the Philippine National Bank, a government-owned commercial bank with banking offices widely distributed over the Philippines. In the postwar period additional indigenous commercial banks were established, as well as the government-capitalized Development Bank of the Philippines, which performs investment banking functions. As of the end of 1957 the domestic credits of the Central Bank, commercial banks, and the Development Bank of the Philippines, totaled ₱3.4 billion, or approximately 84 per cent of domestic credit outstanding.[21]

Other financial institutions include insurance companies, which at the end of 1958 numbered 121. Of these, 71 were domestic companies. Outstanding domestic investments of insurance companies at the end of 1958 totaled ₱242 million. Investments of insurance companies included loans, 40 per cent; government securities; 33 per cent; and other investments, 29 per cent. Also of importance is the Government Service Insurance System, which operates a retirement system for civil servants. As of the end of 1958 outstanding domestic investments of the GSIS amounted to ₱349 million. Investments of the GSIS included real estate loans, 49 per cent; other loans, 20 per cent; and government securities, 31 per cent.

Next in importance is the government-capitalized Agricultural Credit and Co-operative Financing Administration (ACCFA), which provides subsidized credit to the rapidly expanding network of Farmers' Co-operative Marketing Associations (FACOMAS). The outstanding credits of ACCFA totaled ₱86 million by December 31, 1958. Still another important source of agricultural credit are the Rural Banks. These are subsidized to a limited extent by government subscription of their capital and by rediscount privileges at the Central Bank. At the end of 1957, 106 rural banks had domestic credits totaling ₱28 million.

In the field of agricultural credit a structure of institutions has de-

[21] Not including credits of agricultural moneylenders and book credits of retail merchants.

veloped which departs from the form as well as the substance of the Western institutional framework. Basic to the financing of agricultural production and marketing is the moneylender. The moneylender is typically the landlord or the middleman who assembles the crop for transportation to domestic markets or abroad. Because of the prevalence of tenancy and the impaired tenure rights of nominal landowners, advances against crops are not available from conventional credit institutions but are available at high cost from moneylenders.

There were also at the end of 1958 1,239 postal savings offices with 390,284 accounts with outstanding balances of ₱42 million, seven building and loan associations with domestic loans outstanding of ₱10 million and seventy-six pawnshops in the city of Manila and suburbs with loans outstanding of ₱15 million. Manila has a vigorous securities exchange, where a wide range of corporation securities are traded.

This listing of the different institutions of the Philippine capital market should not leave the impression that these institutions are of the same relative importance and perform the same functions as in the West. Commercial banks exist primarily to finance foreign trade, and their portfolios of nontrade assets are relatively limited. The typical enterprise is family dominated regardless of the legal form, and business capital is traditionally family wealth as augmented by retained earnings. Though capital market institutions are embryonic by Western standards, they have not lagged behind the development of the demand for such institutions. The individual Filipinos saver has not reached the stage where he demands complex institutions to facilitate investment, and Filipino industrialization has not reached the point that complex functional specialization is demanded of capital market institutions.

· IV ·

Economic Survey, 1945-1958

POSTWAR Philippine economic development should be analyzed in terms of three relatively distinct phases or periods. First was the period of relief and reconstruction (1945–1950) after the defeat of the Japanese occupation forces. Second was a period of institutional reform and economic consolidation (1950–1953), which followed the visit of the Bell Mission. The third period (since 1953) has been a period of steady economic expansion distinguished by radical changes in fiscal and monetary policy following the inauguration of President Ramon Magsaysay in January 1954. This period has been marked by aggressive promotion of economic nationalism and resort to deficit financing to accelerate economic growth.

Relief and Reconstruction, 1945–1950

The rehabilitation of the Philippine economy took place in an environment which is accurately described as an emotional and economic binge following the destruction and dislocation of the war and the subsequent liberation. The years from 1945 to 1950 were characterized by a succession of clamorous economic crises superimposed on rapid expansion in production and real income. The economic extremities which beset the Philippine economy during this period were of two basic types. First was the succession of budgetary crises arising out of the failure of the national government to raise sufficient revenues to cover expenditures. Paradoxically, fiscal policy during this period was both conservative and irresponsible. Fiscal policy was conservative inasmuch as government economic activity was conducted at low levels, i.e., government receipts and expenditures averaged 5 to 7 per cent of national income. Budgetary deficits, though large relative to receipts or expenditures, were of minor significance when compared to the levels of economic activity or to the steady growth of output. The failure of the government to impose and to collect sufficient taxes to cover the low levels of expenditures can only be assessed as irresponsible.

The second type of economic crisis which plagued the Philippines was the steady pressure on available foreign exchange resources arising out of an unprecedented demand for imports. The strong import demand resulted from the import needs of rehabilitation and inventory replenishment, the pent-up demand for consumption, and maintenance of the prewar currency parity, which substantially overvalued the peso.

The fiscal and balance of payments problems of the Philippines tended to distract attention from deeper-seated and more disturbing social ills. First was the deterioration of public morality which attended the perversion of government institutions during the Japanese occupation; this was compounded by mismanagement of the transition to civilian administration in 1945 and 1946. Distortion of values and low standards of political morality in these critical periods have persisted as obstacles to the use of political institutions to pursue national economic goals. Second was the division within Philippine society, which had deep roots in tenure arrangements in agriculture and which was manifested in armed rebellion led by the Huks. This crisis reached a peak of intensity in the summer of 1950, when the continuity of the Philippine state was in question.

The Philippines emerged from the war with a substantial part of its physical capital destroyed. Bitter fighting during 1944–1945 together with heavy allied bombing and Japanese demolition resulted in extensive destruction of Philippine housing, plant and equipment, and livestock inventories. The problem of rehabilitation was complicated by the economic dislocation attributable to three years of Japanese occupation. The "Greater East Asia Co-prosperity Sphere" called for Philippine specialization in production of raw cotton largely at the expense of Philippine sugar production. As attrition of Japanese communications continued, Philippine interisland and external trade dwindled, production for export declined, and Japanese propaganda and organization efforts were directed to increasing food production for local consumption. Rapid inflation produced further distortion as Japanese authorities acquired the local resources needed for military purposes by printing their currency requirements—"mickey-mouse money." With the breakdown of Japanese control mechanisms and communications in the closing months of the liberation, inflation became rampant. By August 1945—in spite of repudiation of the occupation currency—available estimates indicate that the Philippine cost of living was approximately 800 per cent of what it had been before the war.[1]

The rehabilitation of the Philippine economy was many-faceted—Filipino and American, public and private. The liberation forces were primarily concerned with military goals and the development of Luzon as a staging base for the anticipated conquest of Japan. This required restoration of basic public utilities, including land and interisland transportation, electric power, water supply, and sanitation, as well as establishment of semipermanent supply facilities, troop housing, and so forth. The indirect contribution of military construction to Philippine rehabilitation, particularly communications, was substantial. Even today the visitor to the Philippines soon becomes aware of this contribution by the ubiquitous "Bailey bridges" and other military-type structures still in use.

A major contribution was embodied in relief supplies which provided urgent requirements of food, housing, clothing, and medical care. A substantial portion of this burden was assumed by the Civil Affairs Program of the United States Army, which distributed food, clothing, medical supplies, seeds, and so forth. This Program also included the transfer of transportation equipment to the Philippine government and to private enterprise and the establishment of schools and hospitals.

The Army Civil Affairs Program was cut back rapidly following the re-establishment of the Commonwealth government on February 27, 1945. Responsibility for Philippine relief was shifted to the United

[1] *Report to the President of the United States by the Economic Survey [Bell] Mission to the Philippines* (Washington, 1950), p. 14. Hereinafter referred to as the *Bell Mission Report.*

Nations Relief and Rehabilitation Administration (UNRRA), and the first shipment of UNRRA supplies arrived on September 14, 1945. Successive UNRRA allocations for Philippine relief and rehabilitation in September and November 1945 and March and August 1946 totaled $11 million plus substantial amounts of used clothing. Over half of all allocations were for food, with major allocations for clothing, seed and farm implements, medical supplies, and shipping charges.

The UNRRA emergency operations were clearly inadequate in terms of Philippine relief requirements. Moreover, announced UNRRA policy was not to deplete its available resources for the relief and rehabilitation of any area whose government was in a position to pay with suitable "means of foreign exchange." An UNRRA subcommittee recommended that "the Philippines be considered at the present time in a position to pay with suitable means of foreign exchange for essential relief and rehabilitation imports." [2]

This recommendation reflected the substantial foreign exchange reserves against which currency was issued by the Philippine government. Existing currency legislation could, however, be changed only with the acquiescence of the United States government and under existing legislation foreign exchange reserves could be utilized by the Philippine government to purchase relief and rehabilitation imports only if they were acquired in exchange for Philippine currency. This in effect meant that the Philippine government could utilize the foreign exchange backing of the peso currency issue only if a budgetary surplus was achieved. In view of low levels of tax collections and imperative demands for essential government services, this was not a practical alternative. [3]

The withdrawal of UNRRA from Philippine relief and rehabilitation activity was followed by emergency United States budgetary assistance to the Commonwealth government which maintained the flow of essential consumer goods under Philippine auspices. In amending the Philippine Independence (Tydings-McDuffie) Act in 1939,

[2] United Nations Relief and Rehabilitation Administration, *UNRRA in the Philippines, 1946–47* (Operational Analysis Paper No. 50; Washington, 1948), pp. 47–51.

[3] The alternative influencing the UNRRA decision was the knowledge that the U.S. Congress could enact legislation making the Philippine currency reserves available for current relief expenditures. The U.S. Congress chose to conserve Philippine foreign exchange reserves in anticipation of independence scheduled on July 4, 1946.

the United States Congress provided for remission to the Philippine government of the proceeds of certain United States taxes, principally the excise tax of 3 cents per pound on imports of Philippine coconut oil. Remission was made contingent upon use of the taxes remitted to adjust the Philippine economy to loss of American trade preferences scheduled under the Tydings-McDuffie Act. In November 1945 the accumulated receipts from these taxes amounting to about $72 million were transferred to the Philippine treasury for use by the Commonwealth government for "general purposes." [4] This injection of foreign exchange enabled the Philippine government to provide essential goods and services and at the same time made foreign exchange available to the economy to pay for required imports.[5]

The first half of 1946 was characterized by far-reaching economic and social developments attending the establishment of Philippine sovereignty. As a result of the election of April 23, 1946, Manuel A. Roxas (Liberal) replaced Sergio Osmeña (Nacionalista) as President with a working majority of both houses of Congress. The Huk provinces of central Luzon had taken the elections at their face value, and the peasantry had sought to further their interests through the Democratic Alliance which supported Osmeña. The refusal of the new Congress to seat a number of Democratic Alliance candidates who had been elected and subsequent neglect of agrarian reform measures drove the Huks underground and increasingly into open rebellion.

The spring of 1946 found the United States Congress considering legislation to consummate the transition to economic and political sovereignty scheduled in the Independence Act of March 24, 1934.[6] The economic provisions of the act defined an orderly transition to Philippine economic sovereignty in which the preferred position of each country in the market of the other would be reduced. Mutual

[4] Public Law 215, 79th Cong., 1st sess. In August 1946 the U.S. Congress authorized the return to the Philippine government of securities valued at somewhat over $6 million. These securities had been deposited with the United States by the Philippine government before the war as surety for military supplies and equipment loaned to the Philippines. During the Japanese invasion this equipment had been lost or destroyed (Public Law 652, 79th Cong. 1st sess.).

[5] For a comprehensive account of relief and rehabilitation activities in the Philippines during 1944 and 1945, see A. V. H. Hartendorp, *History of Industry and Trade of the Philippines* (Manila: American Chamber of Commerce of the Philippines, 1958), pp. 153–205.

[6] Public Law 127, 73rd Cong., 2nd sess.

free trade was to be continued from 1935 to 1940, with annual Philippine duty-free exports to the United States to be limited in the case of sugar to 850,000 long tons, coconut oil to 200,000 long tons, and cordage to 3 million pounds annually. Exports in excess of duty-free quotas were subject to full duty. Imports not specifically limited by quotas could be exported in unlimited amounts duty-free. There were no restrictions on United States exports to the Philippines. During the period 1941–1946 Philippine exports receiving preferential treatment in the United States market—i.e., those not on the "free list" of commodities and therefore subject to United States duties—were to be subject to a Philippine export tax of 5 per cent increasing 5 per cent annually to 25 per cent in 1946. Full United States tariffs were to be paid after July 4, 1946, the scheduled independence date.

While subsequent United States legislation made minor modifications in the economic provisions of the Independence Act, the basic principle of a gradual (10-year) transition to economic independence was maintained.[7] However, the painful process of withdrawing from the sheltered United States market was not experienced by the Philippine economy. The export tax and declining quota provisions were suspended for one year in 1941 and war with Japan further interrupted the transition.

With Philippine political independence scheduled to materialize on July 4, 1946, the United States Congress hastily drafted two important pieces of legislation—the Philippine Trade Act of 1946 [8] and the Philippine Rehabilitation Act of 1946.[9] The Philippine Trade Act of 1946, like its predecessor the Tydings-McDuffie Act, provided for mutual free trade during a transitional period—in the latter case until July 4, 1954. After this period increasing tariff duties were to be imposed by both countries on imports from the other country in increments of 5 per cent annually until full duties would be in effect in 1973. In addition, absolute quotas were continued on selected

[7] On April 14, 1937, a Joint (Filipino-American) Preparatory Committee on Philippine Affairs was created to study the economic problems of Philippine independence and propose legislative changes. The *Report of the Joint Preparatory Committee on Philippine Affairs* (Washington, May 20, 1938), vol. I, included proposals which would have made substantive revisions in the Independence Act. However, the subsequent amending act, Public Law 300, 76th Cong., 1st sess., Aug. 7, 1939, made only minor changes in the scheduled transition to Philippine political and economic autonomy.

[8] Public Law 371, 79th Cong., 2nd sess.

[9] Public Law 370, 79th Cong., 2nd sess.

Philippine exports to the United States. The economically significant quotas on sugar, coconut oil, and cordage were maintained at the levels established in the earlier Independence Act and were based on levels of Philippine exports to the United States in the late 1920's.[10]

In addition to providing for a gradual elimination of the preferred position each country enjoyed in the market of the other, the Philippine Trade Act of 1946 included a number of obnoxious infringements on Philippine sovereignty. These included (a) a commitment not to levy export taxes, (b) a "parity clause" establishing the right of United States citizens to participate in the exploitation of Philippine natural resources with the same rights and privileges as Philippine citizens, and (c) a Philippine commitment not to change the par value of the peso or to suspend the convertibility of the peso without "agreement with the President of the United States."

The Philippine commitment not to levy export taxes was matched by the United States constitutional prohibition of export taxation. The quota limitations on Philippine exports to the United States, the provision for national treatment for United States investors, and limitations on Philippine exchange rate autonomy were not matched by comparable commitments on the part of the United States.[11]

The blatant infringements on Philippine sovereignty of the Philippine Trade Act of 1946 were made palatable to Filipinos by enactment of companion legislation providing for United States compensation for war damage suffered by the Philippines. In November 1943, while the war was still in progress, the United States Congress amended the Tydings-McDuffie Act to provide for the establishment of a joint "Philippine–American Commission on Rehabilitation of the Philippine Islands." The joint commission was to formulate recommendations for rehabilitation and for future trade relations between the two countries.[12] After liberation the question of reconstruction became

[10] In the case of coconut oil, cigars, tobacco, and pearl buttons, instead of imposing increasing tariff duties in 5 per cent increments, the duty-free quota would be reduced at the same rate (5 per cent annually beginning in 1954) until in 1973 all Philippine exports of these commodities would be paying full U.S. duties. Imports in excess of the duty-free quota were permitted, subject to the ceiling of the absolute quota.

[11] For a more extended analysis of the 1946 Trade Agreement, see Frank H. Golay, "The Economic Consequences of the Bell Trade Agreement," *Pacific Affairs*, 28 (March 1955), 53–70.

[12] Public Law 381, 78th Cong., 2nd sess. This resulted from Senate Joint Resolution 94 introduced by Senator Tydings on Nov. 3, 1943.

urgent, and in June 1945 a special investigating mission was sent to the Philippines by the United States War Damage Corporation to estimate losses and prepare recommendations for implementing the payment of war damages. As a result of this investigation, it was estimated that the total loss of private, public, and church properties in the Philippines was approximately $800 million in terms of 1939 values.[13]

The war damage legislation which was finally approved on April 30, 1946, provided for outlays totaling $620 million. A total of $400 million was authorized to compensate private parties for war damage.[14] Claims were to be based on the actual (assessed) values of losses or the cost of repair or replacement, whichever was less. Moreover, it was provided that large claims might be reduced by 25 per cent of the amount over $500. The $400 million authorized for rehabilitation was expected to compensate for about 50 per cent, at prewar cost estimates, of the private damage sustained.[15]

In addition to payment of private claims, the act authorized the allocation of $120 million to "restore and improve public property and essential public services." Moreover, transfer to the Commonwealth government of United States surplus property (excluding military weapons and munitions) of a fair value not to exceed $100 million was authorized. The act also provided for extensive technical assistance by United States agencies in restoring Philippine war damage and technical training of Philippine government personnel

[13] *Survey of War Damages in the Philippines,* Report of the Special Investigating Mission sent to the Philippines in June 1945 by the War Damage Corporation and completed in September 1945, 79th Cong., 1st sess. (Washington, 1945). Estimated war damage included: public property, $195,347,595; Catholic church property, $125,000,000; other church property, $14,000,000; private property, $464,420,000.

[14] Philippine Rehabilitation Act of 1946, Public Law 370, 79th Cong., 2nd sess. See also *Philippine Rehabilitation Act of 1946,* Hearings before the Committee on Territories and Insular Affairs, U.S. Senate, 79th Cong., 1st sess. (Washington, 1945).

[15] U.S.–Philippine War Damage Commission, *First Annual Report for Period Ending December 31, 1946* (Washington, 1947). *The Final Report of the Philippine War Damage Commission* (Washington, 1951) reported that war damage claims by private property owners totaled ₱2.5 billion. The report goes on to say that "the Commission approved claims on the basis of prewar values, as required by law, and was able to pay only 52.5 per cent of the approved amount of claims in excess of $500" and that this represented "22.5 per cent less than the statutory maximum of 75 per cent fixed by the Rehabilitation Act."

in the United States. Finally, it provided that war damage payments in excess of $500 would be authorized only after the Philippines had accepted the companion Bell Trade Act.[16]

The "parity" provision of the Trade Act required an amendment to the Philippine constitution which could not but be noxious to Filipinos generally. However, the tying together of the two acts provided a *quid pro quo* which ensured acceptance of the "parity" amendment.

Two further substantial United States commitments to participate in Philippine rehabilitation were made. First were obligations arising out of the absorption of the Philippine Armed Forces (guerillas) into the United States Armed Forces, Far East (USAFFE), in 1945. As a consequence of this decision, the United States extended a wide range of veterans benefits to Philippine veterans. Disability pensions, hospitalization, and "back-pay" awards as well as the benefits of the "G.I. Bill of Rights" were available to Filipino veterans.[17] During the ten years following 1946 United States Veterans Administration disbursements averaged $124 million annually. In addition, payments of "arrears in pay" and "current pay" to Filipino members of the USAFFE amounted to $473 million in the five years following 1945.

Finally, the United States government agreed in 1946 to extend sufficient budgetary assistance to cover the anticipated Philippine government budget deficit during the first year of independence. This resulted from a visit of President-elect Manuel A. Roxas to the United States in the interval following his election on April 23, 1946, and prior to inauguration of the Philippine Republic on July 4, 1946. While in the United States, Roxas told the United States Congress that the Philippine government would need $400 million in reconstruction loans over a period of five years, including $100 million of fiscal assistance in the first year of independence.[18]

[16] It is beyond the scope of this survey to review the extensive controversy over the obligation of the United States to compensate for Philippine war damage. While the U.S. payments fell considerably short of full compensation for damages, they contributed substantially to the rehabilitation of the Philippines. When the U.S. war damage payments are considered together with the extensive outlays for relief and rehabilitation and the $800 million Philippines-Japan reparations settlement, it is obvious that the Filipinos have been substantially compensated for the material losses of the war.

[17] G.I. benefits were extended to Filipino veterans on the reduced scale of one peso per dollar of comparable obligation to an American veteran.

[18] *New York Times*, May 15, 1946. Roxas added that making independence succeed was as much to the future interest of the United States as it was to the Philippines.

Roxas' proposal had two significant results. First, a budgetary loan of $75 million was extended by the United States Reconstruction Finance Corporation to meet the anticipated deficit in the Philippine government budget in fiscal year 1946–47. Second, while no further loan commitment was made, a joint Philippine-American finance commission was created to "investigate the financial and budgetary problems of the Philippine government and to make recommendations . . . with reference to taxation, budget, public debt, currency, banking reform, exchange and trade problems, reconstruction and development." [19]

Completion of the liberation of the Philippines in 1945 found domestic production paralyzed and distribution between rural and urban areas almost completely broken down. Moreover, there were virtually no commercial imports because of the shortage of shipping, which was in heavy demand to supply staging bases in anticipation of the invasion of Japan. Because of the shortage of goods and the rapid increase in currency in circulation resulting from United States military expenditures, prices were sustained at relatively high levels. In 1945 the average cost of living in Manila was 776 per cent of that of 1937.[20]

The Philippine economy functioned at very low levels during 1945–1946. During 1946 physical production was estimated to be less than 40 per cent of production in 1937. The index of manufacturing production was estimated at 21 per cent and of mining at 2 per cent. In agriculture, which experienced more substantial recovery, 1946 output was estimated at 58 per cent of that of 1937.[21]

With the improvement in internal security and communications in 1946, production began to recover. Moreover, heavy United States military expenditures coincided with increased supplies of ocean shipping, and imports rapidly expanded. During 1945–1946 net United States government disbursements totaled 403 million dollars, and earnings from exports (f.o.b.) amounted to an additional $65 million. The large foreign exchange receipts were largely offset by imports, which in 1946 amounted to $335 million (c.i.f.) as compared to $29 million in 1945. In 1946, with the volume of imports equivalent to 125 per cent of prewar and with agricultural production approximately

[19] *Report and Recommendations of the Joint Philippine-American Finance Commission,* H.R. Doc. 390, 80th Cong., 1st sess. (Washington, 1947).
[20] *Bell Mission Report,* p. 14. [21] *Ibid.,* p. 6.

60 per cent of prewar, the cost of living in Manila fell 25 per cent below the high levels of 1945. For 1946 the average cost of living was estimated to be 585 per cent of that of 1937.

Inauguration of the Republic of the Philippines on July 4, 1946, found the Filipinos in a favorable position to rehabilitate their economy and to organize their society to achieve further progress. First, the United States was committed to heavy disbursements including war damage payments. These payments, with favorable terms of trade, enabled the Philippines to sustain imports at more than double the prewar volume during 1947–1949. Second, Philippine external security was guaranteed for the foreseeable future and Philippine fiscal resources were not subject to heavy drain for defense expenditures.

By 1949 the index of the physical volume of production had steadily increased to 91 per cent of the prewar (1937) level.[22] National income had increased from ₱4.4 billion to ₱5.7 billion, an increase of 30 per cent. Moreover, as this was a period of steadily declining prices—the cost of living index declined from 585 for 1946 to 385 in 1949—the expansion in real national income was substantially greater than the expansion in money income.[23]

In spite of the steady expansion of the Philippine economy, the period from 1946 to 1950 was characterized by a succession of economic crises as the basic social ills developed economic symptoms. First, "reconversion" of the Philippine rural economy was essentially a process of restoring the prewar tenure relations in agriculture and rehabilitating the prewar primary producing export economy. Rehabilitation not only involved individual disappointments and privations, but in the Philippines as elsewhere in Southeast Asia aspirations for economic development and sovereignty tended to suffer frustration. Second, the deterioration in standards of public morality became evident in a succession of scandals involving both politicians and the bureaucracy. "Anomalies" in the handling of surplus property disposal, visas for Chinese immigrants, and, following 1949, corruption in import licensing tended to undermine public confidence in political institutions and processes. Third, with persistent fiscal irresponsibility, the Philippine government refused to levy taxes adequate to cover expenditures and, moreover, failed to collect existing taxes. Finally, there was the decline in Philippine foreign exchange re-

[22] *Ibid.*   [23] *Ibid.,* p. 14.

serves as imports continued to expand while exports made only a partial recovery to prewar levels. In view of the decision to defend the prewar currency parity, the resulting disequilibrium in foreign exchange receipts and payments ultimately proved to be manageable only by recourse to stringent import and exchange controls.

The economic activities of the early postwar Philippine governments were extremely limited in scope and magnitude. Whereas in 1940 Philippine national government revenues amounted to almost $100 million, in fiscal year 1945–46, the first full year after Philippine liberation, tax revenues amounted to only $53 million, of which almost one-third came from taxes on cigarettes. This record becomes even more surprising in view of the sixfold price inflation and expansion in money income.

In October 1946 the Philippine Congress approved twelve tax bills which, it was hoped, would increase revenues by at least $30 million during the coming fiscal year. War profits and black-market gains were to be taxed, and graduated income taxes were to be levied. The low levels of revenue experienced in the initial postwar period tended to persist as collections did not match the increases in tax rates. For example, in fiscal year 1947–48 estimated income tax collections of ₱14 million were only ₱2 million over fiscal year 1939–40 collections even though the corporate rate was 50 per cent higher than the 1940 rate and individual rates were increased by as much as 30 per cent. The Philippine Bureau of Internal Revenue estimated that about 30,000 individuals and corporations were liable under war profits tax legislation, but three months after the date for filing returns only 1,920 returns had been received and of these 1,440 showed no tax liability.[24]

During the five postwar fiscal years to June 30, 1950, Philippine national government revenues from taxation averaged ₱250 million annually, and total receipts averaged ₱294 million. During this same period Philippine national government expenditures averaged ₱376 million, which contributed to the cumulative postwar deficit of ₱461 million. To place these aggregates in perspective it should be remarked that national government tax revenues averaged only 4.5 per cent of estimated national income during the five calendar years ending in 1950, and government expenditures averaged 6.8 per cent.

[24] For analysis of the fiscal operations of the early years of the Philippine Republic, see *Report Joint Finance Com.*

While levels of fiscal activity were low, financing of the deficit proved to be a difficult problem. To begin with, the Philippines remained on an exchange reserve standard until the establishment of the Central Bank at the beginning of 1949. Under this arrangement the Philippine currency issue was backed 100 per cent by foreign exchange reserves and fluctuated in volume with the balance of payments. While the other element in the money supply—demand deposits—showed a much lower reserve ratio, the over-all ratio of foreign exchange to the money supply tended to be relatively high, about 50 per cent. So far as the fiscal requirements of the government are concerned, the principal consequence of the exchange reserve standard was to establish a brake on the capacity of the government to engage in deficit financing. Installment of a managed currency system and establishment of the Central Bank in January 1949 provided only temporary relief to the government from fiscal stringency. Legislation creating the Central Bank included explicit provisions designed to ensure the independence of the Monetary Board in formulating monetary policy and specifically limited the loans and advances which could be extended by the Central Bank to the government.

The restrictive impact of the exchange reserve standard and the conservative Central Bank Act was augmented by the narrow market for government securities. Government bonds were relatively unattractive investments when compared with available alternatives and therefore did not compete successfully for the credit resources of commercial banks or the savings of individuals.[25]

The cumulative deficit of the national government during the first five postwar years is most appropriately analyzed in terms of the annual deficit and the extraordinary financing for the deficit. As has already been mentioned, governmental operations during fiscal years 1944–45 and 1945–46 were sustained primarily by receipt from the United States of approximately ₱180 million ($90 million) which had

[25] While institutional arrangements limited access by the government to the banking system to finance budgetary deficits, the government was able to finance limited functions by the borrowings of government enterprises. Government enterprises were able to borrow from the Philippine National Bank (a government-owned commercial bank) and the Central Bank either directly or through the government-owned holding company—the National Development Company. During the five postwar fiscal years ending June 30, 1950, the capital accounts of government enterprises increased by ₱288 million. New capital subscribed through budgetary appropriations amounted to ₱208 million, while approximately ₱80 million was borrowed from the Philippine National Bank and the Central Bank. See *Bell Mission Report,* pp. 23–24.

accumulated in the Coconut Oil and Sugar Processing Excise Tax Funds. During 1947 the principal extraordinary receipt was ₱120 million, proceeds of part of the United States Reconstruction Finance Corporation loan for budgetary purposes.

During the three fiscal years ending in June 1950 the conversion of the monetary system from an exchange reserve standard to a currency managed by the Central Bank resulted in access by the government to a number of nonrecurring sources of funds. First, the government was able to utilize a part of the resources of the Exchange Standard Fund and the Treasury Certificate Fund in which had been held (in the United States) the foreign exchange resources used to back the Philippine currency issues.[26] These sources provided ₱112 million. Second, the Central Bank Act provided for limited amounts of loans and advances by the Central Bank to the government. By the middle of 1950 government borrowing from the Central Bank for budgetary purposes amounted to ₱146 million. Finally, there were miscellaneous sources of peso funds including various government trust funds which were utilized to meet the cumulative deficit.[27]

In addition to the extraordinary sources of receipts listed above, during the five years to June 30, 1950, the Philippine government also utilized proceeds from the sales of Japanese properties which had been turned over to the government by the United States Foreign Liquidation Commission. Receipts from this source totaled ₱83 million. Finally, there were substantial receipts from liquidation of the surplus property turned over to the Philippine government as provided in the Philippine Rehabilitation Act. Although precise accounting of these receipts is not available, they have been estimated to be between ₱80 and ₱90 million.

The Philippine fiscal crises were clamorous and imperative, not because of their magnitude and difficulty of solution, but because of the refusal of the government to face up to minimum fiscal responsibilities. By the end of 1949 the government seemed willing to let the military go unpaid and the educational system wither for want of funds, and even to succumb to the Huk rebellion, rather than face up to minimum responsibility for governmental functions. The de-

[26] Conversion to a currency system managed by the Central Bank was followed by a decline in the over-all ratio of foreign exchange backing for the money supply. The "saving" of foreign exchange became available to the government to finance budgetary expenditures.

[27] For information on the *ad hoc* financing of the annual deficits, see *Bell Mission Report*, p. 22.

manding economic symptoms were manifestations of a deeper moral crisis. The real crisis was the rapid decline in faith in the honesty and integrity of the government. This loss of faith was measured, not by the refusal of the well to do to pay taxes, but by the growing frustration of the middle and lower classes in the face of mounting evidence that the body politic was incapable of action in the interests of all the Filipinos. It is a depressing commentary that the reforms, when they did come, were to a considerable extent installed from the outside as a result of the Bell Mission and its recommendations. The evidence is not conclusive that the Filipinos had the collective will to put their house in order. The disillusionment with existing political institutions was deep, and the will to try again to make them function was eroding rapidly.

The deterioration in the political environment was in sharp contrast to the rapid economic rehabilitation. Recovery of Philippine production is explained by the unprecedented level of investment sustained between 1945 and 1949. The Bell Mission estimated that during the four years 1946–1949, approximately ₱4.0 billion was newly invested in equipment, stocks, and construction. This amount of investment was approximately one-fifth of estimated national income during 1946–1949. Not only was investment taking place at high levels, but because investment was for the rehabilitation of war damage it tended to be highly productive. The principal types of agricultural investment included bringing back under cultivation land which had gone out of cultivation during the war and the restoration of depleted livestock inventories. Commerce and trade accounted for approximately one-third of the estimated investment, with investment in inventories amounting to 70 per cent of such investment. Investment in industry, transport, and utilities and public works was estimated to total ₱1,160 million, or slightly less than one-third of estimated investment. The remaining investment was accounted for by residential and other nonbusiness construction, which was estimated to equal ₱503 million.[28]

[28] *Ibid.*, pp. 8–11. More recent studies result in a substantial deflation in the estimates furnished the Bell Mission by the Central Bank of the Philippines. The United Nations estimates that gross investment during 1946–1949 totaled ₱2,376 million, including gross private domestic investment of ₱2,059 million and gross government investment of ₱317 million. UN, Technical Assistance Administration, *The National Income of the Philippines and Its Distribution* (New York, 1952), pp. 5–9.

Gross investment during 1946–1949 was prodigious, and accomplishments were very substantial. Nevertheless, the Bell Mission in 1950 reported that

despite the large investment, . . . what has been done so far involves no more than restoration and reconstruction. While the aggregate physical production in 1950 will be nearly the same as in 1937, this is an unsatisfactory level of production for the Philippines. With a population more than 25 per cent larger, the Philippines is now probably producing less than the volume of agricultural and industrial goods it produced thirteen years ago [p. 10].

The levels of net investment maintained during 1945–1949 were sustained by external savings transferred to the Philippines through a surplus of imports of goods and services. During the four years following 1945 the import surplus amounted to ₱2,121 million, which was more than matched by United States government disbursements of $1,401 million.[29]

As compared to 1937, Philippine imports during 1947–1949 averaged 212 per cent in volume and increased fivefold in value. On the other hand, exports during 1947–1949 averaged 63 per cent of the average volume of exports during 1937–1940. In other words, the Philippines during the period of rehabilitation was able to have more than twice the prewar volume of imports in exchange for less than two-thirds the prewar volume of exports. This enormous transfer of real income to the Philippines from the outside could not fail to exert a far-reaching impact on Philippine rehabilitation.[30]

[29] It is, of course, true that the decisions to invest necessary to the rapid reconstruction were essentially Philippine decisions. However, they were not matched by comparable decisions to save. Total net borrowings and net donations from abroad during 1946–1949 amounted to ₱1,575 million. UN, Tech. Assist. Adm., *op. cit.*, p. 5.

[30] It is outside the scope of this chapter to do more than briefly summarize postwar economic developments. It is, of course, true that U.S. disbursements consisted for the most part of payments to individuals, and the amount of economic aid in the sense of grants and loans to the Philippine government was limited. Moreover, a significant part of the U.S. disbursements, particularly military expenditures in 1945–1946, represented payments for Philippine goods and services. Such payments should logically be considered as proceeds of exports to the United States of Philippine goods and services. In terms of the problem of Philippine rehabilitation it is highly significant that the Philippines was able during 1946–1949 to have unrequited imports of goods and services, i.e., imports not compensated for by an exchange of exports, of the order of magnitude of ₱2 billion. This amount was approximately one-tenth of Philippine national income during this period.

Observers of the Philippine scene have tended to analyze postwar Philippine economic problems in terms of inflation, both real and incipient.[31] However, the rapid rehabilitation of production with the unprecedented import surplus financed by United States payments made possible a rapidly expanding supply of goods and services. As a result, the entire postwar period until the outbreak of hostilities in Korea was characterized by declining prices. There was a single inflationary symptom in the Philippines, namely, the steady pressure on the balance of payments. Filipinos tended to spend more abroad than could be sustained by foreign exchange earnings because the purchasing power of their pesos when exchanged for foreign currencies at the unrealistic official exchange rate was greater than the purchasing power of the peso internally. This was the result, not of current inflation, but of the distorted cost-price structure inherited from World War II.[32] In spite of the relatively rapid recovery of production—particularly production for the domestic market—and the steady decline in Philippine prices, the peso remained overvalued.

The price inflation which had been inherited from the liberation period (1944–1945) produced significant shifts in the structure of Philippine production. The relatively favorable prices realized in the domestic Philippine market led to the diversion of resources to production for domestic consumption and the relatively retarded recovery of export production. Recovery of export production was also handicapped by the severe destruction of plant and equipment during the war. Sugar production and gold mining, which during 1937–1940 accounted for 52 per cent of the value of Philippine exports, recovered slowly. Philippine sugar exports during 1947–1949 averaged 217,000 metric tons, or 24 per cent of the average annual exports in 1937–1940, whereas the average annual gold production during 1947–1949, equal to $13 million dollars, was only 20 per cent of production in 1937–1940.

Logs, timber, and iron ore, which formerly were marketed in

[31] The persistence of this point of view is surprising in view of the analysis in the Bell Mission report, which demonstrates clearly and unambiguously the nature of the postwar Philippine inflation. See *Bell Mission Report*, pp. 13–14.

[32] It is, of course, possible to postulate circumstances in which inflation in incomes would impinge on the balance of payments at the same time that the price level was declining. Such a situation would require quite restrictive assumptions. The relative height of the postwar Philippine price level and the maintenance of the prewar currency parity provide a simpler, more persuasive explanation of the pressure on the Philippine balance of payments at the time that the domestic price level was declining rapidly.

Japan, recovered slowly because of the laggard normalization of trade with Japan and the retarded recovery of the Japanese economy. The production of abacá increased slowly because of difficult production problems. Although hard fiber prices tended to be favorable, Philippine abacá production was handicapped by the loss of the technical skills of the Japanese, who provided much of the entrepreneurship and capital in the prewar abacá industry. Changes in the organization of abacá production were followed by serious inroads by the damaging mosaic infection.

The bright spot in the Philippine export picture was the coconut industry. Coconut products enjoyed very favorable prices during the postwar shortage of fats and oils, and production was expanded considerably over prewar levels. Although some part of the expansion of copra exports during 1946–1949 represented production which accumulated during the latter years of the war, a substantial permanent expansion in production occurred as plantings made in the late interwar period came into production.

The volume of exports (excluding gold), which amounted to 19 per cent of the 1937–1940 average in 1946, increased to an index of 66 per cent for 1949. If gold exports are included in the index, the recovery in the volume of exports was only to approximately 50 per cent of prewar levels. The same picture emerges in agricultural production statistics. For those crops consumed domestically, plantings were expanded substantially over prewar ones, but those of export crops had made only a partial recovery by the end of 1949.

The Philippines, in common with primary producing countries in general, enjoyed favorable terms of trade during the postwar period. For example, as compared to 1937–1940, the ratio of the unit value of exports to the unit value of imports was 107 in 1946, 134 in 1947, 158 in 1948 (a peak), and 137 in 1949. Then as a result of the outbreak of war in Korea it rose to 145 in 1950. The improvement in the terms of trade contributed materially to the productivity of Philippine resources engaged in export production but only partially offset the handicap of the prewar currency parity.

With respect to the remaining items in the Philippine balance of payments the prewar pattern emerged. The Philippines tended to have substantial outpayments for shipping charges on imports and large amounts for services and capital charges, including remission of dividends and profits to foreign investors. Nontrade receipts other than United States government disbursements were large in the postwar period relative to prewar experience. This was largely due to an inflow of private foreign investment to rehabilitate war-damaged capacity.

A substantial part of the postwar import surplus was paid for by a drawing down of Philippine foreign exchange reserves. Philippine foreign exchange reserves reached a peak of $647 million at the end of 1945 following the transfer by the United States of the proceeds of the sugar and coconut-oil-processing excise taxes and the various currency reserve funds. After 1945 Philippine foreign exchange reserves fluctuated between $400 million and $450 million until 1949, when reserves drained away at a rapid rate. By the end of 1949 reserves had declined by $160 million from the level of $420 million a year earlier. Over the four postwar years 1946–1949 Philippine foreign reserves were drawn down by almost $500 million to make foreign exchange payments.

The growing crisis in Philippine external payments was brought under control during 1950 by exchange and import controls which rationed the available foreign exchange among various claimants. Effective exchange and import controls were first implemented in December 1949, and during the first half of 1950 the intensity of controls was steadily increased until for the full year 1950 the volume of imports was reduced to 58 per cent of that of 1949.

Although exchange and import controls enabled the Philippines to limit foreign exchange payments to the available receipts, they produced three important complications. First, the Philippine government chose to ration the foreign exchange more or less arbitrarily, with all sales of foreign exchange at the official (two-pesos-per-dollar) rate. Yet in the end the reduction in the demand for imports and other foreign payments had to result from increases in the prices of such goods and services. The recipients of foreign exchange licenses sold the reduced quantities of imports of goods and services at prices the market would bear. The intensification of exchange and import controls during 1950 produced rapidly rising import prices—increases unrelated to changes in the cost of imports in foreign currencies. For example, by April of 1951 the index of wholesale (peso) prices of imported commodities reached 163 per cent of the 1949 level, while the comparable index for domestic commodities was 104 per cent.[33]

[33] The index of wholesale prices of "nonessential" imports reached a peak of 180 (1949 = 100) in May 1951.

Similarly, the index of retail prices of imported commodities reached 148 per cent of 1949 levels in May of 1951 while the retail price index of domestic commodities stood at 104 per cent of 1949 levels.[34] Inasmuch as the unit value of import prices remained steady at 100 per cent in 1950 (1949 = 100) and increased to 111 per cent in 1951, it is apparent that the intensification of exchange and import controls accounted for the principal part of the inflationary increases in import prices.

Second, exchange and import controls contributed to the deterioration in morality and reinforced the growing disillusionment and apathy which permeated the Philippine society. The windfall arising out of exchange and import controls was shared by various participants in importing activities including bona fide importers, "ten-percenters," legislators with influence to peddle, and bureaucrats implementing the controls. The scandals which characterized the administration of exchange controls climaxed a disheartening list of well-publicized, large-scale postwar scandals in the body politic.[35]

A third complication arising out of stringent import and exchange controls was the impact on national government revenues. Government revenues in the Philippines, in common with less-developed countries generally, are highly dependent upon taxation of import values. For example, in 1949 revenues from this tax base accounted for 55 per cent of total revenues. Stringent import controls reduced revenues from this tax base in 1950 by ₱35 million to ₱164 million. Reduction in tax revenues on import values more than accounted for the decrease in national government tax revenues in 1950 of ₱33 million. In view of the fiscal difficulties of the government and the growing Huk threat, the fiscal consequences of exchange and import controls were unfortunate.

Stocktaking and Reform, 1950–1953

The year and a half following the end of 1949 proved to be an eventful period in postwar Philippine economic development. It witnessed far-reaching changes which went far to solve the fiscal and balance of payments problems which had plagued the postwar

[34] For details of movements of relative prices following the imposition of exchange and import controls, see Central Bank, *Fourth Annual Report, 1952*, p. 175.

[35] For a comprehensive list of Liberal party scandals—the issues in the elections of 1951 and 1953—the reader is referred to Coquia, *op. cit.*, pp. 100–109.

Philippines. More important, 1950 saw the beginning of an effective military campaign that reduced the Huk threat to minor dimensions. The dramatic shift in Philippine fortunes in 1950 and 1951 had a number of significant aspects. First, internal political developments in the Philippines produced greater legislative and executive responsibility. Second, international developments produced changes in United States foreign policy, which resulted in firmer economic, military, and political commitment by the United States in the Philippines. Third, the strong international demand conditions following the outbreak of war in Korea sustained a rapid expansion in Philippine export production and trade which had tended to lag behind in Philippine postwar reconstruction and rehabilitation.

The internal security position together with chronic Philippine fiscal and balance of payments difficulties deteriorated alarmingly during 1949. In February of 1950 President Truman, on invitation of President Quirino, agreed to send an economic survey mission to the Philippines to "advise the Philippines on the establishment of a sound and well-balanced economy." Subsequently, a difference of opinion arose over the composition of the mission. The Philippines indicated a strong preference for a joint group such as the earlier Finance Commission, while the United States insisted on a mission composed of Americans. Although President Quirino on March 20, 1950, appointed a commission of distinguished Filipinos in anticipation of joint participation in the announced mission, the United States view prevailed and on June 10 the Economic Survey (Bell) Mission arrived in Manila.[36]

In the meantime the chronic Philippine fiscal crisis had continued to worsen under the impact of stringent import controls, and there was again the prospect that in the absence of extraordinary budgetary receipts the civil service, including the armed forces, would go unpaid and minimum governmental services would not be maintained. As has been pointed out, this situation was attributable, not to inordinate demands on Philippine government resources, but to an

[36] The membership of the Philippine (Survey) Commission included Jose Yulo, former speaker of the House of Representatives, chairman; Pio Pedrosa, Secretary of Finance; Miguel Cuaderno, governor of the Central Bank; Bienvenido M. Gonzales, president of the University of the Philippines; and Filemon C. Rodriquez, manager of the National Power Corporation. The U.S. Economic Survey (Bell) Mission was composed of Daniel W. Bell, chairman, Richard J. Marshall, Edward M. Bernstein, August L. Strand, and Francis M. Quillan.

unwillingness to levy and collect sufficient taxes to provide for the relatively low levels of governmental activity.

Government trust funds were appropriated to continue minimum government services in the spring and summer of 1950. In the fall of 1950 the government was again "bailed out" of the annual fiscal crisis by recourse to extraordinary sources of receipts. Some ₱70 million was diverted to the Philippine government by a United States agreement to fund into a ten-year debt obligation the undisbursed portion of funds appropriated by the United States Congress to make "back pay" payments to Filipino forces inducted into USAFFE in 1944 and 1945.[37] The unexpended back pay funds, which had been deposited in the Philippines, had been immobilized by litigation initiated by Philippine veteran interests and had not been allowed to revert to the United States Treasury as intended by the United States Congress. Similarly, by agreement with the International Monetary Fund the Philippine government was allowed to substitute long-term bonds for the Philippine peso subscription to the fund. In effect, the Philippine government was able to borrow ₱22 million from the International Monetary Fund. These "loans," together with ₱112 million of proceeds from the sale of Rehabilitation and Development Bonds to the Central Bank, enabled the government to meet budgeted expenditures during the fiscal year ending June 30, 1951.

Progress toward a more permanent solution to Philippine fiscal problems occurred during the regular and special sessions of Congress in 1950, when a number of new tax measures were enacted which, it was estimated, would produce approximately ₱90 million of additional revenue.[38] The impact of these new revenue measures

[37] The Romulo-Snyder Agreement of Nov. 6, 1950, committed the Philippine government to return of the dollar funds on a scheduled amortization.

[38] The more important measures were Republic Acts No. 562 of June 17, 1950, imposing a ₱50 alien registration fee; No. 567 of Aug. 30, 1950, sharply increasing stamp taxes; No. 571 of Sept. 5, 1950, increasing duties on gasoline, mineral oils, asphalt, and the like; No. 579 of Sept. 15, 1950, increasing estate, inheritance, and gift taxes; No. 588 of Sept. 22, 1950, raising basic sales taxes, excise taxes on luxury and semiluxury articles, and various license and business taxes; No. 589 of Sept. 22, 1950, increasing specific taxes on alcoholic beverages and cigarettes; No. 590 of Sept. 22, 1950, increasing personal and corporate income tax rates and providing withholding tax. Other tax legislation included Republic Acts No. 436 of June 7, 1950; No. 456 of June 8, 1950; No. 564 of Aug. 11, 1950; No. 565 of Aug. 11, 1950; No. 568 of Aug. 31, 1950; No. 572 of Sept. 5, 1950; No. 574 of Sept. 8, 1950; No. 586 of Sept. 22, 1950; and No. 587 of Sept. 22, 1950.

was felt promptly and helped to offset the decline in government receipts resulting from the intensification of exchange and import controls and the reduction in import values.

The Philippine balance of payments, which was brought under control during the first half of 1950, benefited from shifts in international demand conditions following the outbreak of war in Korea. As compared to 1949, the terms of trade improved and Philippine export production and trade, reflecting the high levels of investment of the earlier postwar period expanded rapidly. The index of the volume of exports in 1950 was 130 per cent of 1949, and in 1951 it rose to 146 per cent. The combination of favorable prices and increased quantities of exports resulted in expansion in export proceeds from ₱508 million in 1949 to ₱820 million in 1951, an increase of 60 per cent. The improvement in foreign exchange earnings combined with relatively intense exchange and import controls produced a rapid increase in foreign exchange reserves. These reached a peak of $391 million in April 1951 as compared to $260 million only sixteen months earlier.

Publication of the Bell Mission report in October 1950 found much of the urgency which had prompted the dispatch of the mission only a few months earlier dissipated in the rapid improvement in Philippine economic prospects. Although the Bell Mission was extremely critical of Philippine economic policies, the report was accepted by the Philippines as an opportunity to initiate changes, with the help and co-operation of the United States, which would contribute to sustained Philippine economic growth.

The Bell Mission reported:

Economic conditions in the Philippines are unsatisfactory. The economic situation has been deteriorating in the past two years and the factors that have brought this about cannot be expected to remedy themselves. Unless positive measures are taken to deal with the fundamental causes of these difficulties, it must be expected that the economic situation will deteriorate further and that political disorder will inevitably result. Whatever is to be done to improve economic conditions in the Philippines must be done promptly, for if the situation is allowed to drift there is no certainty that moderate remedies will suffice.[39]

The mission made far-reaching recommendations in the areas of fiscal policy, agricultural development, and social and administrative

[39] *Bell Mission Report*, p. 1.

reform. To make the program acceptable to the Philippines, the mission proposed that the United States undertake an economic aid program in the Philippines of the order of magnitude of $250 million over five years.

The Bell Mission report was a factual, objective survey of Philippine economic problems. The recommendations of the report established the broad outlines of a series of institutional reforms and policy changes which occupied the attention of the Philippine government in the ensuing four years. The report marked the introduction of much-needed objectivity and continuity in United States economic policy in the Philippines to replace earlier reliance on *ad hoc* expedients to deal with transient symptoms. The Bell Mission report served notice to the Philippines that United States assistance to the Philippines was to "be strictly conditioned on steps being taken by the Philippine government to carry out the recommendations of the Mission."

It would be a mistake, however, to attribute the post-1949 reforms to the Bell Mission, and its successor United States aid mission, as there were even more significant internal changes in the Philippines in 1950. Probably most important was the political independence and statesmanship displayed by President Quirino following the election in November 1949. During the early postwar period the Liberal party, a more-or-less unstable coalition of regional political leaders, was disciplined by the specter of the election of 1949 as well as wholesale distribution of public funds in the interests of the Liberal party politicians. The Liberal party was organized to maintain its legislative majority and perpetuate itself in office by the flagrant use of patronage to ensure party loyalty. Following the election of 1949—an election characterized by widespread fraud and intimidation—the Liberal party coalition tended to fall apart.[40] Assurance of a full term in office afforded President Quirino an opportunity for independent action which he did not have prior to 1949 when his political future was uncertain and his control over the party weak.

The growing independence of Quirino proved to be highly beneficial. For example, he acquiesced in the strengthening of the Commission on Elections, a change which has produced far-reaching improvements in the quality of Philippine politics. He also, possibly

[40] For an informative account of the breakdown of the structure of the Liberal party and the important consequences of these developments, see James J. Dalton, "Ins and Outs in the Philippines," *Far Eastern Survey*, 21 (July 30, 1952), 117–123.

to discipline his rebellious party, did not intervene with his administrative power to influence the election of 1951. Moreover, he vigorously supported the then Secretary of Defense, Ramon Magsaysay, who used the armed forces to ensure an election relatively free of intimidation and fraud.

The most important Philippine accomplishment following 1949 was the reduction of the Huk threat to minor proportions. In 1948 and 1949 President Quirino made unsuccessful attempts to bring about a reconciliation with the Huks, but in 1949 and the first half of 1950 Huk depredations increased. In April 1950 Quirino sent Ramon Magsaysay (Liberal), chairman of the House Committee on National Defense, to the United States to ask for additional military aid under the Military Assistance Agreement of March 20, 1947. The Magsaysay mission was successful, and in the two fiscal years ending June 30, 1954, the Philippines received $47 million of military aid as compared to $20 million in the preceding five fiscal years.

In the meantime the Philippines had taken vigorous steps to meet the Huk threat. The military budget was expanded from ₱116 million in fiscal year 1949–50 to ₱131 million in 1950–51 and ₱185 million in 1951–52. In March 1950 Quirino merged the Philippine constabulary, heretofore primarily responsible for the maintenance of law and order, into the better-trained and better-disciplined army. Responsibility for internal security was assigned to the army. Ten battalion combat teams were created out of scattered army and constabulary companies to take the field against the Huks. On July 1, 1950, Quirino created a National Security Council and on September 1, 1950, Magsaysay was appointed Secretary of National Defense. Under the leadership of Magsaysay and with the full support of Quirino, the armed forces rapidly brought the rebellion under control. The reduction of the Huk threat was substantially a Philippine accomplishment and occurred during a period in which the Philippines dispatched the first of five battalion combat teams to fight with the United Nations forces in Korea.

Finally, the outbreak of hostilities in Korea and subsequent developments in international politics produced a solution to the problem of Philippine external security. In the early postwar period the Philippines, in common with other newly sovereign countries, envisaged an acceptable external security arising out of the United Nations as supplemented by regional consultation on problems of common interest. This basic premise of Philippine foreign policy was manifested in active participation in the United Nations, participation in the Delhi Conference of January 1949, and Philippine initiative in convening the abortive Baguio Conference of May 1950. As the collapse of Nationalist China proceeded, the Philippines became increasingly concerned with the problem of external security and sought to establish a firm United States commitment to defend the Philippines. The Philippines astutely used bargaining power arising out of the desire of the United States for a Japanese peace treaty to obtain the desired commitment, which was embodied in the Mutual Security Treaty signed in Washington, August 27, 1951.

The ensuing period through 1953 were years of far-reaching institutional reform superimposed on steady economic growth. They were years characterized by effective efforts to develop institutions and policies appropriate to sustained economic development. They were years of close and effective co-operation between the United States and the Philippines in problems of Philippine economic development, social stability, and external security. They were years of effective economic statesmanship in the Philippines in which the quality of economic leadership and initiative contrasted sharply with the irresponsibility of the earlier postwar years.

Although improvement in the Philippine economic situation in the last half of 1950 would have supported a more independent position, the Philippine government displayed determination to implement the recommendations of the Bell Mission. On November 14, 1950, President Quirino and William C. Foster signed an Agreement on Economic and Technical Co-operation. The Philippines agreed substantially to implement the Bell Mission recommendations and the United States in turn agreed to furnish technical assistance, to resume negotiation of a treaty of friendship, commerce, and navigation, to re-examine the provisions of the 1946 trade agreement, and to initiate an economic "aid program envisioned at $250 million over five years."

When the Philippine Congress convened at the beginning of 1951, the legislative commitments of the Quirino-Foster Agreement found tough sledding as Congress was involved in complex personal and party disputes involving powerful factions in the numerically dominant Liberal party and the growing Nacionalista minority.[41] However,

[41] *Ibid.*

on March 28, 1951, President Quirino signed Republic Acts No. 600 and No. 601, which increased corporate income taxes and established a special tax on sales of foreign exchange. Finally, on April 6, approval of the Minimum Wage Law (Republic Act No. 602) completed the legislative program considered by the United States to fulfill the Philippine commitment in the Quirino-Foster Agreement.

The tax measures enacted in 1950 and 1951 produced dramatic improvement in the Philippine fiscal situation. National government tax revenues, which had amounted to ₱329 million in fiscal year 1949–50, virtually doubled to ₱655 million in fiscal year 1951–52. The special tax on sales of foreign exchange was particularly productive, receipts from this tax amounting to ₱155 million in fiscal year 1951–52. Increases in tax revenues permitted rapid expansion in social investment and welfare expenditures. Moreover, in the remaining three years of the Quirino administration a substantial cumulative budgetary surplus resulted.

The rapid improvement in Philippine foreign exchange reserves after June 1950 resulted primarily from curtailment of foreign exchange payments. Improvement in the reserve position was followed by a reduction in the intensity of controls, and import quantities and values sharply increased. During the last half of 1951 the import rate was ₱1,100 million annually as compared with ₱586 million in the first half of the year. Such fluctuations in the tightness of control tended to produce uncertainty in business calculations and instability in the prices of imported goods. The experiences of this period led to the establishment of a policy of managing the foreign exchange reserve by quarterly budgeting of receipts and expenditures to maintain net foreign exchange reserves at a more-or-less arbitrary "safe" level of $300 million.[42] Subsequent management of the foreign exchange reserve during 1952–1954 reflected this policy decision, and the international reserve fluctuated narrowly around the minimum safe level.

A second significant development in the area of foreign exchange policy was establishment of satisfactory institutional arrangements for the implementation of exchange and import controls. The windfall profits arising out of import restrictions proved to be a strong motivation of bribery, graft, and corruption, and the administration of import controls became a major postwar scandal. The successive administra-

[42] Central Bank, *Fifth Annual Report, 1953*, p. 107.

tion of controls by the Import Control Administration and the Import Control Board demonstrated that administration of import controls could not be left to this type of political institution. Following the elections in the fall of 1951, the Nacionalista party organized Congress with strong working majorities. Import control legislation was allowed to expire on June 30, 1953, and the administration of exchange and import controls devolved by default on the Central Bank.[43]

Administration by the Central Bank produced rapid improvement in exchange and import controls and went far to restore public confidence in controls as an instrument of public policy. The Central Bank administered import and exchange controls through agent commercial banks which policed the transactions of customers in accordance with existing legislation and administrative orders issued by the Central Bank.[44]

A major achievement of the Quirino administration which is little appreciated was the establishment of the Central Bank and its governing Monetary Board as effective instruments of monetary and fiscal stability. In contrast to the experience of many less-developed countries in the postwar period, the integrity and autonomy of the Central Bank were firmly established during 1950–1953. Conservative limits set in the Central Bank Act to access by the government to Central Bank credit were strictly observed. Under the strong leadership of Governor Miguel Cuaderno these institutions (Monetary Board and Central Bank) made an important contribution to rapid improvement in the Philippine economic environment.

Once the fiscal and balance of payments problems had been solved, the Philippines produced a succession of institutional changes appropriate to further economic progress. First was the creation of an effective agency for planning Philippine development expenditures,

[43] The Central Bank Act (Republic Act No. 265 of June 15, 1948) provides, in Sec. 2, that the Central Bank is responsible for the maintenance of the par value of the peso. Under the authority of Sec. 2 the Central Bank took over the administration of import and exchange controls.

[44] While administration of import and exchange controls by the Central Bank was far superior to previous administrations, the bank came under attack from disgruntled exporters and other interest groups which failed to share in the windfalls arising out of controls. These attacks, which reached a peak of intensity in the winter of 1955, rapidly undermined public confidence in the bank. For a detailed account of the battle over economic policy in the last half of 1955, see Frank H. Golay, "The Philippine Monetary Policy Debate," *Pacific Affairs*, 29 (Sept. 1956), 253–264.

the Philippine Council for United States Aid (PHILCUSA). Not only did this body contribute to an economically rational allocation of United States aid, but, more important, the Philippine Congress accepted the principle of appropriating counterpart funds to meet the peso costs of aid projects. During the three fiscal years ending in 1954 such appropriations totaled ₱103 million.

In the area of agricultural development emphasis was given to the establishment of credit and marketing institutions. On June 6, 1952, legislation was approved creating a system of rural banks.[45] To encourage the extension of banking facilities the legislation called for substantial capital participation by the government as well as rural bank access to the credit facilities of the Central Bank. On August 14, 1952, legislation was approved creating the Agricultural Credit and Co-operative Financing Administration (ACCFA).[46] ACCFA was capitalized by a liberal revolving fund appropriation and has been strongly supported by United States aid. ACCFA was authorized to extend low-cost loans to Farmers' Co-operative Marketing Associations (FACOMAS). FACOMAS in turn extend credit to members to finance agricultural marketings and investments in agricultural development.

The period 1950–1953 did not witness comparable achievements in other areas of agrarian reform. Organized colonization was dormant for lack of funds. Although land reform (distribution of estates to cultivators) was continually discussed, no significant policy changes were made and land reform for all practical purposes was a dead letter. Crop distribution laws and tenure security arrangements, which have been long-standing Philippine agrarian reform policies, suffered from weak enforcement. Two promising changes were initiated under prodding and financial support from the United States aid mission. Administrative changes and equipment were introduced which resulted in efficient and rapid land survey and title registration. These changes contributed to a dramatic increase in the rate of voluntary colonization. Of comparable importance were the establishment of the Bureau of Agricultural Extension [47] and the subsequent organization of an agricultural extension service.

Important changes were initiated in the area of Philippine commercial policy. Philippine dissatisfaction with the 1946 trade agree-

[45] Republic Act No. 720.   [46] Republic Act No. 821.
[47] Republic Act No. 680 of June 24, 1952.

ment had increased as the time approached for the imposition of tariffs on trade between the two countries. The Bell Mission report recognized that the 1946 agreement was an irritant in Philippine–United States relations and the Quirino-Foster Agreement provided for revision of the 1946 agreement. During 1952 President Quirino initiated steps leading to establishment of a Philippine position on revision of the treaty.[48] Closely related was the establishment of the Tariff Commission, which initiated action leading to a comprehensive revision of the Philippine tariff code.[49] The existing tariff had been enacted by the United States Congress in 1909, and subsequent changes had been of minor significance.

Of comparable importance were changes in the area of industrial relations, beginning with the Minimum Wage Law enacted in the spring of 1951 and culminating in the "Magna Carta of Labor." [50] The latter, modeled on the Taft-Hartley Act of the United States, substituted the principle of collective bargaining for the existing, and generally unsatisfactory, system of compulsory arbitration. Equally important, the new law sharply reduced the discretionary authority of the Secretary of Labor, which had been subject to abuse.

The policy of balanced budgets and management of the international reserve at a minimum safe level was matched by conservatism in monetary and credit policy, with the result that the period 1950–1953 was characterized by internal monetary stability and continued economic expansion. During the period 1950 through 1953 national income rose from ₱5,464 million to ₱7,015 million, an increase of 28 per cent. Inasmuch as the cost of living index for 1953 was the same as for 1949, this also tended to measure the increase in real income.[51] The rate of increase in real income was substantially higher than the rate of population growth and afforded a rewarding rate of increase in per capita real income.

In this period export earnings expanded rapidly from $254 million in 1949 to $404 million in 1953, an increase of 59 per cent. This increase was largely accounted for by an increase in volume of 51

[48] For details of these developments, see Central Bank, *Fourth Annual Report, 1952*, pp. 64–67, 398–410.
[49] Republic Act No. 911 of June 28, 1953.
[50] Republic Act No. 875 of June 17, 1953.
[51] The cost of living index admittedly is not the appropriate deflator for national income. In the absence of a better measure, it provides a reasonably reliable indicator of the change in real income.

per cent. Recovery to prewar levels had not, however, been completed by 1953, and export production and trade continued to lag behind other sectors of the economy. Improvement in export earnings and other foreign exchange receipts permitted some relaxation in the stringent import controls, and the volume of imports in 1953 was 23 per cent greater than in 1950 but 27 per cent below the peak levels of 1949.

The rapid domestic economic expansion which had characterized the earlier postwar period continued. During the three years following 1950 the index of the volume of physical production increased by 35 per cent, with agricultural output up by 32 per cent, mining 61 per cent, and manufacturing 40 per cent. Gross domestic investment receded from the high levels of the earlier period of rehabilitation of war damage. During the four years 1950–1953 gross domestic investment totaled ₱2,390 million as compared to ₱2,515 million in the preceding four years. In view of the expansion in national income, the rate of gross domestic investment out of national income declined from 12.3 per cent for the earlier period to 9.0 per cent for 1950–1953.

Although rapid expansion characterized the Philippine economy during 1950–1953, public confidence in the government showed no comparable recovery. This was confirmed by the presidential election of 1953 when President Quirino was turned out of office by a Magsaysay landslide. The principal issues in the 1953 election were graft, corruption, and political immorality. While the graft to be obtained from surplus war property and the blackmailing of Chinese refugees had been exhausted, loss of these sources was more than compensated by opportunities arising out of exchange and import controls. Those individuals receiving import and exchange licenses were awarded a windfall profit, depending upon the tightness of import restriction. Under such circumstances it was not surprising that politicians, corruptible bureaucrats, and "ten-percenters" made strenuous efforts to participate in the gains. In addition, a succession of ill-conceived government enterprises tended to maintain opportunities for graft.

The four years following mid-1950 were years of steady economic expansion superimposed on far-reaching institutional changes. The Philippine government supported and encouraged by the modest United States economic aid program, attacked with great success a number of economic problems that had plagued the postwar Philippines. Although the more clamorous problems were amenable to short-run remedies, the Philippines made little progress in solving two major economic problems: the problem of agricultural poverty and the problem of foreign exchange earnings, the latter of which continued to restrain Philippine economic expansion.

Monetary Policy and Economic Growth, 1954–1958

The election of Magsaysay promised continued rapid economic change for the Philippines. The widespread appeal of the campaign issues of corruption and economic mismanagement implied the need for legislative and institutional changes. Moreover, the Nacionalista party, by capturing both the executive and the legislative branches of the government, was in a position to execute economic plans with minimum concern for their effects on the political fortunes of their adversaries. As compared with the period 1950–1953, however, the pace at which economic and social reforms were introduced was slowed. More vigorous enforcement of existing reforms was a dominant characteristic of the Magsaysay administration.

Magsaysay's deepest personal involvement was with the peasantry, and he made strenuous efforts to carry through a comprehensive program of agricultural reform. Early in his administration he revived the moribund policy of government-organized and government-subsidized land colonization. The National Rehabilitation and Resettlement Administration (NARRA) was organized with high hopes that internal migration and land colonization would relieve population pressure and agricultural poverty.[52] A second major element in Magsaysay's agrarian reform program was land reform, i.e., the distribution of agricultural estates to the cultivators, which was enacted in Republic Act No. 1400 of September 9, 1955. Unfortunately, the political power of the landowners in the Nacionalista party was sufficient to emasculate this program, and accomplishments under the legislation have been quite limited. A third element in the agrarian reform program was the establishment of the Court of Agrarian Relations and the Agricultural Tenancy Commission to regulate tenancy relations and to enforce the more liberal crop distribution arrangements provided in national legislation. Closely related to and com-

[52] Magsaysay's experiences as Secretary of Defense with the rehabilitation of agricultural dissidents in the Philippine Armed Forces Economic Development Corps (EDCOR) settlements undoubtedly encouraged him to think of this policy in terms of the broader problem of agricultural poverty and tenancy.

plementary to the program of agrarian reform was the Community Development Program, which in the absence of congressional financial support Magsaysay initiated in the Office of the President with discretionary funds at the disposal of the executive.

A further contribution to agrarian reform involved extension of the agricultural co-operation movement. The Agricultural Co-operative Credit and Financing Administration, liberally supported by congressional appropriation and by the United States economic aid agency, increased the number of FACOMAS from 66 at the end of 1953 to 502 at the end of 1958, with a total membership of 289,000 farmers. Rural banks, subsidized by the government, were also opened at a rapid rate, reaching a total of 120 by the end of 1958. Outstanding agricultural credit from these institutions expanded from ₱4.1 million at the end of 1953 to ₱91.8 million at the end of 1957.

A major effort was made to change institutions and techniques of government in the interests of efficiency. Republic Act No. 997 of June 9, 1954, established the Government Survey and Reorganization Commission, which in the following eighteen months recommended a series of changes appropriate to more efficient government. A number of the changes recommended by the Commission received congressional approval. Republic Act No. 992 of June 4, 1954, initiated a performance budgeting system to replace the antiquated item budget which had contributed to persistent congressional irresponsibility. Republic Act No. 1161 of June 18, 1954, created a social security system. The reforms promised by these legislative acts did not materialize in their entirety, but they represented a continuation of the process of legislative reform initiated in 1950.

The principal economic change of the Magsaysay administration was abandonment of the conservative monetary and fiscal policies which had tended to prevail throughout the postwar period. In his campaign Magsaysay was highly critical of the failure of the Philippine economy to provide rewarding job opportunities and promised that, if elected, solution of the problem of unemployment would be a principal objective of economic policy. Shortly after taking office at the beginning of 1954, Magsaysay outlined a Five-Year Economic Development Plan (1954–1959), which he estimated would create 1.7 million jobs and would require ₱800 million of investment annually, public investment providing 44 per cent of the total.[53] To carry out

[53] *Manila Bulletin*, March 22, 1954, p. 10.

this program of development, Congress enacted Republic Act No. 1000 of June 12, 1954, which authorized the President to issue up to ₱1 billion of bonds to "finance public works and self-liquidating projects for economic development."

Inasmuch as there exists only a small market for Philippine government securities outside the banking system, Republic Act No. 1000 represented a radical departure from earlier monetary policy which severely limited access by the government to the money-creating powers of the Central Bank.[54] The effect of Republic Act No. 1000 was to stimulate economic expansion at the cost of "unbalancing" the government budget and intensifying balance of payments disequilibrium. In the four years following 1954 Central Bank credit extended to the government increased fourfold from ₱260 million to ₱1,049 million while other Central Bank credit, i.e., loans to banks and credit agencies, expanded by a modest ₱83 million. The rapid expansion of Central Bank credit to finance government deficits provided commercial banks with excess reserves which made possible rapid expansion of bank credit to individuals and businesses from ₱848 million at the end of 1953 to ₱1,588 at the end of 1958.

The impact of the rapid expansion in credit on prices was quite limited. The wholesale price index as of the end of 1958 stood at 102 per cent of the 1953 average. The rise in the Consumer's Price Index was more marked. This index at the end of 1958 stood at 106 per cent of the 1953 average with all of the increase occurring in 1957 and 1958. Inasmuch as disbursement of the proceeds of Republic Act No. 1000 bond issues required considerable time, only about one-half of the proceeds had been disbursed by the end of 1957. With about half of the proceeds of Republic Act No. 1000 remaining to be spent, the impetus to price inflation was intensified throughout 1958 and could be expected to continue unabated in 1959.

A second effect associated with the policy of monetary expansion to finance public economic development was the deterioration in the balance of payments position and the loss of international reserves. During the four years following 1953 the international reserve declined from $296 million to less than $100 million. As might be expected, the principal source of this deterioration was expansion in

---

[54] The Central Bank Act provided for maximum Central Bank credit to the government of ₱200 millions of research and development bonds plus advances limited to 15 per cent of the average annual government expenditures.

import payments, which increased from an average of $480 million annually during 1950–1953 to $600 million annually in 1954–1957, reaching a postwar peak of $691 million in 1957. Exports continued their postwar expansion in volume, but this tended to be offset by price declines from the high levels which prevailed during 1950–1953. The import surplus averaged $188 million annually during 1954–1957 as compared to $112 million in the preceding four years.

A major change in exchange control policy occurred in 1955, when producer-exporter interests were able to open a substantial legislative breach in exchange controls. The inappropriately named "No-Dollar Import Law" provided that marginal exports, i.e., exports in excess of a prescribed historical base, could be bartered for imports outside the exchange and import control system.[55] Heavy political pressure has been exerted by exporting interests to maintain and expand the marginal export barter principle. On the other hand, economic interests with a stake in currency overvaluation and exchange controls have strongly resisted encroachment on exchange controls.

More important in analyzing Philippine balance of payments problems following 1953 were internal political developments which contributed to the failure of exchange controls to maintain the international reserve. During 1955 and 1956 monetary policy came under heavy attack by forces organized and led by exporting interests which were restless under the exchange control system. The Monetary Board, politically sensitive to this attack, chose to relax the intensity of controls and abandon the policy of conservative management of the international reserve.

The capacity of the Central Bank to manage the international reserve deteriorated rapidly during the election year 1957. The Nacionalista candidate for President was the incumbent, Carlos Garcia, who had succeeded to the Presidency upon the death of Magsaysay in March 1957. With his political existence at stake in the election in November, Garcia, abetted by the Nacionalista-dominated Congress, exerted heavy pressure on the Monetary Board to make liberal exchange allocations. The windfall inherent in such exchange allocations helped to ensure the loyalty of political favorites. Moreover, increased supplies of consumer goods helped to maintain price

[55] Republic Act No. 1410 of Sept. 10, 1955. A No-Dollar Import Office was created in the Department of Commerce and Industry to administer the law.

stability and create the illusion of well-being among the less-favored elements in the society.

A second policy change promised by the Magsaysay administration was a reversal of a long-standing policy of government participation in entrepreneurial activity. Magsaysay repeatedly avowed that his administration would depend upon private enterprise and individual initiative and he promised to liquidate unprofitable government enterprises, which had been accumulating since the establishment of the Commonwealth. While such a change was appropriate, the economic importance of the liquidation of defunct and moribund government corporations should not be exaggerated. The distribution of functions between government and private enterprise was not materially changed, and many of the liquidated enterprises were soon replaced by new institutions with similar functions.

A major economic policy goal of the Nacionalista Congress, which became evident as early as 1951, was an acceleration of economic nationalism in the narrow sense of "wresting" various lines of economic activity from alien (Chinese) control. The major legislative move in this direction was the Retail Trade Nationalization Law, Republic Act No. 1180 of June 19, 1954. If fully implemented, this law within one generation will dispossess all aliens (except United States citizens) presently engaged in retailing in the Philippines. More immediate progress in Filipinization of economic activities was achieved by use of exchange and import controls to increase Philippine participation in the import trade, a policy initiated by the first import control act in 1949. Allocating the lucrative import licenses to Filipinos guaranteed their competitive viability.

Nationalist desires were also assuaged by rapid transition to Philippine autonomy over commercial policy. Import controls were used to establish high levels of protection for domestic producers, while the Revised Trade Agreement provided for rapid acceleration in the rate at which Philippine tariff duties were to be collected on imports from the United States. Equally satisfying to nationalist emotions were the provisions of the Revised Trade Agreement which removed the obnoxious infringements on Philippine sovereignty which cluttered the 1946 Trade Agreement.

This period also saw the culmination of the prolonged and frustrating reparations negotiations with Japan. The Reparations Agreement signed on May 9, 1956, provided for total reparations transfers of

$550 million over twenty years, plus a Japanese commitment to make long-term loans to the Philippines totaling $250 million. All except $50 million of the reparations are to be transferred in the form of Japanese goods and services.

The Magsaysay administration chose to seek social change and economic progress primarily within the existing institutional framework. Heavy pressure was maintained in the area of agrarian reform to give substance to the promises embodied in existing and new legislation. Social investment was sharply increased through recourse to deficit financing. Government revenues improved steadily with the collection of duties on imports from the United States as provided in the Revised Trade Agreement and the enactment of the new tariff code. Government expenditures tended to increase slightly as a ratio of national income with the expansion in developmental expenditures authorized in Republic Act No. 1000. Major changes took place in the allocation of government revenues. Outlays for defense declined slightly from the high levels established at the height of the effort to suppress the Huk revolt in 1951–1953. Expenditures for economic and social services expanded rapidly from ₱184 million in fiscal year 1952–53 to ₱431 million in fiscal year 1956–57, with a substantial part of the increased outlays going to education. Finally, there was sharp expansion in investment expenditures by the national government; these expanded from an average of ₱135 million in 1952–53 to ₱323 million in 1956–57.

During the three fiscal years 1952–1954 there was a small cumulative national government budgetary surplus of ₱81 million, but in the succeeding three fiscal years the cumulative deficit amounted to ₱338 million. The budgetary deficit was entirely accounted for by increased investment by the national government, which expanded from a total of ₱421 million in the fiscal years 1952–1954 to ₱778 million in 1955–1957. Direct borrowings by the national government from the banking system were augmented by bank credit extended to government corporations and agencies. Aggregate bank credit extended to the public sector increased from ₱406 million at the end of 1954 to ₱1,008 million at the end of 1957.

As in earlier postwar years Philippine economic policy problems were superimposed on rapid economic expansion. The index of physical volume of production rose by 25 per cent in the three years following 1954, with agricultural output increasing by 20 per cent, mining by 34 per cent, and manufacturing by 40 per cent. The pace of postwar growth in national income was maintained; the 25 per cent increase over the four years following 1953 was substantially greater than the growth in population.

The momentum of the Magsaysay political campaign served to unite the Philippine nation behind the new administration and established conditions favorable to rapid economic progress and social reform. These potentialities for progress were realized to a limited degree. The *élan* evident in the first two years of the administration was noticeably diminished in 1956, and there was increasing disillusionment and bitter political controversy both between Congress and the administration and within the administration.

President Garcia, who succeeded Magsaysay when the latter was killed in a plane crash on March 17, 1957, inherited a set of economic symptoms somewhat similar to those of the early postwar years. The budget was substantially unbalanced, and commitments under Republic Act No. 1000 were such as to ensure that this situation would prevail for some time to come. Exchange and import controls had deteriorated in public esteem. There was growing recognition that reliance on exchange and import controls to defend the prewar exchange parity was a sterile policy with limited potential to contribute to Philippine economic development. Increasing evidence of wholesale evasion of exchange controls plus the legal loopholes in the control system negotiated by favored export groups contributed to a lessening of morale and morality. In view of the new taxes as well as progression in existing taxes, the failure of government revenues to expand relative to the expansion in income strongly suggests that tax discipline was definitely not improving.

Important aspects of the economic situation deteriorated during 1957 as the Philippines was absorbed in the scheduled presidential election. Garcia, struggling to establish his political independence and power, was neither in a position to, nor interested in, taking the steps necessary to alleviate the growing balance of payments crisis. The Monetary Board was guilty of economic irresponsibility as easy credit policies and liberal exchange allocations were continued until after the elections in November. During 1957 Central Bank holdings of securities and debts of various agencies of the government expanded from ₱474 million to ₱841 million, an increase of 77 per cent.[56] This was in sharp contrast with the extension of credit by commercial banks to individuals and businesses which increased from ₱1,254 million to ₱1,513 million, or by 21 per cent. The international reserve of the Central Bank declined precipitously from $161 million at the end of 1956 to $71 million at the end of 1957.[57]

Immediately after the election in November the Garcia administration inaugurated an "austerity" program of credit restriction and more stringent exchange controls in an effort to restore the international reserve.[58] On December 9, 1957, Central Bank Circular No. 79 was issued providing for cash deposits of (a) 200 per cent against letters of credit for imports of "semiessential" consumer goods and "nonessential" producer goods, (b) 100 per cent against more essential imports, and (c) prohibition of imports of "nonessential" goods. Moreover, a Central Bank circular letter that accompanied Circular No. 79 enjoined the banks not to lend funds to cover the deposit requirements.

The December measures were met by strong protests, and relaxation commenced almost immediately. Imports were, however, reduced from ₱613 million in the last half of 1957 to ₱567 million in the first half of 1958, and foreign exchange holdings of the Central Bank increased by $10.5 million. On the other hand, government expenditures continued at high levels, and Congress passed a budget for fiscal year 1958–59 calling for expenditures of ₱1,347 million as compared to estimated revenues of ₱1,017 million.

The year 1958 saw Philippine attempts to revive the earlier postwar policy of seeking *ad hoc* balance of payments assistance. President Garcia resumed the practice of the political pilgrimage to the United States by the newly elected Filipino President, a practice which

[56] A part of the increase in Central Bank holdings of government securities and debts represented purchases from commercial banks which drew down their holdings by ₱189 million to ₱166 million.

[57] The international reserve is a gross figure. Offsetting the "official" reserve was $40 million, repayable in dollars, which the Central Bank borrowed from U.S. banks during 1957. Inasmuch as no comparable liability appeared in the balance sheet of the bank in 1956, the net international reserve of the bank actually declined during 1957 by $130 million and at the end of 1957 amounted to some $30 million.

[58] The first forceful step in reversing the policy of "credit ease" which the Monetary Board had pursued since 1954 was taken on Sept. 2, 1957, when the rediscount rate was raised from 2 to 4.5 per cent.

had been interrupted by Magsaysay. An avowed purpose of the visit was to obtain dollar credits. Official communiques indicated that substantial dollar credits had been extended to the Philippines. Subsequent developments have shown that such credits were established to cover foreign exchange costs of specific projects and therefore do not serve to ease directly the tight Philippine balance of payments situation. In late 1958 Garcia made a similar state visit to Japan and received a warm reception. Although substantial credits were established in favor of the Philippines as a result of this visit, they also proved to be tied to specific projects and were therefore not available to ease the tight foreign exchange position.

Controversy over exchange rate and exchange control policy continued unabated. Shortly after succeeding to the Presidency, Garcia was confronted by Senate Bill No. 167, which had passed both houses of the Nacionalista-controlled Congress. This legislation provided for extension of the marginal export barter system and would have denied an increasing part of foreign exchange earnings to the exchange control authorities. The proponents of the legislation were undoubtedly aware that such a large legal breach in the government's monopoly of foreign exchange transactions would have made the demise of the control system likely. Confronted by a politically explosive decision, Garcia chose to veto the bill.

A major element in the "austerity" program initiated after the election in 1957 was repeal of the No-Dollar Import Law, which provided for an extensive and growing volume of barter transactions outside exchange controls. Repeal of the law was strongly supported by the administration, but Congress adjourned in 1958 without taking action. During the last half of 1958 continuation of relatively tight money policies, minimum restraints on government expenditures, and stringent import and exchange controls gradually re-established control over the balance of payments. The administration under the leadership of the Monetary Board continued efforts to repeal the barter export legislation. In addition, the administration strongly supported a return to the earlier exchange premium tax, with proposed rates as high as 50 per cent.[59] It was widely acknowledged

[59] It will be recalled that the initial "special tax on sales of foreign exchange" was enacted in 1951 following a Bell Mission recommendation. This tax was replaced as a result of the Revised U.S.–Philippine Trade Agreement by a special (temporary) import tariff.

that only by such a *de facto* devaluation would it be possible to continue some semblance of import and exchange controls and the structure of economic policies dependent upon these controls.

In 1959 Congress did repeal the No-Dollar Import Law (Republic Act No. 2262 of June 19, 1959) and did enact an exchange premium tax with flexible rates of from 25 to 40 per cent (Republic Act No. 2609 of July 16, 1959). The extensive list of exemptions to the exchange premium tax makes it doubtful, however, if this tax will go far to relieve the pressure on the balance of payments.[60] Equally important, Congress enacted new legislation continuing the marginal export barter policy (Republic Act No. 2261 of June 19, 1959) initiated by the No-Dollar Import Law. Although this policy is subject to considerable administrative discretion, there are few grounds for believing that marginal export incentives will not be maintained and that exchange control discipline will not continue to deteriorate.

Reappearance of Philippine balance of payments and fiscal problems after a brief period of stability should surprise no one. The stability of 1951–1954 was due essentially to fiscal conservatism and stringent exchange and import controls. Abandonment of these policies was followed by reappearance of the previously suppressed balance-of-payments crisis. It is abundantly clear that the key to solution of the immediate and clamorous Philippine economic problems is the supply of foreign exchange. The Philippine approach to this problem can best be described as a policy of mendicancy and erratic belt-tightening. Such a solution can only handicap economic expansion with growing foreign exchange requirements arising out of high levels of investment.

The Philippine economy is basically sound. Economic expansion has taken place at a rewarding rate in the postwar period although the distribution of income will persist as a socially divisive influence. The Philippines has benefited enormously from foreign savings, which have, in the aggregate, accounted for the principal part of Philippine net capital formation in the postwar period. Up to now Filipinos

[60] The exchange premium tax is tied to an administration commitment to devise and implement a program of progressive "decontrol," i.e., progressive dismantling of exchange and import controls. By early 1960 Congress was increasingly restive over the failure of the administration and the Monetary Board to live up to this commitment. See below pp. 138–139.

have been willing to place primary reliance on external capital, and policy has concentrated on maximizing the flow of extraordinary balance-of-payments assistance—war damage, reparations, economic aid, etc. This policy choice has probably consigned the Philippines to a lower rate of growth than can be sustained by more effective organization of national capacities.

· V ·

Dimensions of

Economic Progress

RELIABLE appraisal of Philippine economic progress is, of course, dependent upon the availability and quality of Philippine statistics. Fortunately for this study, Philippine statistics are plentiful and relatively good.[1] Gaps in statistical knowledge have been closed rapidly since the establishment of the Central Bank, inauguration of the United States economic aid program, and reorganization of the National Economic Council. A statistical problem of some magnitude is, however, created by a plethora of statistics in a number of fields —particularly foreign trade and payments. A confusing multiplicity of statistics results from collection by different agencies using diverse definitions. Similarly, constant refinement of statistical techniques and extensions of coverage make it necessary to search for the latest revised series.

Philippine statistics also reflect nationalism. Filipinos are sensitive and eager for recognition, and they present their best side to the world. As a result, a number of unfortunate gaps and misleading series exist. One prominent example is the choice of 1937 as the base

[1] Higgins comments on "the relatively large number of trained people, plus an unexplained Filipino passion for statistics" (*op. cit.,* p. 742).

year for foreign trade comparisons. It happens that in 1937 Philippine exports were abnormally low and the prices received very favorable. As a result, the official statistics substantially overstate postwar Philippine export performance and substantially understate the improvement in the terms of trade. Other examples include the meaningless aggregation of current and capital expenditures of all kinds into a category labeled "economic development" in the official presentation of the national government budget and the relatively poor quality and inadequate coverage of price series.[2]

Table 14. National income, population, and cost of living

	National income [a] (₱ million)	Population [b] (million)	Per capita income (pesos)	Cost of living [c] (1953 = 100)
1946	4,202	18.4	228	150
1947	5,364	18.8	285	112
1948	5,511	19.1	289	105
1949	5,464	19.5	280	99
1950	5,922	19.2	299	102
1951	6,487	20.3	320	111
1952	6,554	20.6	318	103
1953	7,015	21.0	334	100
1954	7,145	21.4	334	99
1955	7,624	21.8	350	98
1956	8,414	22.3	377	100
1957	8,818	22.7	388	102
1958	9,232	23.1	400	105

[a] UN, ECAFE, *Economic Survey, 1958.*

[b] UN, Statistical Office, *Demographic Yearbook, 1958.* Estimates are for mid-year. Mid-year population in 1937 was estimated to be 15.4 million.

[c] UN, Statistical Office, *Statistical Yearbook, 1958.*

The reader should be cautioned that comparisons of the Philippines with other countries using the official peso exchange rate are virtually worthless. Rates of change, trends, and so forth can be compared, but absolute levels cannot.

The use of statistics inevitably lends an aura of preciseness to economic analysis which, in the present study, is both unintended and unnecessary. The statistics presented herein are adequate to estab-

[2] Filipinos, with few exceptions, react with surprise and skepticism when their attention is called to the declining price trend indicated by postwar price series.

Table 15. Measures of economic progress in the Philippines [a]

	Prewar	1950	1952	1954	1956
Index of population [b]	100 [c]	128	134	139	144
Agricultural production index [d]	100 [e]	103	130	136	143
Fish catch (000 MT)	81	226	318	365	416
Cotton yarn production (000 MT)	1.9 [f]	.3	.5	.7	.8
Cotton fabric production (000,000 meters)	10.5	8.8	6.4	13.0	16.6
Cigarettes (000,000,000)	3.3	7.5	11.5	14.9	15.7
Newsprint consumption (000 MT)	16 [g]	n.a.	n.a.	25	34
Cement production (000 MT)	167	298	316	321	444
Lumber production (000 cu. meters)	2,340 [h]	n.a.	995	850	1,131
Electricity, installed capacity (000 kw)	123	224	n.a.	362	488
Installed hydro-electric capacity (000 kw)	20	52	59	85	186
Electricity, energy produced (000,000 kwh)	209	538	660	960	1,130
Coal production (000 MT)	41	159	139	120	152
Estimated consumption of commercial sources of energy in coal equivalents (000 MT)	832 [h]	n.a.	2,084	2,590	4,213
Apparent consumption of steel in terms of crude steel (000 MT)	125 [i]	n.a.	141	238	319
Consumption of nitrogenous fertilizers (000 MT)	7	14	27	13	36
Railway traffic (000 passenger km)	433	400	374	417	603
Railway traffic (000,000 freight ton-km)	162	170	132	143	157
Motor vehicles, passenger (000)	30 [h]	45	50	54	66
Motor vehicles, commercial (000)	18 [h]	55	55	60	69
Merchant shipping (000 grt)	111	144	148	154	134
Commercial aviation (000,000 passenger km)	3	187	213	130	141

[a] UN, Statistical Office, *Statistical Yearbook, 1955* and *1957.* Prewar is 1938 except as indicated.
[b] UN, Statistical Office, *Demographic Yearbook, 1958.*   [c] Mid-year 1937.
[d] UN, ECAFE, *Economic Survey, 1955* and *1958.*   [e] Average 1934–1938.
[f] 1941.   [g] Average 1938–1939.   [h] 1937.   [i] Average 1934–1936.

blish trends and indicate orders of magnitude.[3] More precise interpretations are usually unwarranted. The statistics have been carefully selected and documentation is sufficient to enable the reader to investigate references and establish definitions. However, in a number of cases alternative and more-or-less conflicting series exist.

The Philippine economy has sustained rapid expansion throughout the postwar period (Table 14). Prewar levels of aggregate output were restored by 1951 and the next seven years witnessed steady progress (Tables 15, 16). Postwar Philippine economic growth has shown remarkable stability in the face of moderate export price

Table 16. Indexes of the physical volume of production [a]
(1955 = 100)

Year	Combined index [b]	Agriculture	Manufacturing	Mining
1949	56.3	59.8	46.9	47.5
1950	62.4	64.4	56.6	61.1
1951	72.0	73.8	66.4	76.2
1952	77.4	79.4	69.9	93.7
1953	84.0	85.2	79.0	98.3
1954	92.7	94.0	88.8	92.0
1955	100.0	100.0	100.0	100.0
1956	108.6	106.1	115.7	110.8
1957	116.2	110.2	125.0	123.7
1958	n.a.	112.2	134.6	122.5

[a] Central Bank, *Statistical Bulletin,* 10 (Dec. 1958), p. 141, table 68.
[b] *Ibid.,* 9 (Dec. 1957), p. 155, table 74.

fluctuations, and the traditional dependence of the Philippine economy on primary production and trade has been rapidly reduced. More important, fluctuations in domestic economic activity have remained of minor significance.

The first four postwar years of rehabilitation witnessed rapid recovery of Philippine productive capacity. Such a picture does not emerge from the national accounts as national income remained relatively stable during 1947–1949. When account is taken of the rapid decline in Philippine prices during this period, the growth of real national product from extremely low wartime levels is quite impressive (Table 17).

[3] In a number of cases, processing of national statistics by specialized agencies of the United Nations has removed ambiguities and established comparability.

The period following 1949 has been one of stability in Philippine price indexes, and the growth in real product has probably corresponded closely to growth in money product. In the nine years following 1949 national income increased by approximately 61 per cent from ₱5,464 million to ₱9,232 million in 1958. During this period the Philippine population is estimated to have increased from 19.5 million to 23.1 million, an increase of 18 per cent. Per capita national product amounted to ₱280 in 1949 and ₱400 in 1958, an increase of 43 per

Table 17. Selected price indexes [a]
(1953 = 100)

	Cost of living	Wholesale prices: Manila			
		General	Domestic goods	Exported goods	Imported goods
1937	26	30	28	33	n.a.
1938	26	28	31	24	n.a.
1939	27	29	33	23	n.a.
1940	28	26	30	19	n.a.
1946	150	199	264	92	n.a.
1947	112	134	123	106	n.a.
1948	105	140	146	129	n.a.
1949	99	101	107	91	78
1950	102	98	99	99	94
1951	111	110	108	103	119
1952	103	101	100	82	105
1953	100	100	100	100	100
1954	99	95	94	88	97
1955	98	92	92	81	92
1956	100	95	94	84	100
1957	102	99	99	88	106

[a] UN, Statistical Office, *Statistical Yearbook, 1955* and *1957*.

cent. Measured in this fashion, the Philippine economy has performed remarkably well and there can be few grounds for a critical appraisal of public policy.

Philippine expansion in the nine years following 1949 has been widely distributed (Table 18). The largest absolute increase took place in the agricultural, forestry, and fisheries sector, where income increased by ₱1,056 million or by 46 per cent. Expansion in agricultural production was somewhat greater than the expansion in income originating in agriculture because of declines in prices of agricultural

Table 18. National income by industrial origin [a]
(₱ million)

Industrial category	1949	1950	1951	1952	1953	1954	1955	1956 [b]	1957 [b]	1958 [b]
Agriculture	2,308	2,505	2,787	2,806	3,009	3,118	3,161	3,175	3,230	3,364
Mining	40	55	79	98	107	105	121	122	142	138
Manufacturing	440	502	630	639	834	850	1,001	1,195	1,292	1,474
Construction	276	239	237	221	236	205	230	296	328	281
Trade	709	752	838	809	780	781	861	999	1,057	1,096
Transport. and communication	193	205	228	242	242	235	250	286	322	327
Public administration and defense	377	386	431	487	544	574	648	679	685	705
Other services	1,121	1,278	1,257	1,252	1,263	1,277	1,352	1,662	1,762	1,847
National income at factor cost	5,464	5,922	6,487	6,554	7,015	7,145	7,624	8,414	8,818	9,232

[a] UN, ECAFE, *Economic Survey.*
[b] R.P., NEC, "An Analysis of the National Income Accounts of the Philippines for the years 1957 and 1958," *Statistical Reporter,* 3 (April 1959), 12.

commodities, both those consumed domestically and exported. In the nine years following 1949 agricultural production in real terms increased by 88 per cent.

The most rapid expansion following 1949 took place in the mining sector. This was due for the most part to the fact that the postwar recovery of this sector was very slow, and in 1949 the index of mining production was only 32 per cent of 1937. During the nine years following 1949 income originating in mining increased from ₱40 million to ₱138 million, an increase of 245 per cent. The increase in physical production was more modest, amounting to 158 per cent, and at the end of 1958 the Philippine mining industry had not fully recovered to prewar levels.

Since 1949 and the establishment of high levels of protection by stringent import and exchange controls manufacturing output has expanded rapidly. In the nine years following 1949 income originating in manufacturing rose from ₱440 million to ₱1,474 million, an increase of 235 per cent. The increase in the physical index of manufacturing output was somewhat more modest, amounting to 187 per cent.[4]

The services sector of the Philippine economy expanded rapidly in the nine years following 1949 from ₱1,498 million to ₱2,552 million, or by 70 per cent. Government services expanded by ₱328 million to ₱705 million, an increase of 87 per cent, whereas other services (including housing) increased by ₱726 million to ₱1,847 million, an increase of 65 per cent.

Income originating in transportation and communications increased between 1949 and 1958 by ₱124 million, or 69 per cent. The trade sector expanded by ₱387 million, or 55 per cent, while income originating in construction increased by ₱5 million, or 2 per cent.[5]

Although Philippine expansion has, in the aggregate, been rapid, a number of aspects of postwar development cause concern. First, in spite of expansion in the national product, an expansion sub-

[4] The Philippine index of manufacturing production probably reflects substantial upward bias. Rapid expansion in manufacturing output has reflected the high levels of protection arising out of exchange and import controls. Introduction of new commodities in the Philippine index of production involves weighting which reflects the large element of protection in the prices of these commodities.

[5] Construction was taking place at high levels during the early postwar period because of the large U.S. war damage payments to rehabilitate wartime capital destruction.

stantially greater than the rate of population growth, no reduction in poverty in the Philippines seems to have occurred over the past two decades. Such a conclusion arises out of the fact that the majority of Filipinos are dependent upon agriculture for a livelihood, and though agricultural production has shared in the postwar expansion in output, per capita output of agriculture has only recovered to 1934–1938 levels. When this fact is combined with the relative stability in the proportion of the population engaged in agriculture, it means that the productivity of human resources engaged in agriculture has increased modestly if at all.

The principal part of agricultural production is consumed on the farm by the cultivator and his family, and real income is therefore measured by productivity. A minor part of food production and all of export production enters the market, and real income is the resultant, not only of productivity, but of the terms of trade at which agricultural output is exchanged for other production. With respect to production of export crops, the internal terms of trade have been relatively unfavorable since the prices of these commodities have been determined in the world market, whereas internal prices have tended to reflect the substantial overvaluation of the peso. With the exception of coconuts, export crops have tended to lag behind prewar levels of production.

The prices received for agricultural produce marketed domestically have been relatively favorable, and this situation is reflected in the relative expansion of such production. However, one consequence of this expansion has been slow deterioration in the internal terms of trade for such output. In recent years output per head of population dependent upon agriculture has been no greater than levels attained in the late interwar period (1934–1938), while the relative expansion of cereals and foodstuffs for the domestic market has tended to prevent any improvement in the terms of trade for agricultural produce entering the market.

Second, Philippine economic expansion has not achieved significant diversification of Philippine export production and trade. Philippine exports are almost exclusively primary products. In 1937–1940 the three principal Philippine exports, all primary products, accounted for 78 per cent of the total value of Philippine exports, whereas in the period 1956–1958 the three principal exports of primary commodities accounted for 76 per cent of the total value of exports.

More important in terms of future Philippine economic progress is the failure of the Philippines to share in the postwar expansion in world trade. When gold is introduced into the volume index of Philippine exports, it is apparent that Philippine exports have no more than recovered to prewar levels and in per capita terms are substantially below prewar levels. In view of Philippine aspirations for rapid economic growth and of the import requirements for capital formation, there can be few grounds for satisfaction over Philippine export performance in recent years.

Third is the low level of capital formation during the postwar period (Table 19). Gross domestic investment during the nine years 1950–1958 totaled ₱6.8 billion or 10 per cent of national income. During this period depreciation has been estimated at ₱3.7 billion, leaving net investment of ₱3.1 billion, or 4 to 5 per cent of national income.[6] In view of the high rate of Philippine population increase and of our knowledge of the capital requirements of progressive economies, postwar capital formation in the Philippines cannot contribute to optimism regarding future Philippine economic progress.

If we look behind aggregate capital formation, further economic problems can be discerned. First, the contribution of Filipino savings to capital formation is surprisingly small. During the postwar period 1946–1958 the savings of foreigners in the form of donations and investment provided ₱2.8 billion, while the net savings of Filipinos provided only ₱1.5 billion of the resources necessary for net investment (Tables 20–22). If we take into account the extensive contribution of the Chinese community to gross investment, it is apparent that the willingness of Filipinos to invest productively is extremely low.

Consumption as a ratio of the total means available to Filipinos has tended to remain a stable percentage of the total means available as production and money incomes have expanded. In the nine years following 1948 the ratio of total consumption to available means ranged from 89.4 per cent to 95.4 per cent (Table 19). This means, in effect, that during a period in which income was expanding rapidly the marginal propensity to consume did not decline significantly. To the extent that this statistical impression is reliable, it means that

[6] With the exception of the period 1947–1949, when U.S. war damage payments formed a relatively high proportion of gross investment, the proportion of gross investment to gross national product has remained relatively stable.

Table 19. Distribution of gross national expenditure [a]

(₱ million)

Year	Gross domestic product	Imports less exports of goods and services	Gross national expenditure	Consumption expenditure		Ratio of consumption to total expenditure	Investment expenditure				Ratio of gross investment expenditure to total expenditure
				Private	Government		Gross fixed capital formation		Increases in stocks	Total	
							Public	Private			
1947	5,964	360	6,324	5,221	406	88.9	53	478	167	698	11.1
1949	6,196	514	6,710	5,594	450	90.0	198	401	67	666	10.0
1950	6,655	−77	6,578	5,533	476	91.3	188	297	84	569	8.7
1951	7,415	55	7,470	6,371	540	92.5	162	330	68	560	7.5
1952	7,576	55	7,631	6,479	600	95.4	161	325	34	552	4.6
1953	8,111	−5	8,106	6,816	631	89.4	165	394	100	659	10.6
1954	8,283	50	8,333	6,960	654	91.4	167	396	156	719	8.6
1955	8,820	188	9,008	7,501	718	91.3	173	451	165	789	8.7
1956	9,571	8	9,579	7,919	800	91.0	193	555	112	860	9.0
1957	10,118	279	10,397	8,585	828	90.5	202	657	125	984	9.5

[a] UN, ECAFE, *Economic Survey, 1956 and 1958.*

Table 20. Combined capital account
(₱ million)

	Annual average 1946–49	Annual average 1950–53	1954	1955	1956	1957	1958 [a]	Total 1946–58
Gross domestic investment [b]	629	585	719	789	860	984	1,071	9,277
Depreciation [b]	299	375	407	430	441	477	486	4,934
Net domestic investment	330	210	312	359	419	507	585	4,343
Foreign savings								
Net borrowing abroad [a]	81	−54	111	257	61	297	95	928
Net donations to Philippines [a]	251	122	52	64	78	124	98	1,909
	332	68	163	321	139	421	193	2,837
Philippine savings								
Depreciation	299	375	407	430	441	477	486	4,934
Net Philippine savings	−2	142	149	38	280	86	392	1,506

[a] R.P., NEC, "An Analysis of the National Income Accounts of the Philippines for the Years 1957 and 1958," *Statistical Reporter*, 3 (April 1959), 8–14.
[b] UN, ECAFE, *Economic Survey*. Rows do not add exactly because of rounding.

Table 21. Balance of payments, 1950–1957 [a]
($ million U.S.)

	1950	1951	1952	1953	1954	1955	1956	1957	1958
Current transactions									
Imports, c.i.f.	377	534	480	529	538	607	565	691	634
Exports, c.i.f.	331	418	338	386	392	390	438	430	483
Balance of trade	−46	−116	−142	−143	−145	−218	−127	−261	−151
Investment income remitted, net	−15	−24	−29	−55	−57	−67	−65	−64	−54
Other invisibles, net	−26	−12	−2	9	2	6	15	42	46
	−87	−152	−173	−189	−200	−279	−177	−283	−159
U.S. government expenditures	260	120	153	158	145	151	147	134	112
Balance on current account	173	−32	−20	−31	−55	−128	−30	−149	−47
Capital movements									
Private	−39	−17	35	47	43	59	58	54	29
Official	−98	52	−7	7	1	80	—	118	14
Monetary gold	−2	−3	−3	—		−6	−6	16	−4
Errors and omissions	−35	—	−5	−24	11	−4	−23	−40	8
	−173	32	20	31	55	128	30	149	47

[a] Central Bank, *Annual Reports*. Columns do not add exactly due to rounding

Filipinos have not been very successful in organizing their economy to divert increments of income to resource accumulation.[7]

Fourth, the low levels of government activity should be a cause for concern. It is generally recognized that government has an important role to play in accelerating economic growth by contributing to the accumulation of resources directly through the government's power to tax and spend.

Table 22. Balance of payments, 1927–1929, 1937–1940, and 1945–1949 [a]
($ million U.S.)

	Average 1927–29 [b]	Average 1937–40 [b]	1945 [c]	1946 [c]	1947	1948	1949
Imports, c.i.f.	303	287	29	335	588	674	673
Exports, f.o.b.	321	317	1	64	265	318	260
Balance	18	30	−28	−271	−323	−356	−413
Other payments, net	−60	−49	—	−29	21	−24	−55
U.S. government expenditures, net	36	92	284	119	335	339	324
Errors and omissions	8	−29	—	−26	−16	4	−16
Net change in international reserves	3	45	256	−207	17	−37	−160

[a] *Bell Mission Report,* p. 35.

[b] U.S., Department of the Army, Armed Services Field Manual, *Philippine Islands,* Sec. 8 (Washington, 1943), p. 63.

[c] Excludes surplus property, UNRRA supplies and aid, certain grants in kind, and allowance for remittances of American military personnel to dependents in the United States.

Philippine fiscal performance has been undistinguished. During the ten fiscal years ending June 30, 1958, government expenditures totaled ₱7.7 billion, or 10.5 per cent of national income in the ten years ending December 31, 1958. Government expenditures have increased relative to the increase in available means from an average of ₱517 million in 1947–1949 to ₱1,068 million for the three fiscal years ending June 30, 1958. However, expansion in recent years has resulted from deficit spending rather than improved revenue performance. Government investment has tended to expand as a ratio of total

[7] It can, of course, mean other things, which will be dealt with in the course of this study. For example, a major part of postwar capital accumulation has taken the form of land brought under cultivation, a fact which is substantially understated in the national accounts.

expenditures in recent years but currently amounts to less than 2 per cent of national income.

There are two basic perspectives from which to view postwar Philippine economic growth. First, one can compare current levels of material welfare with levels prevailing in the late 1930's. Although the evidence is sketchy, the available series (Table 15) suggest that present levels of per capita income are only moderately—perhaps one-fifth—above prewar levels.[8] On the other hand, emphasis can be placed on postwar growth. Here there can be little question of sustained economic growth well in excess of population growth. The right perspective will, of course, depend upon the success with which the Philippines maintains the momentum of postwar expansion.

[8] By the time this study appears, this question should be answered satisfactorily. Marvin Goodstein is completing an index of the volume of Philippine gross national product which will compare present levels of production with levels of the late 1930's.

· VI ·

Exchange Rate Policy

MAJOR aspects of Philippine economic policy are circumscribed by the availability of foreign exchange and the intensity of disequilibrium in external economic relations. More than one-half of national government tax revenues are derived from taxation of import values; monetary policy is preoccupied with management of the international reserve; pursuit of objectives of Philippine nationalism is highly dependent upon exchange and import control; and industrial development, which looms large in Philippine national aspirations, has been aggressively promoted by protection and foreign exchange allocation.

International trade theory, and more specifically the theory of commercial policy, has played an important role in speculation regarding processes of economic growth. The case for free trade, i.e., "neutral" commercial policy, is a case for international specialization, an optimum allocation of resources and the maximization of the real income of the world. Opposing the case for free trade is the theory of protection, i.e., "positive" commercial policy, which assigns national objectives to commercial policy including that of accelerating national economic growth. It is contended that positive commercial policy will influence growth through the following independent relationships: First, protection can be used to raise the prices of imports and import-competing products produced domestically, thereby establishing an incentive for private developmental expenditures in the protected industries. Crucial to the theory of protection is the argument that the structure of international specialization is in large part historical accident and that recourse to protection will enable latecomers to avoid specialization unfortunate for the welfare of the nation. Second, taxation of imports will produce government revenues to finance developmental expenditures, i.e., social investment. Finally, commercial policy can be used to affect the distribution of the gains from trade in favor of the country resorting to protection.[1]

The traditional theory of protection relies upon import taxation for implementation. The claim of the state to the windfall arising out of import restriction is unquestioned. Moreover, any monopoly returns to domestic producers of import-competing commodities arising out of import restriction would tend to disappear over time as output increased. Finally, improvement in the terms of trade which might result from protection would be distributed widely through society. In the relatively stable environment of the international gold standard the case for taxation of foreign trade to implement commercial policy was persuasive.[2]

Speculation with respect to commercial policy has kept apace with the far-reaching changes in economics of the last quarter-century, and recent years have seen the ascendancy of a nationalistic commercial policy of controlled external disequilibrium. The objective of such a commercial policy in underdeveloped countries is to maintain a tolerable equilibrium in external payments while an economic development policy implemented by high levels of investment is pursued. It is recognized that increments of investment, even where financed by additional domestic private savings or taxation, may contribute, in the short run, to external disequilibrium if there is an import component in the additional investment.[3] Moreover, there is an

---

[1] Maximum protection will minimize revenues from import taxation and ultimately will minimize the gains from trade.

[2] Symmetry of analysis of traditional commercial policy requires consideration of export taxation as well as import and export subsidization. However, theoretical analysis as well as implementation of commercial policy has been dominated by protection, i.e., import restriction.

[3] Underdeveloped countries have found that additional investment, financed wholly or in part by foreign loans or economic aid, may contribute to external disequilibrium where the increment of investment involves domestic expenditure

important role to be played by deficit finance and private credit expansion in accelerating economic growth, and it is widely recognized that the controlled disequilibrium of developing countries should properly arise in part from a high level of investment not matched by comparable levels of intended domestic savings.[4]

Underdeveloped countries are handicapped in their efforts to accelerate economic growth by low levels of savings, inelastic supply functions, relatively large marginal propensities to import, and limited foreign exchange reserves. Under conditions of unlimited foreign exchange reserves the investment multiplier in the typical underdeveloped country might not be large inasmuch as the small propensity to save would be counterbalanced by a relatively large propensity to make current account payments. However, in the absence of foreign exchange reserves or foreign financing adequate to sustain a large deficit in the current account, the investment multiplier tends to be large, because governments are forced to limit foreign payments.

The underdeveloped country resorting to exchange and import controls may be faced by the need to intensify such controls steadily. Inelastic supply functions combined with a large investment multiplier tend to (a) generate price increases which impair the competitive position of exports and (b) lead to increased domestic consumption of output previously exported.[5] The resultant decline in foreign exchange proceeds will require intensification of controls to maintain a tolerable external equilibrium. Moreover, controls over trade and payments have proved to be an obstacle to an inflow of foreign investment which would tend to materialize in the initial stages of development.

In the face of such formidable obstacles, countries attempting to

---

as well as foreign exchange expenditure. The increased incomes resulting from the increment of domestic investment expenditure together with the import content of the investment may generate a demand for imports of goods and services in excess of the foreign exchange proceeds of the foreign loan or economic aid.

[4] A recent comprehensive statement of the theory of developmental commercial policy is to be found in Gunnar Myrdal, *An International Economy* (New York: Harper Bros., 1956), pp. 267–288. The footnote references of this work provide a useful bibliography of the extensive literature treating the relationships between commercial policy and economic growth.

[5] Such changes in prices and costs are not essential to the theory of developmental commercial policy. External imbalance will normally result from the tendency of individuals to spend a significant part of increments of income on imports of goods and services.

accelerate economic growth impose stringent quantitative controls over imports (and other payments) to maintain a precarious but tolerable equilibrium.[6] Generally, the rationing of foreign exchange is on the basis of developmental priorities, and an increasing proportion of foreign exchange tends to be reserved for imports of capital goods. Such a theory of developmental commercial policy has considerable relevance and many underdeveloped countries can point to their balance of payments difficulties as evidence of effective attempts to accelerate economic growth.[7]

The foregoing explanation of external disequilibrium essential to the theory of developmental commercial and exchange rate policy has little relevance for the Philippines. The chronic balance of payments crisis that has plagued the postwar Philippines is attributable essentially to the Philippine decision to restore and maintain the prewar currency parity of the peso. This conclusion, which is basic to a major part of the policy analysis of this study, is strongly supported by the following arguments:

First, Philippine developments in the course of the Japanese occupation and the subsequent liberation period produced changes which could not fail to make the prewar exchange parity inappropriate. Although the Japanese occupation currency was repudiated, the capital destruction and economic dislocation of the war and the heavy peso expenditures by the liberation forces in 1944 and 1945 combined to establish a structure of costs and prices at least 5 to 6 times prewar levels. This was in sharp contrast to the movement of United States prices and costs, which increased less than 100 per cent. Inasmuch as the United States accounted for more than two-thirds of Philippine foreign trade, both imports and exports, maintenance of the prewar currency parity stimulated foreign exchange payments and handicapped expansion in export earnings.

In addition to relative inflation in Philippine costs and prices, the

[6] In a formal sense it is incorrect to include exchange controls in commercial policy, since exchange rationing applies to capital transfers as well as to trade and services. It is, however, realistic to consider exchange controls in underdeveloped countries as an aspect of commercial policy in view of the tendency for both marginal restrictions as well as the substantive impact of exchange restriction to be applied to current account items.

[7] Cf. Myrdal, *op. cit.*, p. 270: "Under these circumstances it should, perhaps first be said that there must be something wrong with an underdeveloped country that does not have foreign exchange difficulties."

abrupt termination of Philippine isolation in 1944–1945 produced radical changes in tastes and consumption patterns. Widespread distribution of Western consumption items by United States military forces found ready acceptance by Filipinos. Such changes in tastes were solidified during 1946–1949, when the Philippines enjoyed an unprecedented import surplus as the result of heavy United States disbursements. During the early postwar period complete freedom to consume imports combined with relatively favorable prices effected far-reaching changes in the Philippine standard of living.

Second, Philippine domestic investment has been at relatively low levels. During the early postwar period of reconstruction domestic Philippine investment was maintained at fairly high levels. But the volume of such investment was more than matched by transfer into the Philippines of foreign savings as domestic investment was more than matched by the import surplus on current account. Moreover, half of the estimated domestic investment during 1945–1949 was accounted for by inventory accumulation, primarily commercial stocks, and did not generate income in the Philippines. Since 1949 net domestic investment has averaged less than 5 per cent of national income, and in view of the continued inflow of foreign savings the modest levels of domestic investment can hardly account for the intense balance of payments disequilibrium.

Third, deficit financing by the government has been modest. During 1945–1949 the Philippines was on an exchange reserve standard, and the budgetary deficits not only were small in the aggregate, but were financed by *ad hoc* arrangements in which the deficits were matched by extraordinary foreign exchange receipts. During 1951–1954 government receipts and expenditures were in balance. Since 1954 the national government budget has been unbalanced, but the cumulative deficit has been small when compared with the relevant economic aggregates.

Finally, and most important, Philippine domestic prices have declined through much of the postwar period. The cost of living index which in 1946 was 560 (average 1937–1940 = 100) declined steadily to an index of 367 in 1949. During 1950–1957 the index showed great stability, standing at 378 in 1957. In view of the substantial increases following 1949 in prices of imported goods, it seems clear that prices of domestic goods declined throughout the postwar period to 1957 (Table 17). The down trend in Philippine costs and prices strongly challenges an explanation of Philippine external disequilibrium in terms of high levels of domestic investment generating inflationary increases in income.

The Philippines is the only country suffering extensive capital destruction in World War II which has chosen to defend its prewar exchange rate. Declining Philippine costs and prices and continued inflation in the United States have materially reduced the relative Philippine inflation. The remaining discrepancy in relative costs and prices is, however, a sufficient explanation of the disequilibrium in trade and payments between the two countries. The principal part of the remainder of Philippine trade is conducted with Western Europe and Japan. While Philippine trading partners with few exceptions have reduced their postwar external disequilibrium by currency depreciation, the Philippines has resisted such a step.

Given Philippine exchange rate policy and the maintenance of a tolerable external equilibrium by stringent exchange and import controls, the government is confronted by three conceptually distinct, but closely related problems. First, and most important, is the problem of increasing foreign exchange earnings. Except for half-hearted experiments with export incentives in the form of barter of marginal exports outside exchange controls and subsidization of gold production, this policy problem has been neglected. However, the supply of foreign exchange now and for years to come will remain the principal restraint on Philippine efforts to accelerate economic growth.

Second is the problem of maintaining an acceptable level of exchange control discipline in the face of strong economic incentives to evade controls. The organization of export production has established opportunities for evasion, and the configuration of the islands has encouraged smuggling. More important has been the capacity of exporting and other economic interests to mobilize political influence to legalize transactions outside the control structure.

Finally, there is the problem of integrating exchange and import controls with tariff policy into a rational system of developmental commercial policy. Philippine commercial policy is confronted by two basic problems. First is the allocation of protection. The structure of protection has shifted rapidly in the postwar period as industrialization has been promoted with imagination and energy. Second is the distribution of the windfall arising out of exchange and import controls. In general terms, it has been policy to allocate foreign exchange at the official rate on the basis of commodity essentiality and nationality of the applicant. Imports have been rationed among consumers by the market mechanism, i.e., restricted quantities have been sold at prices the "market would bear," and the windfall has tended to go to those receiving import and exchange allocations. Because of the pressing need for revenue as well as widespread dissatisfaction with the inequities and corruption inherent in exchange and import controls, the government has made erratic attempts to capture the foreign exchange windfall by taxation.

These three policy problems are discussed at length in this and the following two chapters. Repercussions of exchange rate, exchange control, and commercial policies are evident in virtually all aspects of public policy. The restraint arising out of the availability of foreign exchange serves as the dominant, and monotonous, theme of this study.

The following analysis of exchange rate policy is organized around the economic case for a more realistic rate of peso exchange. Such an organization reflects the belief not only that a persuasive case can be made for this policy alternative, but that such an approach provides a convenient framework for analysis of other important policy issues.

Analysis of exchange rate policy has traditionally been concerned with appraising the potential contribution of devaluation to curtailment of payments for imports of goods and services. This is not a dominant consideration in assessing Philippine exchange rate policy. The less-developed country successful in accelerating economic growth —the postwar Philippines is a case in point—will be faced by rising levels of demand for imports of goods and services. A tolerable equilibrium has been maintained in Philippine external payments for the past decade by exchange and import controls. Under the circumstances there is no need—and indeed, it would be highly irrational— to reduce foreign exchange payments below recent levels. It cannot be overemphasized that the principal objective of peso devaluation should be to stimulate export production and trade in order to earn larger amounts of foreign exchange. Increased foreign exchange earnings would be utilized primarily to provide more imports of goods and services.

The Philippines has not shared in the world-wide expansion in exports that followed World War II and that reached 187 per cent of the prewar volume in 1957. Philippine exports recovered slowly to prewar levels, they probably exceeded prewar for the first time in 1956. Although this performance is comparable to that of Burma, Indonesia, India, and Japan, it is inferior to that of many countries with a commodity pattern of trade similar to the Philippines' and whose relative prices, as compared to prewar, are not as inflated as those of the Philippines (Table 23).

In the case of the Philippines, currency overvaluation attributable to maintenance of the prewar exchange parity has handicapped export recovery and expansion. Conservative monetary and fiscal policies and expanding domestic output have interacted to produce declining prices and costs during most of the postwar period. However, the "rationalization" of Philippine costs and prices necessary to make the official exchange rate a realistic parity has been only partially completed.

Moreover, special circumstances have affected expansion of the principal prewar Philippine exports. Gold, which accounted for more than one-quarter of the value of exports in 1937–1940, has been handicapped by the fixed price of $35 per ounce established by United States gold purchase policy. In spite of various schemes for stimulating gold production, Philippine gold production has not recovered to half of prewar production. In the case of sugar, the principal prewar export, Philippine exports are made almost solely to the sheltered United States market under the sugar quota. Philippine sugar production is acknowledged to be high cost and at the current exchange parity is not competitive in other markets. The inefficiency of this industry is due primarily to its organization into small-scale units, an organization perpetuated by the scheme for allocating the profitable United States sugar quota on a historical basis. In the case of abacá, the fourth most important prewar export, recovery of production has been handicapped by radical changes in the organization of the industry. In the interwar period abacá production was organized in relatively large units with Japanese management and capital. Disposal of Japanese holdings after the war resulted in breaking up medium-size plantations into small holdings. Another problem of the abacá industry has been the mosaic disease, control of which was weakened with the changed organization. Under the stimulus of favorable prices copra and coconut products, second most important prewar export, have expanded substantially over prewar levels. Philippine exports of logs and timber, base metals, and canned pineapple have also expanded substantially.

Table 23. Comparative export volume indexes [a]

	Philippines (1937–40 = 100)		World (1937–38 = 100)	Malaya (1938 = 100)	Ceylon (1938–40 = 100)	Cuba (1935–39 = 100)
	Exports excluding gold	Exports including gold production [b]	Export volume	Export volume	Export volume	Export volume
1952	107	95	131	156	134	152
1954	111	97	141	158	142	140
1956	138	118	173	180	144	182
1957	127	109	187	186	137	n.a.

[a] UN, Statistical Office, *Yearbook of International Trade Statistics*. Selection of countries for comparison reflects the availability of statistics as well as comparability of the commodity structure of trade.

[b] Official quantum indexes do not include either gold production or trade. Such exclusion is unwarranted in the Philippine case. Philippine gold production is used either to make payments abroad (imports, profit remission, disinvestment, etc.) or is added to foreign exchange reserves. Philippine gold production during 1937–1940 averaged ₱67.1 million annually or 26.3 per cent of average annual nongold exports of ₱254.6 million during this period. Gold production has been introduced into the index by using the value of gold production in 1937–1940 as the appropriate weight. Gold production (valued at ₱70 per ounce) amounted to ₱32.8 million in 1952, ₱29.1 million in 1954, ₱28.4 million in 1956, and ₱26.6 million in 1957.

What conditions are necessary for devaluation to produce larger amounts of foreign exchange earnings from exports? First, higher peso prices will have to induce expansion in export production. Conditions seem to be favorable to such an expansion. The Philippines is undergoing a rapid revolution in attitudes toward economic activity and productive investment. The postwar expansion in production and export of coconut products, base metals, and forest products as well as the response of tobacco, coffee, and cacao producers to high levels of protection suggests that Filipino producers, large and small, respond rationally to favorable prices.[8] Growing social pressure to break up large land holdings, urbanization, and proliferation of commercial and industrial experiences attributable to protection and Filipinization policies have accelerated emergence of Filipino entrepreneurship. Another factor favorable to export expansion is the relative availability of resources of all kinds. Labor resources include a rapidly growing agricultural work force as well as a growing technically trained population. Natural resources including potentially arable land are relatively abundant, particularly in the frontier areas of land settlement.

Second, will an expansion in Philippine exports produce larger foreign exchange earnings? Although it is conceivable that an increase in Philippine exports could produce a relatively large decline in world prices and therefore in foreign exchange proceeds, such a result is unlikely. The marginal increase in Philippine export production would be sold in world markets at world prices, and a relatively large expansion in Philippine exports would represent a relatively small change in world supplies of any commodity and close substitutes for that commodity. Economists have long understood that regardless of the elasticity of world demand, the demand (over an extended period) confronting a single country supplying only a small part of the supply entering world trade will tend to be relatively elastic.[9]

[8] Depreciation will tend to make profitable the production of commodities that are not profitable at the present peso exchange rate. The relevant appraisal of the response of export production to higher peso prices should include potential as well as existing export commodities.

[9] There are healthy differences of opinion regarding the response of export production and foreign exchange proceeds to devaluation. For example, Governor Cuaderno of the Central Bank has been quoted as follows: "Considering the elasticity of world demand, there is no indication that after devaluing the Philippine peso, foreign exchange earnings in foreign markets of the principal export

The recommendation that Philippine production for export be expanded (particularly if made by a non-Filipino) may be discredited by the contention that the spokesman is advocating a policy that will perpetuate the colonial characteristics of the Philippine economy. Such a position involves the belief that primary production for export and more "desirable" production to replace imports and to supply the domestic market are alternatives—that expansion in export production takes place at the cost of reduced production for the protected domestic market. This is clearly specious in an expanding economy where growth in the labor force is in excess of growth of nonagricultural employment opportunities and land and other natural resources are available for development. Analysis of cases of accelerated economic growth does not indicate that development is accompanied by a decline in primary production and exports; rather there is an absolute increase although a relative decline in the importance of such production and trade. Resources invested in Philippine export production are not necessarily resources denied to Philippine industrialization, although many appraisals of Philippine economic policy reflect such a belief.[10]

What would be the impact of devaluation of the peso on other foreign exchange receipts? In the case of the Philippines, nontrade receipts are dominated by United States government expenditures and private capital receipts. An argument against devaluation arises when substantial amounts of foreign exchange receipts are relatively fixed in peso amounts. An example of this type of payment would be United States Veterans Administration payments of G.I. benefits to Filipino veterans. While G.I. benefits are fixed in peso amounts, such payments have been exhausted in most categories. The remaining categories of Veterans Administration payments—pensions, disability payments, and the like—are denominated in dollars and would not be affected by the peso exchange rate.[11]

---

products of the islands would increase. It does not seem possible also, that the production of commodities, for export, except sugar which has a limited market, would increase appreciably. Moreover, there is no assurance that competitor countries would not take retaliatory measures" (*Manila Bulletin*, May 11, 1956, p. 20).

[10] Such a position reflects failure to understand the rationale for foreign trade. Specialization and exchange are techniques of indirect production which increase productive efficiency.

[11] It should be pointed out that arrangements have been made between the U.S. Veterans Administration and the Central Bank to ensure that all Veterans Adminis-

Another large element in nontrade receipts is United States economic and military aid payments. Would a devaluation be followed by a reduction in the dollar amounts of such payments? There is considerable evidence that relative costs play a minor role in the allocation of United States economic and military aid. The distribution of aid appropriations seems to reflect strategic and political considerations rather than economic considerations. To the extent that this is true, Philippine dollar receipts will be independent of the peso exchange rate. It seems unlikely that the United States would react to a devaluation of the peso by reducing the relative size of dollar allocations to Philippine economic and military aid.

The relationship between devaluation and foreign investment is impossible to predict, although the ultimate effect on foreign exchange earnings should be favorable. Devaluation would improve the profitability of export production and induce foreign investment in this sector, where such investment has been concentrated.[12] Initially, the impact on foreign exchange availability would be of minor importance because the principal part of foreign investment in the Philippines comes out of the retained earnings of existing foreign firms or out of the proceeds of borrowing from Philippine credit institutions. To the extent that foreign investment results from the transfer of purchasing power from foreign countries in order to acquire capital assets in the Philippines—either by purchase or by construction—devaluation would reduce the foreign exchange costs of investment. In this case the immediate effect upon foreign exchange availability would depend upon whether the induced expansion in investment would offset the reduction in dollar unit costs.[13]

On the other hand, to the extent that devaluation increased the peso costs of imported capital goods, foreign investment out of peso earnings and out of proceeds of borrowing in the Philippines would

---

tration payments would be channeled to the exchange control authority. An appropriate devaluation would introduce desirable equity in the treatment of this group of Filipinos, who have been denied access to the free market in foreign exchange. Access to the premium free market is widely, but arbitrarily, distributed within Philippine society.

[12] Postwar growth in Philippine export earnings has been concentrated in nonferrous metals, forestry products, pineapples, and coconut products. The first three have attracted substantial amounts of foreign investment.

[13] To the extent that foreign investment takes the form of capital goods purchased abroad by the foreign investor and exported to the Philippines, such investment does not directly affect Philippine foreign exchange availability.

be reduced. This argument should not be underestimated. A major Philippine policy with respect to investment incentives has been to use the system of exchange and import controls to subsidize imports of capital goods. Substantial subsidization results from allocating foreign exchange for such purposes at the official exchange rate and exempting such imports from taxation of all kinds. Similarly, devaluation will tend to reduce the profitability (in terms of foreign currencies) of both existing and potential foreign investment by making less favorable the rate at which peso profits can be converted into foreign currencies.

It is, of course, unrealistic to analyze the effects of devaluation on foreign investment in isolation. If some combination of tariff and exchange rate policies should make it possible for the Philippines to reduce the intensity of controls on foreign payments, the impact on foreign investment might be substantial. There is considerable evidence that potential foreign investors are reluctant to endure the uncertainties which inevitably accompany the administration of import and exchange controls.[14] On balance it would seem that devaluation would not reduce foreign investment, and over the long run expanded investment in export production and trade might very well induce a substantial expansion in foreign exchange receipts.

Analysis of the impact of devaluation on invisible payments must take into consideration the impact of exchange controls, which have curtailed such payments. At present, a substantial part of such payments is arranged through the free market, where the effective exchange rate substantially devalues the peso. If devaluation should be followed by relaxation of the intensity of controls, the immediate consequence probably would be an increase in foreign exchange outlays for services—in spite of the substantial formal increase in the peso costs of such payments. As has been pointed out, this is a hoped-

[14] For example, R.P., Office of the President, *Report of the Presidential [Philippine] Mission on Foreign Investments* (as reported in a Malacañan Press Release, Feb. 26, 1955) tabulated the most frequently cited requirements for foreign investment in the Philippines. Such requirements (in order of frequency) included: (a) freedom to remit capital; (b) freedom to remit dividends; (c) freedom to remit savings of foreign businessmen upon their permanent return to their country of nationality; and (d) assurance of adequate raw material supply through sufficient exchange allocations. Similarly, the study by the U.S., Department of Commerce, Bureau of Foreign Commerce, *Investment in the Philippines* (Washington, 1955), p. 5, emphasized exchange and import controls as an unfavorable aspect of the Philippine foreign investment climate.

for consequence of devaluation—that an increase would occur in foreign exchange earnings which would support higher levels of Philippine imports and other payments.

The principal argument advanced against devaluation is that it would be inflationary. Following peso devaluation, the foreign currency prices of Philippine imports would remain unchanged, and the peso cost of imports would tend to increase by the ratio of devaluation. Such a conclusion would apply very imperfectly to the Philippines.

Since the end of 1949 the Philippines has been implementing stringent import controls (Table 24). The reduced quantities of imports allowed under import controls have been marketed at prices the market would bear. As a result, since 1950 the peso prices of imports and the prices of domestically produced goods have diverged sharply and persistently. This price divergence cannot be accounted for by changes in the foreign currency prices of imports or by changes in tax rates on imported commodities.[15] The logical and sufficient explanation of the divergence in prices is the impact of import controls and the windfall accruing to importers (and others engaging in import activities) arising out of the restriction of import quantities.

If the peso should be devalued, the initial reaction of importers would be to raise prices in order to maintain customary profit rates. But the capacity of the importer to raise prices may be quite limited. In the first place, if prices are raised, a smaller quantity of imports can be marketed. In the absence of a decline in foreign exchange proceeds, a decline in the consumption of imports following attempts on the part of importers to pass on the increased peso costs will reduce the demand on available foreign exchange. If this occurs, additional amounts of foreign exchange will be available for potential importers who did not receive allocations of exchange under the more stringent controls required prior to devaluation. Unless a decline in foreign exchange availabilities occurs, new importers will presumably have access to foreign exchange saved by the reduction in import quantities.[16]

[15] Implicit in this argument is the belief that reductions in Philippine imports (which might be substantial in terms of Philippine imports of a given commodity) would be small when related to total world trade in a given commodity. Therefore, the impact of the decline in Philippine imports of a given commodity on the world price would be of negligible importance.

[16] For example, it was widely predicted in the spring of 1951 that the imposition of the special tax on sales of foreign exchange would be followed by price increases

Table 24. Data relevant to appraisal of intensity of Philippine import controls [a]
(1949 = 100)

Year	Volume of imports [b]	Index of national income [c]	Retail prices, Manila	Wholesale prices, Manila			Unit value of imports [b] 1948-49 = 100
				All items	Home goods	Imports	
1950	58	110	101	97	92	121	94
1951	73	123	113	109	101	153	106
1952	66	125	106	100	95	136	105
1953	73	128	101	99	93	129	100
1954	81	132	96	94	88	125	96
1955	91	139	93	91	87	119	96
1956	89	153	98	94	89	129	97
1957	100	161	101	98	92	136	100
1958	n.a.	169	106	101	94	141	102

[a] Central Bank, *Statistical Bulletin*, 10 (Dec. 1958), pp. 167, 170, 173, and 174, tables 83, 86, 89, and 90. Home goods are "locally produced commodities for home consumption in Manila."
[b] UN, Statistical Office, *Yearbook of International Trade Statistics, 1957*.
[c] See above Table 14.

This argument is reinforced when we consider the probable consequences of devaluation on foreign exchange proceeds. If Philippine foreign exchange earnings should increase following devaluation, the additional amounts of foreign exchange can either be used to make foreign payments, including imports, or to accumulate as foreign exchange reserves. In view of Philippine aspirations for economic growth and the projected increases in income under development plans, accumulation of foreign exchange at a rate which would reduce imports below current levels would be exceedingly irrational. Therefore, if foreign exchange earnings should increase following devaluation, some part of the increased earnings would probably be used to acquire imports. If this should be the case, it would clearly be deflationary, i.e., other things being equal, increased quantities of imports could only be sold at lower peso prices.

A second inflationary effect of devaluation would arise out of the increase in peso prices of exports. To the extent that Philippine export commodities are consumed domestically, the peso prices of these commodities would tend to increase by the ratio of devaluation. Although this undoubtedly would be inflationary, the consequences should not be exaggerated. For example, coconut oil, logs, timber and lumber, and leaf tobacco were the only commodities exported in 1953–1954 in which a major part of production was consumed domestically.

During 1953–1956 the value of domestic consumption of major export commodities averaged approximately ₱371 million annually, or about 5 per cent of average annual private consumption expenditures of ₱7,092 million (Table 25). Domestic consumption of other export commodities is not economically significant. It becomes evident that the inflationary impact of devaluation on the peso prices of export commodities would directly affect only a relatively small part of Philippine consumption expenditure.

What would be the impact of devaluation on the price of rice, a staple of great importance in the Philippine standard of living? Discussion of exchange rate policy in the Philippines has emphasized

---

as importers and retailers passed on the tax. Actually, liberal foreign exchange allocations caused the prices of imports to decline steadily following imposition of the exchange tax. Analysis of the peso prices of imported goods since 1949 supports the conclusion that import policy and not foreign exchange costs is the ultimate determinant of peso prices of imports. See Central Bank, *Third Annual Report, 1951,* pp. 14–17; *Fourth Annual Report, 1952,* pp. 14, 175.

that rice is an imported commodity, that the price of imported rice would tend to rise by the ratio of devaluation, and that the price of marginal rice imports would determine the price for rice domestically produced. The Philippines is on the margin of rice self-sufficiency, and imports during 1953–1956 averaged 37,350 metric tons, or 2.3 per cent of the average annual production.[17] It is true that in a competitive free market there would be only one price for rice, and the price of all rice consumed in the Philippines would be set by the price of marginal rice imports.[18] It should, however, be pointed

Table 25. Production, trade, and consumption of export commodities (annual average, 1953–1956—000 metric tons)

Commodity	Pro- duction [a] I	Exports [b] II	Domestic con- sumption [c] III	Value of exports f.o.b. (₱ million) IV	Estimated value of domestic consumption (₱ million) [d] V
Copra	952	718	234	242	79
Coconut oil	147	66	81	33.4	41
Leaf tobacco	27	9	18	6.6	13
Sugar, centrifugal	1,191	860	331	205	79
Timber, logs, and lumber (000 cu. meters)	4,307	1,307	3,000	69	159

[a] Central Bank, *Annual Reports.* The figures are for crop years.
[b] See above Table 9. The figures are for calendar years.
[c] Column I minus Column II.
[d] Ratio of consumption to exports (Column III: Column II) multiplied by value of exports (Column IV).

out that by monopolizing the rice import trade the government is presently insulating the domestic economy from the impact of the price of marginal rice imports.

Virtually all the countries of the world implement agricultural price policies which insulate domestic agricultural markets from world markets. In countries such as the United States, the United

[17] UN, ECAFE, *Food and Agricultural Price Policies in Asia and the Far East* (Bangkok, 1958), pp. 95–100.
[18] No producer in a free market situation would sell his rice for less than he could obtain abroad, i.e., he would have the alternative of exporting his rice.

Kingdom, and most of Western Europe domestic prices are maintained above world markets and the producer is thereby subsidized. In Burma, Thailand, India, Ceylon, and some other countries, the reverse is true, and the consumer is subsidized by domestic prices below world prices. It is inconceivable that the Philippine government, following devaluation, would not continue to isolate the Philippine economy from the potential inflation inherent in the small quantity of marginal rice imports.

Another aspect of the relationship between exchange rate policy and inflation may be summarized as the "incipient inflation" argument. This involves the belief that, whereas the directly inflationary consequences of devaluation would be important, more disastrous would be the impact on resistance to inflationary economic policies. It is, of course, true that the potential benefits of devaluation would be dissipated if devaluation was not co-ordinated with relatively conservative monetary and fiscal policies, which would tend to maintain the price incentives established by devaluation.

The importance of this argument in the case of the Philippines should not be understated. For example, export producers have been allied with proponents of expansionary monetary and fiscal policy in opposing current exchange rate policy. The latter recognize that the exchange parity and the strong vested interests in currency overvaluation are the principal obstacles to utilization of expansionary fiscal and monetary policies.[19]

It should be pointed out that the "incipient inflation" argument is not an argument against devaluation but an argument against policies which would dissipate the potential benefits of devaluation. Devaluation is not a panacea and would be effective only where necessary monetary and fiscal discipline exists. This is the tragedy of Philippine exchange rate policy since 1949. The inflationary impact of devaluation has been visited on the Philippines by import restrictions, while conservative monetary and fiscal policies probably have restrained economic growth. In other words, high levels of monetary and fiscal discipline have been exercised since 1949, but they were exerted on behalf of an exchange rate policy that became increasingly bankrupt as Philippine economic growth labored under the handicap of limited foreign exchange receipts. Optimum timing of an appropriate exchange rate policy change is undoubtedly some distance in the past.

[19] Cf. Golay, "The Philippine Monetary Policy Debate."

In view of the essential conservatism of the Philippine political and economic elites as well as the strong residue of colonial influence in economic policy making, appraisal of exchange rate policy might very well include the assumption that an appropriate devaluation would not be followed by monetary and fiscal license.

The argument for devaluation advanced here should not be construed as a case for dismantling the structure of controls. The utility of exchange and import controls has been widely demonstrated since the beginning of World War II. Many countries have learned to utilize exchange and import controls to contribute to a wide range of economic policies only remotely related to the maintenance of equilibrium in external payments.[20]

However, if the Philippines successfully maintains its relatively rapid postwar economic expansion, the expansion in income (both money and real) will result in at least a comparable growth in the desire to import goods and services. The obvious escape from this impasse is to direct economic development toward the production of substitutes for imports and to the production of exports. With regard to the former, there has been no lack of protection in the Philippines, and economic expansion in this direction has been rewarding, although the rate of expansion has not mitigated the intensity of controls. The latter alternative has been neglected (or ignored) by the Philippines in spite of the growth in foreign exchange requirements of postwar development. Again it should be emphasized that the case for devaluation is not the traditional case for the elimination of balance of payments disequilibrium, although a more realistic exchange rate would contribute to such an objective. An appropriate devaluation should not aim at reducing foreign exchange payments below existing levels but at providing the wherewithal necessary to expand imports to sustain Philippine aspirations for rapid economic growth.

This leads to a further observation regarding the timing of the dismantling of the control system. No economist would argue that the effects of devaluation would be instantaneous. This would be particularly true of the effects of devaluation on export proceeds. Foreign exchange earnings would increase only as production in-

[20] For example, dual-pricing systems have been highly productive of government revenues in the postwar period of strong demand for primary products. Distribution of the windfall arising out of import restriction has enabled newly sovereign and relatively weak governments to pursue economic policies that they were unable (or unwilling) to implement by conventional fiscal techniques.

creases, i.e., to the extent that supply is elastic. The output of some Philippine export commodities might respond relatively quickly to the stimulation of devaluation, e.g., lumber production and some mineral output. For the bulk of Philippine export commodities, the expansion of supply could only be relatively slow. The beneficial consequences of devaluation would accumulate for a prolonged period following devaluation. For this reason it might be desirable to retain indefinitely the structure of import and exchange controls.

Producer-exporters, particularly spokesmen for the Philippine sugar industry, have attempted to make a case for devaluation on grounds of equity. They have argued that it is inequitable that they be required to surrender their export proceeds to the Central Bank at the rate of two pesos per dollar, while the foreign exchange, which in terms of the relative purchasing power of currencies is worth much more, is allocated to importers at the official rate. This argument has no place in the case for devaluation developed here. The decision to devalue should reflect the interests of all Filipinos and not the interests of any economic pressure group.

Present levels of Philippine export production and trade are not unprofitable. The low levels of export production and trade reflect the response of entrepreneurs to the rates of return inherent in the official rate of exchange for the peso. This is the fundamental explanation of the relatively retarded levels of Philippine export production and trade. The basic argument for devaluation is that it would stimulate relatively stagnant export industries and thereby increase foreign exchange earnings. Therefore, with the important exception of the sugar industry, devaluation should be permitted to exert maximum effect upon the profitability of export production. Strong pressure to divert to the government by export taxation any windfall on current levels of exports arising from devaluation can be expected.[21] Such taxation should be strongly resisted as it would counteract the potential benefits from devaluation.

The Philippine sugar industry is clearly a special case. Exports of sugar under the Philippine quota in the United States market as well as sales in the domestic market have been highly profitable. This arises out of the fact that the United States implements a sugar price policy designed to bring about domestic (United States) sugar production equal currently to about one-fourth of United States sugar

[21] The peso proceeds from current (predevaluation) levels of exports would tend to increase in proportion to the ratio of devaluation.

consumption.[22] Inasmuch as the United States is at a comparative disadvantage in the production of sugar, to provide a sufficient incentive to bring about the desired domestic production, sugar imports into the United States are limited by absolute quota. This policy results in a price for sugar in the United States substantially above the world market price of sugar. The principal beneficiaries of this policy are the sugar producers in those countries assigned a quota in the United States market.[23] The monopoly windfall to Philippine sugar producers with quotas in the United States market has been extended to all Philippine sugar production by Philippine sugar price policies which result in a domestic price (excluding transportation differentials) equivalent to the United States price.

The profitability of Philippine sugar production quotas is readily confirmed. First, Philippine sugar exports in both the prewar and postwar periods have tended to be stabilized at the level of the United States quota and to be made almost exclusively to the United States. Second, an active market exists for unused annual quota rights, and the privilege of exporting sugar to the United States is given a monetary value. A number of owners of sugar quota lands do not grow sugar; they live off the proceeds of the rentals of quota rights to bona fide sugar producers.[24] The proponents of devaluation must recognize that the sugar industry, already profitable because of

[22] During 1948–1953 continental United States produced 11.8 million metric tons of sugar. This amounted to 27.8 per cent of U.S. sugar availability during this period (UN, FAO, *Yearbook of Food and Agricultural Statistics, 1954,* vol. VIII, pt. 1, "Production," and pt. 2, "Trade").

[23] Whether intended or not, a major consequence of U.S. sugar price policy has been to subsidize the Philippine economy to the extent of the difference between the proceeds of Philippine sugar exports to the United States and the value of these exports in the world sugar market. During much of the postwar period this subsidy has amounted to 40–50 per cent of Philippine sugar export proceeds. Currently, it is 2–3 times the magnitude of the U.S. aid program. It is difficult to conceive a less efficient way to subsidize the Philippine economy, which must rely on a trickling down process to diffuse the monopoly profits of the sugar industry to the rest of the economy. The windfall arising out of U.S. sugar price policies, to which the claim of the Philippine people is paramount, has exerted only a fraction of the potential contribution that it might have made to Philippine economic growth. The Philippine government and the United States must share the blame for the failure to divert this windfall to the Philippine government where it belongs. The United States in effect tried to guarantee this inefficient process by prohibiting Philippine export taxation in the 1946 Trade Agreement.

[24] For example, Jose M. Gomez, president of the National Association of Sugar Cane Planters, reported that unused quota rights had a value equivalent to 2–3 cents (U.S.) per pound (*Manila Bulletin,* June 15, 1956).

access to the sheltered United States market, is a special case. The stimulus of devaluation should be allowed to exert maximum influence on marginal production but should not be allowed to swell the existing monopoly returns to this industry.[25]

Possibly the most important considerations which should enter into an appraisal of Philippine exchange rate policy are political and not economic. The structure of political power inherited by the sovereign Philippines was typical of colonial primary producing economies, with a preponderance of power residing in exporting industries—sugar, gold, coconuts, abacá, and so forth—which had been the principal goals of colonial economic development. Inasmuch as the transfer of sovereignty was not revolutionary, the political power structure was transferred intact. With the lapse of time indigenous elements concentrated in the sugar industry acquired political power incommensurate with their numbers or economic importance.[26] Exporter-producers have a strong stake in continuing colonial specialization in primary production and maintaining economic incentives for the export industries. Moreover, they tend to find a large community of interest with the economically conservative agricultural landowners concentrated in production of rice.

The accelerated social changes—urbanization, internal migration, and increasing political sophistication—as well as the appearance of countervailing economic interests created by exchange and import controls have tended to erode the traditional power structure inherited from the colonial period. The competition between the traditional elites and rising urban and entrepreneurial interests has been joined over exchange rate policy.

In this struggle a victory for the exporting interests which would be signaled by devaluation of the peso would have more than economic consequences. It would enhance the power of the Sugar Bloc and their cacique allies, who by their experience and interests are

[25] Evidence of the capacity of the sugar industry to expand exports under the stimulus of economic incentives is indicated by sugar exports to countries other than the United States under the No-Dollar Import Law, which provided for the barter of marginal exports outside the control system. Centrifugal sugar exports to countries outside the United States increased sevenfold to 117,000 metric tons in the first full year of the export incentive system.

[26] The influence of the sugar bloc was enhanced in the early postwar struggle between the Liberal party and the Nacionalista parties in which the Liberal party, with strong participation and financial support by the sugar industry, came out on top.

poorly equipped to provide the leadership necessary to maintain economic growth. The sympathies of the literate Philippine population have resided with the opponents of devaluation largely because of an awareness that the alternative leadership would not be productive of progress. Many Filipinos verbalize their opposition to a change in the official exchange parity in terms of their suspicions that the proponents of devaluation are pursuing their self-interest without concern for the welfare of the country as a whole.

This aspect of an appraisal of exchange rate policy should not be minimized. Optimum timing of devaluation—as is usually the case— is clearly in the past. Controversy over this policy has been allowed to polarize to the point where the adverse political consequences of such a change may very well offset economic considerations in appraising this policy. It is unfortunate that this issue has acquired a character such that a decision which is probably warranted on economic considerations should be rejected for political reasons. However, though devaluation may in the short run represent a political setback to those elements of the Philippine society most capable of providing economic leadership, it is unlikely to halt the processes of social change which have been initiated and which are necessary to rapid economic growth.

Exchange rate policy in the Philippines as elsewhere will have important consequences for income distribution, and the exporting interests will be the principal beneficiaries.[27] Such a result can be expected from any policy that establishes economic incentives, and existing exchange controls have important consequences for income distribution. Consideration of income distribution should not be a decisive factor in appraising exchange rate policy inasmuch as progressive income taxation as well as taxation of sugar exports to the United States under the quota are available to achieve income distribution goals.

Another consideration which should be introduced in appraisal of exchange rate policy is the impact on government revenues. Devalua-

[27] President Garcia engaged in poetic license when in 1957 he vetoed Senate Bill No. 167, which provided for export incentives implemented by import certificates, by concluding that the effect of the bill would be to make the "rich richer and the poor poorer." Doubtless the sugar bloc and other exporters and producers would have benefited. On the other hand, a rewarding increase in foreign exchange proceeds, income and imports, would not have made the poor poorer, but rather the opposite.

tion would tend to result in an immediate increase in import (peso) values equal to the ratio of devaluation. Inasmuch as the bulk of import duties are based on import values, devaluation would produce substantial increases from tariff duties and various other taxes which use import values as the basis for taxation. To the extent that devaluation results in expanded foreign exchange earnings, this should be followed by expansion in imports and an increase in tariff revenues. Tending to offset the increase in government revenues arising out of devaluation will be the increase in the peso costs of government imports as well as any increase in the structure of peso costs and prices that might follow devaluation.[28]

Finally, appraisal of Philippine exchange rate policy must introduce pragmatic considerations which may have been dominant in the postwar period. Since 1945 the Philippines has benefited from average annual imports at least double the prewar volume in exchange for average annual exports no greater than the prewar volume. This has been possible because of large-scale United States disbursements under various *ad hoc* and continuing programs. It is quite conceivable that the Philippines has maximized postwar foreign exchange availability by economic "brinkmanship," to which the United States was vulnerable. There can be little question that the availability of foreign exchange has been directly related to the intensity of Philippine external disequilibrium as well as to other emergencies of various types.

This consideration may provide a rationalization for postwar exchange rate policy, but it is of rapidly diminishing importance. In 1950 the United States abandoned the earlier policy of *ad hoc* balance of payments and budgetary assistance, and present disbursements occur under continuing, relatively predictable programs. More important, United States payments were cut in half in 1951 and have not increased absolutely since that time. Such payments have declined rapidly in relative importance, and because of their continuing, semipermanent nature are not amenable to upward manipulation by crisis.[29]

[28] Since foreign exchange for government imports is allocated at the official exchange rate, the control system has had the result of increasing the government's command over resources from a given level of peso receipts.

[29] Such a conclusion must have been brought home to Filipinos by the negligible economic results of President Garcia's pilgrimage to the United States in the spring of 1958.

It will be recalled that the current exchange premium act (Republic Act No. 2609 of July 16, 1959) obligated the Monetary Board to initiate gradual removal of exchange and import controls.[30] The Monetary Board's plan for decontrol was made public on April 18, 1960.[31] Exchange decontrol is to be accomplished by allowing an increasing proportion of total foreign exchange receipts to be traded on a free exchange market with full decontrol to be achieved not later than 1964. Decontrol of imports and other foreign exchange payments is to be scheduled by exchange control category with full decontrol not later than 1964.

The plan also calls for legislation repealing the current export barter law (Republic Act No. 2261 of June 19, 1959) which permits the barter of marginal exports outside the control system, elimination of the extensive list of exemptions to the exchange premium tax,[32] and an enabling act authorizing the President to impose an export tax of not more than 40 per cent.

On April 25, 1960, Central Bank Circulars Nos. 105 and 106 initiated the decontrol program. All foreign exchange, as before, is to be sold to the Central Bank. In the case of export proceeds, receipts from invisibles, and United States government payments, 75 per cent of the foreign exchange receipts will be converted at the official rate of two pesos per dollar with the remaining 25 per cent converted at a so-called free market rate determined by the Central Bank. Proceeds from the sale of gold and receipts from tourism will be converted at the free market rate. The Monetary Board initially established the free market rate at 3.2 pesos per dollar.

Foreign exchange and import licensing is continued without change for the following import categories: highly essential commodities, essential producers' commodities, semiessential producers' commodities, and decontrolled commodities.[33] Exchange for other import control categories and for invisible payments will be sold at the free market rate plus the foreign exchange margin fee of 25 per cent.

[30] See above p. 98. Republic Act No. 2609 provides: "In implementing the provisions of this Act, along with other monetary and fiscal measures to stabilize the economy, the monetary authorities shall take steps for the adoption of a four-year program of gradual decontrol (Sec. 2)."

[31] *Phil. Newsletter,* April 18, 1960, pp. 3–6.

[32] Republic Act No. 2609, Sec. 2.

[33] During 1956–1958 imports in these categories accounted for 75.3 per cent of foreign exchange allocations for imports (Central Bank, *Tenth Annual Report,* 1958, p. 129).

The Monetary Board's plan of decontrol makes no mention of a change in the official exchange parity. The request for authority to impose heavy export taxes suggests that the monetary authorities hope to establish some semblance of a "decontrol equilibrium" by some combination of the present exchange parity, export taxation, and tariffs. There is little likelihood that such a system would receive the necessary congressional approval or, if approved, would be permanent.

It seems safe to predict that the decontrol process will result in an effective exchange parity which reflects the realities of the Philippine situation. The effective parity may involve some combination of a free market in foreign exchange with minimum exchange procurement by the government for high priority imports, e.g., government imports and consumer price control items. Equally likely is the probability that at some stage in the decontrol process the monetary authorities will assess the situation as favorable and junk the scheduled decontrol in favor of a new official exchange parity appropriate to Philippine economic development.

The basic argument for devaluation is that it will stimulate export production and thereby increase foreign exchange earnings. The Philippines has not shared proportionately in the world-wide expansion in trade which characterized the postwar period. Not only have the export industries remained relatively depressed, but the limited foreign exchange earnings have required the Philippines to exist on lower levels of imports than would have been necessary if export potentials had been more fully developed.[34]

The principal argument advanced against devaluation is that it will be inflationary. To the extent that devaluation produces an increase in foreign exchange earnings, it will permit an expansion in Philippine imports which have been restricted by stringent import and exchange controls. An increase in imports would not be inflationary as it would increase the supply of goods and services available to the Philippine economy.

[34] For example, Governor Cuaderno has been cited as being of the opinion "that the adoption of the so-called dollar retention system would cause more hardships to the national economy, especially in this country which does not earn enough foreign exchange to pay for the importation of capital goods and materials needed by established industries" (*Manila Bulletin*, May 11, 1956, p. 20).

· VII ·

Exchange Control and the

Supply of Foreign Exchange

GOVERNMENT monopolization of foreign exchange transactions through exchange and import controls has replaced import taxation as the principal instrument of developmental-commercial policy. The traditional role of protection has been subordinated to use of exchange rationing to contain the external disequilibrium which accompanies accelerated economic growth.

Exchange allocations are universally based on a scale of essentiality, with liberal allocations for high priority imports of capital goods, essential food items, and industrial raw materials. Allocations for less essential and luxury imports are less liberal, and in many cases allocations are not made. Major policy problems arise out of substantial discrepancies in the purchasing power of the national currency which result when restricted quantities of imports are rationed by the price mechanism.

The windfall inherent in effective exchange and import controls has a divisive impact on society.[1] Exchange and import controls are re-

[1] Exchange and import controls are effective whenever total expenditures of foreign exchange are reduced below the level that would prevail in the absence of such controls.

sented beyond the export community because their effects are haphazard, wasteful, and discriminatory. They are haphazard because the selection of both commodities imported as well as individuals awarded the windfall frequently involve economically irrational criteria. Waste enters because the windfall is dissipated to fixers, corruptible bureaucrats, politicians, and the like and because frenetic activity inevitably attends such controls. Exporters resent controls as a discriminatory tax on their foreign exchange earnings, and individuals whose foreign exchange applications are denied resent the discretionary allocation which usually prevails.[2] On the other hand, the distribution of the windfall creates strong economic interests which can be mobilized to support both controls and the government implementing them.

Economists at this point are prone to point out that logical alternatives exist to overcome these objections to exchange and import controls—multiple exchange rates or the auction of foreign exchange. Either alternative is capable of diverting the windfall arising out of exchange restrictions to the government.[3] The durability of exchange and import controls with a minimum number of allocation rates is due to three consequences of this system which have tended to acquire utility. First is the direct revenue effect of exchange and import controls. To the extent that foreign exchange is used directly by government to import, the government derives additional command over resources. In less-developed countries with relatively weak governments and limited tax bases there is a tendency to tax indirectly where conventional taxation is not politically feasible. Second is the contribution of exchange and import controls to the promotion of economic nationalism. By the allocation of foreign exchange, subject to stringent restriction, to Filipino importers and retailers, they are

[2] A major cause of the abortive Indonesian rebellion of 1957–1958 was the dissatisfaction over exchange and import controls. The principal part of available foreign exchange was diverted from the export economy concentrated in Sumatra and Celebes to the seat of political power in Java.

[3] An appropriate structure of tariffs could accomplish the same objective. Tariffs receive little consideration in discussion of developmental commercial policy because of an alleged lack of flexibility. However, in view of their certainty and the minimum incentive to corruption, they may very well represent the most effective way of rationing the available foreign exchange in less-developed countries. They have an important advantage in the quality of protection afforded domestic producers. Such protection is looked upon as permanent and stable and therefore has maximum protective effect.

given a windfall that ensures their competitive survival. Third is the utilization of exchange and import controls to promote industrialization. Import controls are used to establish high levels of protection, and the windfall inherent in effective exchange and import controls can be utilized to subsidize entrepreneurial initiative.

The unwillingness of governments of less-developed countries to capture the windfall inherent in restriction of foreign exchange payments by import duties, exchange premiums, and so forth produces strong incentives to evade the control system.[4] Erosion of the government monopoly of foreign exchange depends upon three factors—the length of time such controls have been in effect, the opportunities to evade controls, and the capacity of those economic interests adversely affected by such controls to mobilize political power to change the system.

The experience of less-developed countries with exchange and import controls is analogous to experience with price control and rationing in time of war and national emergency. The effectiveness of such controls declines with the lapse of time and the dilution of patriotic discipline. In the contest of wits between the exchange control authority and the entrepreneur earning foreign exchange it would be a mistake to sell the latter short. The lapse of time allows the exchange control authority to close loopholes, but it also gives the businessman an opportunity to find other loopholes.[5]

The extent of evasion of exchange and import controls will depend not only upon the strength of the motivation but also on the existence of factors favorable to evasion. Spatial dispersion of export production is a factor favorable to evasion through export undervaluation and smuggling. Export production, particularly plantation agriculture, mining, and forestry industries, tends to be located in frontier areas. Export crops are shipped directly, in many cases, from private port facilities. The spatial dispersion of such production increases the

[4] If the windfall is diverted to the government by taxation, individuals can appropriate the difference between the foreign and domestic prices of imports only by smuggling or by living abroad. Taxation of foreign trade values is relatively easy to enforce because of the ease with which foreign commerce can be supervised.

[5] Central Bank Circular No. 20 of Dec. 9, 1949, established the basic control over foreign exchange receipts. For a running account of the battle to maintain exchange control discipline, the reader is directed to the "Exchange Policy and Management of the International Reserve" section of the successive *Annual Reports* of the Central Bank. The bank is responsible for the management of exchange control.

difficulty of supervision necessary to effective exchange and import controls.[6]

The nature of the organization of export production can be a major factor in evasion. Generally speaking, peasant production of exports will show a higher order of exchange and import control discipline. If the procurement and marketing of such produce is organized competitively, the dispersion of production and relatively small-scale export operations will tend to discipline the industry. Export valuation will be policed by the quotations of competitive producers, and the small scale of operations will minimize collusion between exporters and their foreign trading partners.[7]

At the other extreme, export production will be organized in large-scale, capital-intensive plantations, mines, lumbering operations, and the like. Optimum conditions for evasion of exchange and import controls probably exist where export production on a large scale is in the hands of direct private foreign investment, i.e., a wholly owned foreign subsidiary. This would be true, for example, of oil production in Indonesia and chromite and pineapple production in the Philippines. Where production is sold to the parent concern, the discretionary nature of the pricing process facilitates evasion of controls. Moreover, the discretionary definition of profit in relations between parent and subsidiary presents a similar opportunity.

Still another important factor of great influence on the effectiveness of exchange control is the quality of the control administration. Currency overvaluation is a powerful incentive to corruption, and public officials in Southeast Asia, like public officials in our own country, have not proved incorruptible. Bureaucratic discipline tends to be relatively low because of lack of administrative experience during the colonial period. Moreover, the generally low pay scales of civil servants hardly conform to the expectations generated by successful nationalist revolutions. In the case of the Philippines, the incentive

---

[6] For example, during recent years it has been estimated that up to one-half of the foreign exchange earnings from exports from Sumatra have evaded the Indonesian exchange and import control system.

[7] It is frequently argued that evasion of controls is widespread in the assembly and shipment of small holders' export produce because of the important role in this activity of the Chinese minority with their capacity for sharp business practices. The virulence of economic and political nationalism and the harshness of punitive measures against this minority tend, however, to maintain relatively high exchange control discipline.

to evade exchange and import controls is unusually strong, conditions favorable to such evasion exist, and the prevalence of evasion is widely discussed.

The statistical evidence of export undervaluation is difficult to organize, and the results of statistical tests, while suggestive, are inconclusive. Comparative data are readily available on the unit values of exports, and Philippine unit values can be compared with those of other countries for evidence of export undervaluation. Ideally, such a comparison should involve countries which, in contrast to the Philippines, do not have exchange and import controls. Such a requirement could not be met inasmuch as exchange controls are universally applied in tropical Asia. More important, however, than the formal existence of exchange and import controls is the effectiveness of controls as measured by the divergence between the purchasing power of currencies internally and externally.

The unit values of exports of coconut products, pineapples, and lumber from the Philippines, Malaya, and Ceylon have been compared for evidence of export undervaluation. The three countries have specialized in agricultural production and trade, and per capita export proceeds are relatively high.[8] Malaya and Ceylon have devalued their exchange rates substantially as compared with prewar parities, whereas the Philippines has chosen to maintain the prewar parity.[9] Exchange controls in Malaya and Ceylon are maintained primarily to control capital movements, and import quantities are relatively unrestricted.[10] Finally, Philippine exchange controls did not serve to limit import and other foreign exchange payments prior to 1950. Under such circumstances one would expect to find, following 1949, increasing divergence between the reported unit values of Philippine exports and those of Malaya and Ceylon.

This type of test is useful in only a limited number of cases for various reasons. For example, sugar, the second major Philippine ex-

[8] During 1953–1955 the average annual per capita value of export proceeds amounted to $22 for the Philippines, $45 for Ceylon, and $205 for Malaya.

[9] During 1951–1955 the Malayan dollar parity was 32.67 U.S. cents as compared to an average parity of 55.47 during 1937–1939. Similarly, the post-1949 parity of the Ceylonese rupee has been 21.00 U.S. cents as compared to an average parity of 35.63 during 1937–1939.

[10] This is readily verified by comparison shopping of imports in the three countries. Tourists consider Malaya and Ceylon to be shoppers' paradises as compared to the Philippines. The same generalization applies to a wide range of industrial imports as well as to less essential consumer goods.

port crop, is marketed almost exclusively in the United States and the sugar industry has traditionally been closely regulated to police the quota. This regulation, involving fixed quota quantities and well-publicized prices, has minimized the opportunities for the evasion of exchange and import controls by undervaluation of export shipments. Sugar interests have sought to mobilize political power to obtain special treatment or to destroy the exchange and import control system.[11]

The third major export crop is abacá. The Philippines produces approximately 90 per cent of the world supply of this commodity, and it is not feasible to compare Philippine unit values of this commodity with those of other producers. Production is dominated by small holders' output, and abacá is marketed widely throughout the world. Wide distribution of production, assembly, and marketing probably acts as a check upon evasion of controls.

The principal postwar export crop of the Philippines has been coconuts, which are marketed as copra, coconut oil, desiccated (shredded) coconut, and copra meal.[12] Copra is predominantly a small holders' crop and is produced throughout the islands. The assembly of copra for export is dominated by Chinese. Individual firms are relatively small and spatially dispersed. In the case of copra, Philippine prices are well synchronized with those of Malaya and there is no evidence that the imposition of effective controls was followed by a relative decline in Philippine unit values. Prewar as well as postwar relative price relationships are maintained.

The organization of coconut oil, desiccated coconut, and copra meal production contrasts sharply with that of the copra industry. The principal part of Philippine coconut oil exports is produced by subsidiaries of United States and other foreign firms. These firms are relatively large and few in number, which facilitates collusion in pricing. More important, evasion is facilitated by the arbitrary nature of pricing between parent and subsidiary company. Copra meal, which is a by-product of coconut oil production, is marketed under similar arrangements. Desiccated coconut, like coconut oil, is produced almost entirely by subsidiaries of foreign firms.

During the prewar period Philippine unit values of coconut oil

[11] See below, pp. 153–157.

[12] Copra meal, the residual product in the manufacture of coconut oil, is a fertilizer.

were closely synchronized with prices paid for coconut oil exports from both Malaya and Ceylon.[13] When compared with Malayan values, there is no evidence of relative deterioration in the unit values of Philippine coconut oil exports following 1949. The reverse is true when Philippine and Ceylon values are compared. Malayan and Ceylonese export unit values of coconut oil in the postwar period ranged from 3 to 6 times the average unit value in the prewar period and tended to be well synchronized with reported unit values of copra. Reported Philippine unit values of coconut oil ranged from 2 to 4 times prewar values, and there was a slight tendency for the gap between the relative prices of copra and coconut oil to narrow as prices of copra declined.

In both the prewar and postwar period Philippine exports of desiccated coconut have been marketed almost entirely in the United States. This resulted from a tariff preference under the trade agreement of 1¾ cents per pound. Desiccated coconut has been almost exclusively produced by direct private United States investment in the form of wholly owned subsidiaries. Philippine reported unit values for desiccated coconut were substantially above those reported by Ceylon in the prewar period, but in the postwar period these positions have tended to be reversed. Moreover, there has been a distinct divergence in the reported unit values of Philippine and Ceylonese desiccated coconut since 1949.

The remaining major Philippine coconut product export is copra meal. Copra meal fertilizer is not reported in the exports of Ceylon and Malaya and is evidently consumed by domestic commercial agriculture. Analysis of the trend in unit values of this product is therefore not feasible.

The fourth major export crop is canned pineapple. The entire export crop is produced on a single, large-scale, industrialized plantation and cannery in northern Mindanao. This industry is a wholly owned subsidiary of an American firm, which ships virtually its entire output to the home firm. Malaya is a substantial producer and exporter of pineapple and affords an opportunity to compare changes in unit values. The results are quite interesting. In the prewar period the unit values of Philippine pineapple exports were approximately twice

[13] During 1949–1957 exports to the United States accounted for 84 per cent of Philippine coconut oil exports. Such exports, within the quota established in the Trade Agreement, are given a preference of 2 cents a pound.

those received by Malaya, whereas in the postwar period the relationship has been reversed. Moreover, Philippine unit values declined following the imposition of exchange and import controls in 1949, whereas Malayan unit values have steadily increased since 1950.

Another type of evidence that can be brought to bear in this case results from comparison of the unit value index with the movement in the wholesale price of canned pineapple as reported by the United States Bureau of Labor Statistics. Unit values realized for Philippine pineapple exports have averaged about 110 per cent of prewar, whereas wholesale prices of this commodity in the United States have averaged 170 to 175 per cent of prewar prices.[14]

Forest products comprise still another important primary commodity export of the Philippines. Lumbering operations are spatially dispersed, with a large number of small- and medium-scale producers. Investment in this industry is predominantly Filipino, although several of the largest units are foreign controlled. Forestry products are exported both as lumber and as logs, with the latter, since 1950, averaging several times the former in value. Philippine exports are predominantly tropical softwoods, with a minor portion of hardwoods. Exports are shipped directly from the producing area, and Japan is the principal market. The reported unit value of Philippine lumber exports has remained fairly stable since 1948, and shipments have expanded rapidly. The experience of Malaya, which has also been an important lumber exporter in the postwar period, contrasts rather sharply with that of the Philippines. Malayan unit values averaged 20 to 25 per cent lower than Philippine during 1948–1950, but in the next five years the relationship was reversed, with Malayan unit values averaging about 10 per cent more than Philippine.[15]

A similar pattern appears in the unit values of Philippine exports of logs and timber as compared with those of North Borneo. North Borneo is close to the Philippines and exports the same varieties of tropical softwoods. During 1948–1950 North Borneo and Philippine values were fairly comparable. Beginning in 1951, the values began to diverge substantially, with North Borneo unit values averaging 25 to 30 per cent higher than those of the Philippines.

[14] U.S. Bureau of Labor Statistics, *Retail Food Prices by Cities.* The average annual retail price per No. 2½ can of pineapple during 1937–1940 was 21.9 cents, whereas during 1951–1954 the price was 38.5 cents.

[15] Malayan exports of lumber amounted to less than $.5 million (U.S.) in the prewar period.

Exports of metals and ores including gold, iron ore, copper concentrates, and chromite accounted for 11.9 per cent of the value of Philippine exports during 1956–1958. The most important Philippine mineral export in recent years has been copper. Copper is not refined in the Philippines and is exported in the form of concentrates of varying copper content and with varying content of other metals. The heterogeneous nature of this export precludes useful statistical analysis.[16]

Iron ore has been an important Philippine export in both the prewar and the postwar periods. Iron is produced in a single large mine and is shipped exclusively to Japan. Malaya also makes substantial iron ore shipments to Japan. Comparison of the reported unit values of iron ore shipments from the Philippines and Malaya indicates close correlation, with some relative improvement in Philippine values. Because of transportation costs, a comparison of f.o.b. unit values is not fruitful.

The Philippines is a substantial exporter of chromite ore, which does not appear in the export lists for either Malaya or Ceylon. Comparison of Philippine unit values with those reported by Southern Rhodesia and the Union of South Africa does not indicate a significant divergence in Philippine unit values. Philippine chromite is produced in a single mine operated by a largely American-owned firm with shipments direct from the mine to refineries in the United States. The only evidence of arbitrariness in the pricing of chromite exports lies in the sharp divergence in the United States wholesale price of chromite ore and in Philippine export unit values. Philippine exports averaged 110 per cent of prewar unit values during the period 1951–1955, whereas the reported United States wholesale price of chromite averaged some 250 per cent of prewar levels.[17]

As might be expected, an attempt statistically to demonstrate a relationship between Philippine import and exchange controls and evasion of such controls by export undervaluation raises more questions than it answers. The usefulness of the test varies from product to product, but in general there can be little satisfaction with the number of country comparisons. Moreover, there are heroic assumptions regarding product homogeneity. In the case of coconut oil, desiccated coconut, sugar, pineapples, and chromite ore, an assumption

[16] This characteristic would also be favorable to evasion of controls.

[17] See *Commodity Yearbook, 1956* (New York: Commodity Research Bureau, 1957), p. 86.

of homogeneity is not unrealistic, both as between countries and over time. In the case of iron ore, copra, abacá, logs, and lumber, such an assumption is less realistic; in the case of copper concentrates it precludes any meaningful comparisons.

Table 26. Comparison of export unit values of selected countries [a]
($ U.S. per metric ton)

| | Copra | | Coconut oil | | | Desiccated coconut | |
	Philip-pines	Malaya	Philip-pines	Ceylon	Malaya	Philip-pines	Ceylon
Average 1937–39	42.5	46.5	81.5	81.5	74.3	125	70
1948	264	308	431	511	465	468	634
1949	170	219	286	367	389	336	418
1950	195	211	308	348	347	331	438
1951	198	243	315	428	413	314	341
1952	135	156	192	585	250	249	616
1953	199	186	288	712	287	318	722
1954	170	174	254	682	286	296	620
1955	148	150	223	539	223	264	497

| | Canned pineapple | | Lumber | | Logs and timber | | |
	Philip-pines	Malaya	Philip-pines	Malaya	Philip-pines	Sarawak	North Borneo
Average 1937–39	130.5	59.4	n.a.	n.a.	n.a.	n.a.	n.a.
1948	249	412	64	36	36	24	15
1949	169	326	43	37	20	22	24
1950	145	268	45	34	19	18	20
1951	152	321	44	49	23	27	29
1952	146	320	42	40	19	26	29
1953	148	329	40	38	21	26	26
1954	138	355	48	50	22	n.a.	n.a.
1955	166	n.a.	49	54	22	n.a.	n.a.

[a] For Philippine trade statistics, see notes to Tables 8 and 9. Prewar trade statistics for Ceylon and Malaya were obtained from U.S. Department of Commerce, *Foreign Commerce Yearbook.* Postwar statistics for Malaya, Ceylon, Sarawak, and North Borneo were obtained from UN, Statistical Office, *Yearbook of International Trade Statistics.*

In spite of the substantial shortcomings in the comparisons, the available evidence shows a significant pattern (Tables 26, 27). Philippine unit values of coconut oil, desiccated coconut, canned pine-

apple, logs, and lumber show a marked tendency to decline relative
to those of other producers of southern and southeastern Asia. In
the case of the first three commodities, the shift in the relationship
of postwar unit values as compared to prewar is marked.

Table 27. Comparison of export unit value indexes of selected countries [a]
(average 1948–1950 = 100)

	Copra		Coconut oil			Desiccated coconut	
	Philippines	Malaya	Philippines	Ceylon	Malaya	Philippines	Ceylon
Average 1937–39	20.2	18.9	18.9	23.3	18.6	30.1	14.1
1948	126	125	129	125	116	124	124
1949	81	89	86	90	97	89	84
1950	93	86	92	85	87	88	88
1951	95	99	94	105	103	84	69
1952	64	63	57	143	62	66	124
1953	92	76	87	174	72	85	145
1954	81	71	76	167	71	79	125
1955	70	61	67	132	56	70	100

	Canned pineapple		Lumber		Logs and timber		
	Philippines	Malaya	Philippines	Malaya	Philippines	Sarawak	North Borneo
Average 1937–39	78.6	17.7	n.a.	n.a.	n.a.	n.a.	n.a.
1948	150	123	138	102	165	113	75
1949	102	97	93	104	92	102	121
1950	87	80	97	94	90	86	104
1951	92	96	96	138	107	125	149
1952	88	96	91	112	88	122	147
1953	89	98	86	108	96	120	133
1954	83	105	104	139	104	n.a.	n.a.
1955	100	n.a.	105	152	100	n.a.	n.a.

[a] See notes to Table 26.

A more refined statistical comparison of the movement of unit
values before and after 1950 does not yield consistent results. Philippine unit values of coconut oil and desiccated coconut show some
relative improvement following 1950 as compared to the earlier post-

war period. On the other hand, the anticipated relative decline in the Philippine unit values of canned pineapple, logs, and lumber did appear.

Although the statistical evidence of export undervaluation leaves much to be desired, there can be little doubt of substantial evasion by this technique. R. Marino Corpus, director of the Export Department of the Central Bank, estimated that the Philippines is losing at least 10 per cent of the annual dollar receipts from exports as a result of overshipment, undervaluation, and misdeclaration of exports.[18] Since the Central Bank is a zealous defender of exchange and import controls, Corpus' estimate is undoubtedly conservative.[19]

A second avenue of exchange control evasion is smuggling. Philippine exports are not well adapted to this inasmuch as they are bulky and of relatively low value per unit of weight and volume.[20] But the configuration of the Philippines and the proximity of North Borneo are highly favorable to smuggling, and a substantial smuggling trade takes place between the Sulu Archipelago and adjacent North Borneo. One report estimated that by 1958 virtually all of the copra production of southern Mindanao and Sulu, estimated to be at least 60,000 tons and valued at $10 million annually, was being shipped to Borneo in small, heavily powered Moro launches. Smuggled goods were being openly peddled in the Philippines as far north as Bacolod and Cebu.[21] On April 10, 1958, a President's Law Enforcement Unit

[18] *Phil. Newsletter*, Jan. 10, 1958, p. 8.

[19] A revealing episode involving evasion of exchange controls by exporters occurred toward the end of 1957. On Dec. 18 the cabinet created a "co-ordinating team" to tighten vigilance over undeclared overshipment and underpricing of exports and the overpricing of imports. The co-ordinating team included representatives of the bureaus of Customs, Internal Revenue, Mines and Forestry, the Philippine Coconut Administration, Fiber Inspection Service, and the Philippine Constabulary (*Manila Times*, Dec. 19, 1957). It was subsequently reported that a cabinet committee was formed to "check on the activity and study performance" of the co-ordinating team. The latter committee included the Secretary of Finance, chairman, Secretary of Defense, Undersecretary of Agriculture, Secretary of Commerce and Industry, and Secretary of Foreign Affairs (*Phil. Newsletter*, Dec. 20, 1957, p. 2).

[20] Gold is an important exception to this generalization, but gold does not have to be smuggled as gold policy provides for special treatment of this industry outside the control system.

[21] *A.C.C. Journal*, 34 (May 1958), 197–199. The report went on to say that Sandakan in North Borneo was reputed to be the largest importer of American cigarettes in the world and implied that the cigarettes were the principal item for which Philippine copra was exchanged.

for the Southern Philippines was created (Executive Order No. 293) to deal with smuggling and evasion of immigration laws. In its first year of operation the antismuggling campaign was reported to have collected ₱5 million in tax revenues and ₱1.5 million in confiscated goods.[22]

Still another substantial foreign exchange leakage results from illegal transactions through which a part of the foreign exchange allocated by the exchange control authority is accumulated abroad. Estimates of the volume of such transactions do not exist, but situations which have been exposed indicate that the leakage is economically significant. For example, in June 1959 in two test cases the Supreme Court upheld the constitutionality of Central Bank implementation of exchange and import controls.[23] In issuing the ruling, the Supreme Court ordered the prosecution of a number of businessmen charged with overpricing imports for which exchange had been allocated.[24] Evasion also takes place through "ship back" procedures. Exchange allocations are obtained for essential or decontrolled imports, but the commodities are not accepted; instead they are shipped back to the point of origin. The foreign exchange does not, however, return to the Philippines.[25] Still another illegal transaction involving imports is misrepresentation to shift an exchange allocation from one category to another. The most prominent exposure of this practice occurred in early 1958 in the case of the Roxas-Kalaw Textile Mills, Inc., which was using exchange allocations for raw materials to import finished products.[26]

[22] *Phil. Newsletter*, June 5, 1959, p. 6. The Central Bank reports that in 1957 recorded Philippine exports to North Borneo of "crude materials, inedible" (largely copra) were $23,100, while North Borneo reported imports in the same category totaling $3,579,626 (*Tenth Annual Report, 1958*, p. 59).

[23] Constitutionality was challenged on the grounds that the Central Bank had acted illegally when it stepped in to continue exchange and import controls at the end of June 1953, when Congress allowed the specific legislative authority to lapse. See above, pp. 84–85.

[24] Officers of Henderson, Trippe and Co. were accused of having obtained two excessive allocations of foreign exchange for importation of cattle from Australia to the Philippines. They were charged with falsely representing the price per head of cattle at $114.20 when in fact the price was $56.20 per head. Officers of the Villanueva Steamship Co. were charged with willful misrepresentation when they alleged that they had purchased a vessel for $1,148,000 when in fact the vessel was acquired for $266,000 (*Phil. Newsletter*, June 5, 1959).

[25] *Ibid.*, Jan. 3, 1957, p. 8.

[26] Columbia University, *Joint International Business Ventures in the Philippines* (Manila, 1958), pp. 133–137. The report concluded, "The organizers went through

The prevalence of evasion is a matter of common knowledge and discussion. One observer recently commented:

There is a great deal of smuggling by persons travelling between Manila and Hong Kong and other nearby ports. There is smuggling of gold and of foreign exchange in the form of checks and drafts, and other outright smuggling of goods through various inadequately guarded provincial shipping points. . . . There is still further circumvention of laws through the bringing in of tax-exempt "personal effects" and "unaccompanied baggage." . . . There is also the abuse of the tax exemption privilege of foreign consular, diplomatic and armed forces personnel.[27]

Approaching in effect the magnitude of illicit evasion has been the steady encroachment on the structure of controls by legislative action. This encroachment has steadily enlarged the volume of transactions outside the control system. As might easily have been predicted, the longer exporting interests lived with exchange controls, the more active they became in exploiting political influence to evade the economic consequences of controls.[28] The sugar industry has been particularly restive. The export market, limited to the Philippine quota in the United States market, was closely regulated by export quotas, and the possibilities of evading the control system by underbilling of export shipments were limited. Moreover, the sugar bloc had long enjoyed political power, and it was natural for this group to use political processes to obtain special treatment.[29]

One avenue of attack on exchange controls has taken the form of legislation ostensibly designed to establish a strong incentive for marginal exports and therefore for export expansion. In view of Philippine political processes and administrative inefficiency, it is safe to

the motions of establishing the textile mills for the purpose of securing foreign exchange at preferred rates of ₱2.00 to $1.00 when the free market rate was closer to ₱3.30 than to ₱2.00. It would seem that the possible returns to capital in actually manufacturing and marketing finished textiles from imported rayon yarn and grey sheeting were not attractive enough, despite available foreign exchange at official rates, government assistance, liberal credit facilities, and a protected local market."

[27] A. V. H. Hartendorp, "Import Control, High Taxes, and Smuggling," *A.C.C. Journal*, 34 (May 1958), 197.

[28] Exporter-producers could not fail to be aware of the discrepancy between the purchasing power of the peso internally and externally.

[29] An impressive testimonial to the political power of the sugar bloc has been the absence of export taxes on sugar in spite of the obvious profitability of the Philippine quota in the sheltered U.S. market.

say that an effective export incentive system would have tended to break down the system of exchange and import controls rapidly. Export incentive legislation was introduced in each session of Congress following 1950, but it was not until the closing days of the special session of Congress in 1955 that a bill providing for exports outside the control system was enacted by Congress and allowed to become law without executive approval.[30] The principal provision of the law (Section 1-d) provided that "no importation into the Philippines and the so-called 'no-dollar remittance' shall be allowed except commodities in exchange for goods exported by persons or firms making the exportation on a straight barter basis when authorized by the Secretary of Commerce and Industry." [31]

In the controversy over implementation of the No-Dollar Import Law it became evident that among those opposed to the law were manufacturers and importers fortunate enough to obtain import licenses. The opposition aroused by the initial barter transactions was followed by attempts to resolve the conflict of interest between importers and exporters. Concessions were made to protect domestic producers of import-competing goods and importers of nonessential imports from the threatened competition of "no-dollar imports." [32] The dispute tended to be resolved in favor of the importers and domestic producers, and the "no-dollar" barter principle was substantially weakened by the provision that barter transactions would be limited to marginal exports in excess of average exports over the previous five years and would be permitted only in exchange for "essential raw materials" and

[30] The No-Dollar Import Law (R.A. 1410 of Sept. 10, 1955). Ironically enough, the title of the law was "An Act to prohibit the so-called 'no-dollar' imports except under certain conditions."

[31] "No-dollar imports" refer to commodities imported for which no foreign exchange is allocated by the Central Bank. Other "no-dollar imports" authorized by the law include: Sec. 1(a), machinery, equipment and accessories, and other capital goods used in "dollar-producing" and "dollar-saving" industries as certified by the Secretary of Commerce and Industry; Sec. 1(b), commodities of a value not exceeding ₱10,000 which are being imported for the personal use of the person or family importing them; Sec. 1(c), commodities brought from abroad by a person who is returning to the Philippines, provided they are not being brought for commercial purposes and do not exceed ₱5,000 in value.

[32] For example, a leading sugar-exporting firm, Victorias Milling Co., in an attempt to test the "no-dollar import" principle applied for permission to export nonquota sugar for assembled radio receivers. This transaction, initially approved, was subsequently rescinded following protests of the small, highly protected Philippine radio industry.

capital goods imports. This decision, though pleasing to importers, seriously weakened the export incentive principle incorporated in the No-Dollar Import Law.[33]

Rules to govern "no-dollar imports" were first issued on October 1, 1955. Barter transactions were limited to producers and producers' associations. Exports allowed for barter were "minor" exports, the excess over the United States quota for goods covered by the Philippine–United States Trade Agreement[34] and the excess over a five-year historical average for other exports.

In December 1955 the No-Dollar Import Office suspended the licensing of such transactions pending "restudy of rules and regulations governing them." In January 1956 the No-Dollar Import Office was instructed to license only barter transactions involving "urgent and essential" imports, all such imports to be disposed of through the National Marketing Corporation (NAMARCO) after payment to the barter exporters of a "price allowing a reasonable profit.[35] Subsequent evolution of barter export policy tended to restore a portion of the incentive, but controversy over the policy resulted in substantial weakening of the marginal export barter principle as provided in Republic Act No. 1410. Under the circumstances the producer-exporter interests resumed their political efforts to obtain favorable treatment.

The next effort to establish the principle of export incentives outside the control system was the enactment of Senate Bill No. 167. This bill providing for a "partial decontrol of imports" and for "desirable incentives to export industries" would have entitled "producers" to import certificates equivalent in value to 15, 80, and 100 per cent of the value of commodities exported.[36] It also provided for the automatic exchange of import certificates for dollar allocations on a one-for-one

[33] "Essential imports," including some food items, industrial raw materials, and capital goods, have enjoyed relatively liberal exchange allocations. Therefore, Philippine prices of these commodities have not increased as have the peso prices of "less essential" imports restricted by controls. It is obvious that if exporters are denied the right to convert marginal exports into imports of "less essential" commodities the economic incentive to make marginal exports to finance "no-dollar imports" would be minimized.

[34] Inasmuch as the sugar quota was the only one of the five quotas on Philippine exports to the United States under the 1946 Trade Agreement to be filled, this provision tended to restrict barter exports other than sugar.

[35] *A.C.C. Journal*, 32 (Feb. 1956), 70.

[36] The value would be 100 per cent only for newly mined gold, 80 per cent for minor exports the total value of which did not exceed ₱6 million in 1952, and 15 per cent for major exports the total value of which exceeded ₱6 million in 1952.

basis. Following a brief but violent public debate, President Garcia
vetoed the bill. In accordance with a promise in his veto message,
on October 4, 1957, he created a Presidential Incentives Committee
"to study ways and means of giving incentives to producers in order
to increase production of essential products and thus to lower prices." [37]

In the meantime revised rules for barter transactions were drawn
up by the cabinet on July 11, 1956.[38] No change was made for United
States quota goods. The five-year average was abandoned, and up to
15 per cent of all major exports were allowed for barter. Barter was

Table 28. Summary of barter transactions [a]
(₱ million)

Actual exports and imports	Actual exports	Actual imports
October 10, 1955–December 31, 1956	53.9	19.6
January 1, 1957–December 31, 1957	85.0	101.5
January 1, 1958–December 31, 1958 Cumulative totals	53.7	63.2

Categories of imports	Cumulative total, December 31, 1958
Essential consumer goods	20.3
Essential producer goods	71.5
Non-essential consumer goods	34.2
Non-essential producer goods	56.5

[a] Central Bank, *Tenth Annual Report, 1958.*

prohibited with countries having no exchange controls and with free
ports, except for the excess of United States quota goods. On November 18, 1957, the No-Dollar Import Office further modified barter
export rules.[39] Fifteen per cent of the total value of major export
commodities was allowed for export to any country. Producers were
permitted to use barter trade proceeds to import 25 per cent in essential producer goods, 25 per cent in nonessential producer goods,
and 50 per cent in essential consumer goods.

[37] Executive Order No. 271 of Oct. 4, 1957. The subsequent report of the Presidential Incentives Committee, *Incentives for Producers,* was released on April 15,
1958. The report is analyzed in the *A.C.C. Journal,* 34 (June 1958), 250–252.

[38] Promulgated in No-Dollar Import Office Circular No. 3 of Oct. 1, 1956.

[39] No-Dollar Import Office Circulars No. 22 and No. 23. Liberalization of barter-export rules during 1957 was undoubtedly influenced by the presidential election
in November.

Barter exports have expanded rapidly and are approaching the statutory maximum of 15 per cent of exports (Table 28). During 1957 barter exports amounted to ₱85 million, or 10 per cent of total exports. As compared to 1956, barter exports of copra and coconut products increased by 224 per cent, sugar 85 per cent, abacá 151 per cent, logs and lumber 34 per cent, and minerals and metals 67 per cent. Barter exports of logs and lumber amounted to ₱32.2 million in 1957, and copra and coconut products amounted to ₱23.0 million.

As of the end of 1957 no-dollar imports other than barter imports amounted to ₱31.1 million, including imports of capital goods of ₱20.1 million and personal goods brought in by returning travelers of ₱11.0 million.

The severe balance of payments crisis of the winter of 1957–1958 brought home to the exchange control authorities the growing threat in marginal barter exports. On January 8, 1958, the cabinet agreed to recommend repeal of the no-dollar import law. Congress, however, failed to act on the cabinet recommendation that year.

In 1959 the necessity for greater realism in Philippine exchange rate and exchange control policies led the executive to recommend to Congress two significant changes. First was revival of the premium tax on sales of foreign exchange, with recommended rates of 20 to 40 per cent. Second was repeal of the marginal export barter principle incorporated in the No-Dollar Import Law. The first proposal bogged down in turbulent controversy until the closing days of the special congressional session. In the final hours of the special session, July 3, 1959, Congress enacted the exchange premium tax law authorizing the requested rates. At the same time Congress provided for an extensive list of commodity imports to be exempted from the premium fee.[40]

The administration's proposal to repeal the No-Dollar Import Law was approved by Congress on April 20.[41] Repeal was tied to a companion measure which re-enacted the marginal barter export principle in a slightly modified form.[42] The new law, "An act to promote economic development by giving incentives to marginal and sub-marginal industries," provides for the barter of marginal exports of virtually all Philippine export commodities. Congress specified (Sec-

[40] Republic Act No. 2609 of July 16, 1959.
[41] Republic Act No. 2262 of June 19, 1959.
[42] Republic Act No. 2261 of June 19, 1959.

tion 3) that marginal exports under the new law could be exchanged in barter for "essential producer goods," "semiessential producer goods," and "essential consumer goods." While implementation of the law will undoubtedly be subject to some administrative discretion, there is nothing in the act to suggest a significant curtailment of the marginal export barter principle.[43]

A second major legal leakage of foreign exchange from the exchange control system results from Philippine gold policy. The gold industry has been particularly successful in making special arrangements under which gold production has realized a favorable exchange rate.

Philippine gold production prior to World War II accounted for an average of one-quarter of Philippine export proceeds. Following devaluation of the dollar in 1933 and the increase in the fixed price of gold to $35 per ounce, Philippine gold output expanded rapidly. Since World War II Philippine gold production, in common with gold production generally, has been handicapped by the unchanged price of gold.[44]

In January 1950 a realistic gold policy was formulated which recognized the existence of premium gold markets.[45] Gold producers were required to sell to the Central Bank at least 25 per cent of the output of gold and gold-bearing metals. Such a policy was realistic in that it recognized that to capture all of the gold output at the official exchange rate would not be administratively feasible and would, moreover, effectively prohibit rehabilitation of the gold industry. Under the new policy the average price received by gold producers would reflect the portion sold to the Central Bank at the official rate and the major portion of output sold at premium prices in accessible free markets. During 1950 and 1951 gold producers were given blanket licenses to export their local production for refining abroad and for the reimportation of the gold after refining.

[43] To minimize urban-consumer resentment of the exchange premium tax, a third law providing for the revival of price controls was passed in the special session of the 1959 Congress. See Republic Act No. 2610 of July 16, 1959.

[44] Prior to 1949 a number of laws had been enacted extending for a limited postwar period tax concessions, waivers of time limits on exploitation, and so forth, to the gold-mining industry. See Republic Acts No. 81 of Oct. 29, 1946, No. 215 of June 1, 1948, and No. 225 of June 5, 1948. Policies of this type were widely adopted to hasten the rehabilitation of various export industries.

[45] Central Bank Circular No. 21 of Jan. 10, 1950.

Under the new policy the Central Bank acquired newly mined gold at a modest rate: gold purchases amounted to ₱4.1 million in 1950, ₱6.6 million in 1951, and ₱5.0 million in 1952. The substantial premium to be realized on gold sales in premium markets led gold producers to seek relief from the requirement of sales to the Central Bank at the official rate. Pending determination of the actual operating condition of gold producers and while alternative policies were under study, the Monetary Board temporarily suspended the gold sale requirement in 1952.[46]

The suspended requirement was not reimposed in 1953. Meanwhile, Republic Act No. 909 of June 20, 1953, provided substantial tax relief for the industry. This did not satisfy the gold industry, which was confronted by declining prices in domestic and world free markets and by the operation of the Minimum Wage Law, which allegedly raised their costs. During 1953 and 1954 a number of proposals to aid gold producers were under consideration, including (a) proposals of a direct subsidy and (b) the use of "export incentive certificates" to be issued by the Central Bank in payment for newly mined gold.

The Monetary Board reluctantly endorsed a "temporary" direct subsidy to gold producers in its annual report for 1953.[47] In June 1954 Congress followed the Board's recommendation and authorized such a subsidy.[48] Funds to carry out the provisions of the act were derived by estimating internal revenue taxes, taxes on sales of foreign exchange, customs duties, and other charges paid by gold producers plus allocation of foreign exchange equivalent in value to the gold sold to the Central Bank. Funds equivalent to the total of these amounts were segregated as the Emergency Gold Assistance Trust Fund and made available to pay the subsidy.

Actual sales to the Central Bank under Republic Act No. 1164 began in January 1955. The Gold Assistance Trust Fund was not large enough to cover the subsidy for all gold produced, and pro-

[46] Monetary Board Resolution No. 664 of Oct. 15, 1952. The suspension was made effective Aug. 4, 1952.
[47] Central Bank, *Fifth Annual Report, 1953*, p. 116. In order that the subsidy not be in conflict with Philippine adherence to the International Monetary Fund Agreement, the Monetary Board recommended that the subsidy not take the form of a fixed increase in the price of gold but be based on production costs. Canada had received IMF approval of a similar proposal.
[48] Republic Act No. 1164 of June 18, 1954.

ducers remained dependent upon the domestic free market for somewhat more than half of their sales. The subsidy policy was renewed
in 1956 with one minor change requiring gold producers to sell not
less than 75 per cent of their output to the Central Bank.[49] During
the latter part of 1956 the free market price of gold in the Philippines
rose rapidly, and gold producers became restless under the requirement that their output be sold to the Central Bank at the fixed subsidy prices. Further modification of gold policy occurred in February
1957, when the Monetary Board approved a plan allowing nonresident owners of "frozen" peso accounts to buy newly mined Philippine gold and, upon sale of that gold to the Central Bank, to receive
foreign exchange at the rate of $35 per ounce.[50] Congress adjourned
in 1957 without renewing the gold subsidy, a move which did not
particularly concern the producers as gold prices tended to remain
above ₱120 per ounce.[51]

Intensification of the disequilibrium in Philippine external payments in 1957 and 1958 was accompanied by steady depreciation in
the free market rate of the peso. During the two years following mid-
1957 the rate has tended to be approximately twice the official rate
of two pesos per dollar. Under such circumstances the gold-mining
industry has had a strong interest in policies which would permit
gold output to be marketed at free market rates, and such a policy
has prevailed.

During the nine years following the establishment of effective
Philippine exchange controls, over four-fifths of Philippine gold production was marketed outside the exchange control system (Table 29).
The leakage of foreign exchange resulting from the gold policy has
averaged approximately $13 million annually since 1951. Concessions

[49] Republic Act No. 1522 of June 16, 1956. Free market prices averaged slightly
below the Central Bank's purchase price so enforcement of this requirement
presented no problem. In the meantime Republic Act No. 909, the original bill
providing special tax relief for the mining industry, expired and was not renewed.
However, the mining industry had earlier obtained enactment of Republic Act
No. 1394 of Aug. 29, 1955, which exempted the mining industry from the special
import tax on imports of machinery, explosives, cyanide, and so forth.

[50] Monetary Board Circular No. 73 of March 4, 1957. Inasmuch as the local
price of gold was around ₱120, such a plan would mean in effect a substantial
devaluation of the peso for the purpose of remitting blocked-peso accounts comprising "excessive" profits of foreign firms.

[51] Central Bank Memorandum to Authorized Agent Banks of Aug. 22, 1957,
liberalized the blocked-peso account policy by recognizing additional blocked
funds which could be converted into foreign currencies by purchases of gold in
the free market.

made to gold producers not only have directly reduced the availability of foreign exchange to the exchange control authority, but have encouraged other exporting groups to seek special treatment for foreign exchange earnings.

The strong economic forces inherent in overvaluation of the peso have been reflected in a steady erosion in the system of exchange controls. Illegal transactions, including export undervaluation and underbilling, import overvaluation and misrepresentation, as well as smuggling, are frequently exposed. Analysis of reported unit values of Philippine exports indicates substantial undervaluation. Equally

Table 29. Gold policy statistics [a]

Year	Gold produced (000 ounces)	Gold purchased by Central Bank (ounces)	Average Philippine premium gold sales (prices ₱ per ounce)
1947	65.5	—	89.2
1948	209.2	—	93.9
1949	287.8	—	94.3
1950	334.0	58.4	108.6
1951	393.6	94.4	123.8
1952	469.4	71.4	106.4
1953	480.6	1.8	104.0
1954	416.1	—	107.7
1955	419.1	172.2	104.7
1956	406.2	—	109.8
1957	380.0	55.0	120.2

[a] Philippine Gold Producers Association. See *A.C.C. Journal,* 32 (Jan. and March 1956), 9, 125; and 34 (March 1958), 122.

important are the legal leakages that exporting interests have been able to arrange by mobilizing political power. The value of barter exports in recent years has exceeded 10 per cent of the export proceeds channeled to the Central Bank. In addition, free market sales of gold have denied substantial amounts of foreign exchange to the Central Bank. On the basis of the available evidence it seems clear that illegal and legal transactions in evasion of exchange controls amount to at least one-quarter, and are probably equal to one-third, of the export proceeds currently channeled to the Central Bank.

While leakage of foreign exchange from the control system is undoubtedly cause for concern to the authorities, the economic consequences should not be exaggerated. First, leakages of foreign exchange from the control system are not lost to the Philippine economy as are foreign exchange earnings which are forgone because of peso overvaluation. Indeed, the leakage presently sustained may very well be the minimum leakage necessary to make exchange controls work in the face of intense external disequilibrium. This position is supported by the steady decline in the free market value of the peso in spite of the expansion in supplies of foreign exchange diverted to transactions outside exchange controls.[52] The capacity of Philippine exchange control authorities to manage the jerry-built partial system of exchange control depends upon leakages which moderate the economic pressures arising out of the unrealistic exchange rate. Diversion of foreign exchange earnings to the black market by legal policies as well as tacit acceptance of extensive evasion is probably necessary to the maintenance of the present semblance of exchange control. It is quite clear that the social goals to which exchange controls contribute—those of economic nationalism—have a sufficient priority to enable exchange control policy to resist formidable economic pressures for change.

As might be expected, the leakages are essentially arbitrary and inequitable. Premium rates of foreign exchange tend to be realized for exports produced by large-scale modern enterprise—gold, lumber, base metals, coconut oil, desiccated coconut, canned pineapple, and so forth. Small holders' production for export—coconuts, abacá, and other items—probably comes under relatively high level of exchange control discipline. It seems clear that "taxation" of export production by exchange controls and currency overvaluation is regressive. Although this should be deplored on grounds of equity, it may contribute to more entrepreneurial activity and therefore to economic growth. In particular, continuing compromise of exchange control has probably been necessary to obtain the levels of foreign investment that have marked the postwar period.

One final comment should be made. To the extent that illegal evasion of exchange controls takes place, it raises significant questions as to the usefulness of unit value, volume, and terms of trade statistics for Philippine foreign trade.

[52] The free market value of the peso has declined in recent years to approximately half the official parity value. One wonders to what level the free market value of the peso would decline if exchange controls should become effective and capture the large amounts of foreign exchange presently diverted to making "illegal" payments.

· VIII ·

Commercial Policy

THE power of the government to regulate and control international trade and payments plays a key role in Philippine attempts to accelerate economic growth. Understanding Philippine economic development turns on recognition of the integration of exchange rate policy, exchange and import controls, and import taxation into a powerful tool for promoting industrialization and economic nationalism. Commercial policy has been primarily concerned with distributing the windfall arising out of import restriction so as to subsidize entrepreneurial activity; relatively little attention has been given to the revenue potential of import limitation.

Import Controls

The Philippines resorted to effective import controls to maintain a tolerable external equilibrium in the face of an unrealistic exchange parity and strong import demand arising out of the dislocations of World War II. Import controls were initially considered to be an *ad hoc* solution to a severe but temporary balance of payments problem. With the lapse of time they have been integrated into longer-term Philippine goals of protection, Filipinization, and industrialization. At present the choice of imports to be restricted, goods and

163

services to be imported, and individuals to be granted import licenses is a critical ingredient in Philippine developmental policy.

The initial commodity classification for purposes of import control was based on essentiality and did not make a functional distinction between commodities. As early as May 1950, however, import control priorities distinguished between "capital goods," "essential producer goods," "essential consumer goods," and so forth. The basic priority assigned to capital goods and import requirements of raw materials was subsequently augmented by the policy of providing tax incentives and foreign exchange subsidies to "new and necessary industries." Similarly, Filipino importers and producers were assigned increasing priority in the allocation of the available foreign exchange. While import control has fluctuated widely in intensity, the basic priorities have remained relatively intact.

Quantitative controls over imports were established by Republic Act No. 330 of July 15, 1948, which authorized the President of the Philippines "to establish a system of import control by regulating imports of nonessential and luxury articles, creating an import control board, authorizing the issuance of rules and regulations to carry into effect such control and penalizing violations of this act." [1]

Control of the importation of "nonessential" and "luxury" articles was initiated on January 1, 1949, by Executive Order No. 193 of December 28, 1948. During the first half of 1949 import control orders were issued which (a) defined the base period for the calculation of quotas, (b) established quota limitations according to the essentiality of the import commodity, and (c) initiated Filipinization of import trade by reserving import quotas for qualified nationals.[2]

The results of import controls in the first half of 1949 were unimpressive. As compared with the first half of 1948, the value of imports increased by ₱20 million to ₱628 million. Of the controlled items, automobiles, automobile tires and parts, and rayon textiles and manufactures actually increased in value.[3]

Continued drain of foreign exchange reserves during the first half

[1] The act affirmed faith in the temporary nature of import controls by terminating executive authority to regulate imports as of Dec. 31, 1949.
[2] See Executive Order No. 209 of March 30, 1949, and Executive Order No. 231 of June 28, 1949.
[3] Controls proved to be relatively effective in the case of tobaccos and manufactures of tobacco, which were reduced in value by approximately 50 per cent.

of 1949 led to the issuance of Executive Order No. 231 on June 28, 1949. This order provided for increased percentage cuts in import categories, elimination of minimum price limits on articles subject to limitation,[4] and the addition of more items to the schedule of controlled items. The protectionist potentiality of import controls was indicated by the inclusion of nails and cement in the list of "luxury and unessential" items. These items were then being manufactured by Philippine government corporations.

While reduced imports of controlled items accounted for a 4 per cent decline in the value of imports in the last half of 1949, Philippine foreign exchange reserves dwindled rapidly. The deteriorating international position, intensified by a capital flight in the last quarter of 1949, called for drastic measures. Effective import controls were initiated by Executive Orders No. 295 of November 29, 1949, and No. 297 of December 24, 1949.[5]

During 1950 imports were reduced to ₱712 million as compared to ₱1,137 million in 1949, a reduction of 37 per cent in value and 42 per cent in volume. Reductions in value were heaviest in "consumption goods," which suffered a cut in value of 55 per cent. Although changes included the reduction of percentage allocations and the inclusion of additional controlled items, basic improvement resulted from the extension of import licensing to all commodities.[6]

Congress allowed the executive authority to "regulate imports" to lapse on April 30, 1950, and it was not until the middle of May that new legislation was approved. Republic Act No. 426 of May 18, 1950, provided, in Section 18, for licensing by an Import Control Administration (ICA), which was subject to policy direction by an Import

[4] For example, under Executive Order No. 193 only automobiles priced above ₱7,000 were subject to percentage cuts, while only rayon textiles with prices above ₱2.35 per yard for mens' and ₱1.50 for womens' fabrics were subjected to percentage cuts. Reduction of import expenditures was frustrated by shifting imports from high-priced imports to imports not subject to cuts.

[5] Because executive authority to regulate imports lapsed on Dec. 31, 1949, Republic Act No. 423 of Jan. 6, 1950, both renewed the authority till April 30, 1950, and made it retroactive to Dec. 31, 1949.

[6] Central Bank Notification No. 10 of Dec. 31, 1949, limited the amount of foreign exchange available for commodities not subject to percentage limitation to 6 per cent per month of the total imports by the importer of such items during 1949. This regulation prevented the shifting of imports from controlled to uncontrolled items.

Control Board selected to represent (a) the Central Bank, (b) businessmen, and (c) consumers. An import license issued by the ICA constituted an automatic foreign exchange license. Import licenses were subject to the overall availability of foreign exchange for imports, which amount was to be certified by the Monetary Board of the Central Bank from time to time (Section 17). The ICA was instructed to fix import quotas subject to narrowly focused congressional instructions (Section 7).[7]

The Import Control Law also provided that, upon certification by the Secretary of Agricultural and Natural Resources and the Secretary of Commerce and Industry that the domestic supply of commodities heretofore imported is sufficient to meet the local demand, the ICB shall impose the maximum percentage reduction on the import quotas for such commodities. The law specified a procedure for introducing new articles or commodities into the schedules or for transfer of a controlled import item from a lower category to a higher category whenever the Import Control Board was "convinced of the necessity of controlling such items to protect local industry or industries" (Section 7).

The act also defined the base for allocating quotas as the average annual c.i.f. value of imports for the three years 1946–1948 (Section 10). Another objective of the law was further Filipinization of import trade, since the ICB was instructed to reserve an increasing portion of import quotas to "bona fide new importers" (Section 14). Only Filipino citizens or corporations with 60 per cent of ownership in the hands of Filipinos could qualify as "bona fide new importers." The portion of the total quota for an article reserved for "new" (Filipino) importers was to increase 10 per cent per year from 30 per cent in fiscal year 1951 to a maximum of 50 per cent in fiscal year 1953.

The improvement in the Philippine external economic position during the last half of 1950 was striking. Effective controls drastically limited foreign exchange payments, while exports, stimulated by strong international demand following the outbreak of war in Korea, rose in value by 29 per cent over 1949. The trade deficit was reduced from ₱629 million in 1949 to ₱59 million in 1950. As a result of these developments, the international reserve of the Philippines increased

[7] Congress provided ten closely printed pages of appendixes listing commodities to be included in various import control categories.

from $260 million at the end of 1949 to $356 million at the end of 1950. The chronic postwar balance of payments crisis was temporarily "solved." [8]

Well-publicized anomalies in the administration of import controls led to loss of public confidence in the Import Control Administration and to enactment of Republic Act No. 650 of May 17, 1951. This legislation, which continued import and exchange controls for the two fiscal years ending June 30, 1953, made important changes in the control administration. Under this new law import commodities were classified into three categories: "decontrolled" items, "controlled" essentials, and a residual category of nonessentials. Administration of control was vested in an Import Control Commission of three members. The commission was empowered to issue import licenses subject to over-all availability of foreign exchange as certified by the Central Bank at the beginning of each half-year. In budgeting the available foreign exchange, first priority was assigned to "any government agency charged with duties and functions of stockpiling essential articles and of stabilizing prices and to all other government institutions." Second priority went to bona fide producers, with business firms and bona fide importers as residual claimants.

On August 28, 1951, a significant revision in import control policy was established by Executive Order No. 471. An additional category of "banned" goods was added.[9] The initial list of banned items included frozen chicken, bacon, ham, fresh fish, and eggs, which were believed to be produced in sufficient quantities locally. Effective July 1, 1952, imports of an additional list of items, including yeast, garlic, onions, and coal fuels, were to be banned. It was expected that local production of banned items would expand promptly under the stimulus of high levels of protection.

During 1952 the protection inherent in import control policy was reflected in additions to the list of banned commodities of such items as cotton weaving yarns, slide fasteners, incandescent bulbs, fluores-

---

[8] The postwar capital flight from the weakening peso was also halted. For example, the "errors and omissions" items in the balance of payments which indicated average "payments" of $20 million annually during 1946–1950 was reduced to zero in 1951.

[9] Republic Act No. 650, Sec. 3, authorized the banning of imports where commodities "are already produced economically and in sufficient quantities in the Philippines."

cent tubes, and tomato catsup.[10] Legislation approved May 9, 1952, initiated rapid curtailment of imports of foreign leaf tobacco.[11]

In 1953 substantial changes were made in the implementation of import control. The existing law, Republic Act No. 650, was scheduled to expire on June 30, 1953, and the Congress, which had passed to Nacionalista control in the elections of November 1951, refused to enact legislation continuing import controls as administered by the Import Control Commission. Anomalies in the operation of controls had become a nationwide scandal. Although the graft and corruption involved in the administration of controls was extensive and should be deplored, they were grossly exaggerated as an issue in the 1953 election. The Nacionalista majority in Congress engineered the demise of the control organization, not only to minimize the opportunity for graft, but to dramatize the issue of corruption that dominated the Magsaysay campaign in 1953.

With the expiration of the import control law the Quirino administration chose to continue import and exchange controls by the exercise of authority established in the Central Bank Act.[12] Central Bank Circular No. 44 of June 12, 1953, provided for selective import control by the Monetary Board.[13] Circular No. 44 provided that, at the beginning of each semester, the Monetary Board would certify to each commercial bank the total amount of foreign exchange available to the bank for the semester (Article 2). The certification included a breakdown by commodity categories and by importers, based on actual letters of credit opened and used during 1952.[14] Applications for the opening of letters of credit were to be considered as applications for licenses to purchase foreign exchange to pay for imports. A banker's committee for licensing import payments, composed of representatives from each commercial bank in Manila, was created to assist the Monetary Board in the implementation of import control.

On June 25, 1953 the Monetary Board issued Regulation No. 1 of *Rules and Regulations Implementing Central Bank Circular No. 44.* Detailed instructions and definitions as well as the schedules of com-

[10] Executive Order No. 521 of Aug. 7, 1952, and No. 530 of Sept. 12, 1952.
[11] Republic Act No. 698 of May 9, 1952.   [12] See above, pp. 84–85.
[13] Reprinted in Central Bank, *Fifth Annual Report, 1953*, pp. 358–361.
[14] A contingency reserve was set aside by the Monetary Board to cover foreign exchange requirements of importers not covered in the regular budget.

modity categories were included. Commodities were classified as "highly essential goods," "essential producer goods," "nonessential producer goods," "essential consumer goods," and "nonessential consumer goods." During the remainder of 1953 frequent changes were made in the schedules to include new items and to adapt the schedules to the requirements of import control.[15]

During 1954 the practice of using import controls to protect commodities domestically produced was continued. Allocations for starch and shoes were substantially reduced, and imports of toys, low-priced pencils, and finished (assembled) cars were banned.

Import controls administered by the Central Bank have continued without basic change to the present time. The annual changes in the classification of import commodities furnish a running account of Philippine industrialization as promoted by import controls. During 1955 automotive storage batteries, ready-mixed paint, cotton and synthetic knitted fabrics, knitted jackets, sweaters, outerwear, and all made-up garments of cotton and rayon were added to the list of commodities for which no dollar allocations would be made.[16] In 1956 commodity reclassification increased the levels of protection for smoking tobacco, cotton and rayon blankets, underwear, slips, and nightgowns, labels gummed or painted, bags and sacks for articles weighing less than 25 pounds, tire-manufacturing and repair materials, automotive tires, abrasive and emery paper and cloth, corrugated aluminum sheets, and plain sheets and foil.[17]

Although the basic nature of controls continued unchanged in 1957, commodity categories were rearranged in accordance with Resolution No. 18 of the National Economic Council, which emphasized the protective nature of exchange and import controls.[18] During the

[15] Pertinent regulations are reprinted in Central Bank, *Fifth Annual Report, 1953,* pp. 362–474.

[16] Central Bank, *Seventh Annual Report, 1955,* pp. 21–22.

[17] Central Bank, *Eighth Annual Report, 1956,* pp. 153–154.

[18] "Be it resolved, as it is hereby resolved: To approve and adopt the reclassification of all commodity imports, and their respective priorities for foreign exchange allocation purposes based on the following criteria; Provided: That any specific article or commodity which is produced locally or for which an acceptable local substitute is available in sufficient quantity . . . shall be . . . transferred to the unclassified imports category (not allocated foreign exchange); and, Provided further: That as conditions normalize and the level of international reserves warrant the decontrolled items should be increased . . . in order to be consistent with the announced policy that controls are never intended to be a permanent feature of the economy" (reprinted in Central Bank, *Ninth Annual Report, 1957,* p. 145).

year seventy-three items were added to the unclassified category and banned for importation. Such items included automotive tires and tubes, cotton textiles and yarns, roasted and soluble coffee, certain steel reinforcing rods, tableware, certain flashlight batteries, lighter fluid, toothbrushes, room air conditioners, and some pottery.[19]

Table 30. Composition of imports [a]
(percentage of total value of imports)

Year	Consumption goods	Material chiefly for consumption goods	Material chiefly for capital goods	Capital goods
1953	48.9	17.9	11.3	21.9
1954	47.6	17.4	11.6	23.3
1955	47.3	16.5	11.4	24.8
1956	39.3	16.7	13.0	31.0
1957	39.6	16.7	14.1	29.6

[a] UN, ECAFE, *Economic Survey*. The series begins with 1953.

Table 31. Distribution of imports by import control category [a]
(percentage of total value of imports)

	1949	1950	1951	1952	1953	1954
All categories	100.00	100.00	100.00	100.00	100.00	100.00
1. Highly essential	3.32	4.67	4.98	3.80	5.50	4.97
2. Essential	46.04	54.60	53.37	59.34	62.34	63.63
a. Producer's	27.28	40.88	36.55	44.71	50.88	51.71
b. Consumer's	18.76	13.72	16.82	14.63	11.46	11.92
3. Nonessential	37.00	30.51	29.80	26.99	24.91	27.66
a. Producer's	22.85	20.58	22.74	19.26	18.01	20.41
b. Consumer's	14.15	9.93	7.06	7.73	6.90	7.25
4. Unclassified items	13.64	10.22	11.85	9.87	7.25	3.74

[a] R.P., Central Bank Survey Commission, *Final Report and Recommendations* (*Minority Report*), (Manila, 1956). Columns may not add exactly because of rounding. Import control categories were subject to rapid change following 1954, and further comparisons are not meaningful.

Frequent changes in the classification of imports complicate the problem of identifying the impact of import controls. There can be no question that Philippine imports of capital goods have increased

[19] The various regulations are reprinted in *ibid.*, pp. 212–351. As of April 1960, the list of banned (unclassified) commodities included 627 items (Central Bank, *Statistical Classification of Commodities* [Manila, 1960]).

both absolutely and relatively since 1950 (Tables 30, 31). There is also some evidence of a relative increase in imports of industrial raw materials. Increased allocations for imports of capital goods have therefore been made at the cost of a relative decline in imports of consumption goods. The correlation between Philippine import performance and that of other Southeast-Asian countries is close. Increases in the proportion of capital goods are common to virtually all countries of the area (Table 32).

Table 32. Composition of imports in Southeast Asia [a]
(percentage of total value of imports)

	Consumption goods	Materials chiefly for consumption goods	Materials chiefly for capital goods	Capital goods
Philippines				
1953	49	18	11	22
1957	40	17	14	30
ECAFE region				
1953	42	30	11	17
1957	30	28	18	24
Burma				
1953	55	16	8	22
1957	37	17	9	37
Ceylon				
1953	67	7	10	15
1957	60	11	13	16
Indonesia				
1953	48	18	6	28
1957	39	22	8	31
Malaya and Singapore				
1953	57	16	13	13
1957	48	22	15	15
Thailand				
1953	48	9	8	34
1957	42	12	11	35

[a] UN, ECAFE, *Economic Survey, 1958.*

Tariff Policy

Current levels of protection in the Philippines are essentially determined by the import controls. Recent years, however, have seen important changes in tariff policy which suggest that the Philippines may be embarked on a transition to a more traditional structure of protection implemented by import taxation.

The original Philippine customs code, enacted in 1909 by the United States Congress, remained in force with minor changes till mid-1957. This law for the most part extended the 1909 United States customs code to the Philippines. An authoritative analysis of colonial Philippine commercial policy concludes:

The Philippine import tariff enacted by [the U.S.] Congress and approved August 5, 1909, . . . was designed to yield the greatest possible amount of revenue consistent with the duty-free status of American goods in the islands. . . . The rates were not identical with those of the United States tariff act of 1909, and were not intended to give all American products entering the islands a degree of protection mathematically equal to that afforded in the home market. There was some attempt to stimulate certain Philippine industries, either established or considered potential, by placing raw materials on the general free list regardless of origin, or by admitting them at low rates of duty although they were duty free from the United States. But the articles and raw materials placed on the general free list of the Philippine import tariff were not of great importance in relation to the whole Philippine import trade. This was all in line with the revenue producing purpose of the tariff, but it was also evident that a great expansion of the general free list or very low rates on imports of non-American origin would have tended either to prevent tariff preferences for American goods or to diminish the possible benefits of such preferences by reducing their magnitude. Under these circumstances it was obviously not possible to protect Philippine industry comprehensively by means of the tariff against potential competition from the United States since protection to a local industry almost inevitably meant protection of the corresponding American product in the Philippine market.[20]

The tariff rates enacted in the Philippine customs code of 1909 were not so important in determining Philippine commercial policy as the duty-free entry of United States goods written into the law. Tariff concessions, the inevitable political and economic concessions to United States investments in the Philippines, and the expanding United States market for tropical produce dominated Philippine economic development. Mutual trade between the two countries expanded rapidly until, in the late 1930's approximately two-thirds of Philippine trade in both directions was conducted with the United States.

[20] U.S., Tariff Commission, *The United States–Philippine Tariff and Trade Relations* (Report No. 18, 2nd ser.; Washington, 1931), pp. 10–11.

The principal consequence of the reciprocal free-trade policy was to limit drastically Philippine recourse to protection as a policy. But the policy did not prevent the development of import values as the major Philippine tax base. Although duties were collected only on non-United States imports, the Philippines resorted to high levels of internal excise taxation to exploit this tax base. While there were a number of interesting cases in which the definitions in excise tax laws effectively distinguished domestically produced from imported commodities, in general internal excise taxes were nondiscriminatory.[21]

The transfer of political sovereignty in the Philippines was matched by detailed plans for the transfer to commercial policy autonomy, which would facilitate the adjustment of the Philippine economy to loss of concessions in the United States market.[22] The scheduled transition to Philippine commercial policy autonomy was suspended in 1940 and subsequently interrupted by World War II. At the conclusion of the war political independence materialized in 1946 as scheduled. In the meantime a new schedule for the transition to Philippine economic sovereignty was drawn up and embodied in the United States–Philippine Trade Agreement of 1946. The economic transition scheduled in the 1946 Trade Agreement did not materialize, and the Revised United States–Philippine Trade Agreement was signed on September 5, 1955.[23]

The principal economic change in the Revised Trade Agreement was to accelerate sharply the rate at which Philippine tariffs would be collected on imports from the United States.[24] The agreement provided that at intervals of three years, beginning January 1, 1956, the proportion of Philippine duties collectible on imports from the United States would be increased by 25 percentage points. Beginning January

[21] The principal exceptions occurred in the case of cigarettes where the use of such terms as "machine packed" and specifications regarding length established tax concessions for domestically produced cigarettes.

[22] See above, pp. 62–64.

[23] See Frank H. Golay, *The Revised United States–Philippine Trade Agreement of 1955* (Cornell Southeast Asia Program Data Paper No. 23; Ithaca, N.Y., 1956). It became quite clear in the process of revising the 1946 Trade Agreement that maintenance of U.S. concessions to Philippine imports was a dominant goal of Philippine policy.

[24] Scheduled rates of U.S. tariffs to be collected on imports from the Philippines were sharply revised downward. For example, as of Jan. 1, 1962, only 20 per cent of U.S. tariff rates will be collected on imports from the Philippines.

1, 1959, 50 per cent of the tariff rates would be collected, the proportion increasing to 75 per cent on January 1, 1962.

In anticipation of the Revised Trade Agreement, the Philippines wrote a new tariff code more appropriate to Philippine aspirations for economic growth. Republic Act No. 911 of June 20, 1953, created a Tariff Commission to "make a thorough study of the tariff system of the Philippines, and not later than one and one half years from the date of assumption of offices of its members, [it] shall submit its recommendations for a revision of the tariff system together with a draft of a bill embodying a revised tariff law." The recommendations of the Tariff Commission in the form of a proposed Tariff Revision Bill were submitted to the House Ways and Means Committee on June 24, 1955.

Among the objectives of the proposed bill the Tariff Commission listed (a) "To raise the standard of living and real income as against money income; (b) To promote the establishment and healthy growth of industries in the country and to protect same; (c) To raise government revenue and (d) to conserve foreign exchange." The proposed tariff code provided in general for lower tariffs, with high levels of protection to domestic producers on a selective basis. Of the 1,229 categories in the proposed law, tariff rates in 845 categories, or almost 70 per cent, were scheduled for reduction. Rates on 264 categories, or 21 per cent, were maintained without change, and rates on 120 items, or less than 10 per cent, were increased. Rates on approximately three-quarters of the items in the latter category were increased to protect local industries; the remaining increases were probably motivated by revenue considerations.[25]

The Philippine Congress failed to act on the proposed tariff revision bill during the regular and special sessions of 1955. Because the Revised Trade Agreement was scheduled to go into effect on January 1, 1956, Executive Order No. 150 was issued on December 31, 1955. This order provided for increases up to several hundred per cent in tariff duties on some eighty-five commodity classifications plus an increase of 30 per cent in all other tariff rates.[26] Congress failed to

[25] Philippine National Bank, Department of Economics, Research, and Statistics, *The Economic Consequences of the Revisions in the 1909 Tariff Proposed by the Tariff Commission* (Manila, 1955). Mimeograph.

[26] Republic Act No. 1196 of Aug. 25, 1954, empowered the President "upon prior investigation by or recommendation of the [Tariff] Commission . . . to decrease by not more than sixty per centum or to increase by not more than ten times the

enact new tariff legislation in 1956 and it was not until the close of the regular session in 1957 that a new tariff code was approved.[27]

The avowed objectives of the revised tariff code included (a) protection of domestic industries, especially "infant" industries, (b) aiding the Philippine economic development program, (c) increasing customs revenues, and (d) preparing for the ultimate elimination of exchange controls.[28] Protection is reflected in high rates on selected items produced in the Philippines. Such rates are somewhat redundant as protection is, and has been, implemented by exchange and import controls, under which such imports have been banned. Similarly, revenue goals were assigned low priority in the new code inasmuch as rates in those categories for which foreign exchange allocations are liberal have been revised downward. For any given structure of import values the 1909 tariff code would probably produce more tax revenues than the revised code.

Analysis of the nine principal categories of Philippine imports in recent years suggests that the Philippine tariff policy is unlikely to make a major contribution to the avowed objectives.[29] These categories, which accounted for 70 per cent of the value of Philippine imports in 1957, include nonelectric machinery (13.1 per cent), textile yarns, fabrics, and made-up materials (12.8 per cent), base metals, mainly steel bars, sheets, plates, and so forth (10.5 per cent), mineral fuels, lubricants, and so forth (9.4 per cent), transport equipment (6.1 per cent), cereals and cereal preparations (5.4 per cent), dairy products (5.1 per cent), electric machinery and apparatus (4.1 per cent), and paper and paperboard manufactures (3.3 per cent).

Nonelectric machinery. With few exceptions, the 1909 rates were higher than those in the revised code. Rates on machinery imports under the 1909 code ranged from 15 to 20 per cent, whereas in 1957

---

rates of import duty however established when in his judgment such reduction or increase is necessary in the interest of national economy, general welfare and national defense."

[27] Republic Act No. 1937 of June 22, 1957.

[28] R.P., Tariff Commission, *First Report of the Tariff Commission to the Congress of the Philippines* (Manila, 1953). See also Montaño Tejam, "Implications of the New Tariff Code," *Economic Research Journal*, 4 (Dec. 1957), 125–128. Tejam served as commissioner of the Philippine Tariff Commission that drafted the proposed tariff revision.

[29] I am indebted to Donald Pond, a graduate student in the Department of Economics and the Cornell Southeast Asia Program, for a preliminary version of the analysis summarized here.

the rate was a uniform 10 per cent. Exceptions to the 10 per cent rate include consumer durables of a luxury nature (dishwashers, 60 per cent; sewing machines, 30–50 per cent; air conditioners, 70 per cent; refrigerators 40–100 per cent), machinery the domestic manufacture of which is in prospect (rice hullers and cone-type mills, 35 per cent), and miscellaneous categories of low priority (automatic packing equipment, 20 per cent; machinery for processing food and drink, 40 per cent).

Textile yarns, fabrics, and made-up materials. In the case of all textile raw materials and textiles a steep progression has been introduced in rates moving from raw materials to finished products. With two important exceptions, the rates under the 1957 law are higher than those under the earlier tariff code. Raw cotton imports were and are free of duty. Under the 1957 law woven cotton fabrics are taxed at varying rates from 10 to 25 per cent, whereas under the 1909 law the rates on comparable categories ranged from 25 to 30 per cent. Woven fabrics of gray rayon are taxed at 50 per cent, while all other rayon and synthetic fabrics pay a duty of 80 per cent. In the 1909 code comparable categories were taxed at rates of 60 or 65 per cent. Cotton knitted goods and cotton garments are taxed at rates of 65 to 70 per cent and 90 to 100 per cent, respectively, as compared to a range from 20 to 30 per cent under the earlier code. Similarly, the rate of duty on imports of cotton yarn has been increased from 15 to 25 per cent to 35 per cent.

Import duties on yarns, knitted goods, and garments are clearly protective under the revised code and recognize the expansion in domestic manufacture of these products. Philippine manufactures of textiles and related products in 1957 were valued at ₱122 million. Such manufactures were concentrated in cotton yarn, knitted goods, and garments.[30] The protection of such industries is established, not by the tariff code, but by import controls which have reduced imports in these categories. The reduction in duties on woven fabrics can only be explained as a sop to consumer opinion. Allocations of foreign exchange in this category have been steadily tightened, and the peso prices of such imports include substantial profits.

Base metals and manufactures thereof. Although comparisons are of limited value because of changes in commodity classifications, it is clear that only minor changes have been made in the taxation of

[30] Central Bank, *Ninth Annual Report, 1957,* p. 35.

such imports. Almost without exception semifinished articles of base metals—bars, rods, tubes, sheets, plates, wire, and the like—pay rates of 10 to 20 per cent, which indicates that the revenue motive is primary. Protection is evident in the rate on concrete reinforcing bars (35 per cent); nails, tacks, nuts, bolts and rivets (20 to 50 per cent); and firearms (40 to 100 per cent)—all of which are produced in limited quantities in the Philippines.

Mineral fuels, lubricants, and the related materials. The most important change here has been to lower the rate on imports of crude petroleum from 10 per cent to 5 per cent. The first Philippine refinery (Caltex) was opened in 1954, and three additional refineries are under construction or planned. The rate on gasoline imports is increased from 20 to 25 per cent, whereas rates on kerosene, tractor fuels, and naphtha have been lowered from 10 to 5 per cent. Import duties in this category are essentially for purposes of revenue. Through duties and excise taxes this category produces large amounts of revenue. Protection to domestic refiners is of minor significance as an incentive as compared to exchange allocation.

Transportation equipment. Import duties on trucks and automobiles have been increased in the 1957 code. Present truck rates range from 15 to 20 per cent as compared to 15 per cent in 1909. Automobile rates range from 20 to 25 per cent as compared to 20 per cent. Selected individual rates reflect important elements of protection for domestic production of transport equipment—assembly of vehicles and manufacture of truck, bus, and "jeepney" bodies. In 1957 the value of such manufactures totaled ₱57 million as compared to imports of transport equipment of ₱75.1 million.[31]

Cereal and cereal preparations. Rates under the revised code are, without exception, higher than previous rates. The rate of duty per 100 kilograms of wheat flour has been increased from ₱.47 to ₱1.25, and for cereal preparations the rate has been increased from 10 per cent to 20 to 45 per cent. Limited protection is still evident in the relatively favorable rate for wheat imports (as compared to flour), which was increased from ₱.25 per 100 kilograms to ₱.375.[32] Increased rates of taxation of imports in this category should produce substantial amounts of revenue.

[31] *Ibid.*

[32] In recent months a flour mill has been established in the Philippines. This enterprise was widely discussed in terms of Philippine access to surplus wheat exported under U.S. Public Law 480.

Dairy products. Rates were slightly lowered for liquid and powdered milk, reflecting the importance of this item in the Philippine diet and the necessity for substantial imports. Revenue considerations were also important, although they are subordinate to welfare considerations.[33] Protection of the domestic margarine industry is evident in sharply raised rates on imports of butter, butterfat, and margarine.

Electrical machinery. As with nonelectric machinery, tariff rates under the revised code are generally lower for electrical machinery used for industrial purposes and are substantially higher for items important in consumption. The general rate for imports of electrical machinery is now 10 per cent as compared to 15 per cent under the earlier code. Protection is evident in a limited number of categories, e.g., incandescent and fluorescent lamps, for which the rate was raised from 15 to 150 per cent. Domestic production of incandescent and fluorescent lamps, radio and television receivers, and other miscellaneous items of electrical equipment is expanding.[34]

Paper and paperboard manufactures. Under the revised code rates of duty on this category have been raised substantially with minor exceptions. The protective motive is suggested by the sharp rise in domestic production of paper and paperboard manufactures over the past few years. In 1955 there were only two domestic producers in this category, whereas in 1957 there were five, with a reported gross output of ₱17 million. In addition, the reported value of manufactured articles of paper and paperboard totaled ₱32 million, while the output of printing, publishing, and allied industries totaled ₱13 million.[35] The revenue motive is evident in the treatment of imports of newsprint, which were taken from the free list and are now taxed at the rate of 25 per cent.

The dominant economic fact emerging from analysis of the revised tariff code is the moderate level of duties. The failure of the Philippines to write higher levels of protection into the revised code is surprising in view of the long history of Philippine protest over the reciprocal free trade relationship with the United States. Equally surprising is

[33] Central Bank, *Ninth Annual Report, 1957,* p. 33. The Philippines produced only ₱10 million of dairy products in 1957 or about one-seventh of domestic consumption.
[34] *Ibid.,* p. 35. Such manufactures were valued at ₱28 million in 1957 as compared to imports of ₱50 million.
[35] *Ibid.,* p. 34.

the failure to use the revised tariff code as an opportunity to divert to the government an increasing portion of the windfall arising out of import restrictions.

Exchange Premium Policy

If imports are restricted by tariff duties which raise their peso prices, the price increases are diverted to the government in tax revenues. If imports of goods and services are restricted by import and exchange controls, comparable increases in the prices of imports tend to occur. In the latter case, capture of the price increases by the government is not automatic but requires action.

The Philippines, in common with other less-developed countries, has great need for government revenues to meet demands for consumption through the budget as well as expanding levels of developmental expenditures. The past ten years have witnessed the erratic evolution of exchange premium taxation, which has had the effect of diverting to the government a portion of the windfall arising out of peso overvaluation and restriction of imports of goods and services.

The Philippines was plagued, as noted earlier, with persistent fiscal and balance of payments problems in the early postwar years. To contribute to the solution of both probems the Bell Mission recommended that

a special emergency tax of 25 per cent . . . [should] be levied for a period not to exceed two years on imports of all goods other than rice, corn, flour, canned fish, canned milk and fertilizer; that if such an emergency import levy is not possible under the Trade Agreement with the United States, either very heavy excise taxes should be imposed or a tax of 25 per cent should be levied on all sales of exchange.

As a result of this recommendation, the Philippine Congress in the spring of 1951 enacted a special tax of 17 per cent on sales of exchange.[36]

The effect of this special tax was to make the peso exchange rate 2.34 pesos per dollar for most transactions and diverted to the government large amounts of revenue. The special tax had one important feature which distinguished it from the tariff and excise tax alternatives

[36] Republic Act No. 601 of March 28, 1951. The act provided for numerous exemptions including a number of foods, textbooks, newsprint, medical supplies, machinery and raw materials to be used in "new and necessary industries," expenses of students studying abroad, and life insurance premiums remitted abroad.

proposed by the Bell Mission in that it taxed payments for invisibles and capital transactions as well as for imports.

The exchange tax proved to be highly productive of revenues, and from 1951 to the end of 1955 total revenues from this source amounted to ₱696 million, or more than one-fifth of national government tax revenues. During the same period foreign exchange disbursements totaled ₱5,804 million; therefore, the average rate of the exchange tax on all foreign exchange disbursements was approximately 12 per cent.[37]

The next development in Philippine exchange premium policy occurred in connection with revision of the Philippines–United States Trade Agreement of 1946. The Revised Agreement provided for a transitional period in which Philippine commercial policy would be increasingly implemented by tariffs, including tariffs collected on imports from the United States. During the transitional period the special tax on sales of foreign exchange was to be replaced by a temporary special import tax of 17 per cent. The rate of the special import tax was to be gradually reduced, and ultimately the tax was to be replaced by the schedule of duties provided in the revised tariff code of 1957.

During 1955 and 1956 the international reserve declined slowly, but in 1957 the drain was sharply accelerated. By early 1958 the reserve had virtually drained away, and in the absence of *ad hoc* assistance from the United States the administration inaugurated an "austerity program" to restore depleted reserves.

To introduce a minimum of realism in the peso rate, the administration, led by Governor Cuaderno, proposed to return to the policy of taxation of sales of foreign exchange. Such action was strongly resisted in both the 1958 and the 1959 congressional sessions. It was not until the close of the special session of the 1959 Congress that legislation providing for a "margin fee" of 25 to 40 per cent on sales of foreign exchange was enacted.[38] The law, which expires at the end of 1961, provides that the Monetary Board shall annually set a premium fee on sales of foreign exchange. The fee was set at 25 per cent for sales of foreign exchange during the last half of 1959.

[37] Note that the exchange tax became effective at the end of March 1951, whereas the total foreign exchange disbursements listed above include the first quarter of 1951.

[38] Republic Act No. 2609 of July 16, 1959.

The recently enacted margin fee on sales of foreign exchange, plus the special import duty provided in the Revised Trade Agreement, plus the accelerated collection of tariff duties on imports from the United States, plus the moderate increases in tariff rates in the revised tariff code of 1957, should go far toward wiping out the present windfall in foreign exchange allocations. At the same time these changes should divert large amounts of revenue to the government.

Such a conclusion must be accepted with important reservations. Tax rates and revenues are poorly correlated in the Philippines. Substantial exemptions to specific taxes have been written into the laws. The intensity of the external disequilibrium has tended to divert the available foreign exchange to high priority uses where taxation is minimized. Also, the wholesale use of tax exemption to encourage "new and necessary" industries has excluded an increasing portion of imports from taxation. Under the circumstances revenues have remained remarkably stable in the face of rapidly increasing tax rates and expanding foreign exchange allocations. For example, peak revenues from the taxation of import values (plus invisibles) was attained in fiscal year 1951–52, and more recent analysis suggests that current revenues from this tax base have only partially recovered to fiscal year 1951–52 levels.[39]

The reasons for the Philippines' failure to use tariff policy to establish high levels of protection and to provide increased revenues are fairly obvious. First, with respect to protection, the Philippines has developed exchange and import controls into a complex, responsive policy instrument. High levels of protection are readily established by minimizing foreign exchange allocations. Discretionary power over protection is centralized in the executive—the Monetary Board and the cabinet—and protection as a policy is removed from congressional controversy and ineptnes. Most important, the effectiveness of protection in promoting Philippine industrialization is augmented by exchange control. Discretionary allocation of foreign exchange at the official exchange rate gives the government a command over resources which could not be realized by conventional techniques of taxation and revenue appropriation.

Second, during the colonial period and the postwar period of independence, the Philippines developed a productive "revenue tariff" implemented by miscellaneous excise-type taxes collected on import

[39] UN, ECAFE, *Economic Survey, 1958*, p. 172, table K.

values. During recent years approximately half of the national government revenues have been obtained from this tax base. Moreover, the scheduled acceleration in the rate at which tariff duties will be collected on imports from the United States should tend to maintain, and even to increase, the proportion of tax revenues from this base.

Third, the belief persists that Philippine external disequilibrium is a transient phenomenon that should be handled by short-run expedients such as exchange and import controls and temporary taxation of sales of foreign exchange. It is difficult for the observer to appraise this consideration which runs through the controversy over international economic policy. There can be little doubt that the Philippines lacks the political stamina to resume the early postwar rationalization of costs and prices necessary to rehabilitate the prewar exchange parity. More important, such a policy would obviously not be in the national interest. On the other hand, the persistence of references to a sound peso and avowals of the temporary character of exchange and import controls suggest that there is a strong strain of nostalgia, if not irrationality, in the national attitude toward commercial policy.[40]

Philippine commercial policy is a complex amalgam of tariff duties, miscellaneous excise-type taxes, and high levels of protection, implemented by import controls. The basic conflict in such a policy is obvious, inasmuch as revenues are minimized by stringent import controls. This policy conflict is more apparent than real. Philippine government is, and has been, minimum government, and the basic economic conservatism of the dominant political elites limits the expansion of governmental functions. Therefore, the search for revenues on the part of the government is not aggressive, and the pressures to divert to the government the windfall arising out of import restrictions are minimized.

[40] Filipino attitudes are complicated by faulty economics and sensitive nationalism, which ascribe both economic advantage as well as status to maintenance of the prewar currency parity.

· IX ·

Fiscal Policy

THE Philippines in common with other less-developed countries has assigned formidable social and economic responsibilities to the national government. The period of independence has witnessed persistent efforts to improve and extend governmental services and at the same time to increase social investment. The importance of taxation is enhanced by the relationship between budgetary deficits, external disequilibrium, and internal costs and prices which limits the use of bank credit to finance budgetary deficits.

The revenue performance of the Philippine government is circumscribed by two basic considerations. First, the Philippines has had a long tradition of minimum government. During the colonial period the dominant Western minority, reinforced by the Chinese minority and the indigenous agricultural aristocracy, was not inclined to expand governmental functions. The prevailing minimum "efficient" level of government functions reflected class fears that expanded government would redistribute income in the direction of greater equality. The postcolonial government has been dominated by the agricultural aristocracy, which, reinforced by the alien elements in the plural economy, has proved an able defender of traditional colonial fiscal policy.

Second is the restraint upon revenues inherent in the structure of the economy and the level of development. The literature dealing with

183

economic development is cluttered with suggestions that revenue performance in less-developed countries is half-hearted. Such a conclusion results from explicit or implicit reasoning by analogy with developed countries which are currently capturing by taxation and spending through the budget one-quarter to one-third of national income. Such a point of view ignores the fact that fiscal performance in the West is largely attributable to the corporation and the withholding device, institutions which have little applicability in less-developed countries. The discipline of self-assessed income tax payers in the West has been nurtured slowly and primarily reflects the high levels of real income which have been attained.

During the postwar period a single major change has occurred in the revenue system (Table 33). This happened during the last half of 1950 and the first half of 1951. In the 1950 special session the Philippine Congress, confronted by the ominous Huk threat, finally faced up to the pressing need for minimum fiscal responsibility and enacted a number of revenue measures. It was estimated that these tax measures would produce ₱90 million of additional revenues, primarily from higher excise tax rates. Shortly thereafter the Quirino-Foster Agreement was signed, in which the Philippines agreed to carry out the fiscal recommendations of the Bell Mission. In the spring of 1951 the Philippine Congress enacted a number of additional revenue bills including a productive tax on sales of foreign exchange.

As a result of these revenue measures, Philippine national government revenues were approximately doubled. This fiscal reform "solved" the chronic problem of budgetary deficits of the early postwar period and at the same time made possible a substantial increase in expenditures, including extension of social services and social investment. Although the increase in revenues was substantial, the level of taxation and expenditure remained relatively modest when compared with levels in other countries trying to accelerate economic growth.

The ratio of tax revenues to national income has not increased since the tax reforms of 1950–1951. This has been true in spite of far-reaching tariff changes, including rapid acceleration in the rate at which Philippine tariffs are collected on imports from the United States. More recently, on July 9, 1959, Congress reimposed the tax on sales of foreign exchange at high rates. The retarded recovery of Philippine exports combined with substantial tax concessions and commodity exemptions to import taxation has limited revenues from new taxes imposed since 1951.

Table 33. Major components of national government tax revenues [a]

(₱ million)

Fiscal year	Total revenue [b]	Tax revenue	Income tax	Customs duty	Transactions and consumption taxes	Licenses, stamp duties, registration fees, etc.	Other tax revenue
1948–49	426	362	54	29	134	145	—
1949–50	381	329	61	26	120	123	—
1950–51	510	443	98	26	169	150	—
1951–52	752	655	123	32	313	187	—
1952–53	700	601	129	28	281	163	—
1953–54	711	644	121	35	309	179	—
1954–55	783	691	129	45	399	103	—
1955–56	857	749	142	113	270	191	33
1956–57	977	821	154	274	155	201	37
1957–58	1,029	847	152	275	163	214	43

[a] UN, ECAFE, *Economic Survey*.
[b] Excluding proceeds of loans, other forms of borrowing, grants and aid, transfers from reserve funds, and counterpart funds.

Within the context of the low levels of taxation, the revenue system is unusually regressive. Income distribution in the Philippines is highly skewed, and the economic organization of agriculture concentrates income in the hands of the landowning class. Agricultural income, which must be self-assessed, is relatively difficult to tax, and Philippine experience bears out this generalization. Moreover, there is no national land tax to substitute for, or supplement, a tax on agricultural income. Real property taxes as administered by local government units are characterized by statutory low rate limits, low ratios of assessed to market values, and frequent tax remission. As a result of these characteristics of income and real property taxation, the principal part of government tax revenue is obtained from excise-type taxes on commodities widely consumed in Philippine society. Income and real property taxes have not provided as much as one-fifth of the revenues at all levels of government during the postwar period.

There is also the problem of tax evasion by Filipinos. Tax evasion is traditional both through underreporting of income and through legal devices providing for tax remission and forgiveness. Philippine income tax laws provide for moderate progression, and yet during the past six years, when national and per capita income has been growing at a rapid rate, the ratio of income tax revenues to national income has not increased.

In terms of the problem of accelerating economic growth, a case might be made for fiscal policies which contribute to the concentration of wealth and income if the possessors of wealth and the recipients of large incomes were potential entrepreneurs. In general, they are not. Because of the status and prestige attached to land ownership, the cacique class is slow to turn to industrial and commercial entrepreneurship. There is, therefore, no strong argument for a regressive tax system favorable to this class. The greater tax discipline of industrial and commercial elements, the relative ease of enforcement of taxes impinging on entrepreneurship, and the wholesale discrimination in the Philippine tax system in favor of the landowning classes result in undertaxation of agricultural wealth and income in comparison with entrepreneurial income. Filipinos as a whole are among the lowest-taxed people in the world, and the Philippine agricultural aristocracy is especially favored.[1]

[1] See L. O. Ty, "Are We the World's Worst Taxpayers?" *Philippines Free Press*, 47 (April 28, 1956), 5. The author states that in FY 1954–55 "only 3,864 out of

Over-all postwar Philippine fiscal policy has been conservative in the sense that total receipts and expenditures have remained a modest proportion of total economic activity (Table 34). Similarly, Philippine public expenditures have been conservative in the sense that budgetary deficits, even in the early postwar years to 1950, were moderate in terms of levels of national income and the expansion in output of the economy. Fiscal policy has also been conservative in the important sense that there has been minimum recourse to inflation to finance public expenditures. In this regard the Philippine experience compares favorably with that of other countries trying to initiate accelerated economic growth. On the other hand, Philippine fiscal policy has been unrealistic in terms of the avowed objectives of public policy and the failure of policy makers to exploit potentially productive tax bases.

Personal Income Taxation

The income tax came to the Philippines in 1913 with the enactment of a United States income tax law following ratification of the Sixteenth Amendment. The initial legislation provided liberal exemptions ($4,000 for married persons or heads of families and $3,000 for single persons) and moderate progression in surtax rates together with a normal tax rate of 1 per cent. The United States income tax law as amended in 1916 retained the income exemptions of the original law, but raised the normal tax rate to 2 per cent and provided greater progress in surtax rates.

The Philippine Income Tax Law, Act No. 2833 of March 7, 1919, enacted the rates and exemptions of the 1916 United States law. In 1920 the Philippine legislature by Act No. 2926 increased the normal tax to 3 per cent and provided for progressive surtax rates from 0.5 to 20 per cent on incomes in excess of ₱10,000. Personal exemptions were set at ₱6,000 for married persons or heads of families and at ₱4,000 for single persons, with exemptions for dependents at ₱400.[2]

The rates and exemptions established in Act No. 2926 remained in force until the approval on November 3, 1936, of Commonwealth Act No. 117, which increased the progression in surtax rates from

---

13,859 landowners who had registered more than 50 hectares of agricultural land for taxation filed taxable income tax returns." Ty concludes: "We as a people are probably the worst taxpayers in the world."

[2] For a detailed survey, see Tax Service of the Philippines, "The Individual and Corporate Income Taxes in the Philippines," *A.C.C. Journal*, 33 (June 1957), 266–269.

Table 34. Public finance statistics [a]

(₱ million)

Fiscal year	National income [b]	National government revenue	Ratio to national income (per cent)	Tax revenue [c]	Ratio to national income (per cent)	Income tax revenue	Ratio to national income (per cent)	National government expenditure	Ratio to national income (per cent)
1946–47	4,783	279 [d]	5.8	201 [d]	4.2	20 [d]	.42	381 [d]	8.0
1947–48	5,438	396 [d]	7.3	302 [d]	5.6	41 [d]	.75	358 [d]	6.6
1948–49	5,488	426	7.8	362	6.6	54	.98	467	8.5
1949–50	5,683	381	6.7	329	5.8	61	1.07	534	9.4
1950–51	6,205	510	8.2	443	7.0	98	1.58	523	8.4
1951–52	6,521	752	11.4	655	10.4	123	1.88	635	9.8
1952–53	6,785	700	10.3	601	8.9	129	1.90	660	9.7
1953–54	7,080	711	10.0	644	9.1	121	1.71	787	11.1
1954–55	7,385	795	10.8	691	9.3	129	1.75	854	11.6
1955–56	8,019	862	10.7	749	9.3	142	1.77	980	12.2
1956–57	8,616	977	11.3	821	9.5	154	1.79	1,057	12.3
1957–58	9,025	1,029	11.4	847	9.3	152	1.68	1,167	12.9

[a] UN, ECAFE, *Economic Survey*.
[b] Average of two calendar years.
[c] Including receipts from taxes apportioned to local governments.
[d] *Bell Mission Report*, tables 13 and 14.

1 per cent to 36 per cent on income levels in excess of ₱10,000, while personal exemptions were lowered to ₱4,000 for married persons and heads of families and to ₱2,000 for single persons. Commonwealth Act No. 117 remained in force until replaced by the National Internal Revenue Code, Commonwealth Act No. 466 of June 15, 1939. The principal change in the National Internal Revenue Code was the reduction of the personal exemption to ₱2,500 for married heads of families and ₱1,000 for single persons. Since the rate of taxation in the initial bracket (up to ₱2,000 of net income) was established at 1 per cent, the principal effect of the legislation was to increase the number of persons subject to taxation.

The next major change in the income tax law resulted from enactment of Republic Act No. 82 of October 29, 1946, which sharply increased rates.[3] In the fall of 1950 rates of taxation were again increased (Republic Act No. 590 of September 22). For example, the rate in the lowest bracket (up to ₱2,000 of net income) was increased by two-thirds, to 5 per cent. The rates established by Republic Act No. 590 expired at the end of 1952 and the lower levels of Republic Act No. 82 were re-established. In 1954 and 1955 the higher rates of Republic Act No. 590 were restored.[4] In 1956 personal income tax rates reverted once again to the lower levels of Republic Act No. 82, and these rates continued in effect through fiscal year 1959.[5]

The rates of the Philippine personal income tax are moderately progressive, with a maximum of 60 per cent on net income in excess of ₱500,000. The personal exemptions of ₱3,000 and ₱1,800 plus ₱600 for each minor dependent are excessively liberal. Such exemptions are more than seven times the average per capita income for married persons who are heads of families and somewhat more than four times the average per capita income for single persons. Moreover, the rate in the first income bracket is quite low, 3 per cent. The Philippine rate does not match the minimum United States rate until net income exceeds ₱10,000. Personal income taxation is excessively liberal whether appraised in terms of welfare standards or of revenue needs (Table 35).

This brief survey of Philippine personal income tax legislation

[3] For example, the rates of taxation on net incomes in all categories up to ₱90,000 increased at least threefold.

[4] Republic Act No. 1094 of June 15, 1954.

[5] Republic Act No. 2343 of June 30, 1959, increased the personal income tax rates on most middle and upper income brackets covering net incomes in excess of ₱6,000.

Table 35. Income taxation [a]
(₱ million—thousand returns)

Fiscal year	Withholding personal income tax [b]			Self-assessed personal income tax			Corporation income tax		
	Number of returns	Taxable returns	Taxes collected	Number of returns	Taxable returns	Taxes assessed	Number of returns	Taxable returns	Taxes collected
1947–48	N.A.	N.A.	N.A.	166	49	21	4.0	2.0	26
1948–49	N.A.	N.A.	N.A.	190	57	22	4.5	2.0	28
1949–50	N.A.	N.A.	N.A.	251	78	23	4.6	2.4	28
1950–51	N.A.	N.A.	N.A.	197	52	41	5.8	2.6	40
1951–52	19	10	11	178	46	31	7.4	2.5	60
1952–53	19	11	10	169	41	27	6.2	2.2	69
1953–54	29	12	9	181	47	24	6.7	2.3	73
1954–55	34	19	14	190	45	41	6.7	2.4	77
1955–56	n.a.	n.a.	15	223	64	44	6.7	2.4	83
1956–57	n.a.	n.a.	14	281	82	44	7.2	2.7	79

[a] R.P., Dept. of Finance, Bureau of Internal Revenue, *Annual Reports of the Collector of Internal Revenue*.
[b] Collection of personal income tax by withholding began Jan. 1, 1951.

has not treated the basic problem of income tax discipline. The personal income tax realizes only a small part of the potential revenues from this source. For example, in recent years the number of tax returns reporting sufficient income to be subject to the personal income tax has been equivalent to less than one-third of 1 per cent of the population. Personal income taxes assessed on both Filipinos and aliens have amounted to approximately six-tenths of 1 per cent of national income in recent years.

Tax discipline as between aliens and Filipinos is distinctly different. In the first year of the Magsaysay administration the annual report of the collector of internal revenue included information on personal income assessed by source of income and nationality of individual.[6] For the fiscal year 1953–1954 the taxable returns filed by Filipinos numbered 43,684, or one out of every 400 Filipinos; the total income reported amounted to ₱604 million, or less than 10 per cent of Philippine national income. Personal income taxes assessed against Filipinos totaled ₱15.9 million, or one-fifth of 1 per cent of national income. Filipinos paid slightly less than half of the total personal income taxes of ₱33.2 million.[7] Moreover, most of the personal income taxes paid by Filipinos were accounted for by the withholding tax assessed against employees of enterprises and civil servants. On income received in 1953, for example, withholding taxes, which were levied against Filipinos, amounted to ₱9.4 million as compared to self-assessed personal income taxes against Filipinos of ₱6.5 million.[8] When the 1954 taxable withholding returns numbering 12,138 are compared with the total taxable returns filed by Filipinos numbering 55,822, it is quite evident that the self-assessed income tax is not a productive source of government revenues.[9]

[6] The Collector of Internal Revenue, J. Antonio Araneta, was forced out of office by congressional failure to include his position in the budget for FY 1955. Araneta made the mistake of trying to collect delinquent income taxes from Representative Ramon Durano, of Cebu. See *A.C.C. Journal*, 30 (June 1954), 227.

[7] R.P., Dept. of Finance, Bur. of Internal Revenue, *Forty-Seventh Annual Report, 1954* (Manila, 1955).

[8] The nationality of the taxpayer in the case of personal income tax collected by withholding is not known. It is a reasonable assumption that business employees and bureaucrats were predominantly Filipinos and that the principal part of the withholding tax was assessed against Filipinos.

[9] Information is available on the Philippine personal income tax by nationality for two additional years. In 1949 personal income taxes paid by Filipinos amounted to ₱7.9 million, or only 44 per cent of personal income tax collections of ₱18.0

The Philippine personal income tax as presently administered is a travesty on tax equity. For example, the ratio of tax returns filed by physicians in 1954 to the number of physicians was only 18 per cent. The comparable ratio for lawyers was 9 per cent, for dentists 4 per cent, and for accountants 36 per cent.[10] In 1954 22 out of 24 senators filed income tax returns, 32 out of 56 governors, but only 47 out of 102 congressmen. The average tax paid in 1954 by the 25,000 "employees"—civil servants, wage workers, and others—subject to the withholding tax was only slightly less than the average tax assessed against the 1,157 physicians filing returns. The average tax assessed against the 1,791 "executives" subject to the withholding tax was twelve times that assessed against physicians filing returns, nine times that assessed against governors, and four times that assessed against lawyers.[11]

Total personal income taxes collected from Filipinos in fiscal year 1953–54 amounted to less than one-sixth of the revenues produced by excise taxation on cigarettes, one-fourth of those on petroleum products, and only two-thirds of those on distilled and fermented liquors. Income tax collections have increased since 1954, but the receipts have declined as a ratio of total tax revenues and also as a ratio of national income.

Corporate Income Tax

During the period March 1, 1913, to December 31, 1918, Philippine corporate income was subject to rates of taxation enacted in the

million. Only one-fifth of 1 per cent of the Filipino population filed personal income tax returns. See Central Bank, *Statistical Bulletin*, 2 (Oct. 1950). In 1956 personal income taxes assessed against Filipinos (income earned in 1955) amounted to ₱28.6 million, or 49 per cent of personal income tax assessed. Personal income taxes were assessed against only one-fourth of 1 per cent of the Filipino population. See Ray E. Davis, *Terminal Report to the Bureau of Internal Revenue* (Manila, Department of Finance, 1958), p. 89.

[10] It is to be regretted that the information provided in the annual report of the Collector of Internal Revenue for FY 1953–54 was not repeated in subsequent reports. In view of the political ordeal of Collector Araneta, who dared to publish such information, the reluctance of the executive to repeat the performance is understandable. The tendency of self-assessed income taxes to decline as a ratio of national income is persuasive evidence that tax discipline in this category has not improved since 1953.

[11] R.P., Dept. of Finance, Bur. of Internal Revenue, *Forty-Seventh Annual Report*, pp. 46–47. For estimates of the numbers of professionals, see Human Relations Area Files, *The Philippines*, vol. II (Subcontractors Monograph, HRAF-16, Chicago 5; New Haven, Conn.: The Files, 1958), table X-6.

United States income tax laws of 1913 and 1916, i.e., at 1 and 2 per cent, respectively. For the calendar year 1919 a basic corporation income tax rate of 2 per cent was established by Act No. 2833. From 1920 to 1935 a basic rate of 3 per cent was established by Act No. 2926, and for 1936–1938 a basic rate of 6 per cent was established by Commonwealth Act No. 117.

The National Internal Revenue Code, Commonwealth Act No. 466, raised the corporation income tax rate to 8 per cent beginning January 1, 1939, and Republic Act No. 82 raised the rate to 12 per cent for the four years ending December 21, 1949. For 1950 the rate was raised to 16 per cent. Republic Act No. 600 raised the corporate income tax to 20 per cent on incomes not exceeding ₱100,000 and subjected the excess to a 28 per cent rate. Originally intended as a temporary measure, the rates established by Republic Act No. 600 were renewed each year by legislation until 1956, when the rates were made permanent by Republic Act No. 1505.[12]

In contrast to the self-assessed personal income tax, the corporate income tax is a relatively efficient way to produce revenue (Table 35). In recent years revenue from the corporate income tax has tended to expand more rapidly than total government revenues and at a rate in excess of the growth in national income. In view of the extensive tax remission under the "new and necessary industries" policy of the government, it seems evident that there is considerable effective progression in the present corporation income tax structure. The performance of the corporate income tax is also related to the rapid improvement in tax discipline of aliens under the impact of Philippine economic nationalism. While statistics are not available on the nationality of the corporate income tax, there can be little question that the ratio of taxes collected on non-Filipino corporations is as high as the comparable ratio for personal income tax collections.

Collections under the corporate income tax have tended to increase steadily, but they account for only about 10 per cent of national government tax revenues and in recent years have averaged only three-fourths of the revenues produced by excise taxation on cigarettes.

Taxation of Import Values

In the Philippines, as in most countries in the early stages of economic growth, import values have been the most productive tax base

[12] See Republic Acts Nos. 868, 1065, 1291, and 1505.

(Table 36). That this should be so is rather surprising in view of the trading relationship imposed on the Philippines by the United States which provided for reciprocal preferential "free trade."

Prior to 1956 the basic tariff law of the Philippines was the Tariff Act of 1909, which was enacted by the United States Congress. The preferential position of United States imports in the Philippine market sharply limited revenues from the tariff since imports from the United States amounted to two-thirds to four-fifths of Philippine imports. The capacity of the United States to dominate the Philippine import market is understandable in view of the fact that the ratio of tariff revenues to the value of non-United States imports during the postwar period to 1956 was 12 per cent.[13]

Because of the so-called "reciprocal free trade" relationship between the United States and the Philippines, taxation of import values has tended to take place under laws that were not called tariff laws. The most important recent tax in this category has been the special tax on sales of foreign exchange, which was enacted in 1951. The tax on sales of foreign exchange at the rate of 17 per cent was highly productive. Although nontrade payments as well as imports were taxed, import payments including insurance and freight which accounted for 85 per cent of foreign exchange disbursements during the five years following 1950 dominated this tax base. During the four years and nine months this tax was collected, it produced ₱593 million, which was equivalent to 17.8 per cent of national government tax revenues during the five fiscal years ending June 30, 1955.[14] The Revised Philippine–United States Trade Agreement of 1955 converted the special tax on sales of foreign exchange to a temporary import duty of 17 per cent on all imports, which is to be gradually absorbed in the Philippine tariff structure.[15]

Collection of regular customs duties on imports from the United States as well as conversion of the special tax on sales of foreign exchange to a temporary import duty has resulted in a remarkable increase in customs revenues. From an average of ₱36 million for the three fiscal years ending June 30, 1955, customs revenues averaged

[13] The average rate on dutiable imports was substantially higher.

[14] In official Philippine statistics revenue from the special tax on sales of foreign exchange is usually included in the reported revenue from the excise tax.

[15] The initial rate of 17 per cent is scheduled to be reduced by annual decrements of 1.7 percentage points until the tax is eliminated in 1966.

Table 36. Taxation of imported commodities [a]
(₱ million)

Fiscal year	Import duties	Special tax on sales of foreign exchange	Excise tax on imported commodities [b]	Compensating tax collected by Bureau of Customs	Advance sales tax collected by Bureau of Customs	Total revenues from taxation of imports	Total tax revenue [c]	Value of imports f.o.b. [d]
1948–49	28.6	N.A.	114.6	4.0	51.7	198.9	362	1,155
1949–50	25.7	N.A.	94.5	3.8	39.7	163.7	329	925
1950–51	26.7	31.8	70.4	5.5	43.1	177.5	443	836
1951–52	32.2	155.4	72.8	9.5	79.6	349.5	655	906
1952–53	28.3	115.1	67.9	10.0	61.8	283.1	601	866
1953–54	34.2	126.4	78.5	10.9	71.6	321.6	644	891
1954–55	44.7	111.9	68.2	8.2	78.8	311.8	681	986
1955–56	182.4	62.4	76.1	10.4	69.6	400.9	738	1,044
1956–57	197.0	N.A.	85.5	13.4	79.6	375.5	821	1,124

[a] R.P., Dept. of Fin., Bur. of Internal Revenue, *Annual Reports*, and Bur. of Customs, *Annual Reports*.
[b] Including Highways Special Fund excise taxes collected on imports of lubricants and gasoline. Excise tax collections on petroleum products listed as "domestic" but actually refined in the Philippines from imported crude oil are included.
[c] See Table 33.
[d] Average of two calender years including the fiscal year.

₱181 million during the following three fiscal years. Further increases in revenues from this source began in 1959, when the rate at which Philippine tariff duties are collected on imports from the United States was doubled from 25 to 50 per cent.

The summer of 1959 saw a return to the earlier Philippine policy of an exchange premium tax. Republic Act No. 2609 of July 7, 1959, provides for a uniform margin fee of not more than 40 per cent on sales of foreign exchange. For 1959 the margin fee was set at 25 per cent. Although the list of imports exempted from payment of the margin fee is extensive, this tax will undoubtedly produce substantial amounts of revenue and will increase the proportion of revenues derived from taxation of import values.

A third tax on import values is the advanced sales tax collected by the Bureau of Customs. The sales tax is imposed at various rates on the basis of the type of article and, in some instances, of price. The sales tax on imports takes two forms. First is the advance sales tax on commodities imported for resale in the Philippines collected by the Bureau of Customs. Second is the compensating tax on imports not subject to resale, e.g., direct imports by business firms and imports for personal use by Filipinos returning to the Philippines and by nonimmigrants temporarily in the Philippines. The sales tax incidence falls heavily upon imports because of the broad exemptions of the major part of Philippine output and differential rates on "nonessential" imports. The basic rate of the sales tax has been 7 per cent since 1950.[16] The broad exemptions tend to minimize revenues from this tax.[17] Sales of watches, household appliances, textiles of silk, wool, linen, and nylon, radios, and other items are taxed at 30 per cent. Sales of jewelry, perfumes, and like items are taxed at 50 per cent, with special rates on sales of automobiles up to 100 per cent on automobiles with a landed cost in the Philippines of ₱10,000 or more.

During the three fiscal years ending June 30, 1957, total revenue from sales taxes on imports, including the advanced sales tax and the compensating tax, averaged ₱87 million. Revenues from sales taxes on domestically produced goods averaged only ₱23.5 million, or approximately 3 per cent of national government tax revenues.[18] The

[16] Republic Act No. 588 of Sept. 22, 1950, Sec. 186.

[17] For example, agricultural products, products exported, fish products, and small retailers are exempted from payment of the sales tax.

[18] R.P. Dept. of Finance, Bur. of Internal Revenue, *Forty-Seventh* and *Forty-Eighth Annual Reports.*

sales tax is more properly a revenue tariff, with the bulk of domestic transactions excluded from taxation by broad exemptions and by discriminatory rates applied to categories which, for all practical purposes, are limited to imports.

Still another tax on import values is the excise tax. As late as 1949 the excise tax on imported commodities accounted for 85 per cent of total revenues from this tax. The most productive commodities subject to the excise tax are distilled and fermented liquors, cigarettes, and petroleum products (principally gasoline). After the imposition of exchange and import controls in 1950 a sharp shift in the sources of excise tax revenues occurred. Production of domestic liquors and cigarettes expanded rapidly because of import restrictions and resulting price increases. Like the sales tax and compensating tax, the excise tax on imported commodities is analogous to a revenue tariff imposed on those commodities for which demand is relatively strong. However, tax rates on imported liquors and cigarettes together with import restrictions have reduced imports of these commodities to such levels that excise tax revenues from these sources have been reduced substantially below the levels that prevailed in the early postwar period.

Except for the single fiscal year 1950–51, when Philippine national government revenues were in the process of rapid expansion following implementation of the Bell Mission recommendations, import values have provided approximately 50 per cent of postwar tax revenues.

Domestic Excise Taxation

The principal remaining source of national government tax revenues in recent years has been the excise tax on domestic commodities (Table 37). Excise taxes are collected in two forms. First is the excise tax collected from manufactures, and second is the sales tax collected from retailers.

Receipts from the excise tax increased rapidly following the imposition of import controls in 1950. The improvement in revenues from this tax was due to three interrelated factors. First, rates of taxation were raised in 1948, 1950, 1952, and 1956.[19] Second, stringent controls on imports and resulting increases in the prices of imported goods have diverted Philippine consumption to domestically produced commodities, especially cigarettes and liquors. Third, com-

[19] Republic Acts Nos. 219, 289, 818, and 1608.

modity definitions in tax legislation have tended to discriminate in favor of domestically produced commodities, thereby establishing higher levels of protection for Philippine producers. For example, the law provides that if cigarettes in the various categories are mechanically packed the tax rate is raised to 220 per cent of the basic rate. Similarly, cigarettes "not wrapped in tinfoil or cellophane and not packed in cartons or tin cans" are taxed at a basic rate substantially lower than the tax rate on cigarettes so packed.

During the three-year period ending June 30, 1957, excise taxes on domestically produced cigarettes averaged ₱106 million annually, or 14 per cent of total national government tax revenues. The remaining domestic excise tax revenues are derived primarily from distilled and fermented liquors, which, during the three fiscal years 1955–1957, produced average revenues of ₱21.7 million, or 2.9 per cent of total revenues. Currently, substantial amounts of excise tax revenues are produced from taxes on imports of refined petroleum products as well as upon petroleum products refined in the Philippines from crude oil imports. During the three fiscal years ending June 30, 1957, revenues from these sources averaged ₱72 million annually. Total excise tax collections during fiscal years 1955–1957 averaged ₱218 million, or 29.1 per cent of national government revenues during this period. During the same period excise tax revenues from domestic manufactures (excluding refined petroleum products) averaged ₱135 million, or 18.0 per cent of national government revenues.

Other National Government Tax Revenues

Additional tax revenues are derived from a proliferation of privilege taxes on movie theatres, common carriers, contractors, warehouses, and so forth. Revenues from these sources averaged ₱60 million annually during fiscal years 1955–1957 (Table 38).

The residence tax is basically a poll tax on citizens over 18 years of age combined with a complex tax in the nature of a surtax on individuals and corporations which is assessed on a basis of both wealth and income. Some five categories of residence certificates are issued for the various categories of taxpayers. The residence tax, a legacy of the cedula of the Spanish period, produced only ₱5.0 million annually during fiscal years 1955–1957. Transfer taxes including estate, inheritance, and gift taxes produced an average of ₱5.6 million annually during fiscal years 1955–1957. The estate tax is levied at rates of

Table 37. Excise tax revenues [a]
(₱ million)

	Distilled spirits and fermented liquors		Cigarettes		Petroleum products [b]		Other commodities		Total	
	Domestic	Imported	Domestic	Imported	Domestic	Imported	Domestic	Imported	Domestic	Imported
1946–47	4.8	4.8	4.5	35.7	4.6	25.2	1.3	1.9	15.2	67.6
1947–48	8.8	4.3	5.2	53.7	—	40.7	1.5	1.9	15.5	100.6
1948–49	13.6	3.4	4.5	61.6	—	47.9	1.6	1.7	19.7	114.6
1949–50	14.4	3.3	9.2	40.4	—	49.2	2.1	1.6	25.7	94.5
1950–51	18.7	1.8	47.0	17.1	—	50.3	2.2	1.2	67.9	70.4
1951–52	21.1	1.8	61.7	14.5	—	55.5	2.5	1.0	85.3	72.8
1952–53	21.0	1.8	73.7	13.5	—	51.4	2.5	1.2	97.2	67.9
1953–54	21.7	2.5	89.6	11.1	.1	63.5	2.4	1.2	113.8	78.3
1954–55	21.4	2.8	91.3	6.6	12.4	47.7	4.2	1.1	129.3	58.2
1955–56	21.5	2.8	105.2	5.4	30.9	40.4	6.9	4.2	164.5	52.8
1956–57	22.1	3.4	121.4	2.3	36.2	48.4	9.7	7.4	189.4	58.5

[a] R.P., Dept. of Finance, Bur. of Internal Revenue, *Annual Reports*.
[b] Includes the excise tax receipts of the Highways Special Fund. The excise tax receipts on "domestic petroleum products" refer to receipts derived from taxes on petroleum products refined in the Philippines, from imported crude oil.

Table 38. Miscellaneous sources of national government tax revenues [a]

(₱ million)

Fiscal year	Business and professional privilege taxes	Residence tax	Franchise tax	Estate, inheritance, and gift tax	Documentary stamp tax	Revenues from public forests	Wharfage fees and tonnage dues
1949–50	53.6	4.1	1.4	3.0	4.3	4.0	3.1
1950–51	54.7	4.3	2.3	3.5	3.8	3.7	4.3
1951–52	46.2	4.7	1.9	4.2	6.1	4.1	4.4
1952–53	43.7	4.0	1.7	3.7	5.3	3.7	5.2
1953–54	45.7	4.2	2.4	3.0	4.6	4.3	5.8
1954–55	47.7	4.3	2.9	4.8	6.8	4.4	5.7
1955–56	54.4	4.6	2.8	6.4	7.0	4.8	n.a.
1956–57	69.4	6.0	2.9	5.5	6.2	5.4	n.a.

[a] R.P., Dept. of Finance, Bur. of Internal Revenue, *Annual Reports*.

from 1 per cent on net estates from ₱5,000 to ₱12,000 to 15 per cent of net estates in excess of ₱1 million. In addition, an inheritance tax is imposed at graduated rates that vary by type of beneficiary. A gift tax is imposed in two parts: the first on the donor and the second on the donee. The rates for the donor component of the gift tax are the same as the estate tax rate. The rates for the donee component of the gift tax are like the inheritance tax rates in that the tax rate varies by type of relationship with a system of coefficients superimposed on a basic rate schedule which is the same as the inheritance tax.

Immigration taxes are a minor revenue producer, although in recent years rates have been sharply increased and increased revenues are being realized. The immigration tax includes an assortment of levies on various categories of aliens who are in the Philippines for one reason or another. The remaining national government tax revenues are derived from wharfage fees, tonnage dues, documentary stamp taxes, and revenues from the public forests. These taxes are stable sources of revenues averaging ₱15–18 million annually during recent fiscal years.

Philippine National Government Expenditure

Because of relatively low levels of national government tax revenues, the limited governmental expenditures in the Philippines tend to be concentrated in current expenditures (Table 39). Only in recent years, with the adoption of a capital budget and acceptance of the policy of financing capital expenditures through budgetary deficits, have expanded levels of social investment been sustained. Tax revenues are presently devoted almost in their entirety to consumption of goods and services through the budget. During the three fiscal years ending June 30, 1958, current operating expenses of the national government averaged ₱773 million as compared to annual average tax revenue of ₱802 million.[20]

The largest item of public expenditure is education, which in fiscal years 1955–1958 averaged ₱252 million, or 23.6 per cent of the average annual expenditures of ₱1,068 million during this period. Large national government outlays for education result from the central government's responsibility for free public primary education. The Philippine educational system is highly centralized, and an estimated 90 per cent

[20] Central Bank, *Ninth Annual Report, 1957*, p. 95.

of public educational expenditures are provided by the national budget. Provincial and other levels of government are responsible for the maintenance of public high schools. However, these are maintained for the most part on a self-supporting basis out of matriculation and tuition fees. Local revenues from matriculation and tuition fees have averaged between ₱15 million and ₱20 million in recent

Table 39. Major components of national government expenditure [a]
(₱ million)

Fiscal year	Total expenditure [b]	Defense	Economic services [c]	Social services [d]	Contributions to local government	Other current expenditure	Investment [e]
1948–49	467	86	n.r.	146	32	99	104
1949–50	534	102	n.r.	175	37	125	96
1950–51	523	125	n.r.	174	29	102	92
1951–52	635	182	n.r.	176	37	115	125
1952–53	660	167	n.r.	184	49	125	135
1953–54	787	160	36	207	48	175	161
1954–55	854	148	103	264	56	111	172
1955–56	980	166	122	268	56	85	283
1956–57	1,057	157	158	282	61	110	289
1957–58	1,167	177	167	317	70	123	313

[a] UN, ECAFE, *Economic Survey.*

[b] Includes net loans and advances but excludes debt redemption, contributions to sinking funds, and transfers to reserve funds.

[c] Includes current expenditure on agriculture, industrial development, scientific and technical research, irrigation, public works, forests, ports, lighthouses, commerce, planning, and so forth.

[d] Includes current expenditures on education, health, social welfare, relief, and so forth.

[e] Capital outlays including maintenance.

years. The principal part of the educational outlays goes to pay teachers' salaries and other current expenses. For example, total current expenditures on social services, including education, in 1954–1957 averaged ₱256 million out of the average annual expenditures on social services of ₱298 million.

Philippine national government expenditures on education amounted to ₱9.2 per capita during fiscal year 1953–54. National expenditures per pupil in publicly supported schools at all levels during fiscal year

1953–54 amounted to ₱54.0. In relative terms, national expenditures on education are impressive. When measured in absolute terms of need, they are unimpressive.[21]

The second largest category of national government expenditure is defense, which averaged ₱168 million annually during fiscal years 1955–1958. Philippine defense expenditures have been maintained at relatively high levels in the postwar period because of security problems arising out of agrarian unrest, communism, and the decline of law and order during the Japanese occupation and the liberation. Philippine budgetary outlays for defense purposes are supplemented by substantial transfers of United States military equipment and weapons as well as by capital construction in the Philippines by the United States under mutual security arrangements.

Outlays for social services other than education are for public health and sanitation, averaging ₱33 million annually during fiscal years 1955–1958, and for charity and social welfare, averaging ₱4 million.

National government expenditures on economic services have expanded rapidly in recent years and in the three years ending June 30, 1958, averaged ₱149 million. Such expenditures include current outlays on agriculture, industrial development, scientific and technical research, irrigation, public works, forests, ports, commerce, and planning.

Other current expenditures during fiscal years 1955–1958 averaged ₱106 million and included substantial amounts of transfer payments of pensions and gratuities, although the principal part of such expenditures represents current outlays for administration. Contributions to meet the expenses of local governments averaged ₱62 million during fiscal years 1955–1958.

Social investment prior to the Magsaysay administration took place at relatively modest levels. Total investment outlays including capital outlays for public works and covering maintenance, the investments of government enterprises, and grants to local governments for investment purposes averaged ₱128 million annually dur-

[21] The relatively large budgeted outlays have not prevented the abandonment of two years of free public schooling since 1935. Moreover, the large budgeted expenditures on public education have not permitted the resumption of the full school day. The restoration of the two grades and the shift of public education to a full day have been strongly recommended by educational authorities, both Filipino and foreign.

ing the four fiscal years ending June 30, 1954. In other words, gross public investment by the national government averaged 1.9 per cent of national income during the period. When depreciation and obsolescence are deducted from gross investment, it is apparent that net investment by the national government was taking place at very modest levels if at all.

The advent of the Magsaysay administration in 1954 was followed by a major change in public investment policy in which the principle of a capital budget financed by proceeds of government borrowing was introduced. In the three fiscal years ending June 30, 1957, investment expenditures averaged ₱295 million, more than double the average annual expenditures of the preceding four years. The increase in annual gross public investment was largely accounted for by the budgetary deficit, which averaged ₱112 million annually. During the previous four years fiscal operations had resulted in a small surplus.

In spite of the introduction of a capital budget, levels of public investment have been low, and much of such investment is not used efficiently. Approximately one-quarter of public investment occurs through the annual public works appropriations bill, which is aptly termed the "pork barrel" bill. Each member of the House and Senate is allocated a share of "pork" for expenditures desired by his constituents. Such outlays include schools and other public buildings, road construction, and minor port works. The expenditures tend to be relatively ineffective in terms of the over-all requirements of social investment for Philippine economic development. For example, it is not uncommon for public works funds to be utilized to construct temporary roads from nowhere to nowhere.

Another source of waste has resulted from inept investment in public corporations of one kind or another. The Philippines has had extensive recourse to public corporations to achieve diverse public goals ranging from agricultural price stabilization to Filipinization of internal commerce, to land colonization, to directly productive manufacturing and industrial establishments. A number of public corporations, of which the National Power Corporation is the most prominent example, have flourished and have provided essential public services efficiently, but a large proportion have failed and in the process have dissipated the capital investment of the government.

During recent years a number of public corporations, including the Development Bank of the Philippines, the National Power Corporation, the National Waterworks and Sewerage Authority, and the Agricultural Credit and Co-operative Financing Administration have been able to borrow through the sale of securities (largely to the banking system) and with the proceeds of borrowing make investment expenditures. During the five years ending with 1958 the public debt of government corporations increased by ₱365 million to ₱543 million.

Local Government Revenues and Expenditures

Philippine governmental functions are relatively centralized, and local government tax bases are restricted in number and productiveness.[22] Because of the high degree of centralization, local governments are dependent upon grants-in-aid and allocations of revenues from the national government for approximately 40 per cent of their receipts.

Intergovernmental financial arrangements in the Philippines are complex. The national government shares several taxes with other levels of government and makes allotments from its revenues for both general and specific functions of the other levels of government. In addition, intergovernmental aids and loans are granted for various purposes (Table 40).

Three levels of local government in the Philippines have significant revenue and expenditure functions. The provinces have practically no independent taxing power apart from the property tax, and even this power is severely restricted. As a result, the provinces are dependent upon national government allocations of one kind or another for approximately three-fifths of their total receipts. The taxing powers of chartered cities are governed by their charters, which are granted by the Congress. The third level of local government is the municipality. Municipalities are authorized (a) to impose municipal licenses upon persons engaged in any occupation or business, (b) to collect fees and charges for services rendered, and (c) to levy just and uniform taxes for local purposes.[23]

---

[22] For example, such services as fire protection, water supply, and sewage disposal, to the extent that they exist, are primarily a national government function.

[23] They are prohibited from levying (a) percentage or sales taxes, (b) taxes on specific articles (excises), and (c) an extensive list of specified taxes, charges, and fees, including taxes on cedulas, documents, printing and publication, telephone and telegraph lines, broadcasting or wireless stations, light, heat, or power; transportation; forest products; mines; manufacturers and wholesalers in liquor

The principal tax base allocated to local government in the Philippines is real property. The full possibilities of this tax base as a revenue source have never been realized. In recent years the real property tax has accounted for only about 20 per cent of all local

Table 40. Local government revenue [a]
(₱ million)

Fiscal year	Revenue from taxation		Operation of commercial and industrial units [c]	Incidental revenue	Allotments and aid from the national government	Total
	Property tax	Other taxes [b]				
1946–47 [d]	19.1	19.3	17.5	12.3	41.0	109.3
1947–48 [d]	25.6	23.1	21.8	19.1	67.4	156.5
1948–49 [d]	28.2	25.6	24.3	25.2	93.3	196.6
1949–50	30.7	16.9	25.9	30.0	70.0	173.5
1950–51	36.3	21.1	25.0	34.7	44.3	161.4
1951–52	34.1	28.0	25.9	33.5	73.1	194.6

[a] Leticia P. Pacis and Odell Waldby, *Philippine Government Receipts and Expenditures, Fiscal Year 1953* (Manila: Univ. of the Philippines, Institute of Public Administration, 1954).

[b] Municipal taxes provide approximately half of these revenues, with tuition and matriculation fees providing approximately two-fifths. Other revenues include cattle registration fees, marriage licenses, fisheries licenses, and so forth.

[c] Public market and slaughterhouse fees provide more than one-half, with public utility receipts accounting for more than one-fourth.

[d] U.S. Economic Survey [Bell] Mission, *Technical Memoranda* (Memorandum No. 9, Taxation), pp. 122–123.

government revenues in the Philippines and for no more than 3 to 4 per cent of tax revenues at all levels of government.[24] During the three years ending December 31, 1953, real property taxes averaged

---

and tobacco; brokers and agents of various specified types; professions; incomes, inheritances, and gifts; and fees for the registration of motor vehicles and for the issuance of all kinds of permits for driving; and customs fees, charges, and dues. The specific prohibitions are so extensive as to nullify much of the taxing power granted under the general authority (U.S. Economic Survey [Bell] Mission to the Philippines, *Technical Memoranda* [Memorandum No. 9, Taxation; Washington, 1950], p. 166).

[24] During fiscal year 1955 real property taxes accounted for 16.3 per cent of provincial revenue, 21.2 per cent of municipal revenues, and 24.8 per cent of the revenue of chartered cities. See R.P., Special Tax Revision Commission, *Property Tax Administration in the Philippines, 1956* (Manila: Bureau of Printing, 1957), p. 1.

P36.4 million. For 1956 real property tax revenues amounted to P40 million, with collections in Manila amounting to P11.8 million, in other chartered cities P8.1 million, and in the provinces P20.1 million.

The law provides that assessment be made at "true and full value," but actual assessments fluctuate widely around such a norm.[25] A recent study indicated that assessment levels in provinces and cities varied widely—from a low of 21 per cent of market value in Batangas to a high of 125 per cent in Zamboanga del Sur, with a median assessment ratio of 42 per cent.[26]

Underassessment is greater for rural property than for urban residential property and is still greater for rural property as compared to commercial property. The ratio of assessed value to market value was 51 per cent in the case of residential property in cities and 58 per cent in the case of commercial property in cities.[27] The study also measured the equity of assessment—assessments within a deviation range of not more than 20 per cent above or below the median were considered satisfactorily equalized. With such a measure, only in Manila were the inequitable assessments less than 50 per cent of those studied and the over-all level of inequitable assessments was 78 per cent.

Little variation exists in the tax rates on real property. In 45 out of 53 provinces the tax rate in 1956 was the statutory maximum of 1 per cent of assessed valuation. The maximum rates for cities are set forth in their respective charters. The actual 1956 levy in 22 cities was 1 per cent, and only five cities levied the maximum permitted by charter.[28]

In view of the low ratios of assessed value to market value (the median is 42 per cent) and of the low tax rate presently imposed on real property in the Philippines, the effective rate of taxes assessed on the market value of real property averages between one-half and two-thirds of 1 per cent. Only some 60 per cent of property taxes are

[25] Commonwealth Act No. 470 as amended covers the present assessment law of provinces and municipalities; that of cities may be found in their respective charters.

[26] R.P., *Property Tax Administration, 1956.* The study was based on analysis of 11,102 sales transactions involving real property in 25 provinces and 28 chartered cities. In 22 per cent of the cases the assessed value was less than 20 per cent of the market value.

[27] *Ibid.,* p. 7.

[28] *Ibid.,* p. 97. The city of Manila applies the maximum rate (1.5 per cent) authorized by its charter.

collected in the year in which they are due, and large amounts of assessed property taxes are waived. Typhoons, earthquakes, and rat infestations have been used as justification for legislation remitting property taxes. In 1956, of assessed property taxes of ₱61.4 million at all levels of government, only ₱40 million was collected. Delinquent real property taxes as of January 1, 1956, amounted to ₱61.4 million, which equaled the total assessment of property taxes for 1956. Of the delinquency of ₱21.4 million for the year 1956, ₱16.8 million was provincial. Similarly, of the cumulative delinquency on January 1, 1956, ₱51 million, or five-sixths, was provincial.[29] Thus, not only is farm land assessed at a relatively lower ratio to market value, but the owners of this land pay a much smaller proportion of their taxes. During much of the postwar period the effective rate of real property taxation to the market value of agricultural real estate has probably been as low as one-fourth to one-half of 1 per cent.

In recent years approximately one-third of real property taxes has been collected in metropolitan Manila, and provincial collections, representing the taxation of agricultural lands as well as residential property in municipalities, have contributed slightly more than half of the total collections. If all the taxes assessed against agricultural land should be fully collected, at current assessments and rates they would amount to no more than 4 per cent of the total tax revenues. Philippine property tax collections in recent years have averaged only one-quarter of the excise tax collections on domestic cigarettes and liquors. In the United States taxation of real property provides approximately 90 per cent of the tax revenues of political subdivisions below the level of state governments. In the Philippines this tax has amounted to no more than one-fifth of the low levels of local government receipts in recent years.

Other local government revenues include municipal licenses and tuition and matriculation fees for high schools. These provide approximately 90 per cent of the revenues in the category of "other taxes." Substantial revenues are listed from the "operation of commercial and industrial units." Inasmuch as these revenues are derived from the sale of water, electricity, and so forth, and are gross receipts rather than net revenues, their inclusion in total tax revenues is questionable. Rentals from markets and slaughterhouses provide more than half of the revenues in this category, with public utilities adding a quarter.

[29] *Ibid.*, pp. 168–169.

Substantial amounts of local government revenue are listed under the category "incidental revenue." Detailed information regarding the sources of revenues in this category is not available.

Failure to levy and collect a realistic real property tax in the Philippines is particularly unfortunate because of the concentration of land ownership and absentee landlordism. Ownership of agricultural land is a reliable index of agricultural income and wealth, and in the Philippines these largely escape taxation. A real property tax with realistic rates and proper enforcement would not only produce large amounts of revenue, but would establish desirable social incentives. Better still would be a progressive real property tax with rates based on the size and the productiveness of holdings.

The visitor in the Philippines is struck by the large amounts of unoccupied urban land and fallow rural land. To a considerable extent this situation results from the low levels of taxation, which minimize the out-of-pocket costs of idle land. Similarly, the visitor is impressed by the distorted land values. For example, urban and suburban land prices in and around Manila probably average two to four times those of equivalent lands around Washington, D.C. It is not uncommon for the market prices of rural land to average ten times the value of the gross annual yield of the land, whereas in the United States the comparable ratio would be only a fraction as large.[30] While these relationships reflect factor proportions favorable to land and capital improvements on land, they also reflect Philippine fiscal policy and failure to levy and collect adequate real property taxes.

The need for reform of real property taxation is obvious both to Filipinos and to students of the Philippines, but there are few grounds for expecting such a reform to materialize. So long as Philippine political parties consist of loose coalitions of regional leaders whose power is based upon the landowning class, there is little likelihood of reform.

---

[30] Oppenfeld *et al.*, *Farm Management*, p. 44, reports an average ratio of annual gross return to market value of crop land of 1:6 for a sample of 3,241 Philippine farms. On the other hand, for the three years 1956–1958 "cash receipts from marketings plus value of farm products consumed by farm households, plus imputed rental of farm buildings" in the United States averaged 31.9 per cent of the market value of agricultural real estate including farm buildings. See *Economic Report of the President*, transmitted to Congress, Jan. 20, 1960 (Washington: Government Printing Office, 1960), pp. 229, 236.

Closely related to the problem of real property taxation is that of decentralizing government functions. Students of the Philippines are agreed that the government is excessively centralized and that opportunities exist to develop local institutions capable of contributing to Philippine economic development through powers to tax, to provide essential social services, and to make social investment.[31] In recent years a number of significant steps have been taken in the direction of government decentralization including the chartering of cities, provision for elected barrio councils, and the Community Development Program. However, the Congress has been very reluctant to relax its control over the power to tax, and the progress of this desirable social reform has not been appropriate to Philippine economic growth.

Public Debt Policy

Philippine public debt policy is a composite policy covering three kinds of debt (Table 41). First is the debt of the national government. This comprises the bulk of the peso debt as well as the principal part of the foreign debt. The existing foreign debt was incurred primarily as the result of *ad hoc* loans to the Philippine government to make peso funds available to cover budgetary deficits during 1947–1950. The foreign debt of the national government reached a peak of ₱317 million at the end of 1950 and has steadily been reduced until as of the end of 1957 it amounted to ₱157 million. As of the end of 1957, the dollar debt of the national government was equivalent to ₱82 million, and that of the National Power Corporation to ₱44 million. In addition, the Central Bank owed the dollar equivalent of ₱30.5 million to the International Monetary Fund.[32]

---

[31] American observers tend to reach such a conclusion by analogy with the experience of the United States where local units of government proved highly effective in mobilizing local resources to provide free public education, transportation facilities, public utilities, and the like. In the Philippines such local services and investments are, to a considerable extent, the responsibility of the national government.

[32] The total of the public debt and the public foreign debt is understated substantially as it does not include dollar obligations of the Central Bank and the Philippine National Bank, which are government-owned. As of the end of 1957 the Central Bank balance sheet showed foreign loans payable of ₱80 million. Moreover, the Central Bank was the guarantor of special credit lines arranged with U.S. banks for the use of Philippine commercial banks to the extent of $22.3 (₱45) million as of the end of 1957.

The Philippine foreign debt amounts to less than one-tenth of the listed public debt, and the service costs have been approximately 1.5 per cent of the foreign exchange budget in recent years.[33] There is widespread discussion in the Philippines of the possibility of marketing government dollar bonds in the United States and other capital markets to raise funds for economic development. To date this source of development funds has not been utilized, probably because of in-

Table 41. Public debt outstanding [a]
(₱ million—end of period)

Year	Total	Level of government			Source		Purpose	
		National government	Local government	Government corporations	Domestic	Foreign	Budgetary	Developmental
1941	141	90	30	21	21	120	—	141
1946	133	82	30	21	21	112	—	133
1947	253	202	30	21	21	232	120	133
1948	606	420	93	93	372	234	420	186
1949	701	512	93	96	467	234	458	243
1950	884	699	87	97	567	317	585	299
1951	816	659	68	88	612	203	538	277
1952	770	617	65	88	591	179	493	277
1953	1,066	826	62	178	867	199	697	369
1954	1,086	786	52	248	905	180	633	453
1955	1,327	969	45	311	1,159	167	590	737
1956	1,535	1,117	37	381	1,374	161	539	996
1957	1,627	1,131	28	466	1,469	157	469	1,156
1958	1,995	1,406	46	543	1,810	185	606	1,389

[a] Central Bank, *Statistical Bulletin,* vol. 10 (Dec. 1958).

creasing costs of borrowing in the United States and the reaction of potential investors to the discretionary Philippine exchange controls.

During the three years after the Bell Mission visit to the Philippines, public debt policy was relatively conservative, and the public debt increased by ₱182 million, or 21 per cent. In the ensuing five years to the end of 1958 deficit financing of developmental expenditures

[33] For example, in 1957 amortization and interest payments on the public foreign debt amounted to $9.4 million as compared to total allocations in the foreign exchange budget of $676 million (Central Bank, *Ninth Annual Report, 1957,* pp. 144–152).

resulted in rapid growth in the public debt, which increased by ₱929 million, or 87 per cent.

A minor component of the public debt is local government debt, primarily borrowings from government-owned banks. Such debt declined from a peak of ₱93 million at the end of 1948 to ₱28 million at the end of 1957. Decline in this portion of the public debt is consistent with the minor economic role of local government in the Philippines.

The increase in the public debt during the past decade is accounted for by loans for developmental purposes, as the budgetary debt at the end of 1957 was only slightly larger than it was at the end of 1948. This conclusion must be accepted with significant reservations, however, as the increase in public borrowing by the national government undoubtedly permitted the allocation of current revenues to retirement of budgetary debt to an extent not possible in the absence of such borrowing.

The increase in the Philippine public debt is "viewed with alarm" in many quarters, but the doubling in the eight years after 1950 was not excessive. This was a period in which national income increased by 50 per cent in real terms, and the ratio of public debt to national income increased only moderately—from 15 per cent in 1950 to 22 per cent in 1957. Moreover, the foreign debt was reduced substantially. The rate of public borrowing has tended to increase since 1953, and such borrowings are accounted for largely by sales to the banking system. These borrowings have remained conservative when related to the growth in output of the Philippine economy.

To conclude this brief analysis of Philippine fiscal policy, fiscal performance should be related to the economic organization. Filipinos have chosen to seek accelerated economic growth through reliance on individualism and private enterprise. Attempts to generate high levels of entrepreneurship and other activities productive of economic growth are concentrated in establishing strong economic incentives. These incentives are dominated by indirect subsidies including tax remission and allocation of the windfall arising out of restriction of foreign exchange payments.

Those appraising Philippine fiscal policy must remember that a recital of receipts and expenditures understates the extent to which the government controls the use of resources. The economic effects of current Philippine fiscal activities are comparable to substantially higher levels of tax collection and government expenditure. By forgoing tax receipts and the foreign exchange windfall, the government is able to dispose of greater amounts of resources than would be possible through taxation and direct subsidization. More important, the incentives established by forgoing taxes may be more effective than they would otherwise be because they are removed from the area of political controversy and resulting uncertainty.

This is not to say that the present fiscal performance should not be improved upon. There is great and obvious need in the Philippines to exploit agricultural production, income, and landownership as tax bases. Substantial additional amounts of revenue could be collected by the government without materially disturbing the system of entrepreneurial incentives. It is, however, essential that the reader be aware that Philippine fiscal performance is inadequately described by cursory reference to statistics of receipts and expenditures.

· X ·

Monetary Policy

THE Philippines in common with other colonies implemented an exchange reserve currency system during the later colonial period. The foundation of the currency system was the Philippine Gold Standard Act of 1903, which established a form of the gold standard. A Gold Standard Fund consisting of silver coins held in the Treasury in Manila and dollar deposits in United States banks was used to maintain parity in peso exchange. This was accomplished by selling drafts on the dollar deposits of the Gold Standard Fund in exchange for pesos while depository banks in the United States sold peso drafts on the Fund held in Manila in exchange for dollars. Under such an exchange reserve standard (the reserve consisted of silver pesos and dollars) the currency issue in the Philippines was directly related to the level of foreign receipts and payments.[1]

The first important modification of the reserve currency standard occurred in 1918 following establishment of the Philippine National Bank when the Gold Standard Fund and Silver Certificate Reserve were combined into a single Currency Reserve Fund. The automaticity of the Currency Reserve Fund broke down because of the provision

---

[1] For a comprehensive survey of Philippine monetary policy during the American period, see George F. Luthringer, *The Gold Exchange Standard in the Philippines* (Princeton, N.J.: Princeton University Press, 1934).

that the foreign assets of the fund could be deposited in the Philippine National Bank. The accumulation of peso deposits in the fund after World War I when the Philippine balance of payments was in deficit did not result in a contraction in the currency in circulation because the foreign exchange assets of the fund were, in effect, being disbursed by the Philippine National Bank in increased loans and credits. As a result, the foreign exchange assets of the fund were drained away in the absence of an automatic curtailment of the money supply.

In 1922 a large Philippine bond issue was sold in the United States to restore the dollar assets of the fund, and the currency law was revised to restore the automaticity of the 1903 act. Under the new legislation Treasury certificates (currency) had to be backed 100 per cent by dollar deposits. In addition, the Gold Standard Fund had to include reserves for not less than 15 per cent of Philippine currency, either in circulation or available therefor. Since Treasury certificates were backed 100 per cent and since some Philippine currency was not in circulation at any given time, total dollar reserves tended to exceed 100 per cent of the currency actually in circulation. This automatic, ultraconservative exchange reserve standard remained in force until 1949.

At the outbreak of World War II the Treasury certificates in the separate Treasury Certificate Fund were recorded and destroyed on Corregidor while the gold bullion was removed by submarine to the United States. As a result, the currency circulation was backed in excess of 100 per cent by gold and dollar assets intact in the United States. After the war the Philippines was in a position to resume the currency reserve standard without change.

Resumption of the prewar currency system was also facilitated by a number of fortuitous developments. First, the United States Congress enacted legislation turning over to the Philippines the proceeds of United States excise taxes on the processing of Philippine copra and sugar. Second, the Philippine Congress amended the basic currency legislation to eliminate the reserve requirement of 15 per cent against Treasury certificates which were backed 100 per cent by the automatic Exchange Standard Fund.[2] This change had the effect of freeing $30 million of currency reserves, i.e., it made this amount of foreign exchange available without a corresponding re-

[2] Republic Act No. 86 of Oct. 29, 1946.

duction in currency in circulation either by a budget surplus or by credit contraction. The importance of these changes arose out of the relationship between the government budget and the money supply. In the early postwar period the incapacity of the Philippine government to raise adequate amounts of peso revenues to cover expenditures would have required a departure from the exchange reserve standard if foreign exchange assets had not been diverted to the Exchange Standard Fund on an *ad hoc* basis. Moreover, the Exchange Standard Fund exchanged large amounts of pesos for dollars in providing United States military forces with their peso requirements.

The limited budgetary deficits of the Philippine government in the early postwar period together with the heavy expenditure by the United States military forces would have been highly inflationary if a deficit in the Philippine balance of payments had not developed. The import surplus on current account increased the supply of goods and services available to the Philippine economy. At the same time the conversion of pesos to dollars served to offset the expansion in currency resulting from budgetary deficits and heavy United States military expenditures. Fortunately, shipping became available promptly after the war, and the Philippine balance of payments rapidly developed a heavy import surplus. As a result, currency circulation, which had expanded to five times prewar levels in 1945, declined rapidly during 1946. Notes and coins in circulation, which totaled ₱882 million at the end of 1945, declined steadily to ₱472 million at the end of October 1946. Currency in circulation remained relatively stable during the remaining period of the reserve currency standard until the establishment of the Central Bank in January 1949. The remaining period of the exchange reserve standard is of interest primarily because of the chronic budgetary deficits and their financing.[3]

Negotiations with the United States over a budgetary loan in 1946 led to creation of the Joint Philippine-American Finance Commission to study aspects of Philippine fiscal and monetary problems. United States members of the commission arrived in Manila in January 1947, and the commission submitted its report in June.[4] The report of the commission included recommendations designed to im-

[3] See above, pp. 70–71.
[4] *Report Joint Finance Com.* The Philippine members were Miguel Cuaderno, Secretary of Finance; Pio Pedrosa, Commissioner of the Budget, and Vicente Carmona, president, Philippine National Bank. U.S. members were Edgar G. Grossman, Arthur W. Stuart, Treasury Department, and John Exter, Board of Governors, Federal Reserve System.

prove the budgetary situation by increasing revenues as well as important changes in areas of exchange rate and economic development policy.

A major recommendation of the Finance Commission concerned the monetary system. The report concluded that the exchange reserve system was "an unsuitable permanent system for an independent Philippines." The commission recommended the establishment of a central bank which would implement a managed currency system.

Following the recommendations of the Joint Philippine-American Finance Commission, steps were taken to establish a central bank. At the request of the Philippine government two members of the staff of the Board of Governors of the Federal Reserve System were detailed to assist in the preparation of central banking legislation.[5] The resulting law was signed by President Quirino on June 15, 1948.[6]

In Article I, Section 2, the Central Bank Act defines the responsibilities of the Central Bank as follows: "(a) to maintain monetary stability in the Philippines; (b) to preserve the international value of the peso and the convertibility of the peso into other freely convertible currencies; and (c) to promote a rising level of production, employment and real income in the Philippines." Monetary policy decisions as well as general supervision of Central Bank operations are vested in the Monetary Board, consisting of seven members, one of whom is the chief executive officer, or governor, of the Central Bank (Article II, Section 7). The Secretary of Finance serves as chairman of the Monetary Board, and the president of the Philippine National Bank and the chairman of the Board of Governors of the Rehabilitation Finance Corporation are ex-officio members. Appointed members must be "of recognized competence in the economics of banking, finance, commerce, agriculture or industry."

In view of the nature of postwar Philippine economic problems, the most significant aspects of the Central Bank Act deal with the management of the international reserve and the access of the government to the Central Bank to finance budgetary deficits.[7] With respect

[5] These were John Exter, who had been a member of the Joint Finance Commission, and David L. Grove, an economist. After the war the Board of Governors of the Federal Reserve System gave extensive technical assistance to various countries who wanted to establish managed currency systems.

[6] Republic Act No. 265.

[7] For a comprehensive analysis of the Central Bank Act, see David L. Grove and John Exter, "The Philippine Central Bank Act," *Federal Reserve Bulletin*, 34 (Aug. 1948), 938–949.

to management of the international reserve, the act provides: "The Central Bank of the Philippines shall exercise its powers under this Act to maintain the par value of the peso and the convertibility of the peso into other freely convertible currencies" (Section 67). Furthermore, "the Central Bank shall maintain an international reserve adequate to meet any foreseeable net demands on the Bank for foreign currencies" (Section 68). Section 70 provides:

Whenever the international reserve of the Central Bank falls to an amount which the Monetary Board considers inadequate to meet the prospective net demands on the Central Bank, or whenever the international reserve appears to be in imminent danger of falling to such a level, or whenever the international reserve is falling as a result of payments or remittances abroad which, in the opinion of the Monetary Board are contrary to the national welfare, the Monetary Board shall take such remedial measures as are appropriate and within the powers granted to the Monetary Board and the Central Bank.

Section 70 further states:

If the resultant actions fail to check the deterioration of the reserve position of the Central Bank, or if the deterioration cannot be checked except by chronic restrictions on exchange and trade transactions or by sacrifice of the domestic objective of a high level of production, employment and real income, the Monetary Board shall propose to the President such additional action as it deems necessary to restore equilibrium in the international balance of payments of the Philippines.[8]

The chronic budgetary crises of the early postwar period were reflected in the provisions of the Central Bank Act limiting access of the government to the lending facilities of the Central Bank. The act provides that direct loans to the government and its political subdivisions be limited to short-term advances for the purpose of

[8] The situation envisaged in Sec. 70 is that of a fundamental conflict between the objectives of domestic and international monetary stability that might require consideration of revaluation of the peso. The procedure for changing the par value of the peso is covered in Sec. 49: "The par value shall not be altered except . . . when the existing par value would make impossible the achievement and maintenance of a high level of production, employment and real income without: (1) The depletion of the international reserve of the Central Bank; or (2) The chronic use of restrictions on the convertibility of the peso into foreign currencies or on the transferability abroad of funds from the Philippines; or (3) undue Government intervention in, or restriction of, the international flow of goods and services."

covering seasonal gaps between revenues and expenditures (Section 95). Such advances have to be repaid before the end of the first quarter following termination of the fiscal year, and they are limited in amount to 15 per cent of the estimated income of the government for the current year. In addition, the act authorized special direct developmental advances to the government until June 30, 1951, not to exceed ₱200 million (Section 137).

The Central Bank Act also established the responsibility of the Bank to "endeavor to control any expansion or contraction in the money supply, or any rise or fall in prices, which in the opinion of the Board is prejudicial to the attainment or maintenance of a high level of production, employment and real income" (Section 64).[9]

To meet the far-reaching responsibilities assigned it, the bank was expected to rely on traditional instruments of Central Bank policy. In order to maintain convertibility of the peso, the Central Bank is required to buy any quantity of convertible foreign exchange offered to it, and sell any quantity demanded from it (Section 73). This responsibility is limited by the provision in Section 74 that

in order to protect the international reserve of the Central Bank during an exchange crisis and to give the Monetary Board and the Government time in which to take constructive measures to combat the crisis, the Monetary Board with the concurrence of at least five of its members and with the approval of the President of the Philippines may temporarily suspend or restrict sales of exchange by the Central Bank and may subject all transactions in gold and foreign exchange to license by the Central Bank.[10]

The Central Bank may grant loans with maturities up to 180 days to commercial banks against paper related to commercial loans and up to 270 days against paper related to production and processing

[9] The Central Bank Act singled out money supply and the cost of living as the appropriate measures of domestic stability (Sec. 66). A percentage change in the money supply (currency in circulation plus demand deposits) of more than 15 per cent over any twelve-month period or an increase of over 10 per cent in the cost of living index obligates the Monetary Board to submit to the President a report on the situation. If the movements are considered "abnormal," remedial measures by the Monetary Board are mandatory.

[10] The U.S. advisors who participated in drafting the Central Bank Act observed: "It is unlikely that this authority will be exercised within the foreseeable future because of the favorable balance of payments and the extraordinarily high level of the international reserve." This observation was made less than six months before the Philippines resorted to exchange controls. Cf. Grove and Exter, *op. cit.*, p. 945.

loans (Section 87). The bank may in addition make advances up to 180 days against various types of securities including government obligations of less than ten years' maturity.

While the Central Bank is authorized to engage in open market operations, the act recognized that such a function must await development of a market for government securities. To develop such a market the Central Bank is given charge of the marketing of all government securities and the administration of a "Securities Stabilization Fund" capitalized at ₱2 million, which is to be utilized to promote private investment in government securities by "increasing their liquidity and stabilizing their value" (Sections 122–126).

The authority of the Central Bank over the reserve requirements of banks includes a number of novel features (Sections 100–107). The Monetary Board may prescribe reserve ratios from 10 to 50 per cent against demand deposits and from 5 to 25 per cent against time and savings deposits. Moreover, in periods of inflation the board may prescribe ratios up to 100 per cent against any future increase in the deposits of each bank.[11] Finally, although required reserves ordinarily have to be held in the form of non-interest-bearing deposits with the Central Bank, the Monetary Board may authorize maintenance of part of the required reserves in other assets, e.g., government securities or foreign exchange. Such authority "could be of considerable value in accustoming banks to invest in Government obligations."[12]

In addition to the quantitative controls over bank credit, the Central Bank is endowed with an extensive arsenal of selective credit controls including authority to (a) regulate interest rates on different types of credit, (b) establish maximum maturities for bank loans and investments and prescribe the kind and amount of security to be required against various types of loans, (c) place ceilings on the amount of bank loans and investments, or certain categories thereof, or place time limits on the rate of increase of such assets, (d) prescribe minimum ratios which the capital and surplus of banks bear to the volume of their assets or to specific categories thereof, and (e) prescribe minimum cash margins for the opening of letters of credit and relate the size of the required margin to the nature of the transactions to be financed (Sections 108–113).

[11] Whenever the use of such special authority results in required reserves in excess of 50 per cent of the demand deposits or in excess of 25 per cent of time and savings deposits, the Central Bank must pay interest on the excess.

[12] Grove and Exter, *op. cit.*, p. 948.

Although the Central Bank Act created an institution suited to the needs of Philippine economic development, it could hardly be expected to eradicate the fundamental economic problems that have characterized the postwar period. Monetary policy has been increasingly dominated by the related problems of management of the international reserve and of financing government expenditures in excess of revenues.[13]

At the end of 1945 the international reserve amounted to $647 million; by the end of 1948 the international reserve had declined to $420 million. During 1949 the rate of decline accelerated, and by December 8 the reserve had declined to $251 million. This decline occurred in spite of controls regulating imports of nonessential and luxury articles.[14] To meet the crisis in the international reserve the Monetary Board on November 17, 1949, issued a regulation requiring a cash deposit of 80 per cent on all letters of credit to purchase luxuries and nonessential commodities.[15] On December 9 a further step was taken when the Monetary Board imposed controls on all gold and foreign exchange transactions.[16] To administer controls on foreign exchange, the Exchange Control Office of the Central Bank was organized.

During its first year of operations the Central Bank provided substantial amounts of credit to the government to finance various government expenditures as authorized under Section 137 of the Central Bank Act. On February 4, 1949, the board passed a resolution that ₱115 million would be made available during 1949. In addition to the "extraordinary advances" provided by Section 137, Section 95 provided that the bank could grant short-term advances to the government. As of December 31, 1949, the maximum permissible amount, approximately ₱37 million, had been loaned to the government.

[13] The preoccupation of the Central Bank with management of the international reserve was anticipated in 1948 by the authors of the legislation: "It would be folly to believe that the Central Bank can fully insulate the Philippine economy from fluctuations in world demand for the raw material exports on which so large a part of the Philippine level of consumption depends. Nevertheless, the impact of world economic fluctuations, particularly those of brief duration, can be cushioned by appropriate central bank policy. The fulfillment of this compensating function will undoubtedly occupy a permanent place in the Bank's activities" (*ibid.*, p. 949).

[14] Republic Act No. 330 of July 15, 1948.

[15] Central Bank Circular No. 19.

[16] Central Bank Circular No. 20. Central Bank Circular No. 21 of Jan. 19, 1950, extended Central Bank control to gold transactions.

In 1949 the expansion in the money supply resulting from government expenditures covered by Central Bank advances and the credit extended to financial institutions of the government was more than offset by the contraction resulting from the drawing down of the international reserve. An unprecedented import surplus and substantial declines in prices of imports and exports contributed to steady decline in Philippine prices (Table 42).

A major turning point in the evolution of Philippine monetary policy occurred during 1950 and 1951. Instruments of control over foreign exchange payments and the international reserve had been developed during the first year and a half of the bank's operation. With the outbreak of hostilities in Korea, Philippine export prices increased steadily from an index of 208 for the first half of 1950 to 240 in the second half of 1950 and 253 in the first half of 1951. Improvement in export prices was accompanied by an expanded volume of exports, which increased from an index of 90 in the first half of 1950 to 109 in the last half and 126 in the first half of 1951. As a result, export proceeds expanded rapidly to take up a large part of the anticipated decline in United States government expenditures resulting from the scheduled termination of war damage payments.

Foreign exchange prices of imports rose steadily during the last half of 1950 and the first half of 1951 to a peak in August 1951. The increase, however, did not entirely wipe out the declines of the 1949 recession, as the unit value index for imports in both 1950 and 1951 was below 1949 levels. The system of controls was applied with such strictness that outlays for imports in 1950 were reduced to 63 per cent of the 1949 level. As a result of these developments, the international reserve increased rapidly after June 1950 and reached a peak of $391 million in May 1951 as compared to the low point of $251 million in December 1949. The excess of foreign exchange receipts over payments was, of course, financed by an increase in the money supply. Filipino recipients of foreign exchange were required by law to surrender their foreign exchange receipts in exchange for pesos.

The budgetary deficits of the central government continued during 1950 and the first half of 1951. The budgetary deficit of the national government for the fiscal year 1949–50 was ₱150 million and for 1950–51 ₱13 million. In 1950 the public debt rose by ₱181 million, an increase of 26 per cent.

Table 42. Money supply and its origin [a]
(₱ million or equivalent)

| End of period | Money supply | | | International reserve | Domestic credits [b] | | Nonmoney supply deposits | Miscellaneous accounts of banking system [c] |
	Currency in circulation	Demand deposits	Total		Government	Private sector		
1946	539	401	940	885		349	250	59
1947	558	457	1,015	907		558	316	65
1948	576	618	1,194	840		690	302	61
1949	570	466	1,035	520	240	574	370	(74)
1950	675	554	1,229	712	327	571	453	(71)
1951	645	516	1,160	608	354	760	591	(35)
1952	630	569	1,198	612	380	762	540	13
1953	666	558	1,224	592	393	848	572	36
1954	677	550	1,227	545	406	939	619	49
1955	670	666	1,336	418	653	1,106	735	107
1956	719	780	1,499	449	828	1,254	893	143
1957	781	817	1,598	280	1,008	1,513	928	279
1958	818	920	1,738	291	1,220	1,589	1,050	329

[a] Central Bank, *Statistical Bulletin*, vol. 10 (Dec. 1958). Prior to 1950 the accounts satisfy the "monetary equation" only approximately.
[b] Not including Central Bank credit extended to commercial banks.
[c] Net liabilities and capital accounts balance. ( ) indicates net asset accounts balance.

Confronted by these developments the Monetary Board seems to have been torn between the desire to take advantage of the export boom and strict import controls to accumulate foreign exchange and on the other hand to meet its responsibilities for domestic monetary stability.[17]

The freedom of action of the Central Bank was limited by the financial situation of the national government and by its securities stabilization function. The Monetary Board could not refuse credit to the government, and during 1951 the bank's holdings of government securities increased by ₱84 million. On the other hand, the immature market for government securities and the state of the government's credit in the face of the Huk and budgetary crises made open market operations out of the question. Regulation of bank credit through the use of rediscount rates was handicapped by the inflow of foreign exchange, which had improved the reserve position of the commercial banks. Excess bank reserves increased from 8 to over 18 per cent of total deposit liabilities in the last half of 1950.

Initially, the Monetary Board resorted to moral suasion. The Rehabilitation Finance Corporation was enjoined to limit its loan operations to projects included in the development program of the government, and commercial banks were requested to limit real estate and consumption loans and to divert more of their credit operations to production. Finally, the Monetary Board resorted to liberalization of imports. Although the board had certified to the Import Control Commission some $92.2 million of foreign exchange for allocation to importers in the last half of 1950, on September 25, 1950, an additional $25.8 million was certified for the last quarter of 1950. Furthermore, on December 20, 1950, the board recommended, and the President approved, the unrestricted importation of several essential items.

Inflationary pressures reached a peak in the first half of 1951. On April 5 and May 11 the President, following a recommendation of the Monetary Board, authorized virtually unlimited importation of some nineteen groups of essential commodities then under restriction. The total available exchange certified for importation amounted to approximately $360 million in the second quarter of 1951.

[17] Restriction of import quantities drove the domestic wholesale price index for imports from 100 for 1949 to a peak of 163 in May 1951. It should be remembered that 1950 was the year which witnessed the maximum effort by the Huks, as well as the deterioration of the fiscal situation which led to the dispatch of the Bell Mission by the United States.

The credit extended by commercial banks to importers sharply reduced bank liquidity. The level of excess reserves, which had reached a peak in October 1950 of 18 per cent of total deposits, was reduced to 10 per cent in March 1951 and to approximately 1 per cent by July. As the demands of importers on commercial bank credit began to strain the resources of banks, the Central Bank extended credit to the commercial banks. During the first eight months of 1951 such advances amounted to ₱59 million.

The liberalization of imports coincided with a decline in foreign exchange receipts from the peak levels of the first quarter of 1951. Substantial foreign exchange deficits reduced the international reserve from the peak level of April 1951, and largely as a result of the reappearance of a large import surplus the Philippine money supply was reduced from ₱1,292 million in April 1951 to ₱1,160 at the end of December.

The extreme fluctuations in external demand conditions, foreign exchange reserves, money supply, and price levels during 1950 and 1951 caused the Monetary Board to seek a nondiscretionary formula under which the international reserve might be "managed." Such a formula would permit the Monetary Board to escape the onus for discretionary fluctuations in quantities of imports and import prices such as occurred during the eighteen months following June 1950. The first severe challenge of the stabilizing capacities of the new managed currency system can hardly be said to have been met successfully. The desire to build up the depleted international reserve delayed liberalization of imports beyond the first quarter of 1951, and as a result Philippine price movements were undoubtedly more extreme than they should have been.[18] In defense of the Monetary Board it should be remarked that the "bust-to-boom-to-bust" cycle also occurred in Indonesia and Malaya, and in Malaya a modified exchange reserve standard was in effect.[19]

[18] The minority report of the Central Bank Survey Commission concluded: "It appears, therefore, that the monetary inflation which began during the second half of 1950 was more an effect of the drastic curtailment in imports and only to a minor extent a result of the boom in world prices following the outbreak of the Korean War" (*Final Report and Recommendations* [*Minority Report*]).

[19] A number of managed currency systems of Western Europe were guilty of equal mismanagement of international reserves during the Korean boom. The United Kingdom, which consumed raw material inventories during the last half of 1950 and then had to replace stocks at peak world prices in the first half of 1951, is a case in point.

The traumatic experiences of the Monetary Board during 1950 and 1951 were reflected in a new formula for the management of the international reserve. The Joint Philippine-American Finance Commission had recommended that a conservative international reserve level be established as the criterion for exchange management policy. The Monetary Board established the amount of $300 million as the minimum safe level.[20]

The ensuing three years of the Quirino administration were characterized by balanced budgets, internal price stability, and minor fluctuations of the international reserve around the so-called minimum safe level of $300 million. Under these circumstances the Monetary Board and the Central Bank were in a favorable position to develop and strengthen the system of financial institutions and techniques of control. During the three years ending December 31, 1953, the money supply was stable, although domestic credits of the banking system expanded from ₱898 million to ₱1,240 million, an increase of 38 per cent. The stability of the money supply in the face of a rapid expansion in domestic credits was made possible by increases in the nonmoney supply deposits of the banking system and limited drawings on the international reserve.

The modest monetary expansion in the period of fiscal responsibility and price stability facilitated a rewarding increase in national income, which grew from ₱5,662 million at the end of 1949 to ₱7,234 million at the end of 1953, a rise of 25 per cent. During this same period export earnings expanded from ₱508 million to ₱808 million, an increase of 59 per cent.

The remaining years of the Quirino administration, 1951–1953, witnessed rapid expansion in banking facilities. Four commercial banks and two savings and mortgage banks were added, bringing the total number of banks in operation to nineteen (fifteen commercial banks, eleven domestically incorporated, and four branches of foreign banks). City and provincial branches and agencies of banks increased from 86 to 124. In addition, nineteen Rural Banks had been established by

[20] In its annual review and recommendations for 1953 it stated: "The international reserve fluctuated within a narrow range at the $300 million mark which is considered sufficient to satisfy the essential requirements for consumer goods and for development, taking into account current trends in foreign receipts and payments as well as the improved pattern of the national product" (Central Bank, *Fifth Annual Report, 1953*, p. 3). On p. 107 of the same report acceptance by the Monetary Board of such a guide to policy is reiterated.

the end of 1953 under legislation approved on June 20, 1952. The rural banks, together with 102 Farmers' Co-operative Marketing Associations showed great promise of relieving a chronic credit shortage in agricultural production for the domestic market.

Even more important than the expansion of banking and credit facilities was the development of the Central Bank and its Monetary Board as effective institutions for the promotion of Philippine economic stability and development. These were formative years for the Central Bank, which had opened for business in January 1949. The conservative restraints on access by the government to the bank's credit resources were strictly observed up to the end of 1953. Under the vigorous leadership of Miguel Cuaderno, who resigned as Secretary of Finance to become governor of the bank, the Monetary Board and the Central Bank made an important contribution to the rapid improvement in the Philippine economic environment. In contrast to the experience of many less-developed countries in the postwar period, the integrity and autonomy of the Central Bank were not seriously questioned during the Quirino administration.

The advent of the Magsaysay administration was followed by far-reaching changes in monetary policy. In his campaign for the Presidency of the Philippines, Ramon Magsaysay was highly critical of the failure of the Philippine economy to provide rewarding job opportunities. He promised that, if elected, the solution of the problem of unemployment would be a principal objective of economic policy. Shortly after taking office, in an address at Far Eastern University on March 20, 1954, he outlined the basic economic policies of his administration. Here again he affirmed that the criterion of economic policy was to be reduction of unemployment—which was estimated at approximately one-half of the Philippine labor force.[21]

President Magsaysay outlined a Five-Year Economic Development Plan which he estimated would create 1.7 million jobs and require ₱800 million of investment annually, public investment providing 44 per cent of the total. The President estimated that the bulk of the required government investment would be provided out of tax revenues and other receipts and the remainder by ₱600 million of public borrowing over the five years of the Plan.

To carry out such a program of development, the Philippine Congress in regular session enacted Republic Act No. 1000 of June 12,

[21] *Manila Bulletin*, March 22, 1954, p. 10.

1954, which authorized the President to issue up to ₱1,000 million of bonds to "finance public works and self-liquidating projects for economic development." Inasmuch as only a small market for Philippine Government bonds existed outside the banking system (i.e., the Central Bank), this act represented a radical departure from earlier monetary and fiscal policies.[22]

The essential change involved in Republic Act No. 1000 was to introduce a capital budget to be financed by sales of government securities to provide a high level of developmental expenditures and social investment.[23] In effect it was planned that the national budget would be unbalanced for the next five years to the extent of the proceeds of the ₱1 billion bond issue provided in Republic Act No. 1000.

At the time of the passage of Republic Act No. 1000 there was considerable impatience in the Philippines with the conservative monetary and fiscal policies of the previous three years. This restlessness was particularly evident in the Nacionalista party, which tended to attribute excessive conservatism to the Bell Mission report and the influence of American officialdom exerted through the economic aid agency and PHILCUSA. The economic stability of the previous four years was widely interpreted as evidence of the capacity of the Philippine economy to absorb inflationary increases in credit without undue impact on money incomes, prices, or external payments. The belief was widespread that the fiscal and monetary conservatism of the Quirino administration had been unnecessary and unwise and that an opportunity to accelerate economic growth through deficit finance existed.[24]

Unbalancing the budget involved the calculated risk that the increased income generated in the economy by the increment of government expenditure would be absorbed by increases in output, increased savings, and increased foreign exchange payments. Subsequent events amply demonstrated that a substantial part of the pressure was ex-

[22] The Central Bank Act authorizes the bank to engage in open market operations in government securities (Sec. 97). This was interpreted as adequate authorization for Central Bank acquisition of securities issued under Republic Act No. 1000.

[23] The Revised Budget Act of 1954, Republic Act No. 992 of June 4, 1954, provides (Sec. 8) that the annual budget be divided into (a) current operating expenditures and (b) capital outlays. The act implies that extraordinary government receipts will be used to finance capital outlays (Sec. 13).

[24] Of course, the Congress which came under Nacionalista control in the elections of November 1951 was inclined to make a minimum response to the efforts of the Liberal administration to provide economic leadership.

erted on the balance of payments. This is not surprising in view of the high foreign exchange component of Philippine investment and the strong desire on the part of income recipients to use increments of income to purchase goods and services abroad.

Republic Act No. 1000 presented formidable problems to the Central Bank and the Monetary Board. In the absence of alternative markets for the government bonds, the issues provided in the law tended to end up in the portfolio of the Central Bank, and in the process the commercial banks acquired reserves that made possible a rapid expansion of private credit. The increase in expenditures by government and business generated increases in incomes, which impinged directly on the balance of payments. In effect, the Central Bank tended to lose control over the reserves of the commercial banks and necessarily became preoccupied with the problem of managing the international reserve.

Management of the international reserve was complicated by growing pressure to change the unrealistic peso exchange rate. Philippine export producers and exporters became increasingly aware that the exchange rate realized from their export proceeds (which legally must be surrendered to the Central Bank at the official rate) was quite unfavorable as compared to the effective rate of exchange realized by importers. The interest of producer-exporters in a realistic exchange parity was reinforced by widespread disillusionment with import and exchange controls resulting from mismanagement and well-publicized anomalies in their administration.

A violent controversy over monetary and exchange rate policy took place during 1955 in the course of which the Central Bank came under heavy attack. The virulence of the controversy was such that the integrity of the Central Bank and the Monetary Board was a major issue, and public confidence in these institutions declined.[25] Although Governor Cuaderno was retained in office by President Magsaysay and his principal opponents were forced out of the government, the independence and autonomy of the Central Bank were jeopardized.

Distracted by the necessity to battle for its independent existence, the Monetary Board and the Central Bank were not in a position to intensify exchange and import controls as was necessary to main-

[25] For a detailed account of this controversy, see Golay, "The Philippine Monetary Policy Debate," 253–264.

tain the international reserve at the "minimum safe level of $300 million." Foreign exchange reserves declined steadily during 1954 and 1955 from $296 million at the end of 1953 to $209 million at the end of 1955.

Issues of government bonds for developmental purposes under Republic Act No. 1000 during 1954–1955 amounted to ₱368 million. Of this amount, the Central Bank acquired ₱166 million, while holdings of other banks increased by ₱138 million, leaving some ₱64 million to be absorbed outside the banking system. The net increase in Central Bank credit to ₱158 million provided the banking system with reserves that supported an increase of ₱356 million in the domestic credits of other banks. The increase in the money supply was a relatively modest ₱112 million because the increase in bank credits of ₱514 million was largely offset by drawing down the international reserve by the equivalent of ₱174 million and by the increase in non-money supply deposits of banks of ₱162 million.

Once the monetary policy controversy of 1954–1955 was settled in favor of the Monetary Board and Governor Cuaderno, the Central Bank was in a position to re-establish some measure of control over the banking and credit system and to prevent further decline in the international reserve. Nineteen fifty-six proved to be a year of stability and retrenchment. Although issues of Republic Act No. 1000 securities increased by ₱260 million, monetary pressures were satisfactorily contained. Central Bank credit increased by ₱57 million, of which ₱55 million was accounted for by government securities. Credit expansion by other banks amounted to ₱260 million, of which ₱114 million represented increased holdings of government securities. Inasmuch as issues of developmental bonds amounted to ₱260 million, it is evident that nonbanking holders increased their holdings by approximately ₱90 million.[26] The money supply increased by ₱113 million, while the international reserve was slowly built up to $225 million.

The year 1957 produced monetary developments which contrasted sharply with those of 1956. After the death of Magsaysay in March 1957 Vice-President Garcia assumed the Presidency, with a presidential election scheduled for November. Political developments led

[26] The revitalized Government Service Insurance System (GSIS) as well as private insurance reserves provided an increasing market for government security issues.

to abandonment of the 1956 policy of retrenchment, tight credit, and stringent foreign exchange allocations. Issues of developmental bonds amounted to ₱160 million. However, Central Bank holdings of government securities increased by ₱334 million as commercial banks rapidly reduced their holdings by ₱218 million.

Expansion of Central Bank credit of ₱372 million accounted for the major part of the expansion of domestic credit of ₱429 million (Table 43). The principal result of the credit operations of commercial

Table 43. Domestic credits classified by origin [a]
(₱ million)

	Central bank		Commercial banks		Selected financial institutions [b]	
	Public sector	Loans & advances to other banks	Public sector	Private sector	Public sector	Private sector
1949	148	40	92	574	22	214
1950	218	10	109	571	24	275
1951	264	42	90	760	25	324
1952	265	46	115	762	26	418
1953	260	19	133	848	26	497
1954	283	63	123	939	25	553
1955	418	13	235	1,106	27	626
1956	473	96	356	1,254	25	677
1957	841	81	168	1,513	25	801
1958	1,049	102	171	1,589	25	878

[a] Central Bank, *Statistical Bulletin,* vol. 10 (Dec. 1958), tables 13, 14, and 19.
[b] Including Development Bank of the Philippines (formerly Rehabilitation Finance Corporation), Agricultural Credit and Co-operative Financing Administration, Government Service Insurance System, private insurance companies, and pawnshops operating in Manila and suburbs.

banks was to expand their loans and discounts while they reduced their holdings of government securities. The money supply increased by ₱99 million. This moderate increase in the face of the rapid expansion in Central Bank credit was possible because of a drawing down of the international reserve by $169 million and a substantial increase in the nonmoney supply deposits and the miscellaneous accounts of the banking system.

The failure to maintain the previous year's stringent exchange controls was undoubtedly attributable to the election in the fall of 1957. Garcia used all his executive powers over budgetary expenditures, bank credit, and exchange allocation to win the Presidency in his own right and to establish himself as leader of the Nacionalista party. The extent of fiscal irresponsibility in 1957 and 1958 is measured by the budgetary deficit for the fiscal year ending June 30, 1958, which amounted to ₱370 million. To finance this deficit required a 73 per cent increase in net credit extended to the government by the banking system to bring the total to ₱884 million. This followed a 37 per cent increase during the 1956–57 fiscal year.

The heaviest part of the fiscal year 1957–58 deficit was incurred in the last half of 1957 when net credit extended to the government by the banking system totaled ₱254 million. At the same time the private sector made heavy demands on bank credit, increasing borrowings by ₱121 million. Inflationary pressures were allowed to exert their main force on the balance of payments, with the result that the international reserve declined by $172 million in the last half of 1957. At the end of 1957 the net gold and foreign exchange holdings of the Central Bank were reduced to a mere $31 million, a very thin cushion compared with the reserve at the end of the Quirino administration.[27]

After the election, the government and the Central Bank turned to the problem of monetary instability, and an "austerity" program was announced. Import allocations were slashed to conserve foreign exchange, and advance deposit requirements for import letters of credit were imposed. These measures came under strong attack as being too harsh, and relaxation began almost as soon as they took effect. Imports were, however, reduced from ₱613 million in the last half of 1957 to ₱567 million in the first half of 1958. Moreover, bank credit to the private sector fell by ₱74 million while nonmonetary deposits rose by ₱47 million.

Deficit financing by the government continued to be heavy, and net bank borrowings and the use of cash balances by the government rose by ₱115 million in the first half of 1958. Commercial banks continued to liquidate their holdings of government securities and in the process built up their holdings of cash and deposits with the Central Bank by ₱140 million. They were therefore in a good position to resume expansion of credit.

The national government budget for fiscal year 1958–59 provided

[27] The reserve of gold and dollars against the note issue declined from 39 per cent at the end of 1956 to 8 per cent at the end of 1957.

for expenditures of ₱1,347 million with only ₱1,017 of actual revenue. The Budget Commissioner later announced substantial reduction in both estimated expenditures and estimated revenues, but a budget deficit of between ₱150 million and ₱200 million could be anticipated.

Although the austerity program established minimum control over external disequilibrium, the government resumed an earlier policy of seeking *ad hoc* balance of payments assistance. The government counted heavily on obtaining large-scale credits abroad that would help finance the balance of payments deficit and offset the inflationary impact of fiscal operations. Credits or promises of credits were obtained by President Garcia and Governor Cuaderno on visits to the United States and Japan during 1958. These credits did not contribute disposable foreign exchange but were tied to specific projects.[28] In March of 1959 a special three-man mission was dispatched from the International Monetary Fund to the Philippines and it was hoped that as a result of this mission the Philippines would be permitted to make further drawings on the Philippine IMF quota, which was increased in the fall of 1958.

The closely related problems of management of the international reserve and financing of government deficits have dominated Philippine monetary policy throughout the postwar period. The power of the Monetary Board to develop techniques of credit control have been circumscribed by the external disequilibrium, and quantitative credit control has tended to play a minor role. With the exception of a brief period in the summer of 1951, commercial banks have consistently held substantial amounts of excess reserves plus very substantial amounts of potential reserves (Table 44).[29]

In the absence of ability to utilize quantitative credit controls, the Monetary Board has been confined to selective credit controls, and there have been a number of significant developments in this area. The first selective credit control order—Central Bank Circular No. 19 of November 17, 1949—required a cash deposit of 80 per cent on all letters of credit for an extensive list of less essential and luxury

[28] The only significant foreign exchange windfall that materialized in 1958 and 1959 was the appropriation by the U.S. Congress of $24 million to compensate the Philippines for the "loss" on peso currency reserves sustained in 1934 when the dollar was devalued.

[29] There has never been a time when the amount of excess plus potential reserves of the commercial banks has not substantially exceeded the amount of required reserves.

234 *The Philippines*

imports. Beginning November 13, 1951, the Monetary Board required that a reserve of 70 per cent of letters of credit outstanding be maintained by banks in foreign exchange, vault cash, excess reserves, and potential reserves. This credit policy continued with minor changes during 1950–1953. In the latter part of 1953, a presidential election year in the Philippines and one of recession in the United States, the

Table 44. Available, required, excess, and potential reserves
of commercial banks [a]
(₱ million)

End of year	Available reserves	Required reserves	Excess reserves	Potential reserves	Outstanding bank borrowings from Central Bank	Government debt holdings of Central Bank [b]
1949	144	93	51	154	40	148
1950	244	116	129	170	10	218
1951	116	97	19	147	42	264
1952	148	108	40	165	46	265
1953	148	114	34	139	19	260
1954	166	118	48	158	63	283
1955	189	137	52	265	13	418
1956	236	164	73	347	96	473
1957	206	164	42	177	81	841
1958	330	174	155	123	102	1,049

[a] Central Bank, *Tenth Annual Report, 1958.*

[b] Including loans, advances, and securities of local governments, government corporations, and public authorities but not including loans and advances to the Philippine National Bank.

Monetary Board liberalized exchange allocations and revoked Circular No. 19 requiring cash deposits against letters of credit; [30] in early 1954 it lowered the rediscount rate from 2 to 1.5 per cent.

From the beginning of the Magsaysay administration to November 1957, the Central Bank continued practically unchanged a credit policy which it described as "active ease." [31]

By the time of the November 1957 election economic instability

[30] Central Bank Circular No. 47 of Oct. 15, 1953.

[31] Central Bank, *Seventh Annual Report, 1955,* p. 62: "In the interest of a faster rate of economic development, a credit policy of active ease was continued. . . . The rediscount rate of 1½ per cent, which was adopted early in 1954 and is the lowest in the world today, was maintained to facilitate bank borrowings and thereby bolster domestic financing."

had progressed to the point where action was imperative.[32] The major change in credit policy resulted from Central Bank Circular No. 79 of December 9, 1957, which required a cash deposit of 100 per cent against letters of credit for imports of "decontrolled, essential consumer goods and essential and semiessential producers goods," 200 per cent against the import of "semiessential consumer goods and nonessential producers goods," plus a marginal requirement of 25 to 50 per cent on "capital goods" and "essential producer raw materials." Austerity measures were relaxed somewhat administratively in 1958, but selective credit and import controls were enforced to the extent necessary to maintain a precarious external balance.

During 1954–1957 the Philippines pursued a policy of aggressive monetary expansion. The absorption by the Philippine economy of about half of the proceeds of bond issues under Republic Act No. 1000 proved to be relatively destabilizing, and by the end of 1957 the safe international reserve of $300 million inherited from the Quirino administration had been dissipated. Although a precarious external balance was re-established in 1958, political controversy over economic policy proposals continues unabated. Legislation enacted in mid-1959 strongly suggests that the existing political stalemate reflected in exchange rate, exchange control, and commercial policies will maintain strong pressure on the capacity of the Central Bank to maintain internal stability.

Postwar Philippine monetary policy has been confronted by three basic, interdependent responsibilities: management of the international reserve, maintenance of domestic price stability, and provision of the credit requirements for economic expansion. The authorities cannot claim to have managed the international reserve with conspicuous success, but they certainly have been successful in fulfilling the other two responsibilities. Philippine prices have remained remarkably stable, and a rewarding expansion in output has been sustained. Moreover, large-scale deficit financing in recent years has enabled the government to participate in resource accumulation.

During the four years following 1949 the peso debt of the government at all levels virtually doubled from ₱467 million to ₱867 million

[32] Initial changes in credit policy were made on April 2, 1957, when the rediscount rate was raised from 1.5 to 2 per cent, and on Sept. 2, 1957, when the rediscount rate was raised to 4.5 per cent; and in addition a 100 per cent deposit against letters of credit for "non-essential" imports was established (Central Bank, *Ninth Annual Report, 1957*, pp. 113–115).

(Table 45). This increase was absorbed by the economy with no adverse consequences for domestic or international stability. Holdings of government debt by banking institutions increased by ₱153 million, but the proportion of the peso debt outstanding held by banking institutions declined from 51 per cent to 45 per cent. Most promising was the increase in holdings by institutional and private savers. Such holdings rose from ₱186 million to ₱448 million, and sales to the public accounted for three-quarters of the increase.

Table 45. Distribution of the peso public debt [a]
(₱ million)

End of period	1949	1953	1957	1958 [b]
Total domestic peso debt, national gov., gov. enterprises and local gov.	467	867	1,469	1,810
Central Bank	148	260	841	1,049
Commercial banks	92	133	175	171
Rehabilitation Finance Corporation	22	26	25	25
Government Service Insurance System	n.r.	63	105	n.a.
Postal savings	28	32	43	45
Social Security System	N.A.	N.A.	25	57
Private insurance companies	n.r.	n.r.	11	6
Other holdings	158	353	244	n.a.

[a] Central Bank, *Ninth Annual Report, 1957.*
[b] Central Bank, *Tenth Annual Report, 1958.*

In the four years following 1953 the government's peso debt increased to ₱1,469 million, a rise of ₱602 million. Holdings of government debt by banking institutions increased by ₱623 million, of which the Central Bank accounted for ₱581 million. The portion of the outstanding peso debt held by the banking system rose rapidly to 69 per cent. During this period the government had considerable success in tapping postal savings as well as the savings of both government and private insurance schemes. Government peso debt holdings of these institutions increased by ₱89 million. Less promising was the response of the public, whose holdings decreased by ₱98 million.

The shift in fiscal policy to deficit financing of developmental expenditures has complicated monetary policy. In recent years issues of government securities have gravitated to the portfolio of the Central Bank. In the four years following 1953 over five-sixths of the rapid increase in the peso debt was acquired by the Central Bank. While this development embodied great potential for domestic instability, expansion of commercial bank credit was relatively restrained, amounting to ₱639 million. At the same time excess and potential reserves of commercial banks increased from ₱173 million to ₱218 million.

Although the Central Bank has lost control over the reserve position of the commercial banking system, the economic significance of excess, and potential reserves should not be exaggerated. Because of exchange rate and commercial policies Filipino entrepreneurs prefer their loan proceeds in foreign exchange, and loan applications tend to be contingent upon exchange licensing. The capacity of banks to expand earning assets is not essentially a function of excess reserves but of the availability of foreign exchange. Under these circumstances Central Bank management of the international reserve is a pervasive, powerful technique of monetary control. Bank reserves can be provided by the Central Bank with minimum fears that multiple expansion of peso credits will result.[33] Also of major importance in recent years to Central Bank credit control has been the restraint established in Section 22 of the Banking Act, which provides that "the combined capital accounts of each commercial bank shall not be less than fifteen per cent (15%) of its total assets, excluding . . . cash on hand, amounts due from banks, . . . and evidences of indebtedness of the Republic of the Philippines and of the Central Bank. . . ." In recent years commercial bank ratios have tended to hover around the prescribed minimum and bank credit expansion has been restrained. On May 27, 1960, in Circular No. 108, the Central Bank, using its authority (R.A. No. 265, Section 113) to define "total assets" for purposes of Section 22, excluded "loans fully secured by hold-out on deposits; customers' liability acceptances covered by margin deposit for letters of credit; and bank premises, furniture and fixtures, depreciated" from total assets, thereby creating additional capacity for commercial bank credit expansion.

A second factor contributing to the Central Bank's capacity to maintain internal stability is the nature of the portfolio of earning assets of commercial banks. Bankers are traditionalists, and conventional asset ratios change slowly. Foreign trade and the agricultural sector have tended to decline in relative importance, but the changes

[33] The Central Bank has broad authority over the reserve requirements which the banks must observe. Reserve requirements, however, have not been changed since the Central Bank reserve requirements were first established on Jan. 10, 1949 at 18 per cent for demand deposits and 5 per cent for time and savings deposits (Central Bank Circular No. 2 of Jan. 3, 1949).

in the earning assets of commercial banks have not kept pace with the structural changes in the Philippine economy.[34]

A third important source of monetary control has been moral suasion by the Monetary Board. All the principal banking offices are located in Manila, and contact between the Central Bank and commercial banks is close. Central Bank influence is heightened by its dominant role in exchange and import control and the agent relationship of commercial banks.

Still another important aspect of the Central Bank's power to maintain internal monetary stability has been the remarkable growth of nonmoney supply deposits. For example, the increase in nonmoney supply deposits in the eight years from 1950 to 1957 amounted to ₱552 million, which was equivalent to almost one-third of the increase in domestic credits of the banking system, which was ₱1,685 million. In other words, almost one-third of the potential increase in the money supply has been offset by relatively immobilized deposits.[35]

During this period national government balances increased by ₱125 million, reflecting improvement in fiscal performance as well as necessary expansion in government working balances. A second source of increase in nonmonetary supply deposits has been the requirement of marginal deposits on import letters of credit. Such deposits accounted for ₱104 million of the increase. A third important source of increase has resulted from the stringent exchange controls on remittance of earnings of foreign investment. As of September 1958, blocked-peso earnings of foreign firms had reached a total of ₱342 million. Of this amount, ₱182 million had been reinvested in the Philippines, and the remainder was presumably being held in banks or in cash.[36] Postwar Philippine monetary stability has benefited from a considerable capacity to offset increases in domestic credits by "forced savings" of foreign investors in the form of blocked-peso accounts. The principal part of the remaining increase in nonmonetary supply deposits is probably accounted for by the normal growth in

[34] Commercial bankers are understandably reluctant to expand their longer-term manufacturing and agricultural credits. On the other hand, the credit needs of the postwar market industrialization in the Philippines have tended to be longer term.

[35] Including national government balances, savings deposits, time deposits, marginal deposits, and foreign currency demand deposits.

[36] *Manila Bulletin,* Aug. 7, 1959.

working balances of business during the past decade of rapid growth in national income.

Philippine monetary management has been relatively successful in maintaining internal stability while providing the credit requirements —both public and private—of rapid expansion. A number of developments will, however, limit the effectiveness of future monetary management. First, economic controversy has circumscribed the autonomy of the Monetary Board. During the Quirino administration the Central Bank was given a breathing spell to train staff, to acquire command over techniques of monetary control, and to establish public confidence, but the developments of the ensuing four years were traumatic for the Monetary Board and the Central Bank. The shift to deficit financing of development expenditures rapidly eroded Monetary Board autonomy. The virulent controversy over exchange rate policy in 1955 left the board politically insecure and suffering from some loss of public confidence. The Monetary Board was not permitted to rehabilitate the control system because the death of Magsaysay precipitated flagrant use of the spoils system in an effort to influence the 1957 election. When the election was over, minimum efforts to apply the necessary austerity were made.

Second, the loss of the foreign exchange cushion has seriously impaired the ability of the monetary authorities to continue postwar policies. The Philippines is reaping the whirlwind of unplanned, haphazard protection arising out of stringent exchange and import controls. The very high levels of protection resulting from exchange and import controls established strong incentives to invest in industries producing substitutes for those imports subject to greatest restriction. Initially, there was great enthusiasm for the industrialization which seemed to be following protection.[37] There has since been growing awareness that those industries most certain of viability tended to be ones using large quantities of imported raw materials, the finished products of which were subject to exclusion. Industrialization has resulted in firm and inflexible commitments on the part of the Central Bank to supply foreign exchange for imports of raw materials.

In the absence of effective policies to increase foreign exchange

[37] Miguel Cuaderno, "The Bell Trade Act and the Philippine Economy," *Pacific Affairs*, 25 (Dec. 1952), 324–325.

availability, foreign exchange earnings are unlikely to expand as rapidly as the demand for foreign exchange. It is quite evident that reduction of imports of such consumer goods as textiles, wheat flour, canned fish, and canned milk ultimately affects incentives and productivity, not to mention political stability. In the past the Philippines has chosen to draw down its international reserve rather than compromise the policy of subsidizing developmental investment. It is now necessary to find *ad hoc* supplies of foreign exchange or to intensify rationing of the available foreign exchange.

There is one additional question to consider. Would the price stability which has characterized the period since the end of 1953 have been possible without liquidation of the Philippine international reserve? Or, to put it another way, if exchange control had been intensified and if allocations of exchange to "new and necessary industries" had been limited, would the capital budget of the government have resulted in price inflation? It is obvious, of course, that the question cannot be answered categorically. The writer is of the opinion that the deficit financing incorporated in Republic Act No. 1000 could have been absorbed by the Philippine economy without significant price inflation in view of the steady expansion in production and real income which has characterized the postwar period. Dissipation of the international reserve was not the price of the unbalanced budget and price stability but was essentially the price of using foreign exchange allocations to promote industrialization. The Philippines has discovered that an overvalued peso permits the Philippine government to obtain command over resources indirectly when it could not raise and appropriate revenues.

In desperation the Philippines has resumed an earlier postwar policy of mendicancy, but with limited success. Current negotiations with the United States over financial claims of more-or-less credibility do not appear promising. If these negotiations produce a substantial amount of freely disposable foreign exchange, the foreign exchange cushion will be re-established. It is more likely that the government and the Monetary Board through some combination of tight exchange controls, smaller government deficits, and credit controls will re-establish a tolerable external balance. Such a prospect, bleak and unpromising, may be the only practicable alternative to vigorous policies to expand Philippine foreign exchange earnings.

· XI ·

Industrialization Policy

INDUSTRIALIZATION—expansion of the share of manufacturing in national product—is a dominant goal of Philippine society. Filipino elites are articulate in condemning the colonial economic policy maintained by the United States and the nature of their colonial economic development. From the beginning of self-government in 1916, and within the over-all restraint of American colonial policy, Filipinos have tried to use the economic powers of the state to initiate industrial development. The postwar period of independence has witnessed aggressive experimentation with policies and institutions designed to promote manufacturing and the emergence of Filipino entrepreneurship. Identification of the ramifications of industrialization policy is essential to understanding of the economic role assigned the state by Philippine society.

It is obvious that the totality of public policy influences the rate of industrialization of the economy and the inclusion of selected aspects of public policy in industrialization policy is more or less arbitrary. For the purposes of this analysis, industrialization policy is considered to include the following: first, the efforts of the state to engage directly in manufacturing and industrial activities in the role of entrepreneur or as provider of capital in combination with private entrepreneurship; second, the efforts of the state to develop func-

241

tionally specialized capital market institutions to allocate scarce credit and foreign exchange resources to industrial investment; third, the use of the powers of the state to manipulate the intensity of entrepreneurial incentives and concentrate income in profits; and fourth, those activities of the state which influence the amount of and the functional specialization of foreign investment in manufacturing.

Philippine industrialization policy attaches little or no priority to manufacturing for export. Philippine manufacturing is high cost for many reasons, and there are now few illusions about the ultimate maturation of infant industries. Such realism reflects, among other things, the competitive potential of Japan, China, Hong Kong, and other areas. For the foreseeable future Philippine industrialization policy seeks to reserve the domestic market for domestic producers and to enlarge the range of Philippine manufactures. There is relatively little emphasis on the processing of raw materials for export, and little or no progress has been made in this direction since the late interwar period.[1]

During the two decades following establishment of the Commonwealth government in 1935, the government created and operated a wide range of manufacturing and industrial enterprises. By the early 1950's the government was operating railroads, hotels, electric power, gas, and water works as well as directly producing coal, cement, steel, pulp and paper, and textiles and yarns and operating a shipyard and engineering shops. In addition, the government had substantial investments in firms manufacturing incandescent bulbs, fluorescent tubes, pulp and paper and in a domestic and international airline and it owned three ocean-going vessels which it leased to a Philippine shipping firm. Through a government-owned holding company the government was, or had been, engaged in the production of nails, lumber, footwear, sugar, textiles and yarns and in food preserving and packaging, and in addition it operated warehouses.[2] Although the extensive list of government industrial activities indicates persistent faith in the capacity of the government to participate directly in

[1] For example, exports of coconut oil, cordage, and refined sugar have not recovered to prewar levels. On the other hand, there have been minor increases in exports of glycerine, desiccated coconut, canned pineapples, lumber, and plywood.

[2] For a chronological list of government-owned and controlled corporations and business agencies, see Hartendorp, *History*, pp. 49–63.

industrialization, the results of this policy were such as to cause the policy to be radically changed beginning in 1954.

It will be recalled that the principal issue in Magsaysay's successful presidential campaign was corruption and inefficiency in government, and not the least charge was that of corruption, nepotism, and mismanagement of government business enterprises. Following the inauguration of Magsaysay in January 1954, the government initiated action to sell those manufacturing plants and other enterprises of the government in which private enterprise was interested and to liquidate public enterprises with a wide variety of price support, marketing, and land colonization functions. On January 15, 1954, the candid *Report on Government Corporations in the OEC Group* prepared by the Office of Economic Co-ordination was published.[3] The *Report* concluded:

The high incidence of political considerations and the "padrino" system in the appointment, promotion and tenure of office of officials and employees, and even in decisions affecting economic planning and implementation and corporate transactions, is the greatest single factor that, with far reaching chain reaction, destroys the morale and discipline of officials and employees, abets inefficiency and corruption, breeds discontent and labor strikes, is the root cause of abuses and heavy losses and waste of public funds and property, and contributes to the loss of the people's faith in government corporations.

[3] The government corporations in the Office of Economic Co-ordination group included the entrepreneurial activities of the government and were divided into:

"Group I—Corporations organized or over which the government acquired ownership or control, to serve as stimuli in vital sectors of the economy where private capital is incapable, unwilling, or hesitant to venture. Including: Cebu Portland Cement Company, Insular Sugar Refining Corporation, Manila Gas Corporation, Philippine Air Lines, National Shipyards and Steel Corporation, and Manila Hotel Company.

"Group II—Corporations organized or over which the government acquired ownership or control, for use as instruments in the prosecution of specific economic and social objectives. National Development Company [the first four enterprises in Group I were subsidiaries of the National Development Company], Government Service Insurance System, Manila Railroad Company, Metropolitan Water District, National Power Corporation, and Peoples Homesite and Housing Corporation.

"Group III—Service corporations organized and entrusted with functions involving the public interest and primarily governmental in character, and as such cannot realize profit from operation. Land Settlement and Development Corporation, National Rice and Corn Corporation, Philippine Sugar Institute, and Price Stabilization Corporation."

It has been repeatedly announced that government corporations are primarily designed as initial stimuli in vital sectors of the economy where private capital is incapable, unwilling or hesitant to venture, and that, except in cases involving the public interest for the protection of the masses, they are not intended to compete with private business or to engage directly in enterprises that ordinarily can well be left in the hands of private capital. This policy has not been adequately implemented in actual case levels. In consequence, certain government corporations, which are retained unduly in fields that should be open to private capital, become deterrents, instead of stimuli, to the full and rapid growth of certain industries. Resources critically needed for pioneering and development in other phases of the economy are, in effect, frozen in those corporations.

. . . Some projects and activities of government corporations involving the expenditure of huge sums of largely borrowed funds have fallen far short of their goals and failed to meet time schedules, resulting thereby in waste and misuse of public funds and properties. These projects and activities lack thorough planning and programming, competent management, direction and supervision, and are hampered by complicated administrative procedures and poor personnel selection and administration.[4]

With respect to the National Development Company, the government holding company for directly productive enterprises, the *Report* concludes:

NDC annual obligations on account of interest amount to ₱1.2 million, and for amortization, ₱2.5 million. The Company is saddled with considerable investments which do not even earn enough profits to cover administrative expenses. The financial structure of the NDC is in extremely precarious situation. NDC is hardened with large overhead and an inefficient management.

The textile and spinning mills, now the only principal enterprise of the NDC, have a high cost of production and can hardly compete with imported textiles. The fact that the government is now engaged in this business has discouraged private enterprise from investing in and developing a local textile industry.[5]

This bleak appraisal of the accomplishments of Philippine industrialization by direct public investment was followed by a reversal of policy. Recent years have witnessed slow but steady liquidation

[4] Pages 3–4.

[5] *Ibid.*, pp. 29–30. As of the end of 1954, paid-in capital and loans by government banks to the NDC totaled ₱54 million, but net worth amounted to only ₱35 million. By mid-1959 the net worth of the NDC had declined to ₱28 million. See *Philippines Free Press,* Feb. 6, 1960, p. 8.

of public enterprises of an entrepreneurial nature. The rate of transfer to private ownership has been limited by the slow appearance of private investors willing to take on the inept investments which prompted the *Report*.[6] It is present policy to limit government investment to public utilities—power, transportation, and the like—and to corporations with governmental functions such as land colonization, marketing, and price regulation. Government investment in electric power production and transportation facilities has tended to increase in recent years and can be expected to expand further using Japanese reparations and economic aid.

A second major industrialization policy has been the active promotion of capital market institutions to allocate scarce credit and foreign exchange resources for industrial purposes. The principal postwar source of industrial finance has been the Rehabilitation Finance Corporation created in late 1946.[7] The Rehabilitation Finance Corporation was authorized "to provide credit facilities for the rehabilitation and development of agriculture, commerce and industry, the reconstruction of property damaged by war, and the broadening and diversification of the national economy." In order to meet these responsibilities the RFC was initially capitalized at ₱300 million to be fully subscribed by the government. The initial government capital contribution was provided by withdrawal from the Treasury Certificate Fund of sums in excess of the legal reserve required for the fund [8] and appropriation of net proceeds from sales of surplus property.[9] In addition to the resources provided by the capital contribution of the Philippine government, the RFC was authorized to issue bonds, debentures, and other obligations up to an amount equivalent to the subscribed capital and surplus.

[6] Time will undoubtedly color the role of directly productive government enterprise in Philippine economic growth, and economists, so inclined, will attribute a dominant role to government investment and initiative. Available evidence suggests that, with few exceptions, government investment was inept and wasteful and that entrepreneurial initiative was probably retarded rather than promoted. The net worth of the National Development Company at the beginning of the Magsaysay administration (₱34.5 million) was less than 5 per cent of the value of the fixed assets of all large (with more than 20 employees) manufacturing establishments in 1956.

[7] Republic Act No. 85 of Oct. 29, 1946.

[8] Republic Act No. 86 of Oct. 29, 1946.

[9] Republic Act No. 87 of Oct. 29, 1946. Surplus property transfers were provided in Title II of the Philippine Rehabilitation Act, Public Law 370, 79th Cong., 2nd sess., April 3, 1946.

On June 14, 1958, Republic Act No. 2081 converted the Rehabilitation Finance Corporation into the Development Bank of the Philippines. The capital of the Development Bank of the Philippines (DBP) was increased to ₱500 million, the increase in capitalization to be provided by appropriation of "fifty per cent of the proceeds from the sale of [Japanese] reparations goods and services." The DBP is authorized to incur debt obligations equivalent to its subscribed capital and surplus. The law also provides that 25 per cent of the "investible funds" of the Government Service Insurance System and the Social Security System shall be invested in bonds of the DBP. Lending operations of the RFC-DBP expanded rapidly, and by the end of 1958 the loans outstanding totaled ₱463 million, of which ₱152 million were classified as industrial loans.

Philippine commercial banking—in the colonial tradition—has been relatively slow to increase its portfolio of industrial loans. The Central Bank has, however, provided considerable initiative in overcoming the traditional reluctance of commercial banks to make longer-term loans. The monetary policy of "active ease" following 1950 facilitated rapid expansion of commercial bank credit, including industrial loans. For example, in the three years ending December 31, 1957, industrial loans of commercial banks increased by ₱138 million to ₱220 million, accounting for 38 per cent of the increase in commercial bank credit outstanding over this period.

Because of the heavy import requirements of capital goods for industrialization, Philippine entrepreneurs desire to borrow, not pesos, but dollars. At the same time the chronic foreign exchange stringency severely limits the capacity of the Central Bank to allocate foreign exchange proceeds for such purposes. On the other hand, a number of sources of dollar credits in the United States—Export-Import Bank, Development Loan Fund, private commercial banks—are available for the specific purpose of financing imports of capital goods. Under the circumstances a number of institutions have been developed to facilitate the potential flow of foreign exchange loans to Philippine entrepreneurs.

The Central Bank has increasingly acted as intermediary between Philippine commercial banks and United States banks in arranging lines of dollar credit. The role of the Central Bank has been to guarantee that foreign exchange will be allocated as necessary to repay such credits. For example, in 1954 the Central Bank arranged credit lines of more than $60 million "to promote the production of export crops and to finance various industrial enterprises necessary to establishing a well-balanced economy." By the end of 1955 a total of $42.1 million of the credit lines had been used by eight Philippine commercial banks.[10]

During 1956 an additional $18 million of credit lines was used, and outstanding credit as of the end of the year amounted to $52.9 million. In September 1956 growing pressure on available foreign exchange led the Central Bank to suspend the availability of credit lines arranged with United States banks. During 1957 no new credits were extended, and outstanding credit was reduced by $30.6 million. Liquidation of such credits during 1957 undoubtedly brought home to the Monetary Board the threat to management of the international reserve inherent in this policy.[11]

Still another institution devised to promote Philippine industrialization is the Industrial Guarantee Loan Fund established in July 1952. Initial capital of ₱10 million was provided by United States aid counterpart funds (pesos) to be administered by the Central Bank in cooperation with the United States aid mission. It was planned to use the fund to guarantee loans made by commercial banks and other credit institutions for approved industrial projects, thus encouraging long-term lending by commercial banks to small and medium-sized industries. Commercial bank interest in the fund has developed slowly. This has been due to the excess liquidity of commercial banks and the greater profitability of short-term commercial lending as well as to the fact that the fund can guarantee only peso loans. Of the initial deposit in the fund, ₱8 million was allocated to the Rehabilitation Finance Corporation and the National Power Corporation.[12]

In connection with the Industrial Guarantee Loan Fund, there was established in February 1955 the Industrial Development Center (IDC), a joint project of the National Economic Council and the United States aid mission. The IDC not only screened applications for loan guarantees but, which was more important, was given control over the allocation of a line of credit created by the United States Export-Import Bank to make foreign exchange loans to approved

[10] Central Bank, *Seventh Annual Report, 1955,* p. 62.

[11] Cf. Central Bank, *Eighth Annual Report, 1956,* p. 127, and *Ninth Annual Report, 1957,* p. 120.

[12] U.S. Dept. of Commerce, Bur. of Foreign Commerce, *Investment in the Philippines,* p. 60.

Philippine applicants. During the first three years of IDC operations foreign exchange loans totaling $31.5 million were approved. Such loans included $10.5 million for textile manufacture, $6.3 million for plywood and veneer, $4.3 million for cement, and $2.2 million for paper products. The dollar loans have been supplemented by a total of ₱31.3 million of peso loans channeled through the special time deposit program of the Industrial Guarantee Loan Fund.[13]

While the Philippines has been aggressive in devising institutions for channeling peso and dollar credit to industrial uses, the most effective industrialization policy has been that of subsidization of "new and necessary industries." Subsidization has taken three forms: (a) tax remission, (b) high levels of protection, and (c) foreign exchange allocation.

The policy of subsidization by tax remission was initiated by Republic Act No. 35 of September 30, 1946, which provided: "Section 1. Any person, partnership, company, or corporation who or which shall engage in a new and necessary industry shall, for a period of four years from the date of the organization of such industry, be entitled to exemption from payment of all internal revenue taxes." During the early postwar period high levels of investment in the Philippines were sustained by United States war damage and other payments, and rehabilitation proceeded rapidly. As might be expected, such investment was made to restore prewar industries, and there was relatively little application of the "new and necessary industries" policy. In July of 1949 the Secretary of Finance clarified interpretation of the act and summarized accomplishments under the act:

The term "new" has been interpreted as referring to those industries which had not been commercially exploited in the Philippines before the War.

The term "necessary" would refer to industries which contribute to industrial and economic development.

To date, the President of the Philippines, under Republic Act No. 35, has approved exemptions from all internal revenue taxes directly payable by industries engaged in the local manufacture of plastic articles, steel windows, kitchen and household utensils, nails, etc.

[13] R.P., Industrial Development Center, *Third Anniversary Report, 1957* (Manila, 1958). As of June 30, 1958, loans amounting to $34.7 million had been extended from U.S. aid funds to 223 firms and individuals. Dollar loans accounted for over half of the total amount. In addition, under the Export-Import Bank line of credit loans totaling $18.7 million to 97 firms had been extended (R.P., NEC, *Joint P.I.–U.S. Economic Development Program* [Manila, 1958], p. 35).

Inasmuch as the Philippines is just entering the initial stage of its industrialization, it may be stated as a general proposition that a wide variety of industries or enterprises which may be established locally would fall within the scope of the exemption granted under the provision of Republic Act No. 35.[14]

The establishment of effective exchange and import controls in 1950 gave effect to the policy enunciated in Republic Act No. 35. By importing commodities in bulk for packaging or for some relatively minor final processing, a "new and necessary industry" would thereby be able to establish a priority for the purpose of exchange allocation which would not normally be available to such industry. The enhanced premium attached to classification as "new and necessary" led to an upsurge in applications followed by further clarification of the qualifications.[15]

The success of the policy led Congress in 1953 to write new legislation liberalizing the grant of tax exemption.[16] The new law provided for full exemption till the end of 1958, 90 per cent exemption in 1959, 75 per cent in 1960, 50 per cent in 1961, and 10 per cent in 1962, after which time tax exemption is terminated.

The circumstances in which tax exemption will be granted to an industry are listed as follows in Section 3:

(1) Where the establishment of the industry will contribute to the attainment of a stable and balanced national economy.

(2) Where the industry will operate on a commercial scale in conformity with up-to-date practices and will make its products available to the general public in quantities and at prices which will justify its operation with a reasonable degree of permanence.

(3) Where the imported raw materials represent a value not exceeding sixty per centum of the manufacturing cost plus reasonable selling and administrative expenses: Provided, That a grantee of tax exemption shall use materials of domestic origin, growth, or manufacture wherever the same are available in reasonable quantity and quality at reasonable prices.

Notwithstanding the provisions of paragraph (3) above, an industry may be classified as necessary: (a) if it is determined that a substantial portion of the imported raw materials may, as local industrialization and technological development advance, be available locally so as to enable the industry to utilize substantially greater quantities of domestic materials or if its products are used principally in the manufacture or preparation of

[14] *A.C.C. Journal,* 25 (Aug. 1949), 331.
[15] See Cuaderno, "The Bell Trade Act and the Philippine Economy."
[16] Republic Act No. 901 of June 20, 1953.

products of another industry or products intended for export; and (b) if the initial investment in machinery and equipment will be at least two hundred thousand pesos.[17]

The second major component of Philippine "new and necessary industry" policy has been the high levels of protection extended by the taxation of import values and stringent import controls. Levels of protection are analyzed in some detail in Chapter VII, and it will suffice at this point to summarize briefly. Levels of protection are, and have been, relatively high in the Philippines. The taxation of import values has traditionally provided half of the national government tax revenues. Although the composite "tariff" resulting from the jerry-built structure of excise taxation was essentially a revenue tariff, it embodied considerable protection. Since 1949, stringent import controls have provided high levels of protection for domestic production of import-competing commodities. Sharp divergence in indexes of prices of imported goods as compared to other prices indicates the over-all levels of protection arising from import controls. Moreover, maintenance of tight import controls has shifted foreign exchange allocations to "essential" imports. On the other hand, the least "essential" of imports are those which the "new and necessary industries" are capable of producing. Therefore the relative movement of indexes of prices of imported goods must inevitably understate the level of protection afforded "new and necessary" industries. Those imports denied foreign exchange allocation and presumably not imported would not appear in the index of import prices, yet protection established for domestic producers would be maximum.

The third component part of the "new and necessary industry" policy has been the use of the windfall arising out of peso overvaluation and import restriction to subsidize such industries. It was early recognized, after the imposition of effective exchange and import controls in 1950, that qualification as a "new and necessary industry" established a prior claim to foreign exchange to import "industrial raw materials."

By qualifying as a "new and necessary industry" the new firm becomes entitled to protection from competing imports. Moreover, to

[17] Detailed regulations for the application of Republic Act No. 901 were issued by the Department of Finance on Aug. 20, 1953. These regulations, with legal analysis of the policy, are to be found in American Chamber of Commerce of the Philippines, *New and Necessary Industries Granted Tax Exemption under Republic Acts Nos. 35 and 901* (Manila, 1958), mimeograph.

the extent such an industry uses imported raw materials, it can appropriate the windfall inherent in the restriction of imports of "unessential" consumer goods which it chooses to manufacture. For example, among the firms approved as new and necessary industries as of mid-1958, 135 firms received approval of 214 applications to manufacture plastic articles. Equally significant, no "new and necessary industry" proposed to manufacture the raw materials for plastic fabricators. New and necessary industries approved to manufacture plastic articles therefore established priority claims to foreign exchange to import plastic raw materials at the official exchange rate. The profitability of the "new and necessary" plastics-manufacturing firm is assured by manufacturing plastic articles out of raw materials imported at the official exchange rate which are then marketed domestically at peso prices reflecting stringent restriction of imports of finished manufactures of plastic.

Similarly, the applications of more than two hundred "new and necessary industries" proposing to produce articles of raw cotton or cotton raw materials received approval. Inasmuch as the Philippines produces negligible amounts of raw cotton, the survival of such "new and necessary industries" will, of course, depend upon foreign exchange allocations for raw cotton imports. The high levels of protection established by import controls on articles fabricated of cotton combined with the fact that raw cotton is on the import free list result in a substantial windfall subsidy to the "new and necessary industry" allocated foreign exchange to import raw cotton.

When appraised in terms of the goals of *national* economic development, the "new and necessary industries" policy should be considered successful (Table 46).[18] As of the end of June 1958, 826 firms had been approved as "new and necessary industries." Inasmuch as a number of firms had filed more than one petition covering separate products or processes, the number of exemption petitions approved totaled 1,083. The list of products the manufacture of which had been approved for tax exemption by the middle of 1958 included more than

[18] For a contrary view, see Higgins, *op. cit.*, p. 515. Higgins concludes: "Exempting new investment from taxes is a policy to be handled with care. . . . An example of injudicious application of this policy is to be found in the Philippines, where a very wide range of enterprises have been classified as 'new and essential' and accorded tax freedom, with no very clear stimulus to private net investment, which remains about 5 per cent of national income. . . . In short, *the present system retards rather than accelerates economic growth*" (italics are Higgins').

Table 46. New and necessary industries granted tax exemption under Republic Acts Nos. 35 and 901 [a]

Nationality of firm	Number of exemption petitions granted	Number of firms	Size of firms: net capital					
			Over ₱1 million [b]	₱500,000 to ₱1,000,000	₱300,000 to ₱500,000	₱100,000 to ₱300,000	Under ₱100,000	Not Identified
Filipino	551	429	17 [b]	34	26 [c]	122	203	27
Chinese	171	144	7	4	5	40	80	8
Filipino-Chinese	152	107	9	10	10	35	42	1
American	48	22	9	3	2	5	0	3
Filipino-American	50	45	7	3	4	12	14	5
Filipino plus mixed nationalities [d]	69	45	15	6	6	14	4	0
Unidentified	30	28	1	0	0	0	3	24
Firms not including Filipinos [e]	12	6	0	2	0	3	1	0
	1,083	826	65	62	53	231	347	68

[a] American Chamber of Commerce of the Philippines, *New and Necessary Industries Granted Tax Exemption under Republic Acts 35 and 901* (Manila, 1958), mimeograph.

[b] Including the following government enterprises: Ilocos textile mills, Davao Ramie Textile Co., and National Shipyards and Steel Corporation.

[c] Including the Philippine Tobacco Corporation, a government enterprise.

[d] Including Filipinos and Americans, also Filipinos and Chinese, in combination with other nationalities.

[e] Including one each of the following: British, Chinese-Pakistan, American-Chinese, American-British, American-Panamanian, and Spanish American.

two thousand commodities.[19] As might be expected, initial Philippine industrialization has been motivated by the domestic market and is dominated by textiles, food manufactures, plastics, and light fabrication of metals. In the category "canned goods," 87 commodity items are listed on 133 applications. In "thread," "yarn," "woven cotton cloth," "twines," "socks," "gloves," "fabrics," and "cotton," 99 commodity items are listed on 216 applications. "Plastic products" includes 135 commodities listed on 214 applications, and "paper," "paper bags," "leather," "glass products," "aluminum" (fabricated products), "rubber products," and "tin cans and caps" include 169 commodity items listed on 339 applications.

On the other hand, "steel products" includes 41 commodity items listed on 81 applications, "veneer and plywood" includes 6 commodity items listed on 21 applications, and "electrical products and appliances" includes 35 commodity items listed on 68 applications.

Although not all the firms approved as "new and necessary industries" have begun operating, manufacturing output has increased rapidly relative to growth in other sectors of the economy. Many new manufacturing enterprises have sprung up throughout the Philippines since 1950. More important for Philippine economic growth has been the appearance of indigenous entrepreneurship and the promising tendency for Philippine entrepreneurs to associate themselves with entrepreneurs of other nationalities. As of mid-1958, slightly more than half of all firms granted tax exemption have been exclusively Filipino, and these firms have accounted for slightly more than half of the approved applications. In addition, mixed firms involving Filipino participation include an additional 197 firms, for which 271 applications have been approved. Firms in which Filipino entrepreneurship is participating account for 78 per cent of the firms granted exemption in which the nationality of the firm is identified and 76 per cent of the approved exemptions in which nationality is identified. The tendency for Filipinos to associate with Chinese in business enterprises offers considerable promise for a rational solution to a difficult social problem. Firms with joint Filipino-Chinese participation, alone or in conjunction with other nationalities, number 128; for these firms 181 applications have been approved. Such firms account for 16 per cent of the identified firms and 17 per cent of the approved applications of such firms.

[19] American Chamber of Commerce (Phil.), *op. cit.*, pp. ii–xxii.

Another remarkable result of "new and necessary industry" policy has been the minor role of purely foreign investment, i.e., investment not including either indigenous Filipinos or Chinese. Of firms identified by nationality, only 3.5 per cent of the total firms and 5.7 per cent of approved applications were accounted for by firms not including Filipinos or Chinese.

The firms are well distributed by size among classifications based on nationality. Although purely Filipino firms account for only about one-quarter of those with net capital in excess of ₱1 million, Filipino firms account for slightly more than half of those with net capital between ₱100,000 and ₱1 million. Moreover, firms with Filipino participation include three-fourths of the 64 firms with net capital in excess of ₱1 million for which nationality is identified.

The tax exemptions granted "new and necessary industries" were scheduled for rapid extinction beginning in 1959. In view of the success of this policy in stimulating Filipino entrepreneurial activity strong attempts to continue the policy can be expected. The greatest obstacle to continuation of the policy will not be congressional unwillingness but the state of the international reserve. Because of extensive foreign exchange commitments and in the absence of *ad hoc* foreign exchange windfalls, the capacity of the government to subsidize future entrepreneurial activity is limited.

Two additional aspects of Philippine industrialization policy should be mentioned at this point. One is the use of United States agricultural surplus commodities under Public Law 480 to subsidize industrialization. In the absence of foreign exchange to purchase imports of wheat, raw cotton, milk powder, hides, and so forth, the Philippines is able to purchase these commodities, in surplus in the United States, in exchange for pesos. Subsequent sale of these commodities to Philippine entrepreneurs at the official exchange rate has enabled the Philippines to extend substantially the scope of the "new and necessary industries" policy. Wheat flour, cotton yarn, textiles, and reconstituted milk industries based on United States agricultural surpluses have been established in recent years. The precarious nature of such industrialization is evident.[20]

[20] The precariousness of this type of development was made clear in July 1959 when controversy arose between the two governments. The United States insisted that peso proceeds from the sale of agricultural surplus commodities should include the exchange premium tax enacted in July 1959, and the Philippines insisted that

Another is the integration into industrialization policy of Japanese reparations transfers. The Reparations Act, Republic Act No. 1789 of June 21, 1957, provides in Section 2(3): "In general, preference in the procurement of reparations goods and services shall be given to private productive projects. . . . Provided, further, that not more than sixty per cent of the total value of reparations . . . shall be allocated to the private sector." The future contribution of reparations to Philippine industrialization will be limited by two related factors. First is the competing claim of the Filipinized importing industry, which finds most profitable the import of "less essential" manufactures subject to tight controls. Second is the nature of Japanese goods and services available for reparations. The type of "industrial raw materials" essential to "new and necessary industries"—raw cotton, hides, milk powder, wheat, and so forth—may not be available in Japan.[21]

A major contribution to Philippine industrialization has been made by foreign investment. Foreign investment in the Philippines has traditionally been dominated by investment in primary production for export. The market motivating such investment has been the market for industrial raw materials in the West rather than the domestic Philippine market. Recent years have seen an upsurge of foreign investment producing for the Philippine market. Today one finds four oil refineries built or building, three tire factories with familiar American names, a half-dozen pharmaceutical plants with foreign participation and names, an aluminum-fabricating plant, and many others.[22]

Congressional and administration policy makers have been increasingly occupied with the evolution of a foreign investment policy compatible with the aspirations of Filipino nationalism. The Philippines has had extensive experience with foreign investment, and there

---

the peso proceeds should reflect the official peso exchange rate. At the height of the controversy sales of agricultural surplus commodities were unilaterally suspended by the United States. See *Phil. Newsletter*, July 10, 1959, p. 2. The report goes on to state: "Meantime, the Monetary Board has authorized negotiations for the importation of cotton from countries other than the United States. A textile industry spokesman said that 'unless negotiations for the supply of raw cotton are concluded by the end of this month, textile mills will have to be supplied around $5,000,000 for direct imports of raw cotton from Egypt and Mexico for use until the end of the year.'"

[21] An important exception would be raw materials for plastic manufactures.

[22] The list of "new and necessary industries" includes an impressive list of firms with participating foreign investment.

is widespread recognition of the benefits in employment and real income which accrue from foreign investment. Moreover, the American Embassy, the United States economic aid mission, and well-organized American economic interests in the Philippines have been vigilant in protecting the residual economic position of foreign investment.

While there are strong aspirations to accelerate economic growth, there is also a strong urge to see that such development is national as well as domestic. From the point of view of foreign investment the most favorable treatment that can be expected is one which will result in Philippine economic development characterized by expansion of Filipino entrepreneurship and investment relative to that of foreigners —including the Chinese minority. Such a development would represent a radical change from the economic development of the Spanish and American colonial periods, which resulted in rapid alienization of the Philippine economy. Inasmuch as Congress has traditionally been the bastion of Philippine nationalism, progress in achieving a foreign investment policy conducive to high levels of foreign investment has been slow.

While conflicts between the specific goals of economic nationalism and a high level of foreign investment are substantial, the principal obstacle to foreign investment has been exchange control. Reconciling the demands for foreign exchange arising out of the profits of foreign firms and the national system of exchange control priorities is a persistent policy problem.[23]

The relationships between exchange control and foreign investment are complex, and generalizations regarding them cannot be made with confidence. Only to a very limited extent does current foreign investment provide an increment of foreign exchange at the disposal of the Philippine foreign exchange control authority.[24] Foreign investment tends to be direct investment made out of the profits of existing firms or out of the peso proceeds of borrowings from Philippine credit institutions. At best, the capital goods import component of invest-

[23] For the purpose of analyzing foreign investment policy, investment by the Chinese minority is not considered as foreign investment. Policy with respect to this type of investment is discussed in Chapter XIV. An important distinction between foreign investment and investment by the Chinese minority arises in the fact that the earnings of Chinese firms do not represent a priority claim to foreign exchange.

[24] The layman's conception of foreign investment involves the belief that the foreign investor uses his currency (foreign exchange) to purchase or create capital assets in the investment-receiving country.

ment by foreigners would be exported directly to the Philippines, as would be the case with new foreign investment. In cases of direct investment out of peso earnings, the foreign investor, to the extent that imported capital goods are required, will be a claimant on the limited supplies of foreign exchange.

In other words, most foreign investment probably does not directly provide even the foreign exchange requirements of such investment. It is, of course, true that earnings of foreign investment represent a claim to foreign exchange and, if the currency is fully convertible, the process of reinvestment of the earnings of foreign investment would release an equivalent amount of foreign exchange for other purposes. Where exchange and import controls are in effect, such a conclusion does not hold. "Excess" earnings of foreign investment tend to accumulate as blocked currency balances. Such balances are a source of foreign investment, but it is unrealistic to contend that such foreign investment directly alleviates pressure on the available foreign exchange. On the other hand, over the longer run—when foreign investment begins to fructify—the supply of foreign exchange will be increased by production for export or of import substitutes.

The initial step in the evolution of a positive foreign investment policy occurred in 1946 with ratification of the "parity amendment" to the Constitution, establishing national treatment for Americans in the "exploitation of natural resources and the operation of public utilities." This policy was largely the work of the last Resident Commissioner, Paul V. McNutt, who was deeply concerned about the position of American business in the Philippines. McNutt, with limited Filipino and American support, had tried to reverse the independence movement in the period immediately after the war under the guise of a "re-examination movement." When he was frustrated in his efforts to promote "re-examination," McNutt turned to the American Congress, which was engaged in drafting legislation covering war damage payments as well as the transition to Philippine economic sovereignty.

The parity provision was opposed by the State Department and by the Philippine Resident Commissioner, Carlos P. Romulo, but McNutt prevailed.[25] Although Filipinos strenuously resisted the parity provision of the Bell Trade Act, once it was enacted, President Roxas

[25] See David Bernstein, *The Philippine Story* (New York: Farrar, Straus and Co., 1947), pp. 229–234.

and other Filipino officials closed ranks and worked to obtain Philippine approval.[26] In a series of narrow votes the Philippine Congress agreed to submit the proposed constitutional amendment to a plebiscite, which was held in the spring of 1947, at which time it received support from four-fifths of the Filipinos voting in the election.

The case for the parity amendment was based almost exclusively on the premise that it would result in a massive inflow of American foreign investment, which would accelerate rehabilitation and economic development. The impact on foreign investment attributed to the parity amendment failed to materialize. Handicapped by peso overvaluation, rehabilitation of foreign investment in the export sector lagged, and there was little inducement for the foreigner to invest in manufacturing for the domestic market. During 1949–1951 deteriorating economic and political conditions led to a net capital outflow. In 1952 and later years the capital outflow was reversed, and the inflow of foreign investment steadily increased. Foreign investment in production for the domestic market has expanded since 1952 in response to the incentives of the "new and necessary industries" policy.

The advent of the Magsaysay administration was followed by a shift in industrialization policy marked by an affirmation of faith in the primary role of private enterprise and by liquidation of government enterprises. As a part of this policy shift the administration took steps to obtain congressional approval of a resolution outlining a positive foreign investment policy including guarantees with respect to profit remission and capital repatriation.[27] The administration's legislative program, as outlined at the beginning of each congressional session following 1953, always included such a proposal, and bills were introduced into each session of Congress.[28] As might be expected, the Nacionalista-controlled Congress evidenced little interest in such a policy resolution.

[26] For example, ex-President Sergio Osmeña, who had recently opposed President Roxas in the presidential election in 1946, as well as Romulo, advocated approval of the parity amendment.

[27] For a survey of administrative attempts to formulate and obtain congressional approval of a "foreign investment policy," see *A.C.C. Journal*, 31 (May 1955), 171–172.

[28] Legislative resolutions enunciating a positive foreign investment policy have become quite fashionable in less-developed countries in recent years. In view of the discretionary nature of exchange and import controls and the intensity of external disequilibrium experienced by less-developed countries, the well-hedged commitments and statements of intent comprising such foreign investment policy statements are of limited value.

The closest approach to congressional approval of a foreign investment bill occurred in 1958. Both houses of Congress approved foreign investment bills,[29] and a conference committee of the two houses agreed upon a combined version of the two measures. The joint conference version was not, however, approved in either the regular or the special session of Congress in 1959. The important provisions in the two bills concerned the remission of profits. The House bill would have limited profit remittances to a maximum of 50 per cent of the realized profits each year, whereas the Senate bill provided for remission of from 25 to 100 per cent of profits, the rate to be set annually by the National Economic Council.

The essence of Philippine foreign investment policy is now found in the treatment of foreign investment by the exchange control authority. This has three aspects: First, to what extent do foreign firms share in the allocation of foreign exchange to import commodities for sale in the Philippines? Second, what is the treatment of foreign firms in the allocation of foreign exchange to import capital goods and industrial raw materials? Third, what is exchange control policy in regard to profit remittance and capital repatriation of foreign firms?

The first aspect of exchange control will be discussed at length in Chapter XIV. It will suffice for the present to say that exchange allocations have been used to Filipinize import trade rapidly.

Exchange control allocations to import capital goods and industrial raw materials did not, prior to 1957, discriminate overtly between national, Chinese, and foreign investment.[30] Since adoption of the Industrial Priority Formula in 1957, discrimination among investors on the basis of nationality has rapidly increased.[31] This aspect of economic policy is discussed at length in Chapter XIV.

[29] Senate Bill No. 80 and House Bill No. 2046. These two bills were originally passed by their respective houses on May 16, 1958, and June 5, 1958. The two bills are reprinted in the *A.C.C. Journal*, 34 (Nov. 1958), 500–504.

[30] Filipinos widely believe that the policy of formal nondiscrimination actually resulted in *de facto* discrimination against Filipinos. Not only were foreign and Chinese investors more "bankable" credit risks, but commercial bank resources were concentrated in branches of foreign banks. Under the circumstances a disproportionate share of the available credit and foreign exchange resources tended to go to non-Filipinos. For example, see the speech of Marcelo S. Balatbat, president of the Chamber of Commerce of the Philippines, before the Rotary Club of Tarlac, Oct. 21, 1958, reported in the *Manila Times*, Oct. 22, 1958.

[31] "A firm that is financed entirely or mostly by nationals [Filipino citizens] will be given preference. . . . This is justified by the fact that there is relatively greater stability in an enterprise that is operated by nationals. Furthermore, the

With respect to the treatment of the earnings of foreign investment, there are both nonformal and formal aspects of policy. One of the most important of the nonformal aspects is the favorable position of such investment arising out of peso overvaluation. Earnings from foreign investment converted into foreign currencies at the official rate of exchange give the foreign investor a gain that is not available to the Filipino or Chinese investor who has no comparable claim to foreign exchange by reason of his profits.

The second important nonformal aspect of exchange control is the effectiveness of enforcement of controls and the extent of evasion. Strong incentives exist to evade the control system, and businessmen can be depended upon to respond to such incentives. Foreign investors have undoubtedly learned to live with the exchange control system, although there are "costs" of evasion which raise the effective rate at which earnings are converted to foreign currencies. The extent of remittances outside the control system and their division between Filipino and foreign investors cannot be estimated with any confidence.

Formal treatment of the earnings of foreign investment can be summarized as follows: During the eight years following the imposition of exchange controls at the end of 1949 allocation of foreign exchange for the remittance of earnings totaled $376 million, or 8.7 per cent of remittances for imports (c.i.f.) during this period. Remittances of earnings averaged $31 million annually during the period 1950–1953 and $64 million during the Magsaysay administration, 1954–1957. During the latter period the ratio of profit remittances to foreign exchange allocation for imports increased to 10.5 per cent as compared with 6.4 per cent in the earlier period.[32]

The profit remittances after 1949 were partly offset by an inflow of new private investment, which amounted to a net inflow of $240 million. During the four years ending with 1957 the inflow of private capital has averaged $54 million annually. In other words, on net balance the earnings on existing foreign investment were largely

---

enterprise would provide or expand better opportunities for training Filipinos to acquire management skills and techniques. This is not to mention the fact that the earnings of nationals are likely to be plowed back into the national economy— something that cannot be guaranteed in the case of the profits of foreign investments" (R.P., NEC, *The Five-Year Economic and Social Development Program for FY 1957–1961* [Manila, 1957], p. 259).

[32] During the eight-year period the errors and omissions item in the balance of payments aggregated $120 million in the direction of outflow.

plowed back into the Philippine economy in reinvestment plus an inflow of new foreign investment.[33] The net drain upon Philippine foreign exchange resulting from transactions involving private foreign investment has been modest in recent years.

During the first four years of exchange control the basic formula for profit remittances was as follows:

> 10 per cent of the foreign participation in current net profit, or 10 per cent of the foreign participation in the capital stock as of December 31, 1948, whichever is higher.

Add:

> 30 per cent of the foreign participation in depreciated fixed assets as of December 31, 1949, or 30 per cent of the foreign participation in the capital stock as of December 31, 1949, whichever is higher.

The sum of the two above will constitute the total amount allowable for remittance out of current earnings. In no case shall the total amount remittable exceed the amount of the net profit realized during the year.[34]

Nonresident owners of properties were permitted to receive a "portion of the income or earnings of said properties not exceeding 20 per cent of said earnings." [35]

The basic policy governing remittances of earnings has been subject to some modification, depending upon the availability of foreign exchange. For example, in 1951, as a result of the increase in the international reserve, the 10 per cent rate provided for investment income was allowed to be computed on the basis of total net profit instead of merely on the foreign participation as in the preceding year.[36]

The first major change in remittance policy resulted from an unpublished Monetary Board resolution of August 30, 1955, which required that the amount of Philippine income taxes and the tax on sales of foreign exchange be deducted from the remittable amount. In other words, these taxes became a charge against the foreign exchange remittable.[37]

---

[33] This conforms to the traditional pattern of foreign investment in less-developed countries. Savings and investments out of the earnings of existing investment have tended to explain the accumulation of foreign investment historically.

[34] Central Bank, *Third Annual Report, 1951*, p. 460. A comprehensive account of policies and procedures for handling applications for exchange licenses is to be found on pp. 459–478.

[35] *Ibid.*, p. 466.   [36] *Ibid.*, p. 72.

[37] For an explanation of the loophole in exchange controls closed by this change, see "A Letter from Andres V. Castillo, Acting Governor, Central Bank, to Office of the President, Sept. 30, 1957," reprinted in *A.C.C. Journal*, 33 (Nov. 1957), 538–539.

A new investment remittance policy was approved in Monetary Board Resolution No. 104 of January 24, 1956. This new policy was correlated "to a system of priorities to effect an optimum utilization of foreign exchange without prejudicing reasonable attractions to foreign investment." The social productivity rating of each firm with foreign investment was calculated by a complicated formula. Remittances of investment income to nonresidents of from 25 per cent to 100 per cent of foreign participation in current net profits of foreign firms were allowed depending upon their social productivity rating reflecting their net contribution to:

(a) National income and employment or the national income effect;
(b) The strengthening of the country's balance of payments position or the balance of payments effect; and
(c) The supply of basic needs of the economy or product essentiality.[38]

The new formula was subsequently modified by a Monetary Board resolution of September 13, 1956, which declared that the policy governing profit remittances applicable to foreign investments made prior to the application of exchange controls at the end of 1949 was to be applicable to postcontrol investments. This resolution had the effect of arbitrarily nullifying the various bilateral agreements made between the Central Bank and individual foreign investors and firms following 1949.[39]

A further revision in the remittances priority formula was made in 1957 to introduce the capital invested as a restraint on the remittable profits. For example, the allowable remittance for a firm with a social productivity rating of 13 to 15 was limited to 100 per cent of current net profits or 60 per cent of foreign capital invested, whichever is the lesser amount.[40]

The policy initiated in early 1956 of relating investment remittances

---

[38] Central Bank, *Eighth Annual Report, 1956,* p. 155. Calculations under the formula resulted in a Social Productivity Rating under which for a rating of 1–3 the allowable remittance was 25 per cent of the nonresidents' share in net profits, whereas for a rating of 13–15 the allowable remittance was 100 per cent of profits. Firms engaged in public service under a government franchise and banks and insurance companies were allowed to remit a straight 40 per cent of the nonresidents' share in net profits. See also "Letter of Castillo," p. 539.

[39] "Letter of Castillo," p. 539.

[40] *Ibid.,* p. 540. For non-Philippine companies, the depreciated book value of capital assets as of the beginning of the fiscal year for which the profit is realized will be used instead of capital invested.

to a social productivity rating continued until September 30, 1958, when all profit and dividend remittances were suspended.[41] The suspension continued in effect until August 25, 1959, when the Monetary Board issued regulations providing for the resumption of remittances.[42] Profits earned prior to September 30, 1958, may now be remitted at 75 per cent of the rate indicated by the social productivity formula provided in Monetary Board Resolution No. 104. Profits earned after September 30, 1958, are remittable at 50 per cent of the same rate.

Philippine policy with respect to the earnings of foreign investment has been relatively liberal since the imposition of exchange controls in 1949. The effectiveness of this policy has, however, been limited by capriciousness, particularly following the foreign exchange crisis of the winter of 1957–1958. Although remittances have been relatively liberal, large amounts of blocked-peso earnings of foreign investors have accumulated. It has been reported that blocked-peso earnings, at the time remittances were suspended in 1958, amounted to ₱342 million.[43] This amount was more than 40 per cent of the earnings on foreign investment for which foreign exchange was allocated following 1949.

Analysis of foreign investment policy cannot produce categorical answers. For example, it is conceivable that exchange control with forced savings in blocked-peso earnings may maximize foreign investment. Moreover, is maximum foreign investment in the national interests as conceived by Filipino society? The evidence is overwhelming that Filipinos are not interested in maximizing foreign investment. Foreign investment is presently faced by difficult problems of adaptation to the requirements of Philippine nationalism, which encroach upon managerial autonomy. It seems clear that the role of foreign investment in future Philippine industrialization will be relatively minor and will depend upon the ability of foreign investors to adapt to the realities of the postcolonial world.

Philippine industrialization, whether measured by growth of output, number of firms, number of plants, or the extent of Filipino participation, has proceeded rapidly since 1950. In 1950 the value added in

[41] Central Bank, Monetary Board Resolution No. 1235 of July 18, 1958.

[42] *Phil. Newsletter*, Sept. 11, 1959, p. 4.

[43] *Manila Bulletin*, Aug. 7, 1958. Analysis of blocked-peso balances was made by Bernardo Ronquillo in his column of financial analysis. It was estimated that some three-fifths of the blocked balances had been reinvested.

manufacturing accounted for only 8.5 per cent of the national income
as compared with 42.3 per cent contributed by agriculture. Eight years
later the value added by manufacturing had increased almost threefold and the contribution of manufacturing to national income was
16.0 per cent as compared to agriculture, which had declined to 36.4
per cent. During recent years manufacturing output has been expanding at an average of 15 per cent annually.

Of the ₱1,474 million of value added by manufacturing in 1958,
93 per cent or ₱1,368 million, was accounted for by manufactures
for the domestic market including the processing of rice and corn
valued at ₱319 million. The processing of sugar and other export products accounted for ₱112 million.[44]

Investment in manufacturing has expanded rapidly in recent years
and in 1958 accounted for 28 per cent of the gross fixed investment of
₱839 million. Gross domestic investment in nonagricultural machinery
and transport equipment in 1958 amounted to ₱369 million.[45]

Philippine industrialization policy is analogous with, but goes one
step beyond, an infant industry policy. New industries not only are
protected from the competition of imports of finished manufactures,
but are heavily subsidized by tax exemption and foreign exchange
allocation. While there is little likelihood that Philippine manufacturing industries could survive without heavy protection, tax exemptions
are scheduled for termination and commercial policy presently is shifting to import restriction by taxation. So far as Philippine society is concerned, elimination of the heavy current subsidization will signal
maturation of "new and necessary industries." Attachment to industrialization as a goal with little or no regard for efficiency may
sacrifice potential economic growth. This is not equivalent to saying
that potential *national* economic development is also sacrificed.

Philippine industrialization is essentially a national development.
Economic nationalism can be expected to contract non-Filipino access
to the largess that has been distributed to promote industrialization.
This will tend to have two consequences. First, it will accelerate the
already discernible shift in the functional role of the Chinese minority
and should hasten their assimilation. Second, it seems quite likely
that Philippine foreign investment policy may come a full circle. Fili-

[44] R. P., NEC, "An Analysis of National Income Accounts of the Philippines for
the Years 1957 and 1958," *Statistical Reporter,* 3 (April 1959), 4.
[45] *Ibid.,* pp. 13–14.

pinos have been vocal in deploring their colonial-type specialization in primary production for export. On the other hand, recent years have brought home the fact that lack of foreign exchange is the principal restraint on economic growth. It is not unlikely that the groping for a foreign investment policy will ultimately lead to more, rather than less, functional specialization of foreign investment in primary production for export. Such a policy would recognize the relationship between foreign investment and the strong demand conditions of industrial markets in industrial countries. It would be ironical if the much-deprecated colonial specialization should emerge as conscious Philippine policy after a brief period of independence.

· XII ·

Agrarian Reform and
Agricultural Development

THE Philippines is confronted by a complex, deeply rooted problem of widespread poverty in agriculture. Philippine agriculture is characterized by (a) low productivity of both land and labor, (b) concentration of land ownership, widespread absentee landlordism, and high rates of tenancy, (c) organization of production into small-scale, technologically backward units, and (d) relatively high land values. The dimensions of the problem of agricultural poverty become apparent when it is realized that, while approximately 70 per cent of the Philippine population is dependent upon agriculture for a livelihood, less than 40 per cent of the national income originates in agriculture. These crude ratios mean that per capita income in agriculture is only about half the national average and is only one-quarter to one-third as high as per capita income elsewhere in the economy. Moreover, it is commonly estimated that at least 20 per cent of agricultural income accrues to noncultivating landlords. As a result, the per capita income of most of the agricultural population—the principal part of the Philippine population—is perhaps no more than one-fourth of the average income outside agriculture.[1]

[1] These estimates are, of course, only orders of magnitude. They are, however,

266

The urgency of the problem of poverty in Philippine agriculture was brought home by the strength of the Communist-led Huk movement, which was recruited in areas of extreme agricultural poverty. Agricultural development as a social goal is reflected in concern expressed by Philippine statesmen about rural problems and the proliferation of laws and institutions created to deal with various aspects of agrarian reform and development. The time essential for the peaceful evolutionary "modernization" of the Philippines may well depend upon solution of the problem of rural poverty.

What is the role of agricultural development in accelerated economic growth in the Philippines? To analyze this problem it is appropriate to consider two distinct components of Philippine agriculture. First is the sector producing for domestic consumption. Major crops in this sector are rice, corn, and sweet potatoes, which provide the principal part of the caloric intake of the Philippine population. The area planted to these three crops in recent years has accounted for approximately 70 per cent of the area under cultivation. These crops, together with tobacco, beans and other vegetables, cacao, coffee, fruits, and nuts, produced primarily for the domestic market, have accounted for approximately 80 per cent of the area under cultivation in recent years.

The other sector of Philippine agriculture is the export sector, including coconuts, sugar, abacá, pineapples, and a number of minor crops such as rubber, ramie, and maguey. The area planted to export crops averages 20 per cent of the land under cultivation with coconut plantings accounting for two-thirds of the acreage planted to export crops.[2]

The significant difference between the two agricultural sectors is not factor proportions and technology, i.e., "dualism," but differences in demand conditions. Philippine export production and resource productivity in export production expanded rapidly during the first three decades of this century in response to strong demand conditions arising primarily out of the preferred position of Philippine exports in the American market. Rewarding expansion in export production

---

sufficiently reliable to outline the problem of grinding poverty in Philippine agriculture.

[2] A substantial part of the production of both coconuts and sugar is sold in the Philippine market. In recent years such marketings have amounted to approximately one-fourth of the production of these crops.

and trade was interrupted by (a) the depression of the 1930's, (b) the destruction and dislocation of World War II, and (c) the United States policy of gradually reducing the mutual trade preferences of the colonial period.

Economic development must ultimately be accompanied by improvements in the productivity of the agricultural sector producing for the domestic market. In countries in which labor is a relatively scarce factor, improvements in labor productivity are necessary to release labor—rarely at a rate in excess of the natural increase in population—for other employment. In countries such as the Philippines where population is increasing more rapidly than employment opportunities outside agriculture, expansion in agricultural production is necessary to prevent a movement of the domestic terms of trade in favor of agriculture. Such a movement in the internal terms of trade would be an obstacle to the concentration of income in profits or government revenues and would tend to perpetuate the existing structure of specialization and production.

In the Philippines in the past, improvements in resource productivity in the domestic market sector have been postponed by the ready availability of land to bring under cultivation. Expansion of output in the twentieth century has been characterized by a static, traditional technology and stability of yields of both land and labor. However, postwar changes in Philippine agriculture cast doubt on the future validity of this generalization. Although the productiveness of labor and land in agriculture is now approximately equal to the levels of the late interwar period, productivity has been increasing steadily from the low levels of 1945–1946. From 1950 to 1958, income originating in agriculture rose by 34 per cent to ₱3.4 billion. This rate of increase was substantially greater than the increase in population. Moreover, the volume of agricultural output increased relative to income generated in agriculture as the unit value index of agricultural output declined from 113 to 99 during this period.[3]

Historically, the role of the agricultural export sector has tended to contrast sharply with the agricultural sector producing for the domestic market. Agricultural production for export tended to keep

[3] Ruben F. Trinidad, "A Measurement of the Nation's Output at Constant Prices," *Statistical Reporter*, 3 (April 1949), 23–31. Agriculture is the only income-originating sector which experienced a price decline between 1950 and 1958. This was a period of remarkable stability in the composite Philippine price series.

pace, not with slow domestic economic development, but with the relatively rapid development in industrialized metropolitan countries. Development of Philippine export production and trade proceeded rapidly between 1900 and 1930. For example, over the first three decades of this century the population approximately doubled, while sugar production more than trebled and coconut production increased probably four- or fivefold. Only abacá and tobacco among the important export crops expanded less than the rate of population growth.

The role of exports in economic development shifted with the depression of the thirties and drastically changed following World War II. Agricultural export production and trade have remained relatively static over the past quarter-century, and the present structure of economic policies and nationalist aspirations for industrial development provide little reason to believe that export agriculture will resume its earlier role.

To the extent that the Philippines has lost—or deliberately forgone—the opportunity to resume agricultural development in the export sector, domestic economic development will tend to establish a ceiling on agricultural development. Future policy emphasis on agricultural development may be frustrated by the rate of growth of domestic demand and failure of economic development to absorb increments of population outside agriculture.

Crop yields in the Philippines are among the lowest in the world and contrast sharply with the productivity of cultivated land in such densely populated and climatically divergent countries as Japan, Egypt, Java, and northern Europe. The low yields of Philippine agricultural land are paradoxical when related to the density of agricultural population. However, this paradox is essentially illusory. First, comparisons of yields per unit of land are economically relevant only if the areas compared are equivalent in potential productivity. This would require that soil fertility, configuration, and climatic factors—including rainfall and sunshine—be, not necessarily identical, but capable of producing an equivalent output with the same inputs of labor and capital. A major obstacle to high levels of labor productivity in Philippine agriculture is the relatively low quality of land inputs, including configuration, fertility, and climatic qualities. Second, the quantity of labor with which land co-operates to produce crops is not measured by heads of population engaged in agriculture but is highly dependent upon qualitative factors which affect labor productivity. Third, even though land and labor inputs may be equivalent, radical differences in productivity of land may be due to differences in the amount of capital with which the given amounts of land and labor co-operate to produce crops.

The basic agrarian problem of low productivity of Philippine agricultural resources is aggravated by the relative weakness of the agricultural laborer-tenant in the distribution of the agricultural product. The marginal product of labor tends to be relatively low—a stable minimum subsistence level. On the other hand, the product attributable to an additional unit of capital-land,[4] which is relatively scarce, tends to be relatively large. This means that, in a situation where labor is the relatively abundant factor, the share of the product accruing to the labor factor tends to be determined by the product attributable to the marginal increment of labor. At the same time the share accruing to capital-land applied to agriculture tends to be established by the product attributable to the marginal increment of capital-land. While there are significant imperfections in the operation of the marginal principle, it is still the basic explanation of the tendency for the laborer-tenant in densely populated agrarian countries to receive an inadequate share of the agricultural product.

The real income of the laborer-tenant tends to be driven to a subsistence level by the competition of underemployed and unemployed agricultural labor for the available land. Moreover, rapid growth of Philippine population in the densely populated agricultural provinces has tended to diminish the size of cultivator-owned farms to the point where indebtedness is the rule rather than the exception. Interest costs in many cases have so impaired the claim of the nominal owner-cultivator to the agricultural product that the share accruing to him may be comparable to the share accruing to the laborer-tenant. In any case it is apparent that the distribution of agricultural product to cultivators will range from the owner-cultivator free of indebtedness, who is entitled to the entire product of the co-operating factors, through various stages of indebtedness to the tenant-laborer who is essentially limited to the product attributable to the marginal increment of labor (Table 47).

The basic problem of poverty in Philippine agriculture can be re-

[4] It is appropriate at this level of abstraction to consider land and capital a single homogeneous factor.

solved into two component problems: (a) the low productivity of Philippine agricultural resources and (b) the socially disturbing distribution of the product of Philippine agriculture. These are separate

Table 47. Land tenure statistics, 1939 and 1948 [a]

	1939		1948	
Number of farms (000)	*1,635*	*100.0*	*1,638*	*100.0*
Owners	805	49.2	861	52.5
Part owners	255	15.6	163	10.0
Tenants	574	35.1	612	37.4
Farm managers	2	0.1	2	0.1
Farm area (000 hectares)	*6,691*	*100.0*	*5,727*	*100.0*
Owners	3,683	55.0	3,519	61.5
Part owners	818	12.2	491	8.6
Tenants	1,681	25.2	1,554	27.1
Farm managers	509	7.6	162	2.8
Cultivated area (000 hectares)	*3,954*	*100.0*	*3,712*	*100.0*
Owners	1,937	49.0	2,016	54.3
Part owners	594	15.0	365	9.8
Tenants	1,282	32.5	1,259	33.9
Farm managers	140	3.5	72	2.0
Average farm area (hectares)	*4.09*		*3.50*	
Owners	4.58		4.09	
Part owners	3.21		3.01	
Tenants	3.57		2.54	
Farm managers	320.34		71.18	
Average cultivated area per farm (hectares)	*2.42*		*2.26*	
Owners	2.41		2.34	
Part owners	2.33		2.24	
Tenants	2.53		2.06	
Farm managers	88.32		31.53	

[a] R.P., DANR, *Philippine Agricultural Statistics*, I, 6. Average sizes of farms in 1948, in hectares, by type of farm were: rice, 3.09; corn, 2.16; coconut, 4.64; abacá, 8.36; and sugar cane, 9.90. Average cultivated area per farm in 1948, in hectares, by type of farm was: rice, 2.10; corn, 1.46; coconut, 3.24; abacá, 4.45; and sugar cane, 7.10.

and distinct problems, and the solution to one may not contribute to the solution of the other. For example, policies may be implemented which increase the productivity of Philippine agricultural resources without alleviating the socially disturbing distribution of the agricultural product. There is no assurance that the labor factor will automatically share in increments of output.[5]

Moreover, it is apparent that measures producing greater equality between cultivators and other participants in the distribution of agricultural production will not necessarily contribute to the productivity of Philippine agriculture. Indeed, in the short run there are grounds for believing that greater equality in income distribution will adversely affect output.[6]

With the basic marginal principle of product distribution in mind, the components of agricultural policy tend to become intelligible. First, you can have agrarian reform measures designed to strengthen the cultivator's claim to the product of agriculture. Alternatively, measures may be designed to increase the productivity of agriculture without concern for product distribution.

Agrarian Reform

One broad area of agrarian reform includes policy measures designed to expand tenure-ownership rights of the cultivator in the land-capital factor. Such measures enable the cultivator to make a stronger claim to the present agricultural product as well as to any improvements in agricultural productivity.

An obvious way to attack this problem is through land reform in which transfer of title to land-capital vests in the cultivator a nominal claim to the entire agricultural product. The Philippines has a long history of experimentation with land reform, culminating in the Land Reform Act (Republic Act No. 1400 of September 9, 1955), which purports to strike at the basic problem of agricultural poverty.

The policy of purchase of large landed estates and resale to cultiva-

[5] It is not unlikely that the private marginal product of agricultural labor through an extended range of population density may be stable at the subsistence level. In this case the competition of labor of low productivity widely distributed through the economy would tend to prevent the labor factor from sharing in increases in output of specific agricultural industries. For example, the rapid expansion in the Philippine sugar industry did not materially improve the welfare of the laborers and tenants in this industry either absolutely or in relation to other agricultural industries. Wage rates of agricultural labor in the sugar-producing provinces of the western Visayan Islands are exceeded by rates paid in all Philippine regions with the exception of the densely populated provinces of the eastern Visayan Islands. See Central Bank, *Ninth Annual Report, 1957,* p. 44.

[6] See Amando Dalisay, "The Effects of Land Reform on Income Distribution," *Economic Research Journal,* 2 (Sept. 1955), 61–67.

tors was inaugurated when Governor William Howard Taft arranged for the purchase of the so-called "friar lands" from the Roman Catholic Church in 1904.[7] After the establishment of the Commonwealth in 1935 this policy was revived as a major part of President Quezon's "Social Justice" program.[8] Commonwealth Act No. 21 of July 11, 1936, authorized the President to purchase, either by negotiation or through expropriation proceedings, homesites on large landed estates for resale to occupants and appropriated ₱1 million for this purpose.[9] It was not until March 2, 1939, that Executive Order No. 191 created the Rural Progress Administration (RPA) to acquire and administer properties under the foregoing legislation.[10]

Before it was dissolved in 1950, the Rural Progress Administration had acquired a total of 37,747 hectares, equal to approximately 2 per cent of the area of tenant-operated farms in 1948.[11] The RPA received no new appropriations in the postwar period. Land acquisitions by the RPA depended upon loans by the government-owned Philippine National Bank and the Rehabilitation Finance Corporation. It was expected that the payments of new owners-cultivators would maintain a revolving fund for continuing land redistribution. During the postwar period, however, RPA operating expenses were approximately equal to laggard collections, and the capital assets of RPA drained

[7] Concentration of land ownership in the hands of the missionary orders in the Philippines and deterioration in landlord-tenant relations on church-owned estates were significant causes of the Philippine Revolution of 1896 and the growth of the nationalist movement.

[8] Outbreaks of violence reflecting agrarian dissidence occurred frequently in the 1930's. Although there was a tendency to dismiss these incidents as due to religious fanaticism, they were probably a continuation of the historical pattern of agricultural discontent.

[9] Commonwealth Act No. 260 of April 18, 1938, appropriated an additional ₱2 million, and Commonwealth Act No. 378 of Aug. 23, 1938, extended authorization to include leasing of the agricultural portion of such estates for subleasing to tenants and appropriated an additional ₱1.5 million.

[10] In 1940 previous legislation was consolidated in Commonwealth Acts Nos. 538 and 539 of May 26, 1940, which formed the statutory basis for land reform policy until 1955. Commonwealth Act No. 539 authorized government purchase and redistribution of farm land as well as homesites on large estates. Appropriations under earlier legislation were renewed, and, in addition, issuance of ₱20 million in "Social Security Bonds" was authorized. Commonwealth Act No. 538 prohibited ejection of tenants from estates pending government purchase.

[11] The RPA was abolished in a sweeping reorganization in 1950. Functions of the RPA were transferred to the Division of Landed Estates of the Bureau of Lands by Executive Order No. 376 of Nov. 28, 1950.

away. Though the rate at which estates were purchased was slow, distribution was even slower, and during the four years ending June 30, 1950, only 641 patents of title were issued.[12] During the remaining years of the Quirino administration land reform was dormant as Congress refused to appropriate funds for this purpose. Distribution of titles to land previously acquired continued at low levels.

The absence of progress toward land reform in the Quirino administration was due in part to the inept Hardie report issued by the United States economic aid mission.[13] This report was factual and informative, but its arrogance ignited sensitive Filipino nationalism. Public opinion was quickly aroused and easily manipulated by political leaders in Congress and the administration to kill land reform as a policy issue.

In March 1954, after the inauguration of President Magsaysay, an Inter-Departmental Committee on Land Tenure was created. Within two months legislation providing for comprehensive reforms had been drafted and introduced in the House of Representatives.[14] The committee's proposal called for the creation of a land tenure authority with power to purchase estates through negotiation or expropriation. Compensation could take the form of (a) interest-bearing amortized land certificates, redeemable in 25 equal annual payments, (b) nonnegotiable fixed maturity land certificates, also interest-bearing and redeemable in full after 25 years, and (c) negotiable land certificates payable to bearer on demand when presented at the Central Bank. Owners accepting negotiated purchase could receive a maximum of 50 per cent in legal tender or negotiable certificates, the rest to be paid in nonnegotiable certificates. Tenants to whom the estates would be sold would assume an obligation to repay to the government, in 25 equal annual installments, the full cost of the land plus 1 per cent of the price to cover administrative costs plus 6 per cent interest.

No action was taken by the landlord-dominated Congress in the regular session of 1954. In the regular session in 1955 the Senate passed a land reform bill, but the House of Representatives adjourned without acting on the administration's proposal. President Magsaysay

[12] R.P., Bureau of Lands, *Annual Report,* June 30, 1955, p. 32.

[13] U.S., Mutual Security Administration, *Philippine Land Tenure Reform, Analysis and Recommendations* (Manila, 1952). Robert S. Hardie, the author of the report, had acquired experience with land reform as an occupation official in postwar Japan.

[14] House Bill No. 2468 of May 6, 1954.

called a special session of Congress in July 1955 to consider the land reform bill as well as other urgent legislation. The Land Reform Act, Republic Act No. 1400 of September 9, 1955, was enacted in the closing hours of the special session.

The Land Reform Act of 1955 is unlikely to disturb existing land tenure relationships. The original intent of land reform has been circumvented by far-reaching congressional changes in administration proposals. The administration proposed that the landowner be permitted to retain 150 hectares, but the legislation provides for the acquisition of land only in excess of "300 hectares of contiguous area." The opportunity to frustrate land reform by minor sales of land to break up contiguous holdings is obvious. Another consequence of this change will be to minimize acquisition proceedings, which must be initiated by petition of a majority of the tenants of the whole estate. Inasmuch as the large exemption reduces very significantly the proportion of tenants who might conceivably benefit from acquisition, the number of petitions will be reduced.[15]

Equally important were changes in the method of compensation of landowners. All mention of fixed maturity or amortized land certificates was deleted, thus placing compensation, in effect, on a cash basis at the discretion of the estate owner. Moreover, issuance of land certificates by the Central Bank is limited to ₱60 million in the first year and to ₱30 million thereafter.[16] During the first year less than 1 per cent of the authorized amount was issued.[17]

The administrative agency of the Land Reform Act is the Land Tenure Administration (LTA). The three-man administration was appointed by the end of 1955. Within one month the LTA had compiled a list of 82 petitions for expropriation. At the end of June 1956

[15] The law does not provide a method of selecting the part of the estate subject to acquisition. The opportunities for corruption, collusion, and litigation, as well as for rivalry and disillusionment on the part of tenants, are virtually unlimited.

[16] Control over expenditures has been a major source of the political power of the cacique class. Overt opposition to class legislation is unnecessary when the intent of such legislation can be easily frustrated by withholding financial support.

[17] If the maximum rate of use of land certificates should be sustained in the future, it would not reduce agricultural tenancy. Negotiated prices of estates acquired will vary, but to date they have been quite liberal. It is doubtful if land under rice production in the densely populated agricultural provinces will be acquired for less than ₱2,000 per hectare. At this price the maximum rate of acquisition would be 15,000 hectares a year. This rate would accommodate, on farms of present average size, only a fraction of the natural increase in the tenant population.

the LTA reported having 251 petitions for expropriation, 60 of which had been investigated. As of June 30 of that year, only one agricultural estate—of 508 hectares and worked by 187 tenants—had been purchased by the government.[18] At least eight estates were subject to final negotiations preliminary to purchase, and by September expropriation suits had been filed against eleven more landowners. In January 1957 expropriation of seven additional estates totaling more than 3,400 hectares was approved by the cabinet.[19]

Cabinet authorization to expropriate is not the final step in acquisition, which may be delayed for a considerable period by negotiations between the LTA and the landowner. Moreover, lengthy litigation may result when negotiations do not result in agreement on price. The landowner has considerable incentive to use expropriation rather than the negotiated sale procedure. First, if he agrees to sell, the LTA can pay half of the purchase price in negotiable land certificates. Second, and more important, is the tendency of the courts to be liberal in compensating landowners.[20]

The LTA has also been besieged by offers of landowners to sell directly and by tenant petitions initiated with landlord connivance and reflecting landowners' desires to sell underdeveloped or low-yield land at favorable prices. Over 42 per cent of the estates offered for sale were outside central Luzon. However, the LTA has husbanded its resources and concentrated its activities in central Luzon.

Once a private hacienda has been acquired by the LTA, there remains the task of distributing the land to cultivators. During fiscal years 1954–55 and 1955–56 the Bureau of Lands and the LTA reported the issuance of 4,370 deeds in favor of tenants. Forty-six per cent of the deeds were for farm lots; the rest were residential.[21]

[18] During the first year and a half of the Magsaysay administration the acquisition of landed estates for redistribution to cultivators was the responsibility of the National Agricultural Rehabilitation and Resettlement Administration (NARRA). During this period NARRA gained title to or filed expropriation proceedings over 3,137 hectares.

[19] *Manila Times,* Jan. 17, 1957.

[20] This policy has been increasingly evident. For example, in the Yaptinchay expropriation case in Cavite Province, "just compensation" was fixed at ₱4,000 per hectare for irrigated rice land. The government found itself in the unenviable position of appealing a decision which it had "won."

[21] Because the Filipino peasant lives in a village near his land, when landed estates are subdivided two deeds are generally needed for each beneficiary cultivator—one for his farm lot and one for his residential lot in the village.

Still another crucial question to be asked of Philippine land reform is whether or not the land redistributed is going to the actual cultivators. Distribution policy is defined in LTA Administrative Order No. 2, which provides that estates may be resold to "any private individual who is qualified to acquire and own lands in the Philippines and who will personally cultivate and/or occupy the lot or lots which may be sold to him." The looseness of the wording of distribution policy has already produced virulent controversy and subversion of the intent of the program.[22]

The reader is entitled to ask whether the program of estate acquisition will not eventually become self-sustaining as annual collections from resales of land provide adequate funds for expanded purchases. Annual collections have varied between ₱960,000 and ₱1,284,000 since fiscal year 1948–49. So far, administrative costs have absorbed the bulk of repayments, reaching a peak of ₱726,000 in fiscal year 1955–56. To date, payments to the Rehabilitation Finance Corporation and the Philippine National Bank have been insufficient to meet interest charges on the accumulated debt of the Landed Estates Division and its successor, LTA.

Effective land reform is still ahead in the Philippines. Redistribution of land to cultivators has so far been successfully circumvented by the cacique class. Inadequate funds have been made available, and procedures under the law tend to result in exorbitant prices for land acquired. Inasmuch as the cultivator is obligated to repay the full purchase price, current land reform procedures will tend to result in a redistribution of income, not from the rentier class to the depressed tenant class, but in the opposite direction.[23] Moreover, the power to expropriate has been so circumscribed as to be practically nonexistent. The highly publicized Land Reform Act of 1955 improves on the earlier Commonwealth Act 539 in a few respects only; in many important details it is definitely weaker. Vigorous implementation of land reform requires deep commitment on the part of the executive. Magsaysay was so committed and he provided initiative and

[22] "Cultivate and/or occupy" was used because the order applied to both farm and residential lots. In the important Dinalupihan Estate case a substantial part of the redistributed estate was assigned, not to cultivators, but to politically influential residents of the area.

[23] This conclusion will be reinforced if conservative postwar monetary and fiscal policies are continued, thereby maintaining stability in the internal purchasing power of the currency.

leadership in this direction. His death and the restoration of executive control to professional politicians precludes continued challenge to the entrenched power of the cacique class.

A second basic policy designed to expand the claim of the cultivator to the agricultural product involves the expansion of tenure rights by legislative fiat. This has been a traditional Philippine agrarian reform policy; it was initiated in the 1930's by the first crop distribution law, the Rice Share Tenancy Act (Act No. 4054) of February 27, 1933.[24] While the provisions of the law governing distribution of the product were complex, the law specified that tenancy arrangements in which the tenant received less than 50 per cent of the net crop were contrary to public policy. The intent of the land tenure law was circumvented by the provision that it would be placed in effect only upon petition supported by a majority of the muncipal councils within a province.

An amending act, Commonwealth Act No. 178 of November 13, 1936, provided for application of the law "by proclamation to be issued by the President of the Philippines upon recommendation of the Secretary of Labor, when public interests so require." By 1941 President Quezon had declared the act in force in ten provinces, and in November 1946 President Roxas extended its coverage to the entire Philippines.

Enforcement of the amended act was frustrated by insecurity of tenure. Where tenants were acquainted with the law and bold enough to demand its application, the reaction of landlords was to threaten ejection at the end of the agricultural year. This defect was remedied by Commonwealth Act No. 461 of June 9, 1939, which provided that no tenant under "any system of tenancy" should be "dispossessed of the land cultivated by him except for any of the causes mentioned in Act No. 4054 (Section 19) or for any just cause, and without the approval of a representative of the Department of Justice." If either party felt aggrieved by the action of the department, he was entitled to appeal to the Court of Industrial Relations.

The next step in the evolution of the policy of government regulation of tenancy relations was Republic Act No. 34 of September 30, 1946. This act provided for an increase in the legal minimum share of the net product accruing to tenants from 50 per cent to 55 per cent when the tenant furnished both work animals and implements

[24] Texts of legislation regulating land tenure and landlord-tenant relations have been assembled in Appendix G of the Hardie report.

and both parties shared expenses equally. The act was inappropriately referred to as the "70-30" law because it provided for such a division of the output in favor of the tenant when the tenant "furnishes the necessary implements and the work animals and defrays all the expenses for planting and cultivation of the land."

The current Agrarian Relations Act (Republic Act No. 1199 of August 30, 1954) specifies that the basic factors of land and labor shall each be awarded 30 per cent of the net crop on first-class land. The net crop is defined as the crop remaining after the costs of fertilizer, pest and weed control, reaping, and threshing are deducted. Five per cent is allocated to the party furnishing the work animals and 5 per cent to the party who contributes the farm implements. Five per cent of the net crop is allocated to cover the cost of final harrowing and 25 per cent to transplanting.

The case for government intervention in distribution of the agricultural product between the owners of the various factors contributing to that product has two distinct elements. First, such intervention might be directed at a situation in which a portion of the tenant's share was being appropriated by the landlord because of superior bargaining power. Such a preponderance of bargaining power might be explained by traditional elements in the society, political power structure, and so forth. Under such circumstances there would be considerable opportunity for the government to redress inequalities through the agricultural tenancy policy embodied in Republic Act No. 1199.

Second, such a policy might be directed at redressing inequities in crop distribution arising out of factor proportions in Philippine agriculture. To the extent that tenancy policy is motivated by this goal, it is directed at a symptom—the distribution of the agricultural product—and neglects the root causes of poverty and inequality. The potentialities for such a policy in an environment of cacique power are not impressive.

In addition to basic policies of land reform and government intervention in crop distribution, a number of additional agricultural policies are motivated, wholly or in part, by the need to improve the cultivators' claim to the agricultural product.

Usurious practices have been widespread in the rural Philippines, and excessive interest charges paid by cultivators (both small owners and tenants) have seriously impaired the cultivators' claim to the agricultural product. A variety of credit institutions have been created and capitalized by government funds to regulate the cost of credit to cultivators.

The possibilities of agrarian reform of this type are measured by the extent to which cultivators are subject to excessive interest and marketing costs. There is considerable evidence of competition in the gathering and marketing of Philippine crops.[25] Government investment in the Agricultural Credit and Co-operative Financing Administration and in the capital of Rural Banks represents the major current effort in this direction. In addition, antiusury legislation and also the regulation of interest charges in tenancy relations have been traditional Philippine policies, although they have not been vigorously enforced. Probably the principal consequence of this policy in recent years has been to divert substantial amounts of subsidized capital to agriculture.

A final element in Philippine agrarian reform policy has been the extension of minimum wage legislation (Republic Act No. 602 of April 6, 1951) to agricultural labor. At present such legislation covers only a small portion of the agricultural labor force working for wages.

Although the Philippine government has put considerable reliance on policies of intervention to improve the cultivator's claim to the agricultural product, the results have not been encouraging. Government activities have been sporadic and unco-ordinated. More important, Congress has remained uncommitted to this social objective and has minimized the impact of reforms by (a) denying resources to enforcement agencies and (b) subverting legislation by ambiguities and escape clauses. The latter have resulted in extensive and expensive litigation which has the effect of denying the intended benefits of the policy to landless cultivators. The Magsaysay administration achieved some progress toward effective agrarian reform of this nature, but it is doubtful if the three-year interlude of his leadership permanently disturbed the pattern of landlord-tenant relations.

Agricultural Development

A second basic approach to the problem of poverty in Philippine agriculture has been to increase supplies of other productive resources

[25] Even in countries such as the United States with highly developed agricultural marketing systems, there are relatively heavy marketing costs. American producers are articulate in their resentment of the portion of the gross receipts of agriculture absorbed in the marketing process.

with which labor works. One obvious solution to this problem is to distribute the Philippine population more widely over areas suitable for cultivation. The vast areas of productive, unoccupied frontier land in the Philippines have served throughout Philippine history as a relief valve for growing population density. The history of Philippine agricultural development is largely a story of voluntary land colonization.

Positive public land policies have been implemented in the Philippines since early in the Spanish occupation, and migration to the frontier area has always taken place.[26] During the American occupation a basic homesteading policy following the United States model permitted colonists to acquire title to limited amounts of land by building a home and bringing the land under cultivation.[27]

Public land settlement has traditionally loomed large in Philippine plans for agrarian reform. In fact, the potentialities of land colonization have been so much emphasized that this opportunity has tended to divert attention and thereby to prevent progress toward land reform and regulation of tenancy. There has, however, been widespread and pernicious subversion of effective public land policy by land-grabbers, who acquire public lands quasi-legally in order to speculate with them or to become absentee landlords.

It has long been a widespread practice for politically influential Filipinos to lease or purchase public lands at a nominal price with no intention of bringing the land under cultivation.[28] While the paper transaction was completed at the Bureau of Lands in Manila, a colonist looking for land would enter the area and, failing to notice any evidence of private ownership, would proceed to cultivate a plot for himself. Frequently his friends and relatives would join him in

[26] The encomiendas included an obligation on the part of the grantee to develop the land included in the grant.

[27] The basic public land laws of 1903, 1919, and 1929 provide for the private acquisition of public lands through homestead, purchase, or lease of limited areas. The Land Registration Act of 1902 and the Cadastral Act of 1907 set up procedures to facilitate the issuance of land titles. More recently, Republic Act No. 1151 of June 17, 1954, created a Land Registration Commission to expedite title issuance. Finally, substantial amounts of U.S. economic aid have been allocated to land surveys, mechanization of title issuance procedures, and construction of roads in frontier areas.

[28] Individuals are permitted to acquire 144 hectares, while corporations may acquire 1,024 hectares. Such transactions can be completed with little continuing cost to the individual or corporation because of the low levels of land taxation in the Philippines.

unwittingly improving another's claim. Then the legal owner or lessee would appear on the scene either offering to sell the land at a fantastic profit or demanding a share of the crop from the cultivators.[29]

Traditionally, the slow pace of administration in the Bureaus of Lands and Forestry has been an important deterrent to land colonization. Under the Public Land Law no application for homestead, sale, or lease may be accepted without (a) certification by the Bureau of Forestry that the land is "disposable agricultural land" and (b) a survey. Since the real colonist could seldom afford a private survey,

Table 48. Disposition of public land [a]
(000 applications—000 hectares)

Fiscal year	Applications received		Applications approved		Patents issued	
	Number	Area	Number	Area	Number	Area
1946	5.1	n.a.	.4	n.a.	.1	n.a.
1947	22.4	n.a.	4.1	n.a.	.2	n.a.
1948	21.2	n.a.	5.6	n.a.	1.1	n.a.
1949	26.0	n.a.	17.3	n.a.	2.3	n.a.
1950	25.9	213.6	11.0	91.1	3.6	41.2
1951	28.1	219.7	13.0	94.6	3.8	36.4
1952	23.7	211.4	9.7	116.7	3.5	36.1
1953	37.3	269.6	11.6	93.6	7.5	74.6
1954	35.0	237.1	20.0	156.2	16.7	147.9
1955	39.3	263.2	24.2	156.9	46.1	306.0
1956	74.2	339.1	49.2	229.2	43.7	227.6
1957	74.2	343.1	50.9	277.9	44.6	255.8

[a] R.P., Bureau of Lands, *Annual Report of the Director of Lands.*

the inactivity of the Bureau of Lands in making government-financed surveys has especially handicapped the bona fide colonist. During recent years this bottleneck has been rapidly reduced (Table 48). Republic Act No. 1305 of June 16, 1955, allocated ₱20 million for the subdivision and survey of public land over the ensuing five fiscal years. This allocation doubled the previous rate of expenditure for public land distribution. In addition, the Bureau of Lands has received mechanical office equipment and extensive technical assistance from the United States economic aid program. As a result, the rate

[29] A practice in the past has been for politically influential people to acquire land alongside the right of way for a new highway in frontier areas. The possibilities for collusion and corruption as well as the economic motivation of such activity are obvious.

at which land patents are issued has been increased from 3,500 per year in 1952 to in excess of 46,000 in 1955. Meanwhile, the annual rate of patent applications has tripled since 1952, and at the present rate of title issuance the backlog amounts to about three years.

Improvement in the administration of public land policy is probably the most impressive accomplishment of Philippine agricultural development policy, and land colonization is proceeding at a rapid rate. Current rates of applications for, and issuance of, land patents suggest that colonization is presently accommodating the principal part of the increase in the rural population, which is somewhat in excess of 300,000 annually.

A second element in Philippine land colonization policy has been the succession of government agencies created to engage in organized colonization. As early as 1917 the government was recruiting colonists, transporting them to frontier areas, and settling them in subsidized colonies. This policy was revived by the Commonwealth government, which organized the National Land Settlement Administration (NLSA) in 1939. At the outbreak of World War II NLSA was operating two settlement projects in southwestern Mindanao and one in northeastern Luzon. A total of 6,170 settler families resided in these three projects.[30]

NLSA was reorganized in September 1945, and Congress appropriated ₱5 million to rehabilitate projects and resume resettlement operations. Little progress was made during early postwar years, and beginning in 1948 the number of settler families in projects began to decline. NLSA annual reports tended to become "short summaries of the overwhelming difficulties which had paralyzed activity by that time."[31] The most persistent official complaint was "lack of funds." Yet NLSA appropriations and operating income from 1945 to July 1, 1949, totaled ₱7.6 million, or approximately ₱10,000 per family settled in the postwar period.[32] Moreover, when NLSA was dissolved in 1950, it was estimated to have debts of over ₱2 million.

The Land Settlement and Development Corporation (LASEDECO) was created by Executive Order No. 355 in October 1950 to take over the functions, assets, and liabilities of the defunct NLSA. LASEDECO was further capitalized by being given title to the remaining part of

---

[30] Karl J. Pelzer, *Pioneer Settlement in the Asiatic Tropics* (New York: American Geographical Society, 1948).

[31] Margaret Ruth Harris Pfanner, "Postwar Land Colonization in the Philippines" (unpublished M.A. thesis, Cornell University, 1958), p. 22.

[32] *Ibid.*, pp. 119–121.

the war surplus property turned over to the Philippine government
by the United States. The proceeds realized from the sale of war
surplus property were inadequate to support extensive colonization,
and by the end of 1953 LASEDECO had resettled fewer than 400
families.[33]

The next experiment with organized colonization occurred in the
latter years of the Quirino administration when the Philippine armed
forces under the leadership of Secretary of Defense Ramon Magsaysay
organized the Economic Development Corps (EDCOR) to rehabilitate
ex-Huks in frontier colonies. EDCOR was politically oriented and accomplishments must be measured in terms of the political impact on
the Huk struggle, as there was little in the experiment which was
directly applicable to the problem of organized land settlement.
EDCOR was heavily subsidized by the use of army personnel and
equipment, yet the direct cost per family settled was in excess of
₱10,000. More important, the number of settler families never exceeded one thousand, a negligible number in terms of the basic
problem of agricultural poverty and tenancy in the rice-producing
areas.[34]

Currently, organized land colonization in the Philippines is the
responsibility of the National Resettlement and Rehabilitation Administration (NARRA), which was created by Republic Act No.
1160 of June 18, 1954, to succeed the discredited LASEDECO. In
contrast to LASEDECO, which had led a hand-to-mouth existence,
NARRA has benefited from liberal peso appropriations and allocations of United States aid. During the first two years of operation
NARRA expenditures totaled ₱13 million. The pace of organized
land colonization was sharply stepped up with the formation of
NARRA, but the box score of accomplishments is hopelessly confused
by the practice of including all existing settlers in the colonization
areas in official claims and it is impossible to identify the number of
settlers actually recruited and transported.[35] Even if the claims of

[33] David O. Wurfel, "The Bell Report and After: A Study of the Political Problems of Social Reform Stimulated by Foreign Aid" (unpublished Ph.D. thesis,
Cornell University, 1959), p. 446.

[34] Pfanner, *op. cit.*, p. 80. Only 246 ex-Huks were resettled in the four EDCOR
settlements.

[35] As of January 1, 1958, it was reported that NARRA had resettled 22,105
families, distributed 18,558 farm lots, and issued 6,966 patents of title (*Manila
Times*, Jan. 6, 1958).

NARRA are accepted at face value, the rate of organized colonization has been perhaps 6,000 families per year, or approximately 30,000 people. This is no more than one-tenth of the current annual increase in the rural population.[36]

The results of the various organized colonization efforts have been disappointing when appraised in terms of economic criteria. Desertion rates and failures have been high. Recruitment policies have been faulty, and site selection has frequently been inappropriate. While these programs have been set up with revolving funds in which liquidation of settler debts would maintain the fund intact and support future colonization, in every case the investment has been dissipated in high administrative costs and settler default. The cost per settler has been excessive by every criteria, but in particular in terms of the rate of population increase, widespread tenancy, and the public funds available for this type of program.

A third major agricultural development policy has been to create specialized credit institutions which tend to reduce capital rationing in agriculture (Table 49). Capital provided for agriculture can be highly productive in a wide range of uses, including improvements on the land, buildings and equipment, fertilizer, livestock, and inventories.

Inadequate investment has characterized Philippine agriculture outside the sector producing export crops. Failure to invest is explained, first of all, by the tradition-bound, subsistence agriculture of the small holder. Second, it has resulted from the low rate of agricultural investment out of rental income. Landlords have a weak tradition of productive investment and tend to divert savings to acquisition of land already under cultivation, to urban real estate, and to foreign assets. Third is the lack of institutional specialization in agricultural credit. Finally, capital rationing has been due to widespread tenancy and the weakness of incentives to introduce additional capital where the principal part of increases in output accrues to the landlord.

The initial move to establish functionally specialized credit institutions in agriculture took place in 1917 with the establishment of the Philippine National Bank (PNB). Growth of the PNB was sporadic and was characterized in the early years by mismanagement

[36] There are strong grounds for believing that the actual rate of colonization under NARRA has not averaged more than 3,000 families a year.

and political intervention. The PNB gradually overcame various difficulties of a political origin and in the postwar period has rapidly acquired stature as an efficient, competently managed, independent
institution. Commercial banking facilities are provided throughout the
Philippines by branches of the PNB. The PNB has tended to concentrate its agricultural loans on the financing of agricultural export
production.

Table 49. Agricultural credit [a]
(₱ million)

	Total	Commercial banks [b]	RFC	ACCFA	Rural banks
Loans granted:					
1950			15.1	n.a.	n.a.
1951	168.7	155.2	13.5	n.a.	n.a.
1952	203.6	179.1	24.5	n.a.	n.a.
1953	228.5	198.1	25.8	2.8	1.9
1954	222.0	184.6	18.7	15.7	3.0
1955	275.4	175.6	24.7	40.5	4.6
1956	297.4	216.1	25.2	44.5	11.6
1957	345.4	246.6	25.8	48.8	24.2
1958	n.a.	251.8	25.1	23.9	n.a.
Loans outstanding at end of year:					
1950	171.7	128.0	43.7	n.a.	n.a.
1951	234.7	184.3	50.4	n.a.	n.a.
1952	293.6	230.2	63.4	n.a.	n.a.
1953	344.3	260.5	79.7	2.7	1.4
1954	368.6	263.2	86.3	16.5	2.6
1955	413.0	269.3	95.9	43.5	4.3
1956	453.1	277.4	104.6	60.7	10.4
1957	532.5	329.2	111.5	71.3	20.5
1958	n.a.	n.a.	120.1	85.6	n.a.

[a] Central Bank, *Annual Reports.*
[b] Including Philippine National Bank. Agricultural loans were for purposes of
production. They do not include commercial loans to carry inventories of export
crops. At the end of 1956 such loans outstanding totaled ₱94.2 million.

Some of the short-term credit needs of agriculture, particularly
in export industries such as sugar, abacá, and coconuts, have been
met by loans from commercial banks other than the PNB. Such credit
has been concentrated in marketing loans and has made little contribution to agricultural development through land improvements and
the bringing of land under cultivation. To meet the need for long-

term credit assistance, the Rehabilitation Finance Corporation was created in 1946. Since its establishment the RFC has been a major source of long-term credit for agricultural production and land improvements.[37]

In recent years a new type of institution to extend commercial banking facilities to rural areas was created by the Rural Bank Act (Republic Act No. 720 of June 6, 1952). The law provides for Rural Banks established by local initiative with a minor capital contribution by the government through the Central Bank. Moreover, Rural Banks are given special discount privileges at the Central Bank. The number of Rural Banks has grown rapidly in recent years, and at the end of 1957 numbered 106, with loans outstanding amounting to ₱35.9 million. Loans outstanding amounting to ₱20.5 million had been made for agricultural purposes, and two-thirds of agricultural loans were in amounts less than ₱1,000.

The difficulties of financing farm operations and land improvements in provinces distant from commercial and banking centers are aggravated by lack of organized marketing facilities and standardization of agricultural products. To meet this problem, the government in 1952 established the Agricultural Credit and Co-operative Financing Administration (ACCFA) to organize farmers into Farmers' Co-operative Marketing Associations (FACOMAS) and to furnish farmer members credit through such associations.[38] FACOMAS grant loans on either a pledge of the farmer to deliver his next crop to FACOMA warehouses or the acutal deposit of palay (unhusked rice) as collateral. The farmer gains both in the relatively low interest rate of 8 per cent and in improved prices for rice, which can be marketed when prices are relatively favorable.

Although FACOMAS were initially established among rice producers, ACCFA has expanded its operations from rice to tobacco and coconuts. The United States aid program has attached considerable importance to the growth of the agricultural co-operative movement and has invested substantially in this program. By 1959, 502 FACOMAS had been organized with a membership of 289,121 farmers. FACOMAS are widely distributed covering farmers residing in 10,631 barrios in

---

[37] Republic Act No. 2081 of June 14, 1958, converted the RFC to the Development Bank of the Philippines. Because of the high priority assigned industrialization, the emphasis of the Development Bank upon agricultural development will undoubtedly be diminished.

[38] Republic Act No. 821 of Aug. 14, 1952.

47 provinces. By the end of 1958 the loans outstanding amounted to ₱85.6 million.

While the co-operative movement has expanded at a very rapid rate, a number of aspects of the movement need improvement. First is the slow development of the co-operative principle of capitalization by the savings of members. To date, the resources of the FACOMAS have been largely derived from the parent organization ACCFA, and the collective savings of members have been quite modest.

Second, expansion of the price-support activities of ACCFA threatens to dissipate the resources of that agency. As the purchasing agency of the government for all locally grown and produced Virginia leaf tobacco, ACCFA in 1956 and 1957 purchased tobacco worth ₱57 million. During recent years prohibition of imports of tobacco have resulted in favorable tobacco prices. However, there is a danger that objectives of co-operation and extension of agricultural credit will be subordinated to price objectives.[39]

Such problems are relatively minor when compared to the threat of political activity in and around FACOMAS. This is not surprising in a country where the co-operative movement is said to be the largest industry. In most localities where it is found, the FACOMA has become the most important organization outside the municipal government. Not only has office in FACOMA become a stepping stone to local political office, but in some towns the reverse is also true. ACCFA supervisors have exerted strenuous efforts to limit political activities by FACOMA officials, but because of the intensity of Filipino political activity, the economic functions of the co-operative movement are constantly threatened.

The most important contribution of the co-operative movement, if it should flourish, will be its impact upon social change in the rural Philippines. Tenants and small holders are being thrust into positions of community leadership by election to FACOMA boards of directors, and landlords' traditional techniques for directing community decision making are being frustrated.

Apprehensions regarding ACCFA and FACOMAS proved to be well

[39] According to ACCFA, the average price before the tobacco-purchasing program was about ₱1.30 per kilogram. The average price of the tobacco purchased by ACCFA in FY 1954–55 was estimated at about ₱2.00 per kilogram. ACCFA purchases which have expanded rapidly from 5 million kilograms in 1954–55 to 15 million kilograms in 1956–57 accounted for approximately two-thirds of production. See UN, ECAFE, *Food and Agricultural Price Policies*, p. 97.

founded when a survey of the co-operative organization by Arthur D. Little, Inc., a United States firm of economic consultants, was made public in March 1949. The survey reported extensive mismanagement of both FACOMAS and ACCFA. Of ₱86 million of outstanding ACCFA loans at the end of 1948, two-thirds, or ₱57 million, were delinquent. Loans to individual farmers accounted for only one-third of the delinquency, with the balance representing loans to FACOMAS. Over four-fifths of the FACOMAS were reported as operating at a loss in early 1959. Inadequately trained and actually dishonest personnel were a major cause of financial difficulties. The loan funds of FACOMAS had frequently been diverted to unauthorized uses involving poor credit risks. Moreover, ACCFA had dipped into its capital to meet operating expenses, and the ₱100 million revolving capital fund had been dissipated or frozen in assets of doubtful liquidity.

The Arthur D. Little report was followed in December 1959 by a report on the activities of ACCFA by the Committee on Good Government of the Philippine House of Representatives. The House committee's report confirmed the findings of the Little report and concluded that ACCFA's failure was due to incompetence or gross negligence often born of complacency. Moreover, an inadequate accounting system had invited graft and deliberate acts of mismanagement. Early in January 1960 President Garcia initiated a house cleaning by appointing a new chairman and Board of Governors for ACCFA.

Both the Little and the House committee reports agreed that the co-operative movement should be salvaged but were realistic regarding the difficulties and costs of the necessary rehabilitation. The Little report in particular was critical of the price-support functions of ACCFA and recommended liquidation of these activities.

Agricultural production per head of population in the Philippines today is little improved over levels attained prior to World War II. On the other hand, agricultural output has grown steadily from the low wartime levels of 1944 and 1945. The increase in agricultural output since the late interwar period has not been due to increases in productivity of either land or labor but to expansion in land under cultivation. This type of development has characterized Philippine agriculture since 1898 and probably did so before. That is to say, in the absence of changes in patterns of internal consumption or an expanding export market, the demand for agricultural output can be expected to grow at approximately the rate of population growth. In the absence of rapid economic development, the rural population will tend to increase at a rate not less than the rate of population growth. Under such circumstances it is not surprising that Philippine agricultural development has taken the form of land colonization rather than improvements in land or labor productivity. This type of development can be expected so long as there remain extensive areas of land available for colonization.

In recent years agricultural research and extension services as well as specialized credit institutions have promoted technological change and investment in agriculture. These developments, together with new political institutions in the rural sector, promise continued social change, which will tend to maintain the growth of production achieved following World War II. Future economic expansion in agriculture will, however, be restrained by the growth of the internal market and the continued deterioration in the internal terms of trade for agricultural output which have characterized the past decade.

Of the various facets of agricultural development policy, the most fruitful by far has been the policy of voluntary colonization. Radical improvements in the procedures for establishing land title patents have only begun to catch up with the backlog of homestead applications. The rate of voluntary land colonization contrasts sharply with the costly and well-publicized attempts at organized and subsidized land colonization. Philippine experience with the latter policy does not suggest that it should be continued. More land colonization would take place if the resources applied to organized land colonization were diverted to improvements in transportation and communication facilities and social investment in educational and medical services in frontier areas.[40]

A second agricultural development policy of considerable effectiveness has been that of establishing specialized agricultural credit institutions. Addition of Rural Banks and Farmers' Co-operative Marketing Associations to the existing commercial banking system, the Rehabilitation Finance Corporation (Development Bank of the Philippines), and the moneylending activities of landlords and market-

---

[40] Organized land colonization has not been characterized by conspicuous success elsewhere in Southeast Asia, although there is an extensive history of experimentation with this policy in many areas.

ing middlemen have given Philippine agriculture a flexible, adequately financed, and extensive rural credit system. The increased use of rural credit extended by these institutions is an encouraging development that should be reflected in agricultural productivity. The agricultural credit system will support a rapid transformation of the tradition-bound, subsistence-dominated agriculture if market conditions together with community development and agricultural extension and research should set off a process of rapid change.

Agrarian reform policies seeking to relieve rural poverty by distributing the product of agriculture more evenly cannot be assessed as successful. Land reform to date has been successfully opposed by the politically dominant agricultural aristocracy. Purchase and redistribution of large estates has made an insignificant contribution to the relief of tenancy. The case for Philippine land reform is obvious. Philippine agriculture is technologically retarded, and tenant-operated farms are among the more backward areas of agriculture. Tenancy as an institution tends to become socially intolerable in an environment of rapid population growth, limited economic expansion, and resource immobility. In such an environment the income of tenant-laborers tends to be driven to a minimum subsistence level. Redistributing the present rental income to the cultivators is a pressing short-run problem facing the Philippines today. It is to be feared that democratic political processes in the Philippines will not achieve a solution to this problem without widespread violence and attendant danger of authoritarianism.

Government intervention to influence the distribution of the agricultural product is a long-standing Philippine policy. Limited progress has been made, and the possibilities of this policy are not impressive. Vigorous enforcement of existing legislation cannot be expected to overcome the obstacles inherent in the cultural and economic environment which contribute to the present inequitable distribution of the agricultural product. Crop sharing by legislative fiat probably cannot substitute for land reform.

It is becoming increasingly evident that Philippine agricultural development is handicapped by the exchange rate policy. With the important exception of coconuts, Philippine export-crop production has lagged behind prewar, and in recent years the acreage planted to export crops has been approximately 10 per cent below 1934–1938 levels. Unless exports are expanded, agricultural production in the

Philippines will tend to be limited to the domestic market. The size of such a market is bounded by present levels of Philippine food and fiber imports plus the normal expansion resulting from population growth and changes in food consumption habits.

An opportunity exists to use exchange rate policy, i.e., changes in the peso exchange rate, to create incentives that will result in expanded levels of capital formation and production in agriculture. Incentives of this type would be relatively productive because they would influence cash crop production rather than the more tradition-bound food production. Similar incentives result from the controversial barter export policy, which permits exporters, in effect, to retain a portion of their export proceeds for imports outside the system of exchange and import controls.

Similarly, the Philippine domestic market can be reserved to Filipino producers by import quotas, import taxation, and so forth. Recent years have seen rapid expansion of Philippine tobacco production following the tightening of restrictions on imports.[41] Coffee and cocao plantings have been heavy lately for the same reason, and there are high hopes that the production of cotton and other fibers can be expanded sufficiently to supply domestic needs. However, even if the domestic market could be reserved for domestic producers, this market would not long support the rate of growth of agricultural production which has occurred in the postwar period.

There is considerable opportunity to influence levels of, and types of, agricultural development through tax policy. Paradoxically, a high land tax not only would introduce a desirable progression in the Philippine tax system, but would minimize the large amounts of land which are presently withheld from production. The absence of out-of-pocket costs when land is idle and the secular tendency for land to increase in value have retarded the development of large holdings of potentially productive land. Taxation of land would tend to reduce land values, which would probably contribute to diffusion of land ownership. A reduction in land prices not only would expand the opportunities for present cultivators to purchase land, but would tend to reduce the costs of land reform and thereby increase the chances of implementation of reform.

[41] Production of Virginia leaf tobacco expanded from 846 metric tons in 1954 to 19,738 metric tons in 1956. Crop area increased from 4,710 hectares to 35,330 hectares (Central Bank, *Eighth Annual Report, 1956,* p. 42).

More important, direct taxation of land could produce large government revenues, which could be expended for productive social investment in agricultural production. Transportation facilities, irrigation, and agricultural extension and research as well as outlays for education and health are areas for social investment which will enhance the productivity of resources engaged in agriculture. So far as agricultural production is concerned, the need for social investment in agricultural production has been alleviated by the availability of new land. As land resources become relatively scarce, agricultural investment policy will undoubtedly shift toward fruitful investments in irrigation, agricultural experimentation and research, and the like.

· XIII ·

Foreign Aid and

Reparations Policy

ECONOMIC aid to the Philippines should be analyzed in terms of two distinct problems and periods: the rehabilitation effort covering 1944 to 1950 and the period of developmental aid following 1950.

The United States rehabilitation effort in the Philippines involved a wide range of institutions and policies.[1] The dimensions of this effort have not been precisely defined, although the major boundaries can be identified. Approximately $1.2 billion of payments can be directly identified with Philippine rehabilitation including war damage payments, $520 million; transfers of surplus property, $100 million; ad hoc budgetary assistance, $216 million; back payments to Philippine forces inducted into the USAFFE, $137 million; United States Veteran's Administration payments, $163 million; and civilian relief, $56 million. In addition, Philippine rehabilitation benefited from the restoration of essential services such as transportation, water supply, and electricity by the United States armed forces. Philippine policy with respect to rehabilitation was virtually nonexistent unless the exchange rate policy which maximized imports can be called a rehabilitation policy.

[1] For a useful survey of the U.S. contribution to Philippine rehabilitation, see Hartendorp, *History*, pp. 167–205, 375–381. Also see above pp. 60–62.

By the end of 1950 economic rehabilitation of Philippine productive capacity was substantially completed, and steps were taken to shift the economic relationship between the Philippines and the United States to a continuing program of developmental aid. Since 1950 a structure of institutions appropriate to successful United States participation in Philippine economic development has been created. Over this same period the economic aid programs and policies both of the United States and the Philippines have displayed flexibility in confronting and solving problems peculiar to Philippine economic development.

It will be recalled that the Quirino-Foster Agreement committed the Philippines to implement the recommendations of the Bell Mission report and the United States as a *quid pro quo* agreed to establish an economic aid program in the Philippines.[2] An Economic and Technical Co-operation Agreement between the two governments was signed in Manila on April 27, 1951, and a United States Special and Technical Economic Mission was immediately dispatched to Manila to initiate the aid program.[3]

The Philippines took a number of important steps to make its participation in the economic aid program effective. The most significant move was the enactment of Republic Act No. 604 of April 27, 1951, which established a counterpart fund to cover peso costs of economic aid programs.[4] Philippine acceptance of the principle of appropriating counterpart funds "in sums commensurate with the dollar value of the goods, and cost of services and technical assistance to be made available to the Philippines from the Government of the United States through the Economic Co-operation Administration" represented an important milestone in economic aid policy. Appropriation of counterpart funds established a firm Philippine stake in the economic aid program which ensured a high degree of co-operation and collaboration. Moreover, in the absence of Philippine appropriation of peso counterpart funds, local currency costs of economic aid would have had to be provided by the sale of economic aid program imports in the Philippines. To the extent that economic aid was allocated to social investment projects, this probably would have required the import of consumer goods salable in the Philippines and would thereby have

[2] The *Bell Mission Report* recommended an economic aid program of $250 million over five years.

[3] See above, pp. 83–84.

[4] Sec. 1 of the Annex to the Economic and Technical Co-operation Agreement of April 27, 1951, committed the Philippines to appropriation of counterpart funds.

reduced the capacity of the aid mission to reserve dollar appropriations for relatively high-priority capital goods imports.

While Philippine counterpart appropriations have not been commensurate with dollar expenditures by the United States, they have been substantial.[5] They have resulted in desirable independence and autonomy for the aid agency and have been adequate to provide the peso costs of the wide range of constructive programs initiated within the economic aid program. In addition, the counterpart fund has been augmented by peso proceeds from sales of United States aid goods imported into the Philippines under various programs. Counterpart appropriations are used exclusively to support "projects," while costs of technical assistance, administrative costs of the United States government in the Philippines, and peso expenditures of the Joint United States Military Advisory Group have been supported by the proceeds of the sale of aid imports.

In Republic Act 604 the Philippine Congress took occasion to define the nature of the economic aid program envisaged for the Philippines. Economic aid policy was defined as that policy which "will provide insofar as possible the greatest good for the greatest number of Philippine people, promote economic opportunity, and remove the causes of social discontent and unrest" (Section 4). A list of specific economic aid objectives followed:

Financing the construction and rehabilitation of roads and bridges and other transportation and communication facilities to promote marketing of agriculture, forestry and mine products . . . ;

Rehabilitation or construction of irrigation systems, flood control, reclamation projects and waterworks systems and artesian wells;

Financing agricultural production and marketing through aids to rural credit and marketing institutions in form of capital and technical assistance;

Expansion of existing industries or the establishment of new ones, including the expansion of power resources, which may be essential to the development of the national economy;

Improvement of living conditions of the mass of the people by increasing their purchasing power through home industries and through the promotion of vocational education, adult and community schools, public health, slum clearance and low cost housing projects;

[5] Republic Act No. 604 of April 27, 1951, appropriated ₱50 million; No. 821 of Aug. 14, 1952, ₱33.7 million; No. 902 of June 20, 1953, ₱20 million; No. 1278 of June 14, 1955, ₱23 million. As of Dec. 31, 1958, Philippine counterpart contributions totaled ₱142 million.

Assistance to dollar producing and dollar saving industries through loans or otherwise;

Assistance to agriculture, industry, public works and public administration through added and improved technical services and training and research facilities;

Financial aid to resettlement projects . . . and facilitation of the distribution of, and issuance of title to, public lands to homesteaders and other lawful occupants;

Financing the purchase of agricultural and/or residential lands for the purpose of subdividing them for resale to actual occupants or tenants, financial aid to tenants in the purchase of land;

Promotion of measures, including fiscal, designed to stabilize the monetary situation and reduce the cost of living particularly for the indigent and extraordinarily low income groups;

Facilitate the importation of goods and commodities essential to the general good of the Philippine people.

Although the statement of economic aid objectives included many unexceptionable platitudes, it was distinctive for emphasis on agricultural development and social investment. This emphasis was undoubtedly due to deep concern for the agrarian unrest arising out of tenancy and poverty which had been the principal source of Huk strength.

As in other countries, the United States aid program in the Philippines is organized to promote "co-operative" action with appropriate agencies of the Philippine government. Economic aid activities are jointly planned by the economic aid mission and the Philippine counterpart planning agency. During the first four years of the economic aid program the Philippine agency for planning the expenditure of dollar aid and Philippine counterpart peso appropriations was the Philippine Council for United States Aid (PHILCUSA). In mid-1955 President Magsaysay, in accordance with recommendations originating in a management-consulting contract financed by aid funds, reorganized the National Economic Council, and PHILCUSA became the Office of Foreign Aid Co-ordination of the NEC.[6]

An important contribution to the success of the United States aid program has been the high quality of personnel assigned to PHILCUSA and the Office of Foreign Aid Co-ordination. During the formative years of these agencies leadership was provided by Jose Yulo, a highly

[6] Executive Order No. 119 of July 1, 1955.

respected and experienced civil servant and statesman. Yulo assembled a competent staff headed by Filemon Rodriguez, an engineer, and Amando Dalisay, an economist, who provided the continuity necessary for effective participation by the aid agency in the transition from the Quirino to the Magsaysay administration. Yulo resigned as Co-ordinator of United States Aid in the late summer of 1953 to run for Vice-President on the Liberal party ticket, and his place was taken by Placido L. Mapa. In January 1954 Magsaysay appointed Filemon C. Rodriguez Co-ordinator of United States Aid and concurrently chairman of the National Economic Council. Following the integration of PHILCUSA into the National Economic Council in July 1955, Alfredo Montelibano succeeded Rodriguez as chairman of the NEC and the latter became head of the Office of Foreign Aid Co-ordination.[7]

During the first four years of the economic aid program the objectives defined in Republic Act No. 604 were adhered to faithfully and the principal part of the expenditures was allocated to agricultural development and social investment—primarily in roads and other transportation facilities with substantial allocations to public health, education, and public administration.

The election of a Nacionalista administration and Congress in the fall of 1953 was followed by significant changes in economic policy. The Philippines had become increasingly restless under the economic aid policies laid down in 1951. In the first place, the Huk threat had been reduced to minor proportions by 1951. Second, rapid improvement in the economic environment and evidence of improving public morality tended to restore faith in democratic institutions and in government at all levels.

Equally important was the growing Nacionalista influence in government. The only significant difference between the Nacionalista and Liberal parties in the postwar period has been in the area of relations with the United States. Although the Nacionalistas are not essentially anti-American, they have a long-standing tradition of skepticism of United States policies and relatively more determination to enhance Philippine autonomy and sovereignty. The economic aid program tended to come under attack as having the effect of maintaining the

[7] In recent years appointments to top positions in the NEC have been increasingly political as the administration has tried to establish a congressional commitment to NEC plans, and Senators Gil Puyat and Pacita Gonzalez have served as acting chairmen of the NEC. Currently, the chairman is ex-Senator Jose Locsin, who was defeated in the elections of 1957.

colonial type of specialization on primary production and neglecting potentialities for Philippine industrialization. Nacionalista agitation for a change in economic aid policy culminated in Concurrent Resolution No. 13 of May 18, 1954, which was extremely critical of the policies and accomplishments of the economic aid program.[8] The Concurrent Resolution stated:

Whereas, from a scrutiny of the projects that have been undertaken . . . it appears that undue emphasis had been placed on agricultural development or on projects related thereto as well as on projects in the field of public administration and social development, the operation and maintenance of which have increasingly imposed financial burdens on the part of the Philippine Government;

Whereas, the present administration is embarking on a continuing five-year economic development program which places a relatively greater emphasis than heretofore on industrial development and that under the said economic development program there is need of promoting the growth and establishment of new and necessary industries; Now, therefore, be it

Resolved by the Senate, the House of Representatives of the Philippines concurring, . . .

1. That it is the sense of the Congress of the Philippines that there is need of shifting the direction of the aforementioned Agreement of April twenty-seven, nineteen hundred and fifty-one, to that segment of the economy requiring the promotion of industrial development so as to achieve a viable and balanced economy in the Philippines;

2. That, in order to achieve the objective of effecting a change in the character and extent of the provisions thereof, it is desirable that at least twenty per centum of such dollar promotion programmed and expanded each year should take the form of machinery and equipment for new and necessary industries in such manner that the peso proceeds realized from the sale of said machinery and equipment to private investors may be utilized to supplement the peso counterpart funds that are provided by direct appropriation by the Congress.

The shift in policy proposed in Concurrent Resolution No. 13 was quickly reflected in the economic aid program. During the three fiscal years following fiscal year 1953–54 dollar outlays for industrial and mining development amounted to $37.6 million as compared to $1.4

---

[8] Of the twelve substantive concurrent resolutions of the congressional session in 1954, nine were addressed to aspects of U.S. relations with the Philippines. The Nacionalista Congress proposed major changes in existing U.S. policies and practices with respect to the Philippines. See R.P., Office of the President, *Laws and Resolutions,* vol. IX (Manila: Bureau of Printing, 1955).

million in the preceding years of the economic aid program (Table 50).
The ratio of outlays for industrial and mining development to total
dollar outlays for economic aid increased from 2.0 per cent to 36.5 per
cent. The sharpest cutback occurred in dollar outlays for agricultural
development, which declined from $25.5 million to $10.4 million or
from 37 per cent to 10 per cent.[9] Similarly, dollar outlays on public
health and education were reduced from a total of $17.2 million to
$9.1 million, and outlays on public administration were also reduced in
proportion to the total. Furthermore, there was a sharp increase in
United States aid expenditures. During the three years and three
months of the economic aid program up to the end of fiscal year 1953–
54 United States dollar aid was extended at an average annual rate of
$23.9 million,[10] whereas in the next three fiscal years the annual rate
was $34.4 million.

The economic aid program has indeed been a co-operative effort
with counterpart funds appropriated by the Philippine government
accounting for 28.3 per cent of total economic aid outlays. As of the
end of 1958, such appropriations totaled ₱142 million with a further
₱58 million of peso counterpart funds accruing from the sale of United
States aid imports. Disbursements from the counterpart fund included:
peso costs of projects, ₱149 million; technical assistance, ₱18 million;
administrative expenses of the United States government, ₱11 million;
and allocations to the Joint United States Military Advisory Group,
₱14 million.[11]

During the six fiscal years ending June 30, 1957, expenditures under
the economic aid program totaled the equivalent of approximately
$240 million. United States dollar aid of $171 million to the end of
fiscal year 1956–57 was equivalent to 28.5 per cent of the investment
outlays by the Philippine government, or about 0.6 per cent of Philippine national income. Total expenditures under the aid program including Philippine peso counterpart expenditures amounted to approximately 1 per cent of the Philippine gross national product in the period
under consideration.

[9] However, if outlays on community development are included in agricultural
development outlays—as they properly should be—the decline in the latter would
be $10.2 million.
[10] This includes net imports of commodities for resale in the Philippines to
generate counterpart funds in the first year of the economic aid program. Total
appropriations for dollar aid to the end of FY 1954–55 amounted to $79.7 million,
of which $11.5 million was allocated through the counterpart fund.
[11] Central Bank, *Tenth Annual Report, 1958*, p. 144.

Table 50. Allocation of economic aid expenditures [a]
($ million or pesos converted to dollar equivalent)

	FY 1951–1954				FY 1955–1957			
	U.S. aid	Philippine counterpart	Total dollar equivalent	Ratio to total	U.S. aid	Philippine counterpart	Total dollar equivalent	Ratio to total expenditure
Agriculture	25.5	10.6	36.1	**34.6**	10.4	5.0	15.4	11.4
Public works including roads [b]	20.7	11.7	32.4	31.1	36.9	17.2	54.1	40.1
Public health	9.6	1.9	11.5	11.0	6.8	.2	7.0	5.2
Education	7.6	2.9	10.5	10.1	2.3	2.3	4.6	3.4
Public administration	3.0	2.9	5.9	5.7	3.1	1.2	4.3	3.2
Industry and mining	1.4	4.4	5.8	5.7	37.6	5.3	42.9	31.8
Community development	—	1.5 [c]	1.5	1.5	4.9	.2 [c]	5.1	3.8
Labor and other	.3	.1	.4	.4	1.1	.3	1.4	1.0
	68.1	36.0	104.1	100.0	103.1	31.7	134.8	100.0

[a] U.S., International Co-operation Administration, in Hartendorp, *History*, pp. 383, 592, 593. The figures do not include outlays of the Technical Assistance Trust Fund of $6.9 million equivalent and U.S. government administrative costs equivalent to $4.1 million.
[b] Includes defense support construction.
[c] Includes expenditures on housing.

Although aggregate expenditures were not large when related to economic accounting magnitudes, the economic aid program exerted an influence in the area of social reform not to be measured in dollars. The leverage embodied in the special United States relationship with the Philippines reinforced the leadership provided by the Philippine executive to produce a number of important social reforms. The early emphasis on agricultural development assisted very materially in bringing the Agricultural Credit and Co-operative Financing Administration and the system of Farmers' Co-operative Marketing Associations into existence and ensuring their survival. Equally important were the expenditures which transformed the Bureau of Lands into an efficient institution for distributing public lands. Early emphasis on road construction has paid substantial dividends in facilitating land colonization and improving the internal marketing of agricultural produce. Similarly, the emphasis on public health and education has provided facilities and services heretofore neglected.

The United States economic aid program has been the principal economic aid institution, but the Philippines has also been the recipient of economic development assistance through other programs. For example, the Philippines has steadily expanded its use of commodities available under the United States Public Law 480 program. Such commodities are sold for local currencies, and a major part of the sales proceeds is made available to finance aid projects. The initial Public Law 480 agreement between the two countries was signed June 25, 1957, and provided for sale to the Philippines for pesos of $10.3 million of surplus commodities including rice ($2.5 million), cotton ($4.9 million), dairy products ($1.1 million), meat products ($.5 million), and inedible tallow ($.5 million), with the remainder to pay the costs of transportation.[12] The United States allocated peso proceeds of the sale as follows: loan to the Philippine government for economic development, ₱10.4 million; allocation for use by Philippine armed forces, ₱4.2 million, and allocation for purpose of educational exchanges,

[12] Public Law 480 was enacted in 1954, but the Philippines did not utilize this type of economic aid until mid-1957. It was widely rumored that earlier negotiations over such assistance had broken down over attempts on the part of the U.S. Department of Agriculture to include Virginia leaf tobacco in the surplus commodities shipped to the Philippines. Such a position on the part of the United States was believed to have resulted from the insistence of influential southern legislators who wanted to retaliate for the Philippine policy of limiting leaf tobacco imports from the United States. For example, see R.P., *Official Gazette*, 51 (July 1955), p. ccxvii.

United States government expenditures, and development of new markets for exports of United States agricultural products, ₱6.0 million.[13]

A second sale of Public Law 480 commodities occurred in June 1958 and included rice valued at $3.6 million plus $.5 million for transportation. The peso proceeds were allocated as follows: United States government expenditures, ₱2.5 million; Philippine armed forces, ₱2.0 million; United States Export-Import Bank to loan to United States business firms investing in the Philippines, ₱2.0 million; and educational exchange, ₱1.7 million.

Philippine enthusiasm for Public Law 480 agricultural surplus commodities has rapidly increased,[14] and steps have been taken to integrate this assistance into Philippine policy with respect to "new and necessary industries." For example, in May 1957 the Monetary Board in approving a foreign exchange allocation for a "new and necessary" flour mill specified that the mill would use Public Law 480 wheat. In July 1957 the NEC in approving the investment applications of two "new and necessary" firms to produce canned milk specified that the powdered milk imports should be provided by Public Law 480 assistance. During 1957 a number of applications for industrial priorities for "new and necessary industries" using cotton as a raw material specified that the cotton was expected under Public Law 480. There is, of course, a good deal of risk in tieing Philippine industrialization to continued availability of surplus commodities, and acceptance of this risk is a Philippine policy decision of considerable importance to Philippine plans for industrialization.

Still another aspect of Philippine economic aid policy is represented by the Industrial Development Center (IDC). IDC, a joint project of the National Economic Council and the United States aid mission, was established in February 1955 to provide technical, managerial, and financial assistance to domestic industries, particularly to small and medium-sized industries. IDC's industrial financing program is fourfold in scope. Direct dollar aid provides foreign exchange to buy capital goods and machinery. Dollar loans are also arranged through

[13] The dispersal of peso proceeds of PL 480 sales is not included in the tabulation of economic aid expenditures in Table 50.

[14] For example, on Nov. 17, 1954, the cabinet "approved in principle" the purchase of 300,000 tons of rice. On Sept. 13, 1957, the Board of Directors of NAMARCO approved purchases of rice and cheddar cheese totaling $2.9 million. On Feb. 5, 1958, the cabinet "approved" the procurement of 100,000 metric tons of rice, 15,000 metric tons of corn, 38,500 bales of cotton, 30 million pounds of skim milk, 16 million pounds of edible tallow, and 34,000 long tons of wheat.

the United States Export-Import Bank. Peso loans arranged through time deposits with commercial banks are made available to industrial firms on a long-term basis. There is also an industrial and livestock loan guarantee program under which IDC guarantees from 50 to 80 per cent to secure approved industrial loans.

As of May 31, 1958, IDC announced that it had extended ₱33.2 million of peso loans to 58 Philippine manufacturing firms and $39.4 million of dollar loans to 223 firms. Export-Import Bank loans of $18.3 million had been arranged, and Industrial Loan Fund Guarantees covering ₱8.9 million on 15 applications had been extended.[15]

IDC has proved to be an effective instrument for promoting economic development by channeling dollar aid and peso counterpart appropriations to private enterprise. IDC has been liberally supplied with funds, and the variety of programs permits it to participate in a wide range of industrial situations.

Still another aspect of Philippine economic aid policy associated with the United States economic aid mission is the investment guarantee program.[16] The guarantee program provides two types of insurance for United States investors. First, the investor is assured that he can convert new investments into dollars. Second, the fund provides dollar compensation for loss due to expropriation or confiscation of industrial investments. Convertibility and expropriation insurance are provided for a premium payment of approximately 0.5 per cent of the guarantee coverage.

Utilization of the ICA investment guarantee program by United States investors has been expanding at a very rapid rate in recent months.[17] Convertibility guarantees covering the Philippine investments of five United States firms and amounting to $4.7 million had been extended as of June 30, 1958. Expropriation guarantees in the same amount had also been made.

[15] See *Phil. Newsletter,* June 19, 1958, p. 2. Approximately four-fifths of the dollar aid was extended to Philippine-owned firms.

[16] The U.S.–Philippine Agreement providing for the extension of guarantees to U.S. investment in the Philippines was signed in Washington on Feb. 20, 1952.

[17] As of the end of 1958 the total of all guarantees under the loan guarantee program amounted to approximately $400 million. In the last half of 1958 guarantees were being issued at an annual rate of $350 million, and pending applications totaled $1,040 million, of which $16.8 million were for investments in the Philippines. Only a minor portion of guarantees and pending applications have applied to U.S. investments in the less-developed countries (International Cooperation Administration, Investment Guarantees Staff, *Quarterly Report* [Washington, 1958]).

Still another aspect of Philippine economic aid policy has been the increasing use of United States Export-Import Bank loans. The initial loan, to meet dollar costs of the Ambuklao hydroelectric project, was negotiated for $20 million in 1952.[18] In early 1956 Governor Cuaderno negotiated with the Export-Import Bank a line of credit of $65 million for the Central Bank. Only a minor part of this credit was utilized in the ensuing three and a half years.[19] The Export-Import credit was renewed and increased to $75 million during President Garcia's visit to the United States June 18–20, 1958.[20] The Philippines has also received short-term credits from the Export-Import Bank for imports of United States agricultural commodities. For example, on June 28, 1957, a loan agreement for $10 million to import canned milk, cotton, and corn was signed in Manila.[21]

Another potential source of economic development assistance which the Philippines has taken steps to utilize is the United States Development Loan Fund inaugurated in November 1957 with a modest appropriation of $300 million. In February 1958 Ambassador Bohlen reported that, although the DLF had received applications exceeding $1.3 billion from some 28 countries, applications for only a relatively small amount and in preliminary form had been received from the Philippines.[22] However, the communiqué issued at the conclusion of President Garcia's visit in June 1958 announced that the "Development Loan Fund would examine specific projects submitted to it to determine whether they would merit Development Loan Fund financing in an amount not to exceed $50,000,000." [23]

[18] The loan agreement was signed on July 23, 1952.

[19] Ambassador Bohlen in a speech before the Manila Lions Club on Feb. 12, 1958, reported that $46 million of the Export-Import line of credit was unused (*Manila Times,* Feb. 13, 1958).

[20] See joint statement by President Garcia and President Eisenhower, issued June 20, 1958. A Philippine press release recapitulating the accomplishments of President Garcia's state visit reported that applications to the U.S. Export-Import Bank for loans totaling $74 million for the construction of a steel mill were in the final stages of negotiation. The steel mill loans had not been approved as of February 1960.

[21] By June 30, 1959, Export-Import Bank loans totaling $119.1 million had been approved, of which $37.2 million had actually been disbursed. See *Phil. Newsletter,* Jan. 8, 1960.

[22] Speech before the Manila Lions Club, Feb. 12, 1958.

[23] The initial DLF loan to a Philippine borrower was a loan of $5 million to the Central Bank for redistribution to small borrowers. On May 19, 1959, the DLF announced the first loan of $5.3 million to a private Philippine enterprise, the Bataan Pulp and Paper Mill. By Sept. 1, 1959, loans to Philippine borrowers

In addition to assistance from diverse United States programs, the Philippines has benefited from assistance extended by a number of international institutions. In November 1957 the Philippines was extended a loan of $21 million by the International Bank for Reconstruction and Development (IBRD) to finance the foreign exchange costs of the Binga hydroelectric project in northern Luzon.[24]

Republic Act No. 1604 of August 23, 1956, appropriated funds and authorized Philippine membership in the International Finance Corporation, an IBRD subsidiary established to channel loans to private investors in less-developed countries.[25] In view of the limited resources of the IFC at the present time, it is unlikely that this institution will be a significant source of Philippine developmental assistance in the near future.

Other international sources of developmental assistance include United Nations technical assistance, which in recent years has been extended at an annual rate of approximately $.4 million.[26] CARE programs have resulted in the transfer of significant amounts of commodities to the Philippines, thereby conserving Philippine foreign exchange for other purposes. For example, CARE announced in January 1958 the initial shipment of 26 million pounds of powdered milk in a $6 million program to provide milk to school children.[27] Similarly, the Philippines has benefited from technical assistance and other aid from a variety of United Nations agencies including WHO, ILO, FAO, and UNESCO. Finally, the Philippines joined the Colombo Plan at the end of 1951. Modest amounts of technical assistance have been received under the Plan.

A related aspect of Philippine economic policy is represented by

totaling $38.1 million had been authorized by the DLF. See *Phil. Newsletter,* May 29, 1959, and Jan. 8, 1960.

[24] Negotiations involving a Philippine proposal for IBRD funds for the hydroelectric power and fertilizer plant at Maria Cristina in northern Mindanao were initiated in 1948. Republic Act No. 357 of June 4, 1949, authorized the National Power Corporation to negotiate such a loan. The IBRD subsequently rejected the Philippine proposal, and the initial Maria Cristina construction was financed by Philippine resources.

[25] The Philippine membership agreement with the IFC was signed by Ambassador Romulo in Washington on Aug. 23, 1957.

[26] On Nov. 22, 1957, the UN Technical Assistance Administration announced that $408,000 had been allocated to the Philippines for technical assistance in 1958 as compared to $406,000 in 1957 (*Phil. Newsletter,* Nov. 22, 1957, p. 6).

[27] *Ibid.,* Jan. 24, 1958, p. 7.

steps taken to utilize Japanese reparations.[28] The negotiation of a reparations settlement with Japan was characterized by a number of false starts and widespread recriminations, and it became an important issue in Philippine domestic politics. For a decade the reparations question was the major issue affecting Philippine-Japanese relations. Initial steps toward a reparations settlement were taken at the San Francisco Conference of 1951, when members of the Philippine delegation met with Japanese representatives for preliminary talks. Although the Philippines signed the draft peace treaty, it quickly became evident that the Philippine Congress did not intend to ratify the treaty until an acceptable reparations agreement had been negotiated.

Actual negotiation of a reparations agreement began in Manila on January 28, 1952, when a Philippine team led by Foreign Affairs Secretary Joaquin Elizalde met with a Japanese group led by Juichi Tsushima, Foreign Ministry Advisor. The talks ended February 14 when the Japanese, having learned the outlines of Philippine demands, returned to Japan.[29]

The next phase of negotiations occurred in December 1952 when Eiji Wajima, chief of the Asian Bureau of the Japanese Department of Foreign Affairs, visited Manila with a counterproposal listing services Japan was willing to supply as reparations. It became clear as a result of the Wajima visit that the two countries were taking radically different positions on the issue. The Philippines tended to insist on agreement on the amount of reparations first, with discussion of the nature of payment later. Japan took the position that Philippine requirements should be determined first, then Japan's capacity to meet these requirements, and only after that the amount itself.[30] By

[28] Discussion of Japanese reparations under the heading of economic aid policy will undoubtedly be misunderstood. This is not to say that Japanese reparations are analogous to economic aid in the sense that they are unrequited transfers. It is clear, however, that rehabilitation of war damage has long since been accomplished in the aggregate. Therefore, the flow of reparations and loans under the reparations agreement represents an important opportunity for the Philippines to accelerate economic growth. In this sense the reparations are analogous to economic aid.

[29] The initial Philippine position consisted of three points: (a) Japan must pay $8 billion, the official Philippine estimate of war damages; (b) part of this sum must be paid before ratification of the peace treaty; and (c) payment should be completed within a period of ten to fifteen years. See *Manila Times*, Jan. 29, 1952.

[30] See *ibid.*, Dec. 22, 25, 1952.

presenting a list of services available for reparations, the Japanese provided the Filipinos with a more realistic base from which to estimate reparations requirements.

The next step was the abortive Garcia-Ohno Agreement of April 15, 1954. Japan agreed to provide reparations in the form of services valued at $400 million. Reparations were to be scheduled over ten years, with possible prolongation another ten years. The agreement also included the ambiguous statement that the "economic value that will accrue to the Philippines" from the reparations services will not be less than $1 billion and will be determined by a joint commission.[31] The Garcia-Ohno plan ran into immediate opposition in the Philippine Senate, and on April 20, 1954, the administration announced that reparations negotiations had been postponed indefinitely. This action merely recognized the impossibility of getting Senate ratification of the Garcia-Ohno plan.

Almost a year elapsed before reparations talks were resumed. On March 29, 1955, a team of Philippine technical experts from various government departments met with a counterpart Japanese team, and for the first time the negotiations entered the phase of specifying commodities and services. The technical conference was completed on May 20, 1955, and negotiation of the total reparations and the division between reparations and loans was taken up by diplomatic teams. Final agreement was not reached until May 9, 1956, when the reparations treaty was signed in Manila.[32]

The Reparations Agreement provides for reparations, i.e., "services of the Japanese people and the products of Japan in the form of capital goods," equivalent to $550 million, to be supplied at an average annual rate of $25 million during the first ten years of the agreement and at an average annual rate of $30 million during the following ten years. The two governments shall fix, "through consultation, an annual schedule specifying the services and products supplied by Japan each year."[33] It was further provided that the Reparations Agreement would enter into force "either on the date of exchange of the instruments of ratification or on the date the Republic

[31] *Ibid.*, April 15, 1954; also *Philippines Free Press*, April 24, 1954, p. 1.
[32] Senate rejection of the Garcia-Ohno Agreement was vindicated by the substantially larger amount of reparations the Philippines received in the final settlement.
[33] An Annex to the agreement lists a wide range of economic development "projects" for which reparations may be scheduled.

of the Philippines deposits its instrument of ratification of the Treaty of Peace with Japan." In addition to the reparations transfers, a separate note provides that the Japanese government will undertake to facilitate $250 million of loans to be made by private Japanese firms and individuals to Filipino firms and nationals on a commercial basis. Loans shall be primarily in the form of capital goods and shall be on terms "as favorable as warranted by commercial considerations." [34]

In the following session of Congress national policy with respect to reparations was defined in Republic Act No. 1789 of June 21, 1957, as the utilization of all reparations payments "in such manner as shall assure the maximum possible economic benefit to the Filipino people and in as equitable and widespread manner as possible" (Section 1). Utilization of reparations transfers shall be carried out in accordance with the broad program, criteria, and priorities established by the National Economic Council and subject to the following criteria (Section 2):

(e) In general, preference in the procurement of reparations goods and services shall be given to private productive projects: Provided, that during the first year . . . all reparations goods and services . . . shall be earmarked exclusively for government projects, and thereafter, government projects shall be given preference only if they concern electrification, firefighting equipment, tele-communication or railroad or would foster the growth of private productive capacity, or are needed in the performance of essential public services, or involve productive projects which private enterprise is not yet capable or desirous of developing but which are urgently necessary in the interest of overall national economic growth. . . . Provided, further, That not more than sixty per cent of the total value of the reparations to be paid by Japan during the twenty-year period shall be allocated to the private sector: Provided, further, That if the private sector does not or cannot make full use of its allocation, then the portion not so used shall be made available to the government.

(f) The proceeds from the sale of reparations goods or the utilization of services shall be placed in a Special Economic Development Fund . . . which shall be available to the Rehabilitation Finance Corporation and the Philippine National Bank for loans for economic and industrial development

[34] For the complete text of the Reparations Agreement, Annex, and accompanying note covering the loan agreement, see the *Manila Times*, May 11, 1956. The Reparations Agreement, the Annex thereto, and the notes exchanged were ratified by Senate Resolution No. 78 of July 16, 1956. The Treaty of Peace with Japan was ratified by Senate Resolution No. 79 of July 16, 1956.

projects as well as for construction, reconstruction, repair and/or improvement of public school buildings. . . . Provided, further, that fifty per cent of such Special Trust Fund shall be available for industrial loans, thirty per cent for agricultural loans and the remaining twenty per cent for public school construction. . . . The sum of twenty million pesos shall likewise be set aside to constitute a revolving fund which shall be used exclusively to aid in the establishment of rural banks . . . ; and the further sum of fifty million pesos for the purchase of landed estates as provided for in the Land Tenure Act.

Philippine reparations policy seems clearly defined. It assigns primary importance to private investment by allocating a maximum of 60 per cent of reparations transfers to private investors. In addition, it provides that the peso counterpart generated by the sale of reparations will be available primarily for industrial and agricultural loans. The policy provides further that yen loans to be facilitated by the Japanese government will go exclusively to private borrowers.[35] To implement national policy Republic Act No. 1789 establishes a Reparations Commission of three members.[36]

As was planned, reparations transfers in the first year of the agreement were concentrated in the public sector. During the first year ending July 22, 1957, contracts totaled $30 million and deliveries half that amount. During the second year ending July 22, 1958, the two countries agreed on procurement totaling $44 million, with deliveries totaling $35 million, which would bring deliveries during the first two years to the agreed rate of $25 million annually.[37]

An important development with respect to reparations occurred in 1957 when a mission of Philippine bankers was sent to Tokyo to make arrangements with the Export-Import Bank of Japan for implementation of the $250 million of economic development loans specified by the Reparations Agreement. It was announced that the Export-Import Bank of Japan would extend the loans on a participation basis with Japanese commercial banks, the participation of the Export-Import Bank of Japan in such loans to be not less than 60 per

[35] Republic Act No. 1789 also provides for reparations transfers of consumer goods under special circumstances to be marketed exclusively through the National Marketing Corporation (NAMARCO).

[36] Executive Order No. 315 of Sept. 1, 1958, prescribed rules of procedure for the Reparations Commission, and Executive Order No. 320 of Nov. 14, 1958, prescribed further operating procedures.

[37] *Manila Times*, March 20, 1958.

cent. Philippine banks will serve as intermediaries between the Japanese banks and the Philippine importing and industrial interests and will guarantee repayment of the loans. Interest is expected to average about 6 per cent, and the term of payment in ordinary cases is expected to be about five years. An initial payment of about 20 to 25 per cent of the contracted value has to be made by the Philippine importer.[38]

Low levels of public morality and efficiency in the early postwar years resulted in widespread apprehension regarding administration of the reparations program. The well-publicized procurement of a yacht for the use of the Philippine President as well as suspension of reparations transfers to World War II Veterans Enterprises, Inc., tended to substantiate such fears.[39] Formal aspects of the reparations program are well conceived to contribute to Philippine economic growth. Private enterprise is scheduled to receive a substantial portion of the reparations transfers and is allocated the entire development loan portion. The growing pressure for social services and public investment should be relieved by reparations transfers allocated to the Philippine government. On the other hand, there is a strong ground swell of rumors emanating from both Manila and Tokyo suggesting that the reparations program may be succumbing to the seamier side of Philippine political activity.

[38] R.P., Office of the President, Malacañan Press Release, July 16, 1957. See *Manila Times,* July 17, 1957.

[39] See *Manila Times,* Dec. 12, 1958. World War II Veterans Enterprises, Inc., was allocated $8 million out of a total of $20 million in reparations in the first two years of the agreement for the purpose of rehabilitating veterans. In late 1959 a major reparations scandal involving acquisition of offshore fishing vessels and fish-canning equipment was revealed. By mid-1960 a major scandal appeared to be materializing in the procurement of ocean-going vessels as reparations. It was alleged that collusion between Filipino politicians and Japanese shipbuilders resulted in substantial overpricing of such vessels. It was reported that thirty ocean-going vessels were being procured as reparations.

· XIV ·

Economic Nationalism

ECONOMIC nationalism is a pervasive Philippine policy objective discernible throughout legislative, executive, and judicial activity. For purposes of analysis it is appropriate to distinguish two broad, and frequently overlapping, categories of economic nationalism. First is economic nationalism, broadly conceived, as manifested in policies designed to promote economic growth in directions conceived to be in the national interest.[1] For example, economic nationalism is reflected in the use of the powers of government to ensure that international specialization and trade are in the national interest. A second variety of economic nationalism is reflected in the determination of Filipinos to Filipinize their economy. Colonial economic development in the Philippines as elsewhere in Southeast Asia was characterized by progressive alienization. Ownership of productive assets outside the subsistence agricultural sector tended to be vested in aliens, including the economically rational Chinese, Japanese, and other Asian minorities as well as the dominant Westerners. Alienization resulted from superior business acumen and willingness on the part of alien

---

[1] The national interest is a dynamic concept requiring the resolution of conflicts between short-run and long-run considerations as well as those arising out of priorities assigned to security, equality, social stability, economic growth, and so forth. Political institutions and processes permit more or less satisfactory identification of the national interest.

312

minorities to save and invest productively. Such qualities were richly rewarded by the colonial laissez-faire economy which began to appear in the latter part of the nineteenth century and which was fully developed during the American colonial era. The relative absence of such qualities in the tradition-bound Philippine culture precluded the appearance of extensive indigenous entrepreneurship.

Filipinization is a policy of de-alienization, i.e., of increasing Filipino participation in, and control of, major areas of economic activity. Filipinization can be promoted by policies which (a) expand Philippine economic activity relative to the normal expansion in alien participation, (b) prohibit further growth in alien ownership, (c) reduce alien ownership by establishing incentives to disinvest, and (d) transfer alien assets to Filipinos with, or without, compensation.

Filipinization is reflected in a wide range of independent policies. For example, in the absence of private initiative and resources the Philippine government has expanded its economic functions to include commercial, industrial, agricultural, and financial enterprises. Expansion of such public activities has found ready acceptance in the past as such enterprises help to satisfy a deep-seated urge to Filipinize productive resources. More important to achievement of Filipinization is the widespread use of public policy to redress handicaps which have limited participation by Filipinos in domestic and foreign commerce and manufacturing. For example, government monopolization of foreign exchange has been developed into a powerful weapon for increasing the share of nationals in import and retail trade. Commercial and exchange control policies have also contributed to Filipinization of production and marketing of exports. In some cases government monopolies established to implement exchange controls and to produce government revenues have nationalized export industries formerly dominated by aliens.

Filipinization is a joint product of policies which in many cases were originally adopted in pursuit of other policy objectives, e.g., the need for government revenues or balance of payments considerations. Recognition of the utility of particular policies to the pursuit of de-alienization introduces an element of stability into such policies which may conflict with the goal of material progress.

Economic nationalism in the sense of attempting to ensure that material progress is national as well as geographic reaches far back in Philippine history. Violence directed at the Chinese community, particularly in Manila, persisted throughout the Spanish colonial era. The sources of Filipino animosity toward the Chinese are complex, but dependence upon, and inability to compete with, Chinese commercial enterprises have undoubtedly contributed to this feeling. The initial upsurge of nationalism in the closing decade of the nineteenth century was due in part to Filipino resentment at alienization of land by Catholic missionary orders. However, the economic provisions of the Malolos Constitution of 1898 did not portend the latter-day development of Philippine economic nationalism.[2] During the American colonial period an issue on which Filipinos were united was the policy of severely limiting land alienization in amount and restricting land purchase to Filipino and United States nationals. Inasmuch as American colonial administrators envisaged economic development of the Philippines through liberal concessions of agricultural and other resources to all comers, the issue of public land policy became an important rallying point for Philippine nationalism.[3] Filipino public opinion triumphed in this controversy, and the policy of restricting exploitation of Philippine resources to nationals has been continually expanded.[4]

From 1898 to 1935 economic nationalism was a moderate and gradualist movement subordinated to the achievement of independence. Filipino nationalists recognized that aggressive economic nationalism might serve to delay the achievement of independence. This point was brought home to the nationalists as a result of the controversy surrounding the enactment and implementation of the so-called "Bookkeeping Acts" and the Manila Public Stalls Ordinance. The Bookkeeping Acts provided that accounts were to be kept in a language familiar to Filipinos. The Manila Public Stalls Ordinance provided that space in the public markets could be leased only by Filipino and

[2] The only provision pertaining to this question provides: "Any foreigner may establish himself freely in Philippine territory, subject to the provisions governing the matter, exercising therein his industry, or devoting himself to any profession for the exercise of which the law does not require any certificates of fitness from the national authorities" (Art. 24).

[3] For an account of Philippine public lands policy, see Alice M. McDairmid, "Agricultural Public Lands Policy in the Philippines during the American Period," *Philippine Law Journal,* 28 (Dec. 1953), 851–888.

[4] It is true, of course, that evasion of limitations on land alienization has been widespread. However, the essence of the policy has been maintained, and it has exercised great influence on the character of Philippine colonial development.

United States nationals.[5] Opposition of the Chinese community in the Philippines as well as official Chinese resistance to these policies had an immediate impact in the Philippines and abroad. The controversy was seized upon by the American opponents of Philippine independence as justification for prolonging the period of preparation for self-government.[6]

Enactment of the Philippines Independence Act was followed by an upsurge of economic nationalism.[7] A Constitutional Convention provided by the Independence Act was convened on July 30, 1934. During this convention the objectives and policies of Philippine economic nationalism became clearly delineated.

The responsibility of the government to promote national economic development was established in a short preamble that defined the three objectives of the government to be established as "to conserve and develop the patrimony of the nation, promote the general welfare, and secure to themselves and their posterity the blessings of independence under a regime of justice, liberty, and democracy." Similarly, the Constitutional Convention, in the Declaration of Principles, established the power and obligation of the state to pursue the economic aspirations of the Filipino people. The Declaration provides: "The promotion of social justice to insure the well-being and economic security of all the people should be the concern of the State."

Filipinization tended to preoccupy the Constitutional Convention. One delegate subsequently reported:

Economic protectionism! This was the battle-cry of the nationalists in the convention ringing in many of the speeches delivered before the body

[5] The Bookkeeping Acts included Acts of the Philippine legislature No. 2972 of Feb. 21, 1921; No. 3292 of Dec. 2, 1926; No. 4176 of Dec. 5, 1934; and Commonwealth Act No. 113 of Nov. 6, 1936. With respect to the original Act No. 2972, the U.S. Supreme Court in Yu Cong Eng *vs.* Trinidad, 271 U.S. 500 (1926), ruled that "the intent of a statute is the law," and that the intention of the Philippine legislature was to force the Chinese from the retail trade business and not to ensure the full collection of taxes. In declaring the act unconstitutional, the Court in effect held that protection is to be extended not only to citizens or those who stand in some peculiar relationship to the government but to everyone within its jurisdiction, which includes aliens.

[6] Cf. Katherine Mayo, *The Isles of Fear* (New York: Harcourt, Brace and Co., 1925), and Nicholas Roosevelt, *The Philippines, a Treasure and a Problem* (New York: J. H. Sears and Co., 1926).

[7] Public Law No. 127, 73rd Cong., 2nd sess., March 24, 1934.

in the exercise of the one-half hour parliamentary privilege and in the course of the debates.

It was primarily with that battle-cry that they won the fight for the rejection of the principle of jus soli for determining the citizenship of children born in the Philippines of foreign parents. It was with that battle-cry that they won the fight for the nationalization of natural resources. It was with the same battle-cry they fought for the nationalization of labor.

It was with this same battle-cry that the nationalists worked for nationalization of retail trade and of the business in rice, corn, and other cereals of food value produced in the Philippines; for the nationalization of public works contracts.[8]

Although the Constitutional Convention displayed frequent outbursts of sentiment for Filipinization, the Constitution, as approved, was moderate in this respect. To a considerable degree this was due to external influences. First, the Constitution had to be approved by the President of the United States, and this requirement restrained overt nationalism. Important American economic interests which had been built up during the colonial period could bring heavy pressure to bear on the decision of the President of the United States.[9] Second was awareness of the necessity to "live" with China and Japan if Philippine sovereignty was to become a reality. In view of the size of the Chinese and Japanese minorities and their ability to bring pressure to bear on their home governments, it was prudent of the Constitutional Convention to moderate its demands for Filipinization.

The national aspirations of the Filipino people were clearly defined in the drafting of the Philippine Constitution. The state was given wide powers to organize Philippine society to achieve the economic aspirations of the people, including the right to demand compulsory civil service of the people and the right to participate in all kinds of economic activity through public investment and the nationalization of existing enterprises.

Similarly, the Constitutional Convention reflected the determination of Filipinos to de-alienize their economy. Filipinos have been aggressive in their efforts to ensure that the Philippine patrimony of natural

[8] Jose M. Aruego, *The Framing of the Philippine Constitution* (Manila: University Publishing Co., 1936), I, 658. Aruego, lawyer and educator, was a delegate to the Constitutional Convention.

[9] J. Ralston Hayden, *The Philippines: A Study in National Development* (New York: Macmillan Co., 1942), p. 41.

resources be reserved to nationals, that commerce and trade dependent upon the internal Philippine market be increasingly reserved for nationals, that professions and labor be nationalized in the sense of reserving an increasing proportion of employment to nationals, that naturalization remain a formidable obstacle to the economic assimilation of aliens, that the acquisition of the rights of nationals by naturalized citizens be deliberate, and that steps be taken to ensure that Filipino entrepreneurship acquires an increasing influence in Philippine enterprises. Economic nationalism in the restrictive sense of Filipinization has been a dominant objective of Philippine economic policy in the postindependence period and Filipinos have displayed energy and initiative in developing techniques and institutions appropriate to the pursuit of this goal. The remainder of this chapter traces the evolution of various Filipinization policies following the establishment of Philippine independence in 1946.

Import Trade Nationalization

The initial goal of Filipinization was the import trade, which, as in colonial countries generally, was dominated by foreign firms. During 1948 and 1949 imports by Filipinos and Filipino firms accounted for only 23 per cent of total imports. Import trade nationalization has been simplified by exchange and import controls and currency overvaluation, and the postwar period has seen rapid expansion in the share of Filipinos in the lucrative foreign exchange allocations (Table 51).

During the period of relief and rehabilitation and the supply shortages of 1946 and 1947 Filipinization of the import trade was implemented by the government-owned National Trading Corporation, the Philippine Relief and Rehabilitation Administration, and the Philippine Relief and Trade Rehabilitation Administration, which imported directly and allocated imports to Filipino firms. As shipping and trade returned to more normal conditions, the capacity of the government-owned trading corporations to promote Filipinization of import trade rapidly declined. During 1948 and 1949 import trade nationalization was limited to flour imports, which were in short supply and were subject to international allocation.

The postwar drain on Philippine foreign exchange reserves was ultimately halted by exchange and import controls, which were applied with increasing tightness to restrict imports and other payments. Restriction of import quantities resulted in increases in peso prices of imports. The importer allocated exchange for imports was subsidized by the discrepancy between the peso cost of imports and their peso selling prices. The policy of using import and exchange controls to Filipinize the import trade was initiated with the first exchange control order, Executive Order No. 193 of December 28, 1948, which provided that 20 per cent of imports would be allocated to "new importers." Although it contained no nationality provision, the effect of the executive order was to modify the historical distribution of imports among established and largely alien firms. Within three months this policy was more firmly enunciated by Executive Order

Table 51. Composition of imports by nationality of importer [a]
(₱ million)

	Total value of imports	Imports by Filipinos, value	Per cent	Imports by Americans, value	Per cent	Imports by Chinese, value	Per cent
1948	1,136	260	23	319	28	438	39
1949	1,134	263	23	333	29	423	37
1950	712	197	28	227	32	221	31
1951	959	354	37	275	30	257	27
1952	852	286	34	252	30	237	28
1953	895	357	40	248	28	220	25
1954	903	380	42	233	26	216	24
1955	1,073	504	47	260	24	237	22
1956	1,019	486	48	290	28	156	15
1957	1,243	669	54	300	24	175	14

[a] R.P., Bur. of Census and Statistics. Republished in *A.C.C. Journal,* vols. 33 (Nov. 1957) and 34 (Oct. 1958).

No. 209 of March 30, 1949, which provided: "Section 5. Not more than twenty per cent (20%) of the quota fixed for each article shall be set aside, to be allocated exclusively to Filipino importers who had no importation during the base period . . . but have registered subsequently as importers of such articles."

Congress moved quickly to enact its own nationalization legislation in 1949. Legislation was introduced providing that 40 per cent of import quotas for each commodity be set aside for Filipino importers and that this ratio be increased 10 per cent per year for three years. During consideration of this bill the American government lodged a formal protest based on Article X of the 1946 Trade Agreement which led to inclusion in the legislation of the following provision: "That nothing contained in this Act shall in any way impair or abridge the rights granted citizens and juridical entities of the United States of America under the Executive Agreement signed on July 4, 1946, between that country and the Republic of the Philippines." [10]

The subsequent legislation, Republic Act No. 426 of May 22, 1950, provided:

Section 14. The [Import Control] Board shall reserve thirty per centum of the total import quota for any article, goods or commodities for the fiscal year 1950–51, forty per centum for the fiscal year 1951–52, and fifty per centum for the fiscal year 1952–53 in favor of bona fide new importers who did not import such items at any time during the years 1946, 1947, and 1948. *To qualify as a new importer, one must be a Filipino citizen or a juridical entity at least sixty per centum of whose stock is owned by Filipino citizens.*[11]

Legislative promotion of import trade Filipinization remained in abeyance during the remainder of the Quirino administration. The failure to specify further increases in the proportion of imports to be allocated to Filipinos probably was an aftermath of the visit of the Bell Mission and the subsequent Quirino-Foster Agreement. Filipinization of import trade continued, however, as exchange allocations to Filipinos increased absolutely and relatively.

When the Nacionalista-controlled Congress allowed the import control to lapse in 1953, the Central Bank stepped in to take over exchange licensing and, in effect, import licensing under responsibility established in the Central Bank Act. On June 12, 1944, following adjournment of Congress without renewing exchange and import controls, the Central Bank issued Central Bank Circular No. 44 entitled "Guiding Principles Governing the Licensing of Foreign Exchange for the Payment of Imports."

The provisions of the new import control regulation relating to

[10] The protest by Ambassador Myron M. Cowen, dated April 28, 1950, and addressed to the Senate Committee on Agriculture, Commerce, and Natural Resources, is reprinted in the *A.C.C. Journal,* 26 (May 1950), 177.

[11] Italics added. Another important provision of Republic Act No. 426 provided: "Section 12. No importer shall be allowed more than thirty per centum of the total import quota for any item except, when such limitation may, in the opinion of the Import Control Board, be detrimental to the public interest." If enforced, this provision would enable the control authority to reserve a larger proportion of imports of particular commodities for Filipino importers.

nationalization were subject to some latitude in interpretation. Central Bank Circular No. 44 provided:

Paragraph 7. Old importers [defined as in business prior to enactment of Republic Act No. 426, May 19, 1950] shall file their applications for letters of credit with the Authorized Agent Banks. . . . In no event shall the total quota [of old importers] after adjustments exceed 40 per cent of the letters of credit established by such customers in 1950.

Inasmuch as 1950 was the year in which import controls were applied most intensively, the circular, if enforced, would have limited the imports of "old importers" to between 20 and 30 per cent of their volume in 1948 and 1949. Obviously, the new import control provided ample scope for continued de-alienization of the import trade, and the statistics readily confirm this development.

A revealing episode in the Filipinization of import trade occurred in 1954 with the enactment of Republic Act No. 1130 of June 16, 1954, creating an Anti-Dummy Board in the Department of Justice. Creation of this board reflected congressional concern for the evasions of import trade nationalization policy. The connivance of Filipinos who shared in the windfall arising out of import restriction but who were in fact fronts for alien merchants enabled the latter to augment their share of scarce imported goods. The appearance of dummies was a logical and inevitable stage in the process of Filipinization.

The next stage in the evolution of import trade nationalization threatened to occur in the congressional session of 1956. Congress turned once again to enactment of legislation providing for increases in the proportion of available foreign exchange allocated to Filipino importers. House Bill No. 4750 introduced by Representatives Roces and Salvador and an identical Senate Bill No. 408 introduced by Senator Alonto reserved for Filipino importers 75 per cent of the available foreign exchange for payment of imports. Inasmuch as Article VII of the Revised Philippine–United States Trade Agreement of 1955 provided for reciprocal nondiscrimination, the proposed legislation had to include Americans and American enterprises as cobeneficiaries.[12] During debate over the proposed legislation the percentage

[12] The Revised Trade Agreement extended the specific provisions of nondiscrimination in the earlier Trade Agreement of 1946 by providing that "the Republic of the Philippines and the United States of America each agrees not to discriminate in any manner, with respect to their engaging in business activities,

reserved for Filipino (and United States) importers was increased from 75 to 90 per cent. This occurred after a Central Bank official called attention to the fact that exchange quota allocations to Filipinos, Americans, and Philippine government entities already exceeded 75 per cent of exchange allocations for imports.[13] When it was demonstrated that the original legislation was unnecessary, the protagonists, unabashed, simply upped the percentage.[14]

The restrictive bill failed of enactment in 1956, but the administrative discretion inherent in exchange and import controls was used to continue import trade nationalization. Filipinization has proceeded rapidly, almost entirely at the expense of the Chinese business community. Though this may be the cause of nationalistic satisfaction, it has meant little progress in expanding levels of imports.

A further step in the Filipinization of import trade occurred on January 5, 1959, when the Monetary Board approved a resolution which (a) reduced foreign exchange allocations for the January–March 1959 quarter of all alien importers except American and all importers of oil and gasoline by 50 per cent of their 1958 fourth-quarter quotas, with notice that such quotas would be entirely eliminated by September of 1959, and (b) restricted to qualified Filipino and American importers only the right to import decontrolled items. This resolution, if enforced, should Filipinize a substantial portion of the import trade remaining to aliens other than Americans.

Retail Trade Nationalization

Alien participation has been a dominant characteristic of Philippine retail trade. Alien firms, predominantly Chinese with minor Indian participation, tend to be relatively large and to account for a disproportionate share of the total retail trade (Table 52). The antecedents of retail trade nationalization reach far back in the long history

---

against the citizens or any form of business enterprise owned or controlled by citizens of the other" (Art. VII).

[13] *A.C.C. Journal*, 32 (May 1956), 203.

[14] An "explanatory note" attached to H.R. No. 4750 stated: "It will be recalled that Congress had already expressly provided in Section 14 of R.A. No. 426, which has already expired, that 30 per cent of the total imports for 1950–51 should be reserved for Filipino importers; 40 per cent in 1951–52; and 50 per cent in 1952–53, or a yearly increase of 10 per cent. If this yearly increase had been continued, 80 per cent of the total import trade would have been allocated to Filipino importers during 1955–56."

of violence that characterized Filipino-Chinese relations during the Spanish colonial period.[15] Two distinct strains of policy can be identified in the postwar period. First is the direct legislative encroachment on the rights of aliens to engage in retail business in the Philippines, and second is the policy of subsidizing Filipino participation in such trade.

Table 52. Retail trade in 1948 by nationality of trader [a]

Nationality of retailer	Number of establishments (thousand)	Per cent of total	Value of assets (₱ million)	Per cent of total	Gross sales (₱ million)	Per cent of total
Filipino	113.6	90	213	67	467	61
Chinese	12.1	10	93	29	295	38
Other	0.4	—[b]	11	3	10	1

[a] R.P., Bur. of the Census, *Census of the Philippines, 1948* (Manila: Bureau of Printing, 1950).
[b] Less than 0.5 per cent.

In attempting to trace the evolution of retail trade nationalization policy, one is beset by the voluminous bills presented in Congress each year as well as widespread use of this issue in domestic political controversy.[16] During the colonial period when the chief executive was an American, such bills were passed with full knowledge that the Governor-General would not approve them, the aim being to embarrass the American authorities. Such bills were easy to draft and appealed to easily aroused prejudices, especially when directed against the Chinese.

There was every likelihood that with the attainment of independence in 1946 the pace of retail trade nationalization would be ac-

[15] As early as 1586 Governor Vera and other prominent Spaniards in Manila had petitioned the Council of the Indies to forbid the Chinese from remaining in Manila to retail their goods, since this business should be in the hands of the Spaniards. In 1722 the Fiscal of the colony observed to the king: "The Sangleys [Chinese] have gained control of all the commerce in provisions and other supplies and of the mechanical trades" (William L. Schurz, *The Manila Galleon* [New York: Dutton, Everyman ed., 1959], p. 96).

[16] See editorial, "This Year's Nationalization Bills," *A.C.C. Journal*, 30 (May 1954), 168. Thirty-one bills were introduced in the House of Representatives, five of which would have outlawed alien participation in retail trade. The others covered a very wide range of economic activity.

celerated. Two factors, however, tended to moderate this policy. First was the preoccupation of the newly sovereign government with the tasks of reconstruction and rehabilitation. Second was the relative ease of entering the import and retail business, a consequence of the destruction and dislocation of prewar firms and channels of trade.[17]

Expanded Filipino activity in retail trade did not prevent legislative moves to de-alienize such trade. Within three months after the formal granting of independence two laws were enacted to curb Chinese participation in retail trade. The first, Republic Act No. 37 of October 1, 1946, provided in Section 1: "All citizens of the Philippines shall have preference in the lease of public market stalls." The effect of this act, which replaced the Manila Market Stalls Ordinance of 1941, was the ejection of 1,435 small Chinese merchants from the booths and stalls of the thirteen public markets of Manila.[18] The second was Republic Act No. 48 of October 3, 1946, amending the bookkeeping provisions of the National Internal Revenue Code (Sections 336 and 356 of Commonwealth Act No. 466) to provide that accounts be kept in a native language, in English, or in Spanish, with harsh penalties for failure to do so.

A few weeks later Republic Act No. 76 of October 21, 1946, was passed with the expressed intention of reducing the rights of American citizens, corporations, and associations to those already vested under the Constitution or extended by treaty agreement or convention with the United States. The act provides in Section 1:

Existing laws or the provisions of existing laws granting privileges, rights or exemptions to citizens of the United States of America or to corporations or associations organized under the laws of any of the States of the United States of America, which are not enjoyed by citizens or nationals of any other foreign State, . . . are hereby repealed unless they affect rights already vested under the provisions of the Constitution or unless extended by any treaty, agreement or convention between the Republic of the Philippines and the United States of America.

The parity provided by Article VII of the 1946 Trade Agreement with the United States and the subsequent amendment to the Philippine Constitution, established national treatment for United States citizens only for the "exploitation of Philippine natural resources and the operation of public utilities."

[17] Hartendorp, *History*, p. 273.   [18] *A.C.C. Journal*, 29 (June 1953), 232.

Subsequent developments established the fact that, though national treatment for Americans engaged in retail trade in the Philippines was not guaranteed by the parity amendment, such a guarantee was effectively established by Article X, Paragraph 4, of the 1946 United States–Philippine Trade Agreement. The latter provided:

If the President of the United States determines and proclaims . . . that the Philippine Government or any of its political subdivisions is in any manner discriminating against citizens of the United States or any form of United States business enterprise, then the President of the United States shall have the right to suspend the effectiveness of the whole or any portion of this Agreement.

Leverage arising out of potential United States retaliation as well as Philippine reluctance to jeopardize enlargement of the Philippine preferential position in United States import trade proved to be an effective deterrent to nationalization policies detrimental to United States business interests in the Philippines.

After 1946 Liberal party Presidents Roxas and Quirino consistently resisted Filipinization of the retail trade by legislative fiat. Therefore, pursuit of this goal took the form of various institutions and techniques for subsidizing Filipino retailers. By 1954 conditions had changed sufficiently for nationalization of retail trade to be enacted into law. First was the ineffectiveness of various subsidization policies to redress the competitive handicaps of Filipinos. The assets of various government agencies created for this purpose were dissipated with little lasting benefit. Second was the rapid change in the international situation and the deepening of the United States commitment to the defense of the Philippines which culminated in the Southeast Asia Treaty Organization. Such a commitment was interpreted by many politicians as carte blanche to proceed to wrest the retail business from Chinese hands. Third was the change in administration in the Philippines which placed the Nacionalistas—with a long tradition of nationalist activity—in control of both the legislature and the executive branch.

In the congressional session of 1954 a wide variety of retail trade nationalization bills were introduced, including six which would have prohibited alien participation in retail trade.[19] In the closing days of the regular session President Magsaysay "certified" an ad-

[19] Philippine National Bank, *Business Letter,* March–April 1954.

ministration retail trade nationalization bill [20] that purported to be a compromise measure. Congress promptly enacted the law, and in spite of vociferous protests by alien economic interests as well as official diplomatic protests President Magsaysay approved the legislation on June 19, 1954.[21] The bill culminated at least four decades of nationalist activity in pursuit of retail trade nationalization.

Republic Act No. 1180 provides in Section 1:

No person who is not a citizen of the Philippines, and no association, partnership, or corporation the capital of which is not wholly owned by citizens of the Philippines, shall engage directly or indirectly in the retail business: Provided, that a person who is not a citizen of the Philippines, or an association, partnership, or corporation not wholly owned by citizens of the Philippines which is actually engaged in the said business on May 15, 1954, shall be entitled to continue to engage therein, unless its license is forfeited in accordance herewith, until his death or voluntary retirement from said business in the case of a natural person, and for a period of ten years from the date of the approval of this Act or until the expiration of the term of the association or partnership or of the corporate existence of the corporation, whichever event comes first, in the case of juridicial persons.

. . . The license of any person who is not a citizen of the Philippines and of any association, partnership, or corporation not wholly owned by citizens of the Philippines to engage in retail business, shall be forfeited for any violation of any provision of laws on nationalization, economic control, weights and measures, and labor and other laws relating to trade, commerce, and industry. . . .

After enactment of Republic Act No. 1180 a number of developments occurred designed to clarify the implementation of the law.

[20] H.R. No. 2523. Presidential certification of a bill as urgent and necessary implies executive approval. Moreover, it is necessary toward the close of congressional sessions to bypass certain normal congressional procedures established to ensure legislative deliberation.

[21] Republic Act 1180. In his message to Congress accompanying the signed bill, the President said: "I have discussed H.R. 2523 [subsequently R.A. 1180], which seeks to nationalize retail trade, with experts and political leaders, and have devoted considerable time to evaluating the arguments for and against the measure. I am fully aware that the bill has imperfections, but notwithstanding this, I am constrained, in concurrence in its primordial objective, to sign this measure. I have taken this action after carefully considering representations from diplomatic sources and alien chambers of commerce for its disapproval, because I firmly believe in the principle that it is for the best interests of our people and posterity. To my mind, there is nothing in this bill that contravenes our fundamental law or our treaty obligations."

On May 12, 1955, the report of the joint executive-congressional committee [22] studying the Retail Trade Nationalization Law recommended that the law be allowed to stand "to give it a chance to show its effect upon our economy." [23]

The legal test of Republic Act No. 1180 was completed in May 1957 when the Philippine Supreme Court upheld the act in the Lao H. Ichong case, with only one out of eleven justices dissenting and with one other justice refusing to participate in the decision.[24] The decision was justified by invoking the police power of the state.

Judicial approval of Republic Act No. 1180 vests the Philippine government with adequate power to wrest the retail trade from alien hands. If enforced, the law will dispossess Chinese and alien business communities, other than that of United States nationals,

---

[22] At the same time he signed Republic Act No. 1180, President Magsaysay issued Administrative Order No. 37 of June 19, 1954, creating an executive committee to study and recommend improvements in the trade nationalization law. Administration Order No. 76 of Nov. 15, 1954, amended Administrative Order No. 37 to expand the Executive Committee to Study and Recommend Improvements of the Law Nationalizing the Retail Trade to a joint executive-congressional committee. The committee was composed of Secretary of Commerce and Industry Oscar Ledesma, Secretary of Agriculture Salvador Araneta, and the Economic Co-ordinator, Alfredo Montelibano (for the executive), Senators Gil Puyat, Edmundo Cea, and Quintin Paredes, and Representatives Daniel Romualdez, Arturo Tolentino, and Eugenio Perez.

[23] *Manila Times*, May 12, 1955. The report cited the following reasons for not recommending changes in the law: "One year is too short a time to pass judgment on the law, public opinion is strongly against its repeal, and the constitutionality of the law having been challenged, the decision of the Supreme Court should be awaited." The committee recommended that the Department of Commerce and Industry should be given a chance to implement the law to the fullest extent possible and that a "continuing body of technical personnel should be created to study ways and means to do so." It also recommended that a National Marketing Corporation be created by law to extend aid to Filipino retailers "so as to enable them to take over the trade"; finally, the committee said it was "of the belief that action on all nationalization bills now pending in Congress should be deferred."

[24] *Lao H. Ichong v. Jaime Hernandez, Secretary of Finance, and Marcelino Sarmiento, City Treasurer of Manila*, G.R. No. L-7995, May 31, 1957. The Court said: "We are fully satisfied upon a consideration of all the facts and circumstances that the disputed law is not the product of racial hostility, prejudice or discrimination, but the expression of the legitimate desire or determination, of the people, through their authorized representatives, to free the nation from the economic situation that has unfortunately been saddled upon it rightly or wrongly, to its disadvantage. The law is clearly in the interest of the public, nay of the national security itself, and indisputably falls within the scope of police power, through which and by which the State insures its existence and security and the supreme welfare of its citizens."

within one generation. This policy has long been sought by Filipinos, and it undoubtedly represents a goal widely held in Philippine society. The sympathies of the Westerner instinctively go out to the Chinese— the underdogs in this situation—who seem to be penalized for their thrift and industry. Indeed, the gains to be realized from expropriation are a significant factor in Filipino attitudes toward the Chinese minority. On the other hand, a little reflection will also result in sympathetic understanding of Filipino aspirations.

A co-ordinate aspect of retail trade nationalization policy has been the succession of institutions created to subsidize Filipino retailers and thereby expand Filipino participation in this economic activity. This policy was initiated during the Commonwealth period by the creation of the National Trading Corporation (Executive Order No. 249 of January 4, 1940), which was capitalized by an appropriation of P5 million. NTC functioned as a wholesale supplier of merchandise for Filipino retailers. One of its purposes, as was publicly stated by the president of the NTC was to "break the stranglehold of foreign retailers" upon Philippine trade.[25] During the early postwar years NTC resumed its activities, and in 1945 and 1946, when shipping was in short supply and when relief and rehabilitation supplies were being channeled through the Philippine government, NTC was able to divert available supplies to Filipino retailers.[26]

With rapid improvement in the postwar shipping and supply situation, the power of National Trading Corporation and its successor, the Philippine Relief and Trade Rehabilitation Administration, to favor Filipino retailers was rapidly dissipated. Evaporation of the capacity to subsidize Filipino retailers by allocating commodities in short supply and the drying up of relief supplies reduced PRATRA's activities to negligible proportions. Moreover, recurring fiscal crises prevented Congress from appropriating funds for direct subsidization of Filipino retailers.

Revival of the policy of subsidizing Filipinos engaged in retail trade had to await the return of conditions similar to those prevailing in 1945–1946 when allocation of goods to Filipino retailers carried an

[25] *Manila Bulletin,* Oct. 18, 1940.

[26] The Philippine Relief and Rehabilitation Administration (PRRA) was created by Commonwealth Act No. 716 of Nov. 1, 1945. On Sept. 10, 1947, Executive Order No. 90 created the Philippine Relief and Trade Rehabilitation Administration (PRATRA) to take the place of the National Trading Corporation and PRRA.

inherent subsidy that did not require the appropriation of revenues by Congress. Such a development occurred in 1950 when the Philippines resorted to import controls. The following June, Congress enacted a price control act (Republic Act No. 509 of June 13, 1950) which provided:

Section 5. Whenever any article, goods or commodity is in short supply, or whenever there exists reasonable ground to believe that it will disappear in the open market, or whenever there is an uncontrolled inflation of prices, the PRATRA . . . may, with the approval of the President, import directly such article, goods, or commodity for distribution in the local market through such channels *as it may choose,* and such importation shall not be subject to any quota requirement provided for by any economic control legislation.

Shortly after the enactment of price control Executive Order No. 350 of October 3, 1950, abolished the PRATRA and created the Price Stabilization Corporation (PRISCO) to take over the price control and retail trade nationalization functions of the former. Authorized capitalization of PRISCO was set at ₱30 million, which would serve to (a) maintain price supports on rice and corn, (b) as a revolving fund to finance imports of commodities, and (c) as a revolving fund to make loans to Filipino retailers. The powers of PRISCO to use import control to nationalize retail trade proved to be limited, and PRISCO tended to be preoccupied with the use of its import control functions to de-alienize import trade.[27] Although the transfer of the importing business to Filipino hands was rapid, the windfall created by import restriction was passed on to Filipino retailers only to a limited extent.

The Nacionalista victory in the election of 1953 initiated new moves to Filipinize retail trade. The Retail Trade Nationalization Act (Republic Act No. 1180 of June 19, 1954) was followed by Republic Act No. 1292 of June 15, 1955, which provided:

Section 1. It shall be a national policy to encourage Filipino retailers.
Section 2. For the purpose of providing credit facilities for the promotion and development of the Filipino retail trade, there is hereby created a revolving fund to be known as the "Filipino Retailers' Fund" which

[27] On Dec. 21, 1950, Executive Order No. 384 vested in PRISCO import licensing for a list of 26 articles "in short supply." This list was subsequently enlarged by Executive Orders Nos. 423 of March 9, 1951, 446 of June 9, 1951, and 603 of June 26, 1953.

shall be under the administration of the Secretary of Commerce and Industry, or any other office that the President may designate, with the provincial, city and municipal treasurers as his deputies.

Section 3. Importers of prime commodities shall sell to Filipino retailers at the same mark-up as their sales through their present trade channels at least thirty per cent of their imports. . . .

Section 5. It shall be the function of the Retailers' Fund to help in the promotion and development of the Filipino retail trade by assisting Filipino retailers in securing liberal credit facilities, extending to them technical assistance, teaching them merchandising techniques and skill, and, in general, equipping them with the necessary tools to compete more effectively with aliens in the retail business to the end that Filipino merchants may wrest control of this important phase of the national economy from the hands of the foreigners. . . .

Section 10. There is hereby appropriated . . . the sum of twenty million pesos to constitute the revolving fund provided for in Section two of this Act.

Approval of Republic Act No. 1292 was followed two days later by approval of Republic Act No. 1345, which dissolved the Price Stabilization Corporation and created a successor, National Marketing Corporation (NAMARCO). The legislation provided:

Section 1. It is hereby declared to be the policy of Congress to assist Filipino retailers and businessmen by supplying them with merchantable goods at prices that will enable them to compete successfully in the open market so that they may have greater participation in the distribution system of our economy. In order to do this, it is necessary that a government corporation be created for the purpose of engaging in the activities of procurement, buying and distributing merchantable goods to Filipino retailers and businessmen not for the purpose of making a profit but to render an essential public service in order to promote the social and economic welfare of the Nation.

Section 2. There is hereby created a private corporation under the name of the "National Marketing Corporation" which, in short, shall be known as the "NAMARCO." . . .

Section 5. The NAMARCO is authorized and directed:

(a) To procure and buy commodities for distribution at reasonable prices to Filipino retailers and businessmen in order to promote their greater participation in the distribution system of the national economy. . . .

Section 6. The NAMARCO shall have an authorized capital of thirty million pesos to be subscribed entirely by the Republic of the Philippines.

By Republic Acts Nos. 1292 and 1345 the Philippine government created two institutions to give effect to the Filipinization of the retail trade envisaged in Republic Act No. 1180.[28] In other words, Acts No. 1292 and 1345 recognize that retailing is an essential economic activity and that it is necessary, not only to eliminate alien retailers, but to promote aggressively a substitute Filipino trade organization. The structure of policy, so far as legislation is concerned, is complete, and the next few years should provide sufficient evidence to appraise the results of the policy.

Nationalization of "New and Necessary Industries"

A basic conflict between the goals of Filipinization and economic development is becoming increasingly evident in Philippine industrialization policy. Filipinos recognize that it is possible to augment national capital formation by the saving and investment of non-Filipinos domiciled both within the Philippines and abroad. However, Philippine investment policy has increasingly discriminated in incentives extended to nationals vis-à-vis aliens.

Philippine industrialization policy includes a broad spectrum of measures influencing industrial investment both national and domestic. For example, exchange control has important consequences for such investment and inevitably involves discrimination in the treatment of foreigners and nationals. Exchange rate policy has been critically important in influencing the direction of postwar Philippine specialization. Similarly, public policy with respect to resource exploitation can be critically important to both the level and direction of capital formation.

A basic component of Philippine investment policy has been the subsidization of "new and necessary industries" by granting tax concessions and foreign exchange allocations. Initial implementation of this policy was nondiscriminatory, although wide administrative discretion was inevitable in assessing qualifications as new and necessary industries.

[28] Republic Act No. 1601 of Aug. 14, 1946, amended Republic Act No. 1315 to provide that NAMARCO was "to establish and operate distribution offices and agencies and/or to enter contracts with wholesale business throughout the Philippines for the purchase and distribution of such commodities that may be deemed essential for carrying out the purposes of the Corporation authorized in this Act: Provided, *that the distribution of such commodities shall be done through Filipinos only*" (italics added).

Following the imposition of exchange and import controls, conditions arose which enhanced the value of qualification as a new and necessary industry. The protection arising out of Philippine exchange and import controls proved to be intensive and was highest for "less essential" commodities. This commercial policy tended to establish strong incentives for "industries" which could perform some minor processing, such as packaging, of imported "raw materials," the importation of which in final form was embargoed or heavily restricted. Under these conditions, applications for qualification as new and necessary industries increased and included industries which would be subsidized by the allocation of foreign exchange to import so-called "industrial raw materials."

The initial appearance of overt economic nationalism in industrialization policy occurred in the Five-Year Plan adopted by the National Economic Council in early 1957.[29] The plan included a "System for Determining Industrial Priorities"

intended to govern the extension of credit by government banking and financing institutions, the grant of foreign exchange allocation, tax exemption, acquisition and distribution of reparations materials, application of foreign aid to industrial development, the allocation of scarce materials owned or produced by the government or government corporations, and other action involving other forms of government assistance or protection to industry.[30]

The Industrial Priority Formula provides:

A firm that is financed entirely or mostly by nationals (Filipino citizens) will be given preference. This criterion does not necessarily bar foreign investment, which would be contrary to the desire to attract foreign investment. It simply means that all other considerations being the same Filipino nationals will enjoy preference in the allocation of scarce resources. This is justified by the fact that there is relatively greater stability in an enterprise that is operated by nationals. Furthermore, the enterprise would provide or expand better opportunities for training Filipinos to acquire management skills and techniques. This is not to mention the fact that the earnings of

[29] R.P., NEC, *The Five-Year Program for FY 1957–1961*. The plan reports: "But the pursuit of the goal towards optimum production will be limited by the scarcity of some of the resources necessary for development including specifically capital and foreign exchange. Therefore, it is necessary to formulate and implement a system of industrial priorities to ensure that the projects that are selected for preferential development will be those that will generate the highest measure of social benefits" (p. 253). The proposed system of determining industrial priorities was approved by the President on Jan. 9, 1957.

[30] *Ibid.*, p. 262.

nationals are likely to be plowed back into the national economy—something that cannot be guaranteed in the case of the profits of foreign investments.[31]

In the list of principles of the priority system is the following: "In general, investments of aliens shall have priority over investments by foreigners, but investments of nationals shall have priority over all." [32]

The next step in the evolution of a nationalistic policy governing the allocation of various types of government concessions to encourage investment occurred in the fall of 1958. On August 21 the National Economic Council issued Resolution No. 204, which provided:

Whereas, it is the policy of the Government to encourage Filipinos to engage in enterprises and industries vital to the economic growth, stability, and security of the country;

Whereas, this policy should be, as a national program, vigorously implemented so as to enable Filipinos to eventually attain a substantial share of the commerce and industry of this country, whether such enterprises are presently controlled by non-Filipinos or otherwise;

Whereas, the allocation of foreign exchange is now the most effective instrument by which the above objective can be realized;

Now, Therefore, be it resolved as it is hereby resolved by the National Economic Council:

First—That the National Economic Council adopts this program for the promotion of substantial Filipino participation in the aforementioned enterprises not only for those that are now in existence, but for such commercial and industrial activities as may be required in the future;

Second—That toward the attainment of this objective, the National Economic Council adopts the following guiding principles in the allocation of foreign exchange;

(a) That in instances where there are applications for foreign exchange allocations for the establishment of an enterprise whether it be commercial or industrial in nature, and there are among the applicants qualified Filipinos or enterprises owned at least 60 per cent by Filipinos, preference shall be given to the Filipino applicants.

(b) That in instances where Filipino enterprises seek to enter a field now predominantly in the hand of non-Filipinos, such steps shall be taken as will enable Filipino enterprise to participate in such field or activity at the earliest opportunity.

Third—That in carrying out the above objectives, and taking into account the need for foreign capital in certain phases of the development of a country's economy, due recognition shall be accorded to joint-venture enter-

[31] *Ibid.*, p. 259.
[32] *Ibid.*, p. 265. Chinese residing in the Philippines are classified as aliens.

prises of foreign and Filipino capital, in which the Filipino participation is
—or eventually will be—at least 60% of the capital stock ownership.

A week later in Resolution No. 206 of August 28, 1958, approving
the proposal of a joint Filipino-Gulf Oil Company refinery proposal,
the National Economic Council provided:

Be it further resolved: To make of record, as a supplement to NEC Resolution No. 204, the sense of the National Economic Council that it considers it
in consonance with the national policy that the current production levels
as well as those production levels authorized for construction of alien-owned
or controlled oil refineries in the Philippines shall be maintained and that
foreign exchange allocated by the Central Bank to each of these refineries
shall not exceed the amounts allocated during FY 1957.

It was subsequently reported, on September 5, that the National
Economic Council had taken steps to set up "absolute production
ceilings" for all alien firms. The "proposed restrictions would require
such firms to operate under quotas based on their current volume
of business in the Philippines." These restrictions would not be applicable, however, "where Filipino capital might be either unwilling
or unable to meet the investment requirements"; in such cases the
established (alien) firm would be authorized to expand its facilities
"temporarily." [33]

If the policy enunciated in NEC Resolutions 204 and 206 is implemented, it will accelerate Filipinization of future industrial expansion. It will extend Filipinization of import and retail trades to manufacturing. Heretofore non-Filipinos have managed to share in the
high levels of protection to domestic production as well as in the
heavy indirect subsidies resulting from tax exemption exchange control and currency overvaluation.

Nationalization of Resources

Still another area of investment policy in which economic nationalism
has been evident is that governing exploitation of natural resources.
There can be no question regarding the intent of the Constitution,
which in Article XII provided:

Section 1. All agricultural, timber, and mineral lands of the public domain, waters, minerals, coal, petroleum, and other mineral oils, all forces
of potential energy, and other natural resources of the Philippines belong
to the State, and their disposition, exploitation, development, or utilization

[33] *A.C.C. Journal,* 34 (Sept. 1958), 401.

shall be limited to citizens of the Philippines, or to corporations or associations at least sixty per centum of the capital of which is owned by such citizens, subject to any existing right, grant, lease, or concession at the time of the inauguration of the Government established under this Constitution. Natural resources, with the exception of public agricultural land, shall not be alienated. . . .

Section 5. Save in cases of hereditary succession, no private agricultural land shall be transferred or assigned except to individuals, corporations, or associations qualified to acquire or hold lands of the public domain in the Philippines.

Resources development policy was clarified on November 15, 1947, when the Supreme Court in the Krivenko case established the doctrine that "private agricultural land" included urban land of either residential, commercial, or industrial character.[34] Prior to the Krivenko decision aliens had been permitted to acquire urban property by tolerance of the Philippine executive. During September 1953 the Supreme Court in a series of decisions affirmed the Krivenko ruling and established as a principle of Philippine constitutional law the rule that no alien living in the Philippines could acquire title to his residence or place of business.

During the American colonial period titles to mineral lands were initiated by discovery of minerals therein. The right to such a claim could be held indefinitely upon performance of at least ₱200 worth of annual development work on the claim. This policy was terminated by the Philippine Constitution, which reverted to the Regalian doctrine of state ownership. On November 7, 1936, Commonwealth Act No. 137 was approved which provided:

Section 3. All mineral lands of the public domain and minerals belong to the State, and their disposition, development, or utilization shall be limited to citizens of the Philippines, or to corporations, or associations, at least sixty per cent of the capital of which is owned by such citizens.[35]

[34] *Alexander A. Krivenko* v. *The Registrar of Deeds, City of Manila,* Case No. 1-630. The decision is reprinted in R.P., *Official Gazette,* 44 (Feb. 1948), 471–552.

[35] The new law (Commonwealth Act No. 137) substituted 25-year government leases for outright patents and required a locator to determine within four years whether or not his claim was worthy of being leased. It also provided that the area of mineral ground that could be located by any one individual should be limited to three claims on the same vein or lode, each claim to be 300 by 300 meters. Not a single mineral claim had been patented under Commonwealth Act 137 by the end of 1951.

In view of the unambiguous nationalism embodied in the Constitution, subsequent developments in mineral resources policy have tended to take the form of modifications to permit limited alien participation in the exploitation of such resources. The first such development occurred in 1946 when a plebiscite was held which resulted in approval of the so-called Parity Amendment, which established national treatment for citizens, corporations, and associations of the United States in the exploitation of natural resources and the operation of public utilities.

The resistance of Philippine resource policy to attrition is well illustrated by the various administration-led attempts to modify the policy. For example, resource policy has been modified in minor ways in order to establish conditions under which foreign investment would engage in oil exploration in the Philippines.[36] In 1957 an attempt was made to modify the policy in order to encourage foreign investment in the development of extensive nickel deposits in Surigao.[37] Both the Petroleum Act of 1949 and the Surigao Minerals Reservation Act of 1957 provide for alien participation, other than American, as minor stockholders in firms eligible to execute independent contracts for exploitation under government supervision. In both cases the concessions have not produced extensive non-Filipino investment. In view of the essential elements of Philippine resource policy, it is not surprising that foreign investment in the exploitation of Philippine natural resources has been limited to concessions negotiated prior to the establishment of Philippine autonomy. Filipinos are determined to reserve the future exploitation of natural resources to nationals, and to date there are few indications that this policy will be substantially modified.

Assembly and Marketing of Agricultural Products

Still another objective of de-alienization policy has been elimination of alien middlemen from the assembly and marketing of agricultural crops. A major effort has been made to Filipinize procure-

[36] The first Petroleum Law (Act No. 2932 of Aug. 31, 1920) was so restrictive that it was twice suspended for five years (in 1938 and 1944). For other developments in the evolution of oil policy, see Commonwealth Act No. 351 of Aug. 22, 1938, Joint (Congressional) Resolution No. 5 of June 20, 1947, and the Petroleum Act of 1949, Republic Act No. 387 of June 18, 1949.

[37] The Surigao Mineral Reservation Act of 1957, Republic Act No. 1828 of June 22, 1957.

ment and marketing of rice and corn.[38] To accomplish this goal, the government created the Agricultural Credit and Co-operative Financing Administration (ACCFA), which allocates budgetary appropriations, Central Bank credit, and economic aid funds to build up a system of Farmers' Co-operative Marketing Associations (FACOMAS) to replace traditional marketing and credit institutions.[39]

Although the language of the legislation creating the ACCFA is moderate, the role of the ACCFA in Filipinizing the rice trade was made clear when in a cabinet meeting on March 20, 1957, Osmundo Mondoñedo, general manager of ACCFA, reported that "alien palay traders have been totally eliminated in Bulacan, and that their participation in the trade in Pampanga and Pangasinan had been reduced to 50 per cent and in Tarlac and Nueva Ecija to 30 per cent, and that with the added funds it was safe to predict that they would soon be ousted from the whole of Central Luzon." [40]

Still another phase of the nationalization of domestic trade in agricultural commodities has been the tobacco policy initiated by the enactment of Republic Act No. 698 of May 9, 1952. This act provided that imports of foreign leaf tobacco should be rapidly reduced, thereby limiting the domestic market to Filipino producers. The evolution of tobacco policy was completed in 1954 by the enactment of Republic Act No. 1194, which had the effect of terminating tobacco imports. Equally important, Republic Act No. 1194 provided that "all locally grown and produced Virginia-type leaf tobacco shall be purchased by the Government through the ACCFA. . . . The Central Bank through the Rehabilitation Finance Corporation, shall grant the ACCFA the necessary loans with which to effect the purchase of said tobacco" (Section 1). Filipinization of the domestic trade in tobacco has been accomplished with relative ease. This has been due to the government monopoly created to carry out this policy

---

[38] Since the Philippines is predominantly agricultural and rural, the principal part of rice production never enters commercial channels. For example, in crop year 1953–1954, the Agricultural Credit and Co-operative Financing Administration estimated that only 25 per cent of the crop was marketed. See "The Rice Problem and Nationalization of the Retail Trade," in Philippine National Bank, *Business Letter*, March–April 1954.

[39] See above, pp. 287–288. Filipinization of the procurement and marketing of rice and corn is not the exclusive, or even the principal, function of ACCFA. However, there is ample evidence that Filipino society takes satisfaction in the role of ACCFA in pursuit of this goal.

[40] *Manila Times*, Feb. 21, 1957.

and to import controls, which have maintained the profitability of Virginia-type tobacco production and domestic manufacture of cigarettes.

In the 1960 regular session Congress passed a bill (House Bill No. 3295) providing for the nationalization of trade, milling, and warehousing of rice and corn. The bill provided that aliens presently engaged in retailing these commodities could continue in business for six months; in wholesaling, one year; and in milling and warehousing, two years. The bill also provided that the Philippine National Bank, the Development Bank of the Philippines, the Social Security System, and the Government Service Insurance System would each contribute ₱50 million to establish a revolving fund to make loans to Filipinos and Filipino enterprises to enable them to replace the alien elements in the industry. President Garcia vetoed the bill, objecting both to the abruptness of the proposed Filipinization and to the use of insurance trust funds for loans involving excessive risk.

In the 1960 special session Congress enacted a substitute law (R.A. No. 3018), which the president signed on August 2, 1960. The law provides: "Section 1. No person who is not a citizen of the Philippines, or association, partnership or corporation, the capital or capital stock of which is not wholly owned by citizens of the Philippines shall directly or indirectly engage in the rice and/or corn industry. . . ." Aliens engaged in retailing and wholesaling may continue in business for two years from January 1, 1961, "for the purpose of liquidation," while aliens engaged in milling and/or warehousing are allowed three years to liquidate (Section 3). To enable Filipinos to replace alien elements in the industry, a revolving loan fund of ₱100 million contributed equally by the PNB and the DBP is created (Section 4).

Nationalization of agricultural production is a logical step in Filipinization. However, the "fields to conquer" are limited.[41] It is probably safe to predict that alien activities in the assembly and marketing of copra and abacá will come under attack in the future. It is also apparent that the problem will be difficult because these are export commodities, and Philippine commercial policy cannot be used to reserve foreign markets to Philippine enterprise. Two steps have been taken in this direction. First, the activities of ACCFA have been ex-

[41] The sugar industry has been progressively Filipinized since the termination of American colonial rule, as disinvestment has reduced foreign participation to minor proportions.

tended to coconut production, and FACOMAS of coconut producers
have been organized. Second, Republic Act No. 1392 of August 23,
1955, exempts textiles made of 100 per cent Philippine ramie from
the payment of tariff duty. The act requires that both the fiber and
finished goods be marketed through designated government agencies,
so as to eliminate alien middlemen and provide ramie goods directly
to Filipino retailers. As in the case of tobacco, the domestic market
is reserved to Philippine producers by commercial policy.

Naturalization

An important aspect of Filipino economic nationalism is the reluctance of the Philippines to promote the economic assimilation of
aliens. Throughout the period of Philippine self-government evidence
has accumulated that Filipinos do not envisage naturalization as a
culmination of the process of assimilation. Rather, naturalization
initiates a probationary period—of at least the lifetime of the naturalized citizen. Only after his death may his Philippine-born descend-
ants acquire the economic rights of native-born Filipinos.

It will be recalled that the Philippine Constitutional Convention
rejected the principle of *jus solis,* i.e., place of birth, and adopted
the principle of *jus sanguinis,* in which citizenship and nationality are
governed by the rule of descent of blood. The Constitution provided
that the legislature was empowered to draft naturalization laws.

Following the establishment of the Commonwealth, the legislature
provided for naturalization in Commonwealth Act No. 473 of June
17, 1939. Philippine naturalization policy is strict and reflects a determination to prevent any abuse or misuse of acquired citizenship.
The philosophy is expressed time and time again that the naturalization laws are to be strictly observed and that the rights and privileges
of citizenship should be extended only to those who are deserving of
them.

Among requirements for qualification for naturalization are the
following:

1. He must not be less than twenty-one years of age on the day of the
hearing of the petition.

2. He must have resided in the Philippines for a continuous period of not
less than ten years.

3. He must be of good moral character and believe in the principles
underlying the Philippine Constitution and must have conducted himself

in a proper and irreproachable manner during the entire period of his residence in the Philippines in his relation with the constitutional government as well as with the community in which he is living.

4. He must own real estate in the Philippines worth not less than five thousand pesos, Philippine currency, or must have some known lucrative trade, profession or lawful occupation.

5. He must be able to speak and write English or Spanish and any one of the principal Philippine languages.

6. He must have enrolled his minor children of school age, in any of the public or private schools recognized by the Office of Private Education of the Philippines where Philippine history, government and civics are taught as a prescribed part of the school curriculum during the entire period of the residence in the Philippines required of him prior to the hearing of his petition for naturalization as a Philippine citizen.

The following description of persons who will not be accepted for naturalization reflects Philippine reluctance to naturalize members of the Chinese minority: "Persons who, during the period of their residence in the Philippines, have not mingled socially with the Filipinos, or who have not evinced a sincere desire to learn and embrace the customs, traditions, and ideals of the Filipinos."

The naturalization laws have been strictly interpreted and enforced by the courts. Some of the most illustrative and significant cases in recent years have been those dealing with the requirement that the applicant enroll his minor children in approved Philippine schools. The roots of this educational requirement are to be found in the following decisions:

The law demands the enrollment of applicants' children in our schools, not only to ensure that they are trained in our way of life, but also as evidence of the petitioner's honest and enduring intention to assume the duties and obligations of Filipino citizenship. If the applicant for naturalization is really inspired by an abiding love for his country and its institutions (and no other is admissible) he must prove it by acts of strict compliance with the legal requirements. It may mean hardship and sacrifice, but citizenship in this Republic, be it ever so small and weak, is always a privilege; and no alien, be he a subject of the most powerful nation in the world, can take such citizenship for granted or assume it as a matter of right.[42]

The requirement that the applicant must have enrolled his minor children of school age in public or private schools recognized by the Office of Education wherein Philippine history, government and civics are taught or

[42] *Pidelo* v. *Republic*, G.R. No. L-7796, Sept. 29, 1955.

prescribed, and must have so enrolled them during the entire period of residence, in the Philippines required of him prior to hearing of his naturalization petition, is considered an important one, not subject to avoidance, compliance with which can be excused but rarely, if at all.[43]

The following cases, which speak for themselves, illustrate this strict interpretation of naturalization statutes by Philippine courts:

Although all but one of a Chinese applicant for naturalization's nine children had been enrolled in and attended government approved schools in the Philippines as required by this section, the remaining one was a minor who lived in China and was there attending an English school, failure of such one child to meet the schooling requirement as prescribed by the statute was enough to defeat the application of petitioner, in the absence of evidence of physical impossibility.

Claims of Chinese applicants, otherwise eligible for naturalization, that it was impossible to get their minor children out of China, have repeatedly been held of no force as against the statutory requirement.[44]

Perhaps the most important development in Philippine naturalization law since the establishment of the Republic has been the tightening of the principle of *jus sanguinis* with regard to children born in the Philippines of mixed (Filipino-alien) marriages. During the American and Commonwealth periods a succession of court decisions had established the principle that a child of an alien father and a Filipino mother was a Filipino. In 1947 this policy was reversed by the Supreme Court, which overruled a previous decision in the same case. The Court decided that "children of Chinese alien fathers born in the Philippines as the fruit of wedlock with a Filipina do not thereby acquire Philippine citizenship.[45]

Philippine economic nationalism is also reflected in policies with respect to deportation. The grounds for deportation are relatively

[43] *Hao Lian Chu* v. *Republic*, 48 O.G. 1780 (L-3265, 1950). See also *Quing Ku Chay* v. *Republic* (L-5477, 1954).

[44] *Hao Lian Chu* v. *Republic*, 48 O.G. 1780, G.R. No. L-3265, 1950; and *Ang Yee Koe* v. *Republic*, G.R. No. L-3863, 1951. See also *Tan Hi* v. *Republic*, G.R. No. L-6269, 1951.

[45] *Tan Chong* v. *Secretary of Labor*, 79 Phil. 249, G.R. No. L-47616, 1947. The decision, discussing the subject at length, admitted that the doctrine of *jus soli* had been recognized in many Philippine decisions. The Court came to the conclusion, however, that this principle was inapplicable because of the restrictions on Philippine citizenship found in Sec. 4 of the Philippine Act of 1902 as amended.

stringent and include grounds related to economic activities. Republic Act No. 503 amended the Immigration Act of 1940 to include the following additional types of aliens who might be deported:

Section 38. (11) Any alien who engages in profiteering, hoarding, or blackmarketing, independent of any criminal action which may be brought against him. (12) Any alien who defrauds his creditor by absconding or alienating properties to prevent him from being attached or executed.

In recent years economic legislation has tended to provide deportation for aliens found guilty of evasion. This provision originated with the Import Control Law of 1949, which states:

Section 20. That in the case of aliens, in addition to the penalty herein provided [severe fines and imprisonment], the offender shall be, upon final conviction, subject to immediate deportation without the necessity of further proceedings on the part of the Deportation Board.[46]

Enforcement of this type of penalty is subject to wide administrative discretion, but there is considerable evidence that the penalty is frequently imposed.[47]

Miscellaneous Nationalization Policies

There are many other manifestations of economic nationalism in legislation. In the Constitutional Convention there was strong sentiment for inclusion of a constitutional provision requiring the use of Filipino labor.[48] Since 1946 Congress has been aggressive in Filipinizing licensed professions [49] and has taken tentative steps toward

[46] For similar provisions, see Republic Act No. 509 (Price Control Act), Sec. 12; Republic Act No. 650 (Import Control Act), Sec. 17; Republic Act No. 1168 (Price Control Act), Sec. 9; Republic Act No. 1194 (Tobacco Import Control Law), Sec. 1.

[47] For example, it was reported on July 21, 1951, that President Quirino refused to reconsider an order issued on March 22, 1951, by the Deportation Board for the deportation of 33 Chinese nationals convicted of "profiteering in prime commodities" by the court of first instance in Manila. At the same time President Quirino suspended the deportation of 59 other Chinese and 1 Indian merchant pending rehearing by the Deportation Board (*Manila Times,* July 22, 1951).

[48] Aruego, *op. cit.,* pp. 654–656. The Constitution allows ample scope for nationalization legislation by providing that "the State shall afford protection to labor, especially to working women and minors, and shall regulate the relations between landowner and tenant and between labor and capital in industry and agriculture."

[49] For example, see the Plumbing Act, Republic Act No. 1378 of June 18, 1955.

Filipinization of labor in Philippine enterprises.[50] In the Industrial Priorities Formula the objective of labor nationalization is specifically recognized. The formula provides: "Other considerations being equal, preference shall be given to an industrial project that will make the most use of domestic labor." "Firms that employ more Filipinos per unit of capital invested will be given preference." [51] Labor nationalization has been promoted by judicial decisions. Probably the most significant decision occurred on January 31, 1950, when the Supreme Court, upholding a decision of the Court of Industrial Relations, affirmed that for enterprises domiciled in the Philippines "a majority of the laborers employed should be native."

Insurance, both life and property, has been progressively nationalized.[52] Interisland shipping was nationalized during the American colonial period, and overseas shipping has been a recent objective of Philippine nationalization policy. Still another manifestation of economic nationalism in the sense of reserving the domestic market for Filipinos has been the "flag law" policy, which establishes a preferential position for Filipinos in contracting with their government.[53]

Summary

A long tradition of legislative irresponsibility accumulated during the American colonial period when the National Assembly was the principal forum for economic nationalism. This tradition is now being dissipated—but very slowly. To a considerable extent the more flagrant excesses of nationalist legislation reflect a desire on the part of the author to reap political gain in a society only recently removed from colonialism. Such legislation is introduced, debated, and passed with confidence that the executive, confronted by the necessity of exercising international responsibilities, will either veto it or circumvent it with lax enforcement.[54]

[50] For example, see Art. 26 of the Petroleum Act of 1949, Republic Act No. 387 of June 18, 1949, and Sec. 5 of the Surigao Mineral Reservation Act of 1957, Republic Act No. 1828 of June 22, 1957.

[51] R.P., NEC, *The Five-Year Program for FY 1957–1961*, pp. 245, 260.

[52] Republic Act No. 488 of June 11, 1950.

[53] Commonwealth Act No. 108 of Oct. 30, 1936, as amended by Republic Act No. 134 of June 14, 1947.

[54] During the Magsaysay administration a virulent controversy persisted between the President and the Nacionalista leaders in Congress over the "proper" nationalism for the Philippines. Like Quezon, Roxas, and Quirino, Magsaysay was embar-

At the same time it would be a mistake to minimize the importance of economic nationalism as an objective of social policy. Manifestations of this objective pervade so much of the legislation and occupy so much of the time of Congress that there can be little doubt of the priority attached to nationalism.

It is true that much of the legislation along these lines is comparable with, or was copied from, similar legislation in other countries, particularly the United States. The distinction between the economic nationalism of an industrialized country and that of a developing ex-colonial one is qualitative and is marked. The economic progress that takes place in an industrialized society is capable of submerging much social conflict, because the gap between existing levels of material progress and material aspirations is small relative to past progress and is in dynamic equilibrium. In the Philippines, as in other countries of Southeast Asia, colonial economic development alienized the economy to the point that the resulting social strain is unlikely to be submerged by economic growth within Philippine capabilities.[55]

Further understanding of Philippine nationalism results from awareness of the pluralism of the colonial economy and the difficulty of organizing the society to accelerate economic growth. Alien minorities have not assimilated economically or socially. In general, they consider the host culture inferior and therefore they have remained firm in their determination to isolate themselves and maintain their cultural identity. As a result, the social "demand" for national economic development is weakened by alien resistance to expansion in governmental functions and activities.

This alien resistance to the expansion of governmental activities arises in part from knowledge that increased revenues to provide increased social services will redistribute income in favor of the economically retarded indigenous population. It also reflects an awareness that the alien's self-interest lies in maintenance of an enterprise economy which pays a high premium to individualism. Filipinos, on

rassed by the nationalist excesses of Congress in the face of extensive Filipino external commitments.

[55] Alienization creates social tensions and conflict wherever it occurs. Economic nationalism seems to be primarily a function of the extent of alien control and the functional specialization of alien economic activity. The capacity of economic growth and industrialization to submerge the tensions arising out of alienization is probably quite limited. This conclusion is substantiated by the strong feelings of economic nationalism displayed in the Canadian elections of 1957 and 1958.

the other hand, look upon government as a means to national integration and accelerated economic growth. The racial pluralism of the
Philippine economy is interpreted by Filipinos as a formidable obstacle
to the pursuit of national economic development.

A number of unanswered—and unanswerable—questions concerning Philippine economic nationalism remain. First, to what extent is
nationalism in the Philippines motivated by the urge to expropriate
alien property? There is undoubtedly some content of expropriation
in this Philippine policy, but it would be a mistake to exaggerate this
motivation. Filipinos as a whole do not wish to expropriate, but to
eliminate alien competition, which in an enterprise economy tends to
frustrate the emergence of Filipino entrepreneurship. The "good economy," I am convinced, would materialize for the average Filipino if
alien economic interests withered away to some safe minimum proportion. Unquestionably considerable expropriation will take place
in the implementation of Philippine nationalism, but this is not a
major objective.

Second, is Philippine economic nationalism merely the reflection
of long animosity toward Asian minorities? Would economic nationalism be satisfied by the elimination of the economic specialization
of the Asian minorities? Is the present anti-Chinese stage merely the
initial phase of a nationalism that will later turn against Western
economic interests?

Philippine economic nationalism will be conditioned by many
factors. Philippine proximity to the Asian mainland and the requirements of external security may effectively circumscribe economic
nationalism. For example, the resurgence of economic nationalism after
1954 was undoubtedly due in part to the establishment of a firm United
States commitment to defend the Philippines. Special economic arrangements with the United States including the economically important sugar quota, various economic and military assistance programs, and other factors will tend to maintain the special position
of United States economic interests in the Philippines. Equally important is the tendency of Filipinos to identify with the West rather
than Asia. This ambivalence in Philippine culture will curb the application of economic nationalism against Western economic interests. Economic nationalism will be influenced by the rate of material
progress and the distribution of such progress between nationals and
aliens. If Philippine economic progress should be accelerated, if future

increments of income accrue to nationals, and if functional specialization along racial lines becomes less prominent, it is possible that economic nationalism will become quiescent.

Although there are factors which moderate nationalist pressures against Western (United States) economic interests, there are few indications that Philippine economic nationalism is purely an anti-Chinese phenomenon. The resurgence of anti-Americanism in 1955 and 1956—a resurgence which has remained prominent in recent months— has a complex background involving political and economic issues. To a considerable extent the political issues are a rationalization of the growing resentment of the role of United States interests in the Philippine economy. Transfer of Philippine economic nationalism to Western targets is presaged by the recent controversy over the use of control over foreign exchange allocations to ensure that new enterprises are Filipino.

What is the relationship of nationalization to economic development? Such a question cannot be answered with any high degree of confidence. Negatively, it can be asserted that the colonial economy did not produce a rewarding rate of *national* economic development, and Filipinos are determined to restructure their economy. In the short run economic nationalism reduces accumulation of capital by presenting formidable obstacles to those elements in the society which have traditionally performed the saving and investing. Over the longer run the answer is no longer clear. Evidence is accumulating that the policy of de-alienization accelerates the appearance of Philippine entrepreneurship. The "dummies" of five years ago are the entrepreneurs of today as the economic experience they accumulate is augmented by the diversion of windfall gains to them, placing them in an advantageous position to launch enterprises. Social change has been accelerated in the Philippines over the past two decades. The population has displayed remarkable geographic, social, and economic mobility. Urbanization has hastened the breakdown of traditional family ties and has accelerated the appearance of loyalties to new institutions. It is not at all unlikely that the policy of Filipinization has and will generate indigenous entrepreneurship and by so doing will accelerate economic growth.

· XV ·

Economic Planning

HISTORICALLY, the primary economic functions of Philippine governments have been (a) to establish an institutional and legal environment which relates economic rewards to economic activity and (b) to maintain adequate levels of social services and social investment. In addition, there has been extensive but sporadic experimentation with public enterprises engaged in various types of directly productive activity.[1]

During the Commonwealth period (1935–1946) the principle of government participation in directly productive economic activity became firmly established. The National Development Company, which had been organized in 1919 as a mixed private-government corporation, was converted into a government corporation in 1936. The NDC func-

[1] Establishment of substantial Philippine autonomy by the Jones Act of 1916 was immediately followed by an extension of government participation in economic activity. For example, the Philippine National Bank was created in 1916 to engage in commercial banking. The Manila Railroad Co. was acquired by the government in 1916, primarily because of the financial distress of the railroad, which was built with private funds. The National Coal Co. was established in 1917. The National Development Co. was organized as a semigovernment corporation in 1919. The Manila Hotel Co. was acquired by the government in 1923. The Cebu Portland Cement Co., which was privately organized in 1922, was taken over by the NDC in 1924.

tioned as the holding company for government enterprises. In addition, a number of government enterprises were created as independent entities.[2] Corporations organized during the Commonwealth period prior to World War II engaged in diverse activities including manufacturing, commercial activity, provision of public utilities, banking, agricultural development and colonization, and various price support and subsidization functions. Capital required for government corporations was provided by direct appropriation by Congress and by loans from the Philippine National Bank, both directly to the various corporations and indirectly through the sale of securities of the National Development Company to the Philippine National Bank.

The policy of direct government participation in economic development was still in a formative stage when World War II abruptly terminated the testing of this policy. There is no evidence that the proliferation of government enterprises in the prewar period followed a comprehensive economic plan; rather they materialized to solve specific problems.[3]

In the political and economic confusion accompanying the liberation and the transfer of sovereignty in 1946 the need for careful planning to take maximum advantage of resources which were expected to be made available through Japanese reparations, United States war damage payments, and United States war surplus property allocated to the Philippines was widely recognized. Beginning in 1946 a succession of economic plans were drawn up to serve as guides to Philippine economic development and government participation in that development.

The first economic plan to be published was prepared by Thomas Hibben and other members of the technical staff attached to the Joint Philippine-American Finance Commission.[4] The objectives of the Hibben Plan were outlined as follows:

---

[2] For a list of government enterprises, see Hartendorp, *History*, pp. 49–63.

[3] The National Economic Council was created by Commonwealth Act No. 2 of Dec. 23, 1935, and formed in the early part of 1936. Among the functions of the council were the following: "to advise the government on economic and financial questions, including the improvement and promotion of industries, diversification of crops and production, tariffs, taxation and such other matters as may from time to time be submitted to its consideration by the President, and to formulate an economic program based on national independence." The council did not engage in extensive planning activity.

[4] Thomas Hibben, *Philippine Economic Development: A Technical Memorandum Prepared for the Joint Philippine-American Finance Commission* (Manila, 1947).

to expand domestic production, where quantities warrant, of all goods now imported for the manufactures of which the principal raw materials are now or can be made available locally, to expand production of Philippine export products at prices that will permit competition in the world's markets, and intensive development must be made in the services on which productive enterprises depend—power, transportation and communications.[5]

The Joint-Finance Commission asked for estimates of new investment and economic development in the Philippines during the next five years (1947–1951) that would absorb increases in the labor supply and excess foreign exchange reserves and at the same time expand the national product and prepare the economy for the adjustment called for by the trade agreement with the United States.[6]

The plan period was approximately the period during which rehabilitation payments by the United States would sustain a high level of domestic investment and preferential trade would be conducted on the most favorable terms. The plan envisaged total development expenditures over five years of ₱2,250 million, broken down into ₱722 million for domestic labor and materials, ₱1,240 million for import requirements, and ₱215 million for freight and insurance on imports. The memorandum gave no detailed estimates of proposed sources of investment funds and furthermore made no attempt to allocate responsibility for expenditures between government and private enterprise.[7]

Shortly after the appearance of the Hibben memorandum the Philippine government published a *Proposed Program for Industrial Rehabilitation and Development* prepared by the technical staff of the National Development Company under the supervision of the H. E. Beyster Corporation, a United States firm of industrial consultants.[8] The Beyster Plan stressed rehabilitation and industrialization, and frequent reference was made to utilization of Japanese reparations to achieve specific plan objectives.

Development expenditures over the first five years as proposed in the Beyster Plan totaled ₱1.4 billion. In addition to the proposed investment outlays, the plan envisaged Philippine acquisition from Japa-

<hr />

[5] *Ibid.*, p. 2.   [6] *Ibid.*

[7] The memorandum did suggest that the government apply to the U.S. Export-Import Bank and to the International Bank for Reconstruction and Development, on a project-to-project basis, for the foreign exchange required for the program.

[8] Manila, Oct. 28, 1947; hereafter referred to as the Beyster Plan.

nese reparations of a steel industry with a capacity of 150,000 tons annually, substantial numbers of machine tools, a sulphuric acid plant (41,000 tons), caustic soda plant (23,000 tons), textile plants (250,000 spindles), knitting plants, and so forth.[9]

Over a longer term—up to fifteen years—additional investment expenditures totaling ₱3,200 million were proposed, including ₱1,440 million for housing with the remaining ₱1,760 million divided evenly between social investment, such as for transportation, hospitals, and schools, and industrial investment. The Beyster Plan was liberal with outlays to restore the sugar and mining industries, the principal prewar sources of foreign exchange. A total of ₱755 million was allocated to those two industries.

The Beyster Plan made no provision for agricultural development outside the export sector and was obviously influenced by Philippine aspirations for industrialization. While Japanese reparations were an appropriate source of industrial equipment, rehabilitation of the Philippine economy could hardly be accomplished without greater outlays on agriculture and social services. The Beyster Plan undoubtedly pleased Filipinos with its glib proposals of new industries appropriate to the postwar Philippine economy, e.g., machine tools, ferroalloys, nonferrous foundries, and heavy investment in chemical production. No consideration was given to the problem of raising the required funds, and the plan implicitly assumed that United States war damage payments plus Japanese reparations would dispose of the problem of foreign exchange requirements.

These initial ventures in economic planning undoubtedly provided some gratification of Filipino longings to seize the opportunity arising out of United States economic assistance for rehabilitation and Japanese reparations to transform the colonial-type Philippine economy. Neither report was implemented—the Hibben memorandum because it was American and the Beyster Plan because of its lack of realism. In common with much of the early postwar economic planning in less-developed countries, the Philippine plans were no more than rough estimates of the investment requirements to accomplish broad policy objectives. Little consideration was given to the complementary roles of public and private enterprise or to the problem of directing investment into planned channels and spacing investment over the

[9] Estimated to be equal to 7 per cent of the reparations available for distribution to Japan's former enemies.

period of the plan. When considered in the light of the low levels of government economic activity and lack of government control over United States–financed rehabilitation, the initial plans were little more than ambitious statements of Philippine aspirations for diversified economic activity and industrialization.

Two further developments relating to economic planning occurred in 1947. In June of that year appeared the *Report of the Philippine–United States Agriculture Mission* (U.S. Department of Agriculture, Office of Foreign Agricultural Relations). The *Report* appraised the destructive effects of the war on the country's agricultural economy and proposed plans for the rehabilitation of agriculture and a long-range program of agricultural development. In December 1947 an *Electric Power Program for the Republic of the Philippines* prepared by the Westinghouse Electric International Corporation with the co-operation of the National Power Corporation was published. The report outlined a twelve-year power-development program to be completed by 1960 and took up in detail an initial five-year program. The short-run Westinghouse program was approved by the government and has been followed in public development of electric power, although completion of the projects has been considerably delayed beyond the initial five-year period.[10]

Meanwhile the National Economic Council was reorganized on December 31, 1947, under the chairmanship of Vice-President Quirino. The reconstituted NEC was charged with co-ordination of government economic policies.

The next episode in the evolution of planning policy occurred in 1948 when a *Government Program of Economic Rehabilitation and Development of 1948* was prepared by Secretary of Finance Miguel Cuaderno with the co-operation of Filemon C. Rodriguez, manager of the National Power Corporation. The Cuaderno Plan followed a recommendation of the Joint Philippine–United States Finance Commission that the Philippine government apply to the International Bank for Reconstruction and Development for loans to finance the foreign exchange requirements of hydroelectric and fertilizer plant projects. The Cuaderno Plan was prepared for submission to the IBRD to support the Philippine loan application.

---

[10] The Ambuklao project did not begin power generation until 1957; construction is under way on the Binga project, and Maria Cristina in the second stage has only 50,000 kilowatts of installed capacity.

The Cuaderno Plan called for total developmental expenditures of ₱1,848 million over the five years 1949–1953 (Table 53). Outlays were broken down into peso costs of ₱967 million and foreign exchange requirements equivalent to ₱881 million. The plan included both public and private projects with a majority of the projects designated as the responsibility of public investment.

The aim of the program was to adjust the economy to the progressive application of American tariffs on Philippine exports after 1954 and to cushion the impact of the scheduled decline in United States government payments. It was conceived as the initial stage in a process of

Table 53. Estimated investment requirements of the Cuaderno Plan, 1949–1953 [a]

(₱ million or equivalent)

	1949	1950	1951	1952	1953	Total
	Local currency costs					
Agriculture	60.7	79.1	103.8	97.9	—	341.5
Industry	121.7	132.4	161.5	111.7	98.0	625.3
	182.4	211.5	265.3	209.6	98.0	966.8
	Foreign exchange costs					
Agriculture	51.8	51.0	34.4	28.2	—	165.4
Industry	179.0	159.6	176.6	114.8	86.0	716.0
	230.8	210.6	211.0	143.0	86.0	881.4
Total	*413.2*	*422.1*	*476.3*	*352.6*	*184.0*	*1,848.2*

[a] As reported by R.P., Philippine Economic [Yulo] Survey Mission, *Philippine Agricultural and Industrial Development Program, Revised 1950* (Manila, 1950).

structural adjustment to free the national economy from too great dependence on a few export crops and to fortify it somewhat against fluctuations in the demand for and the prices of these crops in foreign markets. These goals were to be accomplished by extending productive activity from raw material production to industrial processing and by enlarging the scope and possibilities of internal distribution through improved and augmented transportation and communications facilities.

For the first time in Philippine planning consideration was given to the sources of investment funds. The plan discounted the possibility of providing investment funds out of tax revenues. The report considered the question of raising funds by the sale of government bonds to the public. While the capacity for investment service of debt incurred in completion of the long-range projects was considered good, it was doubted that substantial amounts could be raised in the existing market for government securities.[11]

The principal source of funds for planned investment was to be borrowing from the newly created Central Bank. Section 137 of the Central Bank Act provided that the bank could advance not more than ₱200 million to the government for "productive and income producing projects." The plan provided that this amount would be used for direct investment by the government in rehabilitation and development projects and for loans to the Rehabilitation Finance Corporation to support private enterprises "to the greatest extent possible in projects they might be willing to undertake." The establishment of the Central Bank and of new branches of commercial banks in outlying provinces was expected to lead to an increase in funds channeled into the banking system from private savings. Such funds would be invested in private and government securities. Government securities were also expected to provide insurance companies with an important investment outlet for their reserves. Total investment requirements for the program were estimated to be ₱1,848 million, of which ₱507 million was allocated for agricultural development.

The Cuaderno Plan, which originated as an expedient to support the Philippine application for an IBRD loan, survived to provide minimum guidance for the expenditure of ₱200 million provided for economic development in the legislation establishing the Central Bank. Examination of expenditures under Section 137, however, does not support the impression that they conformed closely to any existing plan.[12] Although almost half of the allocations were made to agricultural projects, a considerable part of such funds were dissipated in capital losses of ill-conceived government corporations with commercial and price-support functions rather than agricultural develop-

[11] The report concluded that the development of a government securities market was necessarily a slow process and that considerable educational work had to be undertaken by the Central Bank in order to create such a market.

[12] For details of allocations under Sec. 137 of the Central Bank Act, see Central Bank, *Third Annual Report, 1951*, pp. 134–135. The Philippine application to the IBRD for a loan to meet the foreign exchange cost of the Maria Cristina project was rejected, apparently on the grounds that the market for the power to be generated was inadequate. The Philippines completed the first stage of the project (25,000 kilowatts) using Philippine resources under Sec. 137 of the Central Bank Act.

ment. Only a small portion allocated to manufacturing projects materialized as productive investment.[13] Outlays for public utilities and transportation have proved relatively successful, although the ocean-going fleet and the national shipyard and graving dock have contributed more to national prestige than to economic development.

The Cuaderno Plan of 1948 served still another function. During 1949 and the first half of 1950 foreign exchange and fiscal crises were superimposed on the deteriorating security situation in the face of Huk aggression. Following a visit by President Quirino to the United States in January and February 1950, President Truman agreed to send an economic mission to advise the Philippines on the establishment of a sound and well-balanced economy. President Quirino, confronted by the certainty of critical recommendations by the forthcoming mission, attempted to soften the anticipated report. On March 20 he created a Philippine Economic Survey Mission in the hope that the mission to which Truman had agreed might become a joint Philippine–United States mission. President Truman did not yield and the subsequent Economy Survey (Bell) Mission to the Philippines did not include Filipinos. The Philippine Economic Survey Mission, excluded from the work of the Bell Mission but hoping to soften the impact of the Bell Mission report, set to work to prepare an economic plan which would be evidence of the government's concern for a permanent solution of pressing Philippine economic problems.[14]

In creating the Philippine Economic Survey Mission President Quirino instructed it to "draw up a revised and up-to-date, integrated plan" of

---

[13] The Ilocos textile project has been closed as uneconomic. The Philippine Electrical Manufacturing Co., which was essentially a private enterprise, and the small electric-arc steel-manufacturing industry are presently operating under high levels of protection.

[14] An interesting episode occurred during this period when Professor Ricardo R. Pascual, Philippine delegate to the International Institute of Pacific Relations Conference at Lucknow, India, in the fall of 1950, delivered a paper entitled "Present Day Economic Problems and Their Solution," which was taken in large part from the plan prepared by the Philippine Economic Survey Mission. Six years later in a political controversy involving the University of the Philippines, he was accused of plagiarism. In defending himself against the charge, he reported in some detail the activities of the staff of the Economic Survey Mission in their attempts to counteract the criticism which was anticipated in the *Bell Mission Report*. Pascual's account was substantiated by Amando Dalisay, who had been a member of the staff of the Philippine Economic Survey Mission. See the *Collegian*, University of the Philippines, June 13 and 20, 1956.

economic rehabilitation and development with the end in view of (1) making the country as self-sufficient as it can be in the prime and essential necessities of life, such as food, clothing, transportation and communications services, etc.; (2) accelerating the production of dollar-producing exports so as to achieve within the shortest possible time a stable balance of payments notwithstanding the imminent reduction of dollar receipts from the United States commencing this year; (3) establishing an economy which can withstand the gradual cessation of preferential treatment given to us in the American market under the provisions of the Trade Agreement with the United States; and (4) expanding the productive capacity of our people, thereby increasing their earning power and improving their standard of living.[15]

Table 54. Estimated investment requirements of the Yulo Plan, 1950–1953 [a]
(₱ million or equivalent)

	1950	1951	1952	1953	1954	Total
Local currency costs						
Agriculture	75.8	77.3	73.6	73.6	73.7	373.8
Industry [b]	50.2	58.0	44.0	33.4	—	185.6
	126.0	135.3	117.6	107.0	73.7	559.4
Foreign exchange costs						
Agriculture	49.4	37.2	36.0	30.6	27.3	180.5
Industry [b]	61.2	89.5	57.9	29.8	—	238.4
	110.6	126.7	93.9	60.4	27.3	418.9
Total	236.6	262.0	211.5	167.4	101.0	978.3

[a] *Yulo Plan*, pp. 140 and Appendixes to Chapter VII.
[b] The industrial phase of the revised plan extended only through 1953.

In view of the severe fiscal and balance of payments problems confronting the Philippines, the resulting Yulo Plan of 1950 substantially reduced the planned expenditures of the Cuaderno Plan of 1948 (Table 54). The principal revision in the Yulo Plan was (a) to emphasize agricultural development more strongly, both for domestic consumption and for export, and (b) to cut in half the total planned expenditures.

[15] R.P., Philippine Economic Survey Mission, *Philippine Agricultural and Industrial Development Program, Revised, 1950* (Manila, 1950), p.v. Hereafter referred to as the *Yulo Plan*.

In order to achieve the production targets in agriculture, priority was given to (a) creation of a system of agricultural extension services, (b) strengthening of the experiment station and other research facilities, (c) expansion of agricultural credit facilities of the Rehabilitation Finance Corporation and the Philippine National Bank, (d) financial and technical assistance to colonists, and (e) construction of roads in frontier areas. In contrast to previous plans, large-scale agricultural projects, such as irrigation, were emphasized.

The industrial program of the Cuaderno Plan was revised downward by the Yulo Plan. The Cuaderno Plan envisaged total nonagricultural capital investment (public and private) of ₱1,341.3 million over five years, including ₱625.3 million of peso costs and ₱716.0 million equivalent of foreign exchange costs. The Yulo Plan substantially lowered estimated investment expenditures for nonagricultural purposes to a total of ₱424.0 million for 1950–1954.

Of the scheduled ₱212.4 million of investment in manufacturing, ₱203.4 was to be made by the government through the National Development Company. Major allocations were made for textiles, ₱28.4 million; hydroelectric plants, ₱106.0 million; oil refinery, ₱24.0 million; steel rolling mill, ₱4.5 million; shipyard and drydocks, ₱13.0 million; aluminum plant, ₱4.0 million; and ammonium sulphate, ₱11.0 million.

Investment in mining was planned at ₱22.0 million as compared to ₱65.2 million in the Cuaderno Plan. Investment in public works was planned at ₱73.0 million as compared to ₱213.0 million, with ₱30 million allocated to road construction. Investment in transportation and communications facilities was planned at ₱107.9 million as compared to ₱408.6 million in the earlier plan, with major reductions in foreign exchange outlays for trucks, buses, aircraft, and railroad equipment.

Rather than the Yulo Plan, the Bell Mission recommendations served as the principal guide to public economic policy formulation in the ensuing three years. The Bell report included far-reaching recommendations of fiscal and commercial policy measures to solve the pressing problems of adequate government revenues and balance of payments disequilibrium. Moreover, the Bell Mission recommended an economic role for the Philippine government which departed radically from the role envisaged in postwar planning. In general terms, the report recommended that the government (a) concentrate on the provision of adequate amounts of social services and social investment, e.g., agricultural extension and research, power and transportation facilities, public health and education, and the like, (b) improve existing services, e.g., the issuance of land titles and the management of land reform, and (c) sharply limit direct governmental entrepreneurial activity. The mission recommended liquidation of ineffective government corporations. Government activity in the area of agricultural and industrial development was to be confined to the creation of credit institutions which would channel adequate amounts of financial resources to these areas and the provision of adequate amounts of agricultural and industrial research.

During the ensuing three years a strong effort was made to implement the recommendations of the Bell Mission. President Quirino created a Philippine Council for United States Aid (PHILCUSA) from the nucleus of the Philippine Economic Survey Commission with Jose Yulo as chairman.[16] PHILCUSA functioned as the counterpart and co-ordinating body between the Economic Co-operation Administration and the Philippine government.[17] Economic planning in the accepted sense of the word did not take place during the last three years of the Quirino administration, and there was no "plan" in the sense of investment and resource budgets. However, there was undoubtedly a higher level of co-ordination and consistency in economic policy than had been previously achieved.

Following the inauguration of President Magsaysay in January 1954, there was a resumption of formal economic planning.[18] In his first State-of-the-Nation Message to Congress on January 25, 1954, President Magsaysay recommended that "the NEC be revitalized as a really effective agency to plan and put into effect a truly integrated program for economic development." This was followed on March 20, 1954, by the outline of a five-year economic development program [19]

[16] For the first time there was a successful attempt to obtain some minimum congressional commitment to economic planning activities by including six congressional members in the fifteen-member PHILCUSA.

[17] The personnel of the NEC were absorbed into PHILCUSA in the early part of 1951. The NEC was inactive until early in 1952 when a technical staff was assembled to make studies of problems involved in revision of the U.S.–Philippine Trade Agreement.

[18] On May 30, 1953, President Quirino directed the NEC to review the progress made under the Yulo Plan. This report was submitted by Filemon C. Rodriguez, acting executive director of the NEC, on Dec. 24, 1953, a week before the inauguration of Magsaysay.

[19] *Manila Times,* March 21, 1954.

involving developmental expenditures totaling ₱4 billion. It was estimated that 56 per cent of these expenditures would be provided by private investment. The major part of the government investment would be provided out of budgetary revenues in excess of current expenditures. The remainder of the projected public investment would be provided by a "bond issue of ₱600 million floated over five years to enable us to finance, through borrowing from our own people, high priority productive projects and permanent improvements to be carefully studied and recommended by the NEC."

A month later, on April 28, 1954, *The Five-Year Economic Development Program for Fiscal Years 1955 to 1959* was published by the NEC.[20] The published plan, known as the Rodriguez Plan, was even more ambitious than the plan outlined by President Magsaysay and provided for gross investment during the period of ₱6,767 million and net investment of ₱4,106 (Table 55).

Table 55. Proposed net investment program of the Rodriguez Plan, 1955–1959 [a]
(₱ million)

	1955	1956	1957	1958	1959	Total
Agriculture	131	146	159	182	210	828
Manufacturing	181	198	235	284	350	1,247
Mining	25	31	41	54	69	220
Transportation and Communications	40	64	79	95	115	392
Construction	245	256	268	277	282	1,327
Other	8	13	19	23	29	91
	631	707	800	914	1,054	4,106

[a] *Rodriguez Plan* (Condensed Report), p. 41. Rows and columns may not add exactly due to rounding.

The Rodriguez Plan emphasized the employment effects of the planned expenditures and stated that "the program aims primarily to provide jobs for the unemployed, to increase the level of production and the standard of living of the people, and to pave the way for the attainment of an independent economy free from the uncertainties of world market fluctuations." The plan emphasized industrialization and deprecated the value of agricultural development:

[20] R.P., NEC, *The Five-Year Economic Development Program for Fiscal Years 1955 to 1959* (Condensed Report), (Manila, 1954).

There is need for a positive program of exploitation of indigenous resources and of processing them for local use to replace imports and thus provide for the expanding demand for food and other necessities of the growing population. Experience has amply demonstrated that agricultural expansion alone cannot effectively solve our pressing unemployment problem nor materially raise the standard of living.[21]

The basic objective of the Rodriguez Plan was to increase employment by 1.44 million to 8.5 million and to reduce unemployment from 1.4 million to 0.6 million or from 15 per cent to some 6 per cent of the labor force. The emphasis upon the employment effects of the Rodriguez Plan undoubtedly resulted from the virulent controversy which was then raging over the Minimum Wage Law enacted in the spring of 1951. Opponents of the law were attacking it on the basis of extensive Philippine unemployment and the retarded recovery of exports, which, it was claimed, were handicapped by high labor costs. The Rodriguez Plan answered the opponents of the Minimum Wage Law by contending that

the Plan proposes that the basic problem is not one of rationalization of Philippine costs, but it is necessary that overall production should be increased continuously by sufficient additions to investment at a level high enough to insure and maintain high employment levels and at the same time assure higher real income for the individual.

Another significant change in objective was the emphasis given to the role of private enterprise:

Under the program, the government's resources should be devoted mainly to the development of agriculture, public works, irrigation and power, social services, and a few basic industries which are vital to the economy but which, for the present, are unattractive to private capital. Private enterprise should be relied upon to expand its activities in industry and commerce and in production and distribution, with the government giving assistance and encouragement as well as direction.

The Rodriguez Plan proposed net investment over the five fiscal years 1955–1959 of ₱4,106 million. Foreign exchange costs were estimated at ₱2,094 million and peso requirements at ₱2,012 million. The over-all net investment program was further divided into public investment of ₱1,737 million and private investment of ₱2,369 million. Public net investment was allocated as follows: agriculture, ₱175

[21] *Ibid.*, p. 5.

million; manufacturing, ₱555 million; transportation and communications, ₱66 million; construction, ₱850 million; and other, ₱91 million.

For the first time in Philippine economic planning an attempt was made to plan the financing of the over-all investment program. Private savings were estimated at ₱1,882 million, private credit expansion at ₱547 million, public savings through the budget and the retained earnings of government corporations at ₱1,087 million, government borrowing at ₱500 million, and foreign aid at ₱150 million. It was estimated that the plan would increase real national income from ₱7,500 million to ₱11,088 million, or by 58 per cent or by 10 per cent per annum.[22] The Rodriguez Plan suffered the fate of earlier Philippine economic plans, i.e., it was largely ignored. The administration was never firmly committed, and there was no legislative commitment.

A major change in government policy occurred in 1954. It will be recalled that, with the exception of the ₱200 million for development expenditures provided in the Central Bank Act, government access to borrowing from the banking system had been narrowly circumscribed.[23] After the election of President Magsaysay the Nacionalista Congress enacted Republic Act No. 1000 of June 12, 1954, which provided for the issuance of ₱1,000 million of bonds to finance developmental expenditures. Scheduling the expenditure of bond issues occupied Congress and the administration in 1955 and 1956, but these expenditures were apparently not made in accordance with the Rodriguez Plan.[24]

A major planning episode during the first two years of the Magsaysay administration involved the work of the Government Survey and Reorganization Commission. The commission, composed of four senators, four representatives, and four members appointed by the President, was created by Republic Act No. 997 of June 9, 1954. It was directed to survey the entire administration and prepare a comprehensive plan of reorganization. Under the law the reorganization

[22] It was estimated that net investment of ₱4,106 million would be accompanied by an increase in national income of ₱3,588 million. This in turn implies an incremental capital to output ratio of 1:1.15.

[23] After the 1951 election the essential economic conservatism of the government was reinforced by a Nacionalista-controlled Congress, which proved reluctant to meet financial requests of the Quirino administration.

[24] A detailed tabulation of authorized expenditures and the progress of bond sales under Republic Act No. 1000 is to be found in *A.C.C. Journal,* 33 (May 1957), 212.

proposals would become effective if not disapproved by either house of Congress.

The commission, which made extensive use of a firm of American consultants financed by the United States aid program, submitted sixty-one plans for changes in the organization of the national administration. Fifty-three of the plans were recommended to Congress by the President, and thirty-three received congressional approval.[25]

The next stage in the evolution of economic planning policy occurred in January 1956 when the National Economic Council was reorganized by President Magsaysay in accordance with Executive Order No. 119 of July 1, 1955.[26] The NEC was reorganized to include an Office of National Planning, an Office of Foreign Aid Co-ordination, and an Office of Statistical Co-ordination and Standards.[27]

During 1956 the Office of National Planning of the NEC was engaged in preparing still another five-year plan. The completed *Five-Year Economic and Social Development Program for FY 1957–1961* was adopted by the NEC on January 3, 1957, and was subsequently approved by the cabinet.[28] The 1957 Plan represented the

[25] The remaining plans were rejected by Congress. The plans of the Government Survey and Reorganization Commission were published in more than thirty monographs, each dealing with a department or agency of government or with a problem of administration. These monographs comprise a valuable description of Philippine administrative organization as well as an assessment of the organization and proposals for change.

[26] R.P., Government Survey and Reorganization Commission, *Economic Planning, Plans Nos. 10 and 11* with supporting findings and recommendations, was published on Feb. 28, 1955. The commission found that "economic planning in the Philippines is inadequate and ineffective. This is attributable in large measure to poor governmental organization. Numerous entities are concerned with economic planning and development, but their authority is scattered and loosely defined, and their activities have little effective co-ordination or systematic direction (p. 11). The Commission recommended: "One national planning entity should co-ordinate the economic activities of the nation, both public and private. It will need to co-ordinate national fiscal and budgetary policies with credit and monetary policies, tariff and tax policies, public and private investment practices, labor and management practices and many other phases of the economic and social life of the nation."

[27] The membership of the NEC was set at ten and in order to obtain congressional commitment to economic planning, four members, two each from the House and the Senate, were included in the Council.

[28] R.P., NEC, *Five-Year Economic and Social Development Program for FY 1957–1961* (Manila, 1957). Hereafter referred to as *The 1957 Plan. The 1957 Plan* included as a Supplement, a Three Year Production Program prepared by Senator Jose C. Locsin, an ex-officio member of the NEC in 1956–1957.

culmination of a prolonged and confusing postwar period of experimentation with planning. It was both ambitious in terms of past performance and involved the application of advanced planning technique (Table 56).[29] It defined three major problems of the Philippine economy. "First, there is underproduction both for consumption and export. Second, the level of unemployment is certainly high and apparently rising. Third, there is a chronic disequilibrium in the balance of pay-

Table 56. Estimated gross national product and public expenditures and investment in the 1957 Plan [a]
(₱ million)

	1957	1958	1959	1960	1961	Total
Gross national product	10,077	10,712	11,387	12,107	12,874	57,157
Government current expenditures	714	771	832	899	971	4,187
Government net investment [b]	385	393	401	408	413	2,000
Debt service	110	121	133	146	161	671
Estimated national government expenditure	1,209	1,285	1,366	1,453	1,545	6,858
Estimated national government ordinary receipts	950	1,045	1,146	1,254	1,369	5,764
Excess of expenditures over ordinary receipts	259	240	220	199	176	1,094
Internal borrowing	119	126	127	140	152	664
External aid and loans	104	91	95	97	104	491

[a] R.P., NEC, *The 1957 Plan*, p. 98.
[b] The excess of estimated government investment of ₱2 billion over the cost of specific projects recommended for public investment amounting to ₱1,860 million is to be utilized for a program of government guarantees of long-term credits extended by the banking system to private enterprise for high priority projects (*ibid.*, p. 74).

ments." The plan surveyed current economic problems with considerable candor and presented a concise, informative picture of economic progress since 1950.

The 1957 Plan recognized the problem of continuity in postwar economic planning by stating that

[29] Philippine economic planning during 1956 benefited from the participation of Dr. Benjamin Higgins, who was posted to the Philippines by the UN Technical Assistance Administration. Professor Higgins has had extensive experience in economic planning in Indonesia and Libya.

This program constitutes in essence the first revision of the Five-Year Program [Rodriguez Plan] of FY 1955–59 approved by the President in 1954. It is, therefore, also a continuing program intended to be revised and updated every year by dropping off the program for the year just passed, revising that for the remaining four years, and adding another year to form the new program period.

Public investment during the five years was projected at ₱1,860 million, increasing moderately from an estimated ₱365 million in fiscal year 1956–57 to ₱385 million in fiscal year 1960–61. Public investment was allocated as given in Table 57.

Table 57. Proposed public investment in the 1957 Plan [a]
(₱ million)

	1957	1958	1959	1960	1961	Total
Agriculture	54	59	62	64	68	307
Agricultural services	27	30	32	33	36	158
Irrigation construction	27	29	30	31	32	149
Industries	107	85	81	84	76	433
Manufacturing	97	73	67	68	59	362
Mining	11	13	14	17	18	71
Services (utilities)	179	190	196	204	211	980
Transp. and Comm.	85	91	95	97	98	466
Public works [b]	42	43	43	44	44	216
Public utilities	52	56	58	63	69	298
Social development	25	27	28	30	30	140
Health	11	13	14	14	14	66
Education	13	13	13	14	14	667
Labor and social welfare	1	1	1	2	2	7
	365	361	367	282	385	1,860

[a] R.P., NEC, *The 1957 Plan*, p. 24. Rows and columns do not add exactly because of rounding.
[b] Consists of flood control, public buildings, and housing projects.

Planned public investment was ambitious in terms of past levels of performance and recognized the need to expand the essentially low level of government economic activity. For example, during the four fiscal years ending June 30, 1957, government investment, including a substantial amount of investment financed from the sale of Republic Act No. 1000 bonds, averaged ₱235 million annually, as compared to a proposed average annual public investment of ₱372 million. On the other hand, estimated levels of total revenues were quite realistic as Philippine national government revenues have averaged 8 to 10 per cent of gross national product since 1951. The expenditures provided in the plan likewise represented a moderate expansion over the levels of the earlier postwar period and called for substantial deficit financing. If fully implemented, the program of public investment would have represented a modest contribution to the capital requirements of rapid Philippine economic progress. The philosophy behind the public investment program emphasized private initiative and enterprise, and public expenditures were concentrated on government services and social investment.[30]

The following criteria or working rules were to be applied in planning investment expenditures:

1. Because per capita income is low, the production of low-cost essentials should receive preference over the production of luxury items.
2. Because the Philippines has relatively little capital and much manpower, projects requiring large amounts of labor in relation to capital should receive preference, other things being equal.
3. Because only limited amounts of foreign exchange are available, foreign exchange-saving and foreign exchange-earning projects requiring a high proportion of domestic funds should have preference over those requiring a high proportion of foreign funds.[31]

To determine priorities among competing projects for purposes of allocating scarce public investment resources, limited foreign exchange, or bank credits, the NEC derived a quantitative formula as follows:

Industrial Priority $= R_1 + R_2 + R_3 + R_4$ where

$$R_1 = \frac{e\,(W + r + i + p)}{K} =$$ value added to national income as corrected by an essentiality factor to account for the impact of the project on external economies and for other social benefit considerations, the whole per unit of capital resources utilized.

[30] "In order to bring about the essential conditions that will induce private entrepreneurial activities and encourage greater private investment in desirable development projects, public financing of economic and social overhead projects and those that will create the necessary long-term basis for supplementing private enterprise is provided" (*The 1957 Plan*, p. 22).

[31] *Ibid.*, p. 30.

$e =$ essentiality factor determined according to (1) economic importance of the product either as a commodity for export or for domestic use, (2) source of raw materials and supplies used, (3) source of capital equipment, and (4) source and nationality of financing.

$W =$ compensation of all officials, employees, and laborers adjusted for portion paid to non-Filipinos.

$r =$ rent adjusted for payments remitted abroad.

$i =$ interest paid adjusted for payments on foreign borrowings.

$p =$ profit accruing to Filipinos.

$K =$ total investment in the firm with the peso component adjusted by the factor of 0.7.

$$R_2 = \frac{F.E.\,s/e - F.E.\,c}{K} = \text{contribution to the reduction of balance of payments disequilibrium.}$$

$F.E.\,s/e =$ foreign exchange saved or earned.

$F.E.\,c =$ foreign exchange cost.

$$R_3 = \frac{0.5 \times \dfrac{rmd}{rmt} \times rmd}{K} = \text{domestic materials utilization ratio.}$$

$rmd =$ value of domestic materials and operating supplies used in production, excluding the value of the imported component of domestically processed intermediate products whenever such imported component exceeds value-wise 50 per cent of the value of that intermediate product.

$rmt =$ value of the raw materials and supplies used in production. The coefficient $0.5 \times rmd/rmt$ represents a measure of the additional economic value generated by the utilization of the domestic materials and supplies.

$$R_4 = \frac{Id \times 2000}{K} = \text{contribution to alleviation of domestic unemployment.}$$

$Id =$ number of paid Filipino workers (officials, employees, and laborers employed during at least 300 days a year).

The Industrial Priorities Formula is an impressive framework on which to exhibit the various factors relevant to appraisal of investment alternatives. The preciseness of the formula is, however, illusory, and the high degree of uncertainty inherent in estimation of the many variables will continue essential administrative discretion in the allocation of foreign exchange and bank credit.

The public investment program assigned a relatively low priority to agricultural development. Of the outlays on agricultural services, over one-half, ₱89 million, were allocated to "land improvement," which presumably referred to policies to extend the cultivation of land in frontier areas where relatively fertile lands are available. It was estimated that the agricultural development program would (a) attain self-sufficiency in food items, (b) meet about 65 per cent of the requirement of fiber materials for clothing, and (c) maintain the present volume of agricultural exports.

Public investment in manufacturing was to be concentrated in Lanao Province in northern Mindanao where the projects would serve as a market for the expanded hydroelectric capacity of the Maria Cristina project. All of the investment in chemical production (₱129 million) plus the principal part of ₱59 million allocated to investment in an integrated pig-iron smelting and steel mill was to be made in Lanao Province. A substantial part of the public investment in manufacturing and mining was allocated to the establishment of a cement industry integrated with the pig-iron smelting and steel mill using raw materials in Mindanao. A cement plant of 6 million bags of annual capacity costing ₱31 million, a coke plant of 85,000 metric tons costing ₱10 million, and ₱51 million assigned to coal development were included in the program of public investment.

The principal part of the remaining public investment in this category seemed less well conceived. Such investment included ₱26 million allocated to development of the ramie industry in Mindanao plus ₱67 million allocated to the establishment of a machine tool plant, an industrial machinery plant, and a ball- and roller-bearing plant (all in Manila) and for completion of the dock and shipbuilding yard in Bataan Province. The remainder was allocated to "improvement and expansion of industrial research," ₱30 million, and to geophysical and geological surveys, ₱20 million.

Of the allocation to investment in transportation and communications, ₱330 million was for highway construction, ₱52 million for modernization of the Manila Railroad Company and extension of its lines to the Cagayan Valley, with the remaining ₱84 million for port works, airports, airways, and telephone, telegraph, and radio communications.

Public works expenditures included ₱100 million allocated to school construction, ₱66 million to other public buildings, ₱25 million to flood control, and ₱25 million to public housing. Investment in public utilities was concentrated in electric power, which was allocated ₱208 million, approximately 90 per cent of which was to go to hydroelectric power development. The program provided for completion of Ambuklao, Binga, and Units No. 2 and No. 3 of Maria Cristina, projects originally planned for completion in the first phase of the Westinghouse Program of 1947. When completed, the power projects of the plan would result in an additional 270,000 kilowatts of capacity. The remaining ₱90 million allocated to public utilities was to go to improvements in water supply.

Public investment in education was directed toward vocational agricultural and trade schools, ₱14 million; comprehensive high schools, ₱20 million; teacher training, ₱14 million; and elementary schools, ₱15 million. Over half of the public investment in public health was allocated to hospital and laboratory construction, ₱38 million, with the principal part of the remainder going to control malaria, tuberculosis, and schistosomiasis, ₱8 million, and rural health and dental services, ₱17 million.

The basic objective of the plan with respect to private activity was defined as follows: "Public policies and the government's own economic activities should be such as to induce a level of private developmental net investment" of at least ₱3,200 million.[32] The bulk of private investment was expected to come from private savings in the form of retained business earnings and institutional savings, individual savings, the flotation of new corporate securities, extension of public credit, and direct foreign investment. Additional financing was expected through the banking system.

The plan proposed that national government tax revenues should increase during the plan period by ₱537 million to ₱1,369 million, or from 9 per cent of gross national product to 15 per cent. However, to maintain strong incentives to private investment, the plan recommended (a) increased assessment of real property and a progressive surtax on wholly or partially unused land; (b) a system of accelerated and postponed depreciation to be incorporated in the income tax

[32] Not including private investment which does not require financing, e.g., improvements undertaken through the direct labor of farmers, natural increase in livestock, and so forth.

law; (c) amendment of the income tax law to provide for deductions from taxable income of earnings reinvested in high priority enterprises, life insurance premiums, savings deposited in special medium or long-term accounts, savings invested in long-term government and private corporate securities, and donations to industrial and economic research institutions.[33]

The plan proposed that tariff policy be used to maintain the structure of protection which has developed over the past nine years through the use of exchange and import controls.[34] Such a policy would have had as its principal effect the production of governmental revenues, since the monopoly windfall now directed to the recipients of import licenses would presumably have been diverted to the government.[35]

Outside the above-mentioned recommendations with respect to fiscal and commercial policy plus minor recommendations concerning banking policy,[36] the plan did not concern itself with the implementation of private investment goals.

The foreign exchange requirements for the five-year program of public investment totaled $327 million and were allocated at the rate of $63–$69 million per year. Foreign exchange requirements of the public investment program would, in part, be provided by United States aid, which since June 1951 has averaged $22.5 million annually,

[33] Inasmuch as the plan recommends primarily changes that tend to reduce tax revenues, it is difficult to see where the large increase in total revenues and the sharp increase in the marginal rate of taxation is going to come from.

[34] "The three main regulatory purposes of the tariff as an instrument of trade policy can only be achieved if the criteria in fixing rates of duty agree closely with the commodity classification, as well as the pattern of foreign exchange allocation the Council (NEC) may adopt, and which the Central Bank will implement from time to time" (*The 1957 Plan,* p. 83).

[35] It is not unlikely that the plan fails to elaborate on the important revenue effects of its recommendations out of awareness that strong opposition to implementation of the plan can be expected from those interests presently favored by exchange and import controls. Playing down the revenue consequences of the plan would minimize such opposition. Probably the most significant fiscal development in the Philippines in recent years has been the rapid expansion in tariff revenues following the Laurel-Langley Agreement and revision of the customs code. Similarly, the exchange premium tax enacted in June 1959 will tend to produce substantial amounts of revenue.

[36] Primarily in regard to Central Bank selective credit control plus a system under which reserves of commercial banks would be increased through time deposits of the government to ensure that bank credit is extended to high priority projects.

plus $21 million annually from Japanese reparations. A projected foreign exchange budget for the plan period estimated foreign exchange available for imports of from ₱5,700 million to ₱6,400 million as compared to estimated allocations for direct imports of consumer goods of ₱1,827 million, for industrial raw materials for existing industries of ₱2,600 million, for capital goods and raw materials for new industries of ₱915 million, and for direct development requirements of the public sector of ₱634 million. To obtain the estimated foreign exchange requirements of the program a new source was proposed, i.e., the sale of Philippine bonds in United States security markets to the amount of ₱266 million.

The foreign exchange budget reflected rather pessimistic estimates of the possibilities of expansion of export earnings, and alternative estimates ranged from a continuation of the present volume and proceeds to the high estimate that export production would continue a constant ratio of total output.

The 1957 Plan, technically speaking, represented a considerable advance over previous plans because of its concern for the sources of funds both budgetary and foreign exchange. The objectives of the plan were ambitious in terms of past performance. Net investment, both public and private, was expected to total ₱5,060 million, or approximately ₱1,000 million annually, and to increase from ₱865 million in 1957 to ₱1,135 million in 1961. During the two years prior to the beginning of the plan the Philippine gross national product averaged ₱9,228 million annually, out of which consumption expenditures, both public and private, totaled ₱8,461, and estimated depreciation amounted to ₱436 million, leaving net investment of some ₱330 million annually. In terms of past levels of net investment, the levels projected in the plan represented remarkable increases. Indeed, by the last year of the plan, the rate of net investment was to rise to three and a half times the level achieved in the last year prior to the plan.[37]

[37] The authors of the plan suggest one escape from this statistical impasse when they remark that "net investment figures implicit in the available statistics on gross investment and depreciation seem to be highly improbable, if the national income and production statistics are accepted as not too inaccurate. It is, therefore, estimated that present [1956] net investment is of the order of ₱700 million, public and private" (*The 1957 Plan*, p. 70, n. 1). In other words, current social accounts with respect to capital formation are estimated to be at least 100 per cent in error. The basis for such an appraisal arises out of attachment to the incremental capital-output ratio concept. The official social accounts indicate an

In terms of the experience of countries experiencing rapid economic growth, the planned rates of Philippine savings and net investment were quite modest. Total net investment over the plan period of ₱5,060 million was expected to result in an increase in gross national product of ₱2,800 million, indicating an expected incremental capital output ratio of somewhat less than 2.0. Such a relationship would, of course, be highly favorable to Philippine economic progress, but it was quite conservative when compared with recent Philippine experience.[38]

The plan projected a radical increase in savings. If Philippine social accounts are reliable, the average rate of savings out of gross national product would increase from approximately 4.2 per cent in 1955–1956 to 8.8 per cent in 1961, a remarkable increase.[39] However, if we accept the estimate of the authors of the plan that 1956 net investment was of the order of ₱700 million, the plan would project an increase in the average rate of savings from 7.4 per cent of the gross national product in 1956 to 8.8 per cent in 1961.

Like earlier plans, the 1957 Plan had little impact on government economic activity.[40] The dominant role of Congress and of the cabinet in allocating funds for public investment was undisturbed. The 1957 Plan did not obtain congressional sanction, and implementation was fragmentary. Public investment during the three fiscal years ending June 30, 1959, amounted to ₱867 million as compared to planned public investment of ₱1,093 million.

Government investment during the remaining years of the plan

---

incremental capital-output ratio of less than unity in recent years. Such a possibility proved too great a strain for the credulity of the NEC.

[38] During 1952–1956 the Philippine national accounts, for what they are worth, indicated gross investment of ₱3,621 million, estimated depreciation of ₱1,671 million, or net investment of ₱1,950 million. During this period gross domestic product increased from ₱7,415 million to ₱9,546 million, an increase of ₱2,131 million or an incremental capital-output ratio of slightly less than 1:0. Investment in the plan is not strictly comparable to the historical national accounts as the latter include increases in stocks and estimated investment by farmers not requiring finance, whereas the plan estimates exclude such investment.

[39] Of the projected increase of ₱3,367 in gross national product over the plan period, ₱725 million would be saved. This would result in an incremental rate of saving of 20–25 per cent of national income.

[40] On Jan. 2, 1959, the NEC adopted a plan which appeared in print as *Three-Year Program of Social and Economic Development, for the Fiscal Years 1959–60 to 1961–62* (Manila: The Council, 1959). This plan was subsequently adopted by the cabinet. To the best of the author's knowledge this is the latest in the succession of "comprehensive" economic plans.

period will be dominated by the expenditure of proceeds of bond issues under Republic Act No. 1000. As of March 31, 1957, the bond issues authorized by Congress under Republic Act No. 1000 totaled ₱1,235 million, of which only ₱252 million had been issued by the Central Bank.[41] Comparison of public investment scheduled in the 1957 Plan with the allocation of economic development bond issues suggests there was little co-ordination between the Office of National Planning and the planning of expenditures under Republic Act No. 1000.[42]

The ambitious program of public investment in directly productive manufacturing and mining activities in the plan was submerged in the rapid liquidation of existing government enterprises. The plan allocated ₱433 million to this purpose, whereas only ₱70 million of Republic Act No. 1000 bond issues have been allocated to a pig-iron smelting plant and to investment in the government-owned Cebu Portland Cement Company.[43] Similarly, the 1957 Plan allocated ₱980 million to public investment in transportation and communications, whereas bond issues have provided for only ₱232 million.

On the other hand, ₱230 million of bond issues are allocated to irrigation, while public investment in irrigation in the plan amounted to only ₱5 million. Similarly, over ₱100 million of bond issues are allocated as capital contribution to the Philippine National Bank and ₱102 million to the purchase of landed estates under the land reform program, neither of which were allocated public investment in the plan.

Philippine planning policy has been confused in recent years by the appearance of successive "annual" and "five-year fiscal plans." Fiscal planning was initiated by Executive Order No. 236 of February 13, 1957, entitled, "Prescribing Procedures for the Planning of Development Finances, the Planning of Government Securities and the Disbursement of Proceeds." [44]

[41] On May 3, 1957, the NEC reported to Congress that bond issues authorized under Republic Act No. 1000 exceeded the ₱1,000 million limit established in the act by ₱235 million.

[42] For a tabulation of authorized expenditures under Republic Act No. 1000, see *A.C.C. Journal,* 33 (May 1957), 212.

[43] The emphasis in the 1957 Plan on direct public investment in manufacturing at a time when public policy was moving rapidly in the other direction causes one to wonder whether the staff of the Office of National Planning was reading the newspapers.

[44] Reprinted in Central Bank, *Ninth Annual Report, 1957,* pp. 202–212.

Executive Order No. 236 assigns to the Budget Commission responsibility for "formulating integrated plans of development finances involving the use of Republic Act 1000 and similar funds for the government sector consistent with the overall national development program and policies of the government." A Technical Committee on Developing Financing presided over by the Budget Commission shall "conduct the integrated planning of peso expenditures in relation to reparations proceeds, foreign exchange and international loans." The plans of the Technical Committee are subject to review by a Fiscal Policy Council consisting of the Secretary of Finance, governor of the Central Bank, chairman of the National Economic Council, and the Budget Commissioner.

The Budget Commission has tended to seize the initiative in the area of economic planning using both the mandate of Executive Order No. 236 and the responsibility of the commission for the preparation of current budget proposals. The "five-year fiscal plans" have tended to supersede the "five-year plans" of the National Economic Council as the blueprint for government expenditures for economic development.[45]

Since 1946 the Philippines has produced a succession of planning institutions and economic plans. There have been at least six comprehensive "five-year plans," a "three-year plan," and two "five-year fiscal plans" during this period, plus the Bell Mission report and specialized electric power and agricultural development plans. Planning priorities have been subject to rapid and radical change and have tended to reflect the pressing economic problems of the moment. Running through the successive plans has been a consistent, growing emphasis on industrial development, including social investment in power and transportation facilities.[46]

With the possible exception of the Beyster Plan, Philippine economic planning has been realistic in terms of the capabilities of the Philippine economy. Responsibilities assigned to the public sector have con-

[45] One student of Philippine public administration reports, "Beginning in fiscal years 1958 and 1959, the Budget Commission's 'Five-Year Fiscal Plans' were used as the basis for its budgetary functions and congressional appropriations. The fiscal plans were entirely independent of the plans formulated by the NEC" (Jose D. Soberano, "A Methodology for the Study of National Economic and Social Development Planning in the Philippines," *Philippine Journal of Public Administration*, 3 [July 1959], 369).

[46] The prominent exceptions to this generalization were the Cuaderno Plan of 1948 and Yulo Plan of 1950.

sistently been modest in terms of known techniques of fiscal and monetary policy. Similarly, planned rates of private saving and investment
have been modest in terms of the historical experience of countries
achieving accelerated economic growth. In recent years Philippine economic plans have incorporated advanced planning techniques, and the
criteria for investment priorities have been increasingly refined. On
the other hand, none of the economic plans have been fulfilled. Relatively modest levels of planned public investment have never been
attained. Philippine economic plans cannot be considered as more
than organized statements of minimum Philippine aspirations for accelerated economic growth and industrialization.[47]

Why has economic planning been so ineffective? First, the economic
role assigned to government in the plural Philippine society is limited.
The Philippine government, while highly centralized, is paradoxically
conservative, minimum government. Political power is vested in the
ultraconservative agricultural aristocracy, and expansion of the economic functions of the government has been slow. The implementation
of economic planning depends essentially upon two factors: (a) direct
command over resources exercised by the government, i.e., the size
of the public sector, and (b) the capacity of the government to influence private activity by incentives and coercion. The public sector
of the Philippine economy has not tended to expand as a ratio of
aggregate economic activity. Although the Philippines has displayed
considerable initiative and ingenuity in devising incentives appropriate
to private entrepreneurial activity, widespread use of incentives and

[47] Higgins appraises Philippine economic planning in the following terms: "Perhaps the most important lesson to be learned from experience with development
planning in the Philippines is that if a society is to enjoy economic growth it must
'want' it, in the sense that the leadership group, in and out of government, and
the people as a whole are prepared to take the actions necessary to bring economic
growth about. . . . Yet there is little evidence that the preparation of development plans by the government . . . has accelerated economic growth in the
country. Even if carried out to the letter, they would not have accelerated growth
very much, because they have been too modest. And they have not been carried
out. . . . The plans remain paper plans for the most part" (*op. cit.*, pp. 746–747).
In connection with an analysis of Indonesian economic planning Higgins makes
the surprising appraisal of Philippine economic planning which follows: "Indonesia
lags behind such countries as India, Brazil, the Philippines, Italy, China and
Yugoslavia, where vigorous execution of a development plan is a policy with such
strong public support that no government could afford to neglect it" (*Indonesia's
Economic Stabilization and Development* [New York: Institute of Pacific Relations, 1957], p. 125).

subsidies reflects expediency and not economic planning. With respect to coercion, the opportunities to force planned private economic behavior are limited in a nonauthoritarian environment. Philippine experience with price controls, exchange and import controls, crop distribution laws, and the like does not suggest that a high level of discipline can be achieved and maintained by coercion in the Philippine environment.

The role of planning in Philippine economic development reflects the distribution of political power in the society. In spite of administration support of economic planning as a policy, the implementation of the modest plans has been frustrated by the absence of a congressional commitment to planning. Congress has shown little inclination to expand the government's command over resources and to allocate such resources to achieve plan objectives. Congressional reluctance to support economic planning is due in part to government based on a separation of powers in which congressional responsibility to party and administration is diluted and in which Congress derives authority from its capacity to preserve its power over appropriations.

Second, economic planning was discredited by Philippine experiences with public commercial and manufacturing enterprises as well as agricultural marketing corporations with price functions. In the commercial enterprises, management left much to be desired; nepotism and overstaffing were rampant. Productivity proved to be so low that optimistic estimates of competitive costs of production were not realized. Philippine experience with agricultural marketing schemes was even more disappointing. Overstaffing, inefficiency, and even corruption in management, as well as poorly conceived and inadequate financing, quickly dissipated the resources appropriated by Congress without fulfilling the objectives of the schemes. Liquid assets initially available to such agencies were converted into high-cost inventories, and operations ceased following costly liquidation of stocks.

Traditionally, Philippine economic planning has enabled the government to procrastinate and avoid economic responsibilities. Philippine society, restless with ambitions for accelerated economic growth and hopeful that political leadership would be an effective instrument for achieving national economic ambitions, has been diverted by a succession of plans. The ineptness of the government in fulfilling its economic responsibilities precipitated the Bell Mission, which was followed by a contraction in the scope of economic planning as well as liquidation of a number of public enterprises. The shift in emphasis contracted and narrowly circumscribed the role of government. It was increasingly recognized that in planned economic growth the government should concentrate on (a) the establishment of adequate credit facilities to support private enterprises, (b) the provision of public utilities, i.e., electric power, transportation, education, and public health adequate to encourage private enterprise, and (c) participation in a limited number of industrial enterprises with prestige significance, e.g., the steel industry, shipyards, ocean-going shipping, and international air lines.

Third, the National Economic Council is politically isolated. This has resulted from a number of factors. The NEC and its predecessor planning agency, PHILCUSA, have tended to become identified with the United States economic aid mission. Since 1951 the Philippine Congress has been dominated by Nacionalista majorities. Although Philippine nationalism is a relatively mild variety, it is, as is nationalism elsewhere in Southeast Asia, skeptical of Western actions and intentions. Because the NEC is identified with the economic aid mission, the establishment of a legislative commitment to implement plans formulated by the NEC is made more difficult. Moreover, because of the close co-operation with the economic aid mission, the NEC is handicapped by the traditional United States policy of detachment with respect to comprehensive planning. Economic aid is "planned" on a project basis, and aid is appropriated on an annual basis, which precludes United States participation in longer-term planning. It is American policy to promote more private enterprise, and aid administrators are understandably reluctant to become identified with comprehensive planning.

Fourth, the public is indifferent to the fate of economic plans. The threshold of political and economic discrimination is relatively low, and this factor together with the homogeneity of political parties makes congressional frustration of economic planning relatively easy and politically costless.

Fifth, Governor Cuaderno and the Monetary Board have dominated economic policy making. Cuaderno, strongly supported by diverse economic interests, has been able to retain the confidence and support of Presidents Quirino, Magsaysay, and Garcia. So long as the Philippines remains committed to defending the official 2:1 exchange rate and so long as public and private savings remain at low levels, conflict is inevitable between the monetary authority responsible for economic stability and the developmental planning authority responsible for accelerated economic growth. Up to the present Cuaderno and the Monetary Board have been able to maintain minimum restraints on bank credit financing of economic development, and the public investment goals of the successive plans have been subordinated to the exigencies of monetary policy.

The unwillingness of the Philippine government to raise revenues by taxation and the effective restraints on bank credit expansion have severely limited the capacity of the government to participate directly in the accumulation of producible resources. Economic planning is fashionable and satisfies a widespread longing for some assurance that political leadership is providing the initiative necessary to accelerate economic growth. In view of the Philippine commitment to an entrepreneurial type of economic organization, such a role for economic planning may not be inappropriate.

· XVI ·

Price Control Policies

THE problem of accelerating economic growth is analogous in important respects to economic mobilization for war. In time of war price controls and rationing are used to divert resources to the manufacture of munitions and other high priority uses. Similarly, in accelerating economic growth, price controls and rationing can help to channel resources to capital formation.[1]

Monetary policy—deficit financing and bank credit creation—is a powerful tool for raising the level of resource accumulation. On the other hand, price inflation imposes a formidable restraint on the use of monetary policy in less-developed countries. If government and private investors do not compete with each other and with consumers for the available resources, the problem of increasing investment out of a given level of aggregate income is simplified.

Price controls can be related to the level of voluntary savings in a number of ways. Price controls implemented by rationing will tend to increase saving because of a lag in the adjustment of consumers and investors to shortages of goods. If consumers believe restraints on consumption will be temporary, they will forgo consumption in

[1] Cf. International Monetary Fund, *Economic Development with Stability* (Washington, 1953), pp. 49–57.

the short run in anticipation of a return to normal supply conditions in the future. Price control and rationing thereby can bridge the time lag necessary to the fructification of investment. It is not unlikely that price stability promotes voluntary savings by maintaining their real value during a period of economic expansion. Moreover, patriotic appeals for increased voluntary savings are more effective if price controls and rationing maintain appropriate levels of equity in consumption.

Price control in the Philippines is a horse of another color. Although the Philippines has been under consumer price control almost continuously since the establishment of the Commonwealth government, there has never been effective rationing. Postwar Philippine price controls are intelligible in terms of overvaluation of the peso, extreme disequilibrium in external payments, and the fluctuations in the stringency of exchange and import controls. Such a conclusion is readily supported by analysis of price movements in the postwar Philippines. The cost of living increased to about six times prewar (1937–1940) levels in 1945 and 1946. After 1946 the cost of living declined rapidly until in 1949 it averaged approximately 350 per cent of prewar. Since 1949 the cost of living, with the single exception of the year 1951, has remained remarkably stable, fluctuating narrowly within 4 per cent of the 1949 level.

The cost of living index is a composite index of prices of domestically produced goods and imports. Comparison of these components of the cost of living index shows extreme divergence in price movements. For example, following 1949 wholesale prices of domestically produced, home-consumed goods declined steadily, reaching a low point of 86 (1949 = 100) in 1955. In the succeeding years prices of domestic goods have risen, but they are still well below 1949 levels.[2] On the other hand, wholesale prices of imported goods have risen markedly since the imposition of effective exchange and import controls and have fluctuated within wide limits. In the two years following 1949 the index of wholesale prices of imported goods rose to 153 (1949 = 100). In the ensuing four years the index declined steadily to 118 for 1955. Since 1955 intensification of import controls together with collection of tariff duties on imports from the United

[2] Wholesale prices of export commodities have, except in 1950 and 1951, been equally stable, and movements have been closely synchronized with those of wholesale prices of domestically produced, home-consumed goods.

States has produced a steady increase in the wholesale prices of imported goods. By 1958 the index of such prices had risen to 142.[3]

Moreover, extreme movements in prices of import categories are hidden in the available indexes, which aggregate all import prices into a unit value index. The peso prices of "less essential" commodities receiving minimum amounts of foreign exchange increased relative to those of commodities for which foreign exchange allocations were relatively liberal.[4] For example, following the imposition of effective import controls at the end of 1949, the wholesale price index of imports of beverages and tobacco rose to a peak of 224 (1949 = 100) in June 1951, whereas the index for imports of "manufactured goods" rose to 196 in May. On the other hand, the index for imports of "food" rose slowly to a peak of 131 in September 1952, "mineral fuels" reached 124 in April 1952, and "machinery and transport equipment" reached 173 in April 1952.[5]

Price control was initiated in the Philippines by Commonwealth Act No. 498 of September 30, 1939. The act declared it to be "national policy to prevent scarcity, monopolization, hoarding, injurious speculation, manipulation, private control, and profiteering affecting the supply, distribution, and movement of foods, clothing, fuel, fertilizers, chemicals, building materials, machinery, etc." [6] To implement this national policy, the President was authorized to (a) purchase and distribute commodities subject to "scarcity, monopolization, etc." and (b) to fix and enforce "maximum selling prices." [7]

---

[3] Perhaps the most convincing demonstration of the relationship of exchange and import controls to peso prices of imports occurred in 1951. The special tax on sales of foreign exchange was imposed in April 1951 when the index of wholesale (peso) prices of imports stood at 163 (1949 = 100). Following imposition of the tax, which had the effect of increasing peso costs of imports by approximately 17 per cent, the index of wholesale prices of imports declined steadily and fourteen months later stood at 131. The decline took place over a period in which the unit value index for imports was stable. See Central Bank, *Fifth Annual Report, 1953*, pp. 226, 263.

[4] In extreme cases where imported commodities disappeared from the Philippine market, such commodities would no longer be reflected in the index of wholesale prices of imported commodities. Conceptually, the increase in the prices of such commodities would be maximized.

[5] Central Bank, *Fifth Annual Report, 1953*, p. 226.

[6] This statement of national policy has been retained virtually unchanged in the succession of price control acts, executive orders, and the like.

[7] Under the authority of Commonwealth Act No. 498, President Quezon issued Administrative Order No. 107 of Oct. 2, 1939, creating the Emergency Control Board. Executive Order No. 233 of Nov. 8, 1939, fixed the maximum selling prices

On August 19, 1940, Commonwealth Act No. 600, the Emergency Powers Act, was approved declaring a state of national emergency and investing the President with extraordinary powers "to safeguard the integrity of the Philippines and to insure the tranquility of its inhabitants by suppressing espionage and other subversive activities, by preventing and relieving unemployment, and by insuring to the people adequate shelter and clothing and sufficient food supply." [8] Price control in the early postwar years resulted from executive initiative under the Emergency Powers Act.

The first postliberation price control order, Executive Order No. 24 of November 6, 1944, was issued by President Osmeña when the government was located at Tacloban, Leyte. This order amended the final prewar price control order (Executive Order No. 371 of October 2, 1941) by fixing new maximum ceiling prices for an extended list of commodities and services. There followed in quick succession Executive Orders Nos. 26, 28, 29, 35, 39, 62, 74, and 91 issued by President Osmeña in the confusion attending the liberation and the transfer to civil government. One observer comments: "The Osmeña [price control] orders had little or no effect and he had continually to raise the official price-ceilings to bring them closer to the actual prices paid during a period of continued scarcity of supplies, local and imported. The situation was not relieved until August 1945 when the first ships with commercial cargoes began to arrive." [9]

Rapid recovery of production as well as unprecedented levels of imports following 1945 produced sharp declines in prices. The price control orders, though still in effect, were a dead letter till the end of 1949.

Renewal of agitation for price control awaited the reappearance of conditions comparable to those which characterized 1940–1941 and 1945–1946, i.e., shortages of imported commodities. Such conditions

of a substantial list of commodities. Executive Order No. 249 of Jan. 4, 1940, created the National Trading Corporation, capitalized at ₱5 million. The NTC was authorized to purchase and distribute commodities subject to "scarcity, monopolization, etc."

[8] Commonwealth Act No. 620, approved June 6, 1941, extended the effectivity of the Emergency Powers Act. Commonwealth Act No. 671 of Dec. 16, 1941, declared a state of total emergency and authorized the President to issue rules and regulations to meet it. The amended law, the Emergency Powers Act of 1941, remained in force until terminated by decision of the Supreme Court (*Rodriguez and Tañada* v. *Gella*, Feb. 2, 1953).

[9] Hartendorp, *History*, p. 636.

returned in 1950 with the implementation of effective exchange and import controls. There followed rapid increases in peso prices of imported commodities, with price increases for particular commodities primarily dependent upon the stringency of controls.

A Price Control Act, Republic Act No. 509, was approved on June 13, 1950. The act authorized the President to fix commodity price ceilings until April 30, 1951, and provided for a Price Administration Board (PAB) to recommend maximum prices.[10] The PAB was given extensive powers to examine the records of businesses, and harsh penalties were provided for violations of the act, which were punishable by a fine of not less than ₱2,000 or more than ₱10,000, imprisonment of from two months to twelve years, and deportation in the case of an alien. Any person found guilty of any violation of the act was to be barred from wholesale or retail business for a period of five years for the first offense and permanently for a second or succeeding offense.

The initial price order under the Price Control Act was Executive Order No. 331 of July 7, 1950, which fixed maximum importers' or producers', wholesalers', and retailers' prices for a large number of local and imported commodities. The order ran to nine closely printed pages. Executive Order No. 331 was followed by a dreary succession of price control orders, invariably in an upward direction. Twenty-one price control orders were issued during the remainder of 1950, with an additional twenty orders during the four months of 1951 when the law was still in effect.[11]

Price control was extended by Republic Act No. 608 of April 30, 1951, under which seventeen more price control orders were issued. Republic Act No. 729 of June 18, 1952, extended price control through 1953. This law provided that a large number of government officials down to and including local police and local price administration committees should have the power to examine business records and obtain warrants to search premises. Twenty price control orders were issued under this act in the remaining eighteen months of the Quirino administration.

[10] "Sec. 3. In the determination of such maximum prices, the President and the Price Administration Board shall take into account relevant factors such as speculative fluctuations, general increases or decreases in cost of production, distribution, transportation, storage, and other relevant factors affecting prices."

[11] The relationship of price control to exchange and import controls is evident in the preponderance of import commodities in the successive orders.

Price control was allowed to lapse at the end of 1953 and during the first half-year of the Magsaysay administration there was none. A new price control law, Republic Act No. 1168 of June 18, 1954, incorporated most of the provisions of the earlier laws. Republic Act No. 1168 expired on February 15, 1955, and was not renewed during the remainder of the Magsaysay administration.[12]

At the end of 1955 a radical change occurred in Philippine commercial policy, including a sharp increase in tariff rates provided by Executive Order No. 150 of December 31, 1955, and the collection of tariffs on imports from the United States under the Revised Philippine–United States Trade Agreement. During January importers and retailers generally attempted to raise the peso prices of imported commodities, and the administration threatened to reimpose price control.[13] Continued liberal allocations of foreign exchange tended to limit price increases, and no action was taken.

The next stage in the evolution of Philippine price control policy occurred following the presidential election of 1957. The balance of payments situation deteriorated rapidly during 1957. To bring external payments under control the administration under Central Bank leadership inaugurated a far-reaching "austerity program" in which foreign exchange allocations were drastically reduced and substantial penalty deposits on letters of credit were established.

The "austerity program" produced increases in the peso prices of imported commodities, and considerable pressure developed to re-enact price control legislation.[14] Although the strictness of the

[12] Foreign exchange allocations during the last two years of the Magsaysay administration were relatively liberal, and imports in 1957 reached a postwar peak in volume. Expanded imports were made possible by increased foreign exchange earnings and by drawing down the international reserve. The high levels of imports tended to reduce the pressure for price controls.

[13] On Jan. 17 Magsaysay reported that "spiralling prices" made necessary the enactment of new price control legislation (*Manila Times,* Jan. 18, 1956). Magsaysay voiced similar threats in a conference with a federation of Chinese Chambers of Commerce on Jan. 24. He said, "I want to make it clear that if prices do not stop going up I will not hesitate to take drastic measures. I will do everything necessary to protect the people" (*A.C.C. Journal,* 32 [Feb. 1956], 69).

[14] The *Official Gazette* reported on Jan. 20, 1958, that President Garcia, having received reports that prices of essential commodities "have continued to soar" without any justifiable reason "threatens to ask Congress to enact a price control law." In a speech outlining his "austerity program" made in Manila, Jan. 18, 1958, President Garcia said his administration would take "necessary measures,

austerity measures was rapidly relaxed, Congress proceeded to consider a price control law. By the end of March at least nine such laws had been introduced, seven in the House of Representatives, including an administration bill (H.B. 190), and two in the Senate.[15] In spite of strong administration efforts to obtain a price control law, Congress refused to enact such a measure in either the regular or the special session of 1958.

Intensive efforts to obtain price control legislation were renewed by the administration in 1959. In the political jockeying over exchange premium and export incentive legislation at the close of the congressional session in June, Congress enacted a new price control law to remain in effect until December 31, 1960 (Republic Act No. 2610 of July 16, 1959). As in the past, price control legislation was enacted as a sop to consumer sentiment at a time when the prices of imported consumer goods were under upward pressure. Price increases could be anticipated from the exchange premium tax enacted in 1959, from the doubling of the rate at which Philippine tariffs are collected on imports from the United States, and from continued lag in foreign exchange earnings.

As in past legislation, the current price control law declares that it is national policy

during periods of short supply or of unreasonable price levels to protect the interest of the consumer by preventing, locally or generally, the scarcity, monopolization, hoarding, injurious speculation, manipulation, and profiteering, affecting the supply, distribution and movement of—commodities, control of the prices of which is deemed essential to the public interest [Section 1].

Section 2 authorizes the President "to establish, by executive order, such maximum prices at which commodities may be sold at retail or wholesale, as shall be generally fair, reasonable and equitable" and "to direct the NARIC, with respect to rice and corn, and the NAMARCO, with respect to other commodities, to import the com-

---

drastic if need be, to protect our people from the concupiscence and greed of the heartless." See *Manila Times,* Jan. 19, 1958.

[15] One of the bills, Senate Bill No. 41, "An Act fixing the maximum net profits allowed to wholesalers and retailers in the sale of commodities, creating the Net Profit Control Board, and for other purposes." The explanatory note accompanying this legislative proposal stated: "Whereas it is not possible to fix and control prices . . . the percentage of profits which may reasonably be allowed can certainly be controlled." See *A.C.C. Journal,* 34 (Feb. 1958), 96.

modity in short supply for distribution in the local market." As in the past, the current price control law does not provide for rationing.

Although the Philippines has been under consumer price control during much of the period since 1939, it is safe to say there has been no control of prices. Philippine price control policy is intelligible, not in terms of a determination to control prices, but in terms of the contribution of "price control" to the achievement of other goals. Price control has made exchange and import controls more palatable to Philippine society. Successive stages in the intensification of import restriction have been accompanied by renewed price control activity or the threat of such activity.[16] There have been no price increases and no need for price control for other than imported commodities and domestically produced manufactures using imports of "essential industrial raw materials." Price control policy is also intelligible in terms of economic nationalism and the efforts of a succession of government corporations with price control functions to divert to Filipino retailers a portion of the windfall arising out of import restriction.

Following the establishment of effective import control, President Quirino issued Executive Order No. 350 of October 3, 1950, creating the Price Stabilization Corporation (PRISCO). PRISCO was given the following price control functions:

(a) To undertake the prevention, locally or generally, of scarcity, monopolization, hoarding, injurious speculation, manipulation, private control, and profiteering, affecting the supply, distribution, and movement of all articles, goods, or commodities of prime necessity. . . .

(b) To aid in the promotion of the rice and corn industry of the Philippines through the maintenance of stable prices for said commodities. . . .

(c) . . . and to assist Filipino retailers and businessmen, such as supplying them with merchantable goods at prices that will enable them to compete successfully in the open market.

The price control functions of PRISCO were largely neglected, and the agency used its import control functions to promote Filipinization of import trade. While PRISCO imported some commodities

[16] The economic sophistication of the Philippine electorate is such that price control alleviates the unrest over the increases in import prices and the corruption, anomalies, and discrimination in import and exchange control administration. It is undoubtedly an aspect of "face" which permits the statesmen-politicians to enact price control legislation, to appropriate funds, and to hire staff to enforce legislation which has repeatedly proved to be unenforceable.

for allocation to retailers, the limited funds available to it restricted such activities.

The essential limitation to the activities of PRISCO, lack of capitalization, was remedied when its successor—National Marketing Corporation (NAMARCO)—was established. Republic Act No. 1345 of June 17, 1955, provided that NAMARCO should be capitalized for ₱30 million, to be paid in three equal annual installments. Among the price control functions assigned to NAMARCO were the following:

(a) To procure and buy commodities for distribution at reasonable prices to Filipino retailers and businessmen in order to promote their greater participation in the distribution system of the national economy;

(b) To stabilize the prices of commodities in short supply by supplying commodities to the general public through Filipino businessmen.

In addition to the substantial government capitalization of NAMARCO, the act provided: "The NAMARCO shall be exempt from all taxes incidental to its operation" (Section 16). Substantial capitalization, tax concessions, and the windfall inherent in importing under conditions of stringent exchange controls and currency overvaluation have made NAMARCO a powerful instrument for nationalization of the import and retail trade. With respect to price control functions, NAMARCO is inherently ineffective inasmuch as the objectives of Filipinization of trade and consumer price control are in direct conflict. Filipino merchants charge what the market will bear, and prices tend to reflect the tightness of controls.[17]

In addition to consumer "price controls," the Philippines has acquired experience with a wide range of institutions and policies designed to influence prices of primary commodities produced both for domestic consumption and for export.

In the case of rice, the National Rice and Corn Corporation (NARIC) was first established as a subsidiary of the National Development Company in 1936, was reactivated after the war in 1945, became an independent government corporation in 1947, merged with PRISCO in 1950, and was reactivated as an independent corporation by Republic Act No. 663 of June 16, 1951. NARIC in its various forms

[17] NAMARCO has probably limited increases in the prices of consumer goods by establishing a strong vested interest—Filipino importers and retail merchants —with both a stake in liberal exchange allocations for consumer goods and a political voice to support this interest. With the tendency for exchange allocations to go to "new and necessary industries," the Filipinization of import and retail trade has probably limited the attrition in exchange allocations in these categories.

had two principal objectives: (a) to develop the rice industry and
(b) to stabilize the prices of rice and corn. Current legislation
(Republic Act No. 663, Section 2) entrusts to NARIC

(1) The maintenance of a stable price consistent with the average cost
of production, with the purchasing power of the people, and with the national economic policy of the government;

(2) The prevention of speculation in trading and of the exploitation of
the consumers;

(3) The study, promotion, and execution of such measures as will solve
the problems that may arise from over-production of rice and corn.

NARIC has traditionally been consumer oriented, and one of its
principal functions has been to maintain inventories of rice and corn
in urban centers, primarily in Manila. Moreover, NARIC has been
assigned the important import monopoly of rice.[18] Although the
Philippines in recent years has been practically self-sufficient in both
rice and corn, rice imports have served as a safety valve to maintain
price stability.[19] Naric suffered large capital losses in the early postwar period, but in recent years the corporation has operated with
considerable success in minimizing both price fluctuations and imports.
In accomplishing these goals, NARIC has been enormously assisted
by the well-capitalized Agricultural Credit and Co-operative Marketing Administration (ACCFA), which has contributed to the stability
of rice and corn prices by providing crop loans and adequate storage
facilities. Probably the best testimony to the success of NARIC is
the growing opposition of the politically powerful National Federation
of Rice and Corn Planters.[20]

Still another agricultural commodity which is subject to government price policy is sugar. Government policy is to maintain the price

[18] For an analysis of Philippine price policies with respect to rice, maize, and
tobacco, see UN, ECAFE, *Food and Agricultural Price Policies*, pp. 95–100. The
study concludes: "NARIC's price policy seems to have been geared more to the protection of consumers than to support of farmers' incomes."

[19] *Ibid.* During 1953–1955 imports of rice averaged only 1.4 per cent of domestic
production.

[20] In the 1957 session of Congress the federation was able to push through
Congress Republic Act No. 2017 of June 22, 1957, which subjects NARIC imports
of rice and corn to full import duties. Philippine tariff rates on rice and corn,
which are prohibitively high, facilitate government monopolization of these commodities and contribute to the maintenance of Philippine prices above world
prices. The government was able to circumvent Republic Act No. 2017 by importing small marginal rice and corn requirements through NAMARCO, which
is specifically exempted from payment of import duties.

of domestic sugar at levels approximating those received for Philippine sugar exports to the sheltered United States market. To implement sugar price policy, marketing quotas are established for four categories of sugar, i.e., exports to the United States, sugar for the domestic Philippine market, exports under the Philippine quota under the International Sugar Agreement, and sugar in the residual free international market. In recent years the domestic price has been substantially above world market prices of sugar, often approximately double the world market price. Such a policy is enforced by a prohibitive duty on sugar imports.[21]

Still another commodity which has been subject to price policy has been Virginia-type leaf tobacco. The government has been quite successful in reserving the domestic market for this tobacco, which is used in cigarettes, by restricting imports. At the same time favorable prices for domestic producers are maintained by ACCFA, which purchases domestic production.

Republic Act No. 1194 of August 25, 1954, provided that all locally grown and produced Virginia-type tobacco was to be purchased by the government through ACCFA.[22] The act set prices for flue-cured Virginia-type tobacco at from ₱1.50 to ₱3.60 per kilo and for sundried at from ₱.80 to ₱1.50. These prices were quite favorable to tobacco producers, and production has expanded rapidly since 1954. ACCFA stocks of tobacco, particularly of the lower grades, have tended to accumulate, and ACCFA is confronted by large inventory losses.

Tobacco price policy has favored producers and has strongly stimulated production. It is, however, becoming increasingly evident that the prices supported are too high to clear the market in the absence of effective production controls. It would be deplorable if ACCFA after such a promising start should be assigned price support functions that compromise its integrity and dissipate its capital.[23]

[21] Comparable levels of protection are maintained on imports of coconut products, including soap and edible oil. Domestic marketings are not, however, limited by marketing quotas. Relative ease of entry and the fact that these commodities are exports have tended to result in domestic prices approximating world prices.

[22] Monopolization of tobacco procurement by the government also assists in enforcing the very high rates of taxation of cigarettes and other tobacco products by reducing the possibilities of evasion by bootlegging.

[23] A further step in this direction occurred with Executive Order No. 129 of Sept. 23, 1955, under which ACCFA was instructed to purchase domestic production of ramie. During the fiscal year ending June 30, 1957, ₱7.0 million was expended to acquire and export ramie fiber and to import finished ramie textiles.

Finally, gold price policy should be mentioned. During the early postwar period, recovery of gold production was encouraged by permitting gold producers to market their output in the premium markets that prevailed during that period. As more normal conditions returned and premium prices in "free gold markets" declined, Philippine gold producers turned to political action to obtain special treatment, including tax remission. This political activity culminated in Republic Act No. 1164 of June 18, 1954, which provided a direct subsidy to gold producers designed to bring total proceeds from the sale of gold to from ₱105 to ₱112 per ounce, depending on the qualification of the producer for subsidy.

Following mid-1956, the free market price of gold tended to rise above ₱120 per ounce. Producers then arranged to resume marketing their output outside the system of exchange controls at the relatively high premium price. Congress adjourned in 1957 without renewing the gold subsidy law.[24]

The Philippines, like other countries, implements a wide variety of price policies. For purposes of analysis, it is convenient to think of such policies in terms of two broad categories: first are those designed to maintain stability (i.e., limit increases) in the cost of living; second are those designed to maintain minimum prices for producers. Such policies are essentially in conflict since one type of policy is designed to establish a ceiling and the other a floor under prices. In the Philippines the area of conflict is limited because of the division of production into exports and domestic goods.

Through much of the postwar period the Philippine economy has been subject to what was purportedly consumer price control. Price controls have never been combined with rationing or physical resource planning and therefore have been unrelated to the developmental functions usually assigned to such a policy. Such controls are intelligible in terms of three considerations.

First, they were resorted to in response to a situation of short supplies of imports such as occurred in 1940 and 1941, during 1946–1949, and in 1950 and thereafter when the Philippines faced up to the necessity of bringing the balance of payments under a tolerable

---

[24] In the first half of 1958, when prices of metals tended to decline in world markets, Senator Gil Puyat introduced a bill entitled "The Base Metals Incentive Act of the Philippines." It provided for price supports for copper and iron ore as well as inventory loans for producers of other base metals. Congress adjourned without passing the bill.

equilibrium. Price control initiated in 1950 was designed to make the stringent import controls more palatable. It correctly recognized that rapid increases in the peso prices of imported goods following curtailment of imports of such goods were not warranted by increases in foreign prices of such goods and that increases in peso prices represented a windfall profit. The situation was correctly diagnosed, but the remedy was virtually worthless. The capacity of legislatures to frustrate the profit motive by fiat is limited.

Second, Philippine consumer price controls are closely related to the pursuit of goals of economic nationalism. The succession of agencies—NTC, PRATRA, PRISCO, NAMARCO—ostensibly created to channel the flow of consumer goods and to maintain stocks conducive to a desirable price stability have increasingly been utilized to divert to Filipino retailers the windfall inherent in import restriction. The prices of imported commodities essentially reflect their scarcity, which is a function of the availability of foreign exchange. Diverting such imports to Filipino retailers will not contribute to consumer price control; the Filipino retailer can be depended upon to charge what the market will bear.

Third, the only Philippine consumer price control worthy of mention has resulted from policies implemented with respect to rice and corn. Heavy social investment in storage and marketing facilities, as well as readiness to resort to imports to provide marginal supplies of rice, has tended to promote a desirable price stability. At the same time it should be remarked that government monopolization of imports of rice enables the Philippines to implement a policy which results in Philippine rice prices substantially above international prices. In the case of sugar, the government by regulating marketings in the domestic market keeps sugar prices approximately equal to the price received for Philippine exports of sugar to the United States. This price is substantially above world market prices of sugar.

With respect to price floors for producers, public policy has been more aggressive. Where such policies have been applicable, steps have been taken to reserve the domestic market to domestic producers. A wide range of protective measures ranging from embargoes to prohibitive import duties have tended to provide strong producer incentives. Moreover, producers of a wide range of commodities— from gold to leaf tobacco—have benefited from various subsidies, both direct and indirect.

· XVII ·

The Welfare State

ALTHOUGH Philippine economic development is highly dependent upon individual initiative and private enterprise, the government has displayed relative willingness to enact legislation ostensibly designed to redress inequalities in the distribution of economic power and to establish legal safeguards for the economically weak. Extremes of inequality in the distribution of wealth and income suggest that the Philippines is not a welfare state; yet, paradoxically, the Philippines has an extensive structure of welfare legislation and institutions.

Current legislation governing the employment of women and children prohibits the employment of children under fourteen years except in light employment which is not harmful to their health and does not interfere with school attendance.[1] Rules are prescribed for the employment of children under sixteen and under eighteen and for maternity leaves with pay.[2] Moreover, Republic Act No. 1131 provides (Section 7): "The employer shall not discriminate against

---

[1] Republic Act No. 679 of April 15, 1952, as amended by Republic Act No. 1131 of June 16, 1954. Previous legislation governing the labor of women and children includes Act No. 3071 of March 16, 1923, Commonwealth Act No. 647 of June 14, 1941, and Republic Acts Nos. 239 of June 10, 1948, and 270 of June 15, 1948.

[2] Women employees nursing children are given time off at least half an hour twice a day, and establishments where 15 or more married women are employed are required to establish an adequate nursery.

any woman in respect to terms or conditions of employment on account of her sex and shall pay equal remuneration for work of equal value for both men and women employees."

Legislation providing for employer's liability and workmen's compensation for industrial accidents was originally enacted in 1908 and has been continually strengthened since that time.[3] Existing laws, Republic Act No. 772 of June 20, 1952, and Republic Act No. 889 of June 19, 1953, provide adequate financial support for the Office of Workmen's Compensation in the Department of Labor and a schedule of compensation for industrial injuries. Employers are required to pay accident and death compensation benefits over a period up to four years and in amounts up to ₱4,000. Additional liability equal to 50 per cent of the compensation fixed in the laws is established when an employer has failed "to install and maintain safety appliances" or "to take other precautions for the prevention of accidents or occupational disease."

The Philippines has a long history of legislation requiring employers to provide free medical and dental treatment for employees.[4] Current legislation, Republic Act No. 1054 of June 12, 1954, provides that establishments with more than 300 laborers must hire the full services of a physician and a dentist and must maintain a dental clinic and an infirmary or emergency hospital. If employees number between 200 and 300, the establishment must keep a stock of emergency medicines and must retain the services of a physician and dentist. If employees number between 30 and 200, a stock of emergency medicines in the charge of a nurse must be maintained.

In addition, the Philippines has enlightened legislation providing for (a) the priority of wage claims in cases of insolvency and other wage-claim measures, (b) limitation of the hours of work, (c) employees' safety, (d) adequate notice in case of termination of employment, and (e) vacation and sick leave for government employees.[5]

[3] See Acts Nos. 1874 of June 19, 1908, 2473 of Feb. 5, 1915, 2711 of March 10, 1917, and 3428 of Dec. 10, 1927, which provided for employer's liability, and also Act No. 3812 of Dec. 8, 1930, and Commonwealth Acts Nos. 84 of Oct. 26, 1936, and 210 of Nov. 20, 1936, which provide for workmen's compensation.

[4] See Act No. 3961 of Dec. 2, 1932, Commonwealth Acts Nos. 324 of June 18, 1938, and 445 of June 3, 1939, and Republic Acts Nos. 46 of Oct. 3, 1946, and 239 of June 10, 1948.

[5] For an excellent brief survey of protective labor legislation see Abelardo G. Samonte and Tomas C. Alhambra, "Labor Services," in H. B. Jacobini and associates, *Governmental Services in the Philippines* (Studies in Public Administration,

Republic Act No. 761 of June 20, 1952, provided for a National Employment Service, and Republic Act No. 865 of June 16, 1953, protects labor from contract abuses.

In addition to welfare measures which provide minimum safeguards to labor, the Philippine government has often intervened to regulate employer-employee relations in both industrial and agricultural tenancy disputes. During the 1920's and 1930's Philippine labor met increasing employer resistance as it acquired cohesiveness and strength. Stimulated by external developments including the militancy of the CIO movement in the United States, Philippine labor leadership became increasingly radical. Industrial relations deteriorated until in 1934 idleness from strikes and lockouts reached a peak of 662,399 man-days.[6] Under the leadership of President Quezon legislation was enacted providing for compulsory arbitration of labor disputes.[7] This legislation created the Court of Industrial Relations (CIR), which was given jurisdiction over all labor disputes causing, or likely to cause, a strike or lockout involving more than 30 workers. Controversies could be submitted to the CIR by the Secretary of Labor or by either party to the dispute, and pending consideration by the CIR all strikes and lockouts were enjoined. The powers of the CIR extended to tenancy controversies as well as to industrial labor disputes and included power to fix minimum wages and rentals or crop shares, subject to approval of the President and the Supreme Court on appeal.[8]

A second major piece of labor legislation, Commonwealth Act No. 213 of November 21, 1936, limited access to compulsory arbitration to "legitimate" labor organizations "duly registered and permitted to operate by the Department of Labor." The law provided that

---

No. 3; Manila: University of the Philippines, Institute of Public Administration, 1956), pp. 373–425.

[6] R.P., Bureau of Census and Statistics, *Statistical Handbook of the Philippines, 1903–1953* (Manila: Bureau of Printing, 1954), p. 31.

[7] Commonwealth Act No. 103 of Oct. 29, 1936. Article XIII, Sec. 6, of the Constitution provides: "The State shall afford protection to labor, especially to working women and minors, and shall regulate the relations between landowner and tenant, and between labor and capital in industry and agriculture. The State may provide for compulsory arbitration."

[8] Commonwealth Act No. 254 of March 4, 1938, enlarged the court to three judges. Commonwealth Act No. 559 of June 7, 1940, again enlarged the court to five judges and strengthened the powers of the court with respect to strikes and lockouts.

registered labor organizations "shall have the right to collective bargaining with employers for the purpose of seeking better working and living conditions, fair wages, shorter hours and, in general, to promote the material, social and moral well being of their members."

While collective bargaining was permitted, excessive reliance on compulsory arbitration tended to develop as the CIR was aggressive in asserting its jurisdiction. In the first year after the establishment of the CIR idleness from strikes and lockouts dropped to 18,097 man-days. Organized labor was restless under the delays in the compulsory arbitration process, but this system of industrial regulation was in the tradition of autocratic, centralized authority. More important, CIR decisions tended to include wage awards that were probably not attainable by the economically weak labor unions.

The Bell Mission report was critical of labor conditions and the weakness of and abuses within the labor movement; it recommended "that the rights of workers to organize free trade unions to protect their economic interests be established through appropriate legislation."[9] In the meantime the policy of compulsory arbitration and regulation of the labor movement by the Department of Labor was discredited by the arbitrary and politically inspired activities of the Secretary of Labor, Jose Figueras. Figueras, who took office in September 1950, used the hysteria aroused by the Huk movement and his power to withhold registration to promote the National Confederation of Trade Unions to serve his political ambitions. In fiscal year 1952 a total of 391 union registrations were dropped, revoked, or suspended, or more than twice the number of such actions in the previous five years.[10] In mid-1953 Figueras resigned to run for the Senate on the Liberal ticket. He suffered the fate of the other Liberal party candidates in the Magsaysay landslide.

In 1953 Congress enacted an Industrial Peace Act, Republic Act No. 875 of June 17. This act, subsequently called the "Magna Carta of Labor," was formulated by Congress with the advice of the Department of Labor, representatives from labor organizations, and tech-

[9] *Bell Mission Report*, pp. 91–96. The report concluded: "There is entirely too much dependence on the Court of Industrial Relations as a substitute for legitimate collective bargaining. The wide discretionary powers of the Court must be curtailed in order to promote industrial harmony."

[10] R.P., Dept. of Labor, *Labor Golden Book, 1953* (Manila, 1953), p. 10.

nical advisers of the United States aid mission. Drafted in the general spirit of the Taft-Hartley Act, the legislation replaces the system of compulsory arbitration with collective bargaining.

National labor policy is declared to be (Section 1)

to eliminate the cause of industrial unrest by encouraging and protecting the exercise by employees of their right to self-organization for the purpose of collective bargaining; . . . to promote sound stable industrial peace and the advancement of the general welfare . . . through the process of collective bargaining; to advance the settlement of issues between employers and employees through collective bargaining by making available full and adequate government facilities for conciliation and mediation; . . . to avoid or minimize differences which arise between the parties to collective bargaining by prescribing certain rules to be followed in the negotiation and administration of collective bargaining agreements.

Labor unions must still be registered in order to receive rights and protections outlined by the law, but they are adequately protected from arbitrary action by the Secretary of Labor. The CIR has been converted from a judicial body into a quasi-judicial body. It may no longer issue injunctions against strikes. Compulsory arbitration is outlawed except when, in the opinion of the President of the Philippines and as certified by him to the CIR, a labor dispute adversely affects the national interest. The law provides for expansion of the Labor Department's Conciliation Service. Strikes are permitted if a dispute cannot be settled either by direct negotiation or through the efforts of the Conciliation Service, after a 30-day cooling-off period.

This "Magna Carta" has gone far toward establishing a legal environment in which democratic labor unions can flourish. Full understanding of national policy on the part of government, labor, and management will require time. Acceptance of trade unionism is growing, union leaders are developing, and a number of successful collective bargaining relationships have been established. But while the formal legal aspects of Philippine industrial relations have been changed, the substantive aspects have resisted change. In particular, the CIR, supported by a number of significant higher court decisions, has continued to exercise a considerable part of its compulsory arbitration powers. One observer concluded: "The inertia of bureaucratic habits, the Filipino tradition of looking to government first for the solution of private problems and the continued important role of lawyers in union leadership, all conspire to preserve some of the old patterns, despite a new law." [11]

A second major aspect of labor policy is minimum wage policy. Government intervention to establish floors under wages first occurred with Commonwealth Act No. 374 of October 7, 1936, which fixed a minimum wage rate for national government employees. A month and a half later, on November 21, 1936, Commonwealth Act No. 211 was approved which provided that "all laborers employed by corporations, person, or persons in any public work shall receive a minimum daily wage of one peso. In the case of provincial and municipal public works, the province or municipality may pay lower wage if financial conditions of the province or municipality so demand." [12] During the period of postwar rehabilitation minimum wage policy was dormant as the rise in the structure of Philippine costs and prices made the prewar minimums meaningless. Moreover, the rapid recovery of Philippine production was accompanied by steadily declining prices and a given level of money wages resulted in a rewarding increase in real wages.

The Bell Mission report was very critical of the gross economic inequalities in Philippine society and recommended "that a minimum wage for agricultural and other workers be established to provide subsistence standards of living." [13] In the subsequent Quirino-Foster Agreement the Philippine government agreed to give selected recommendations of the Bell report—specifically, tax and minimum wage laws—serious and immediate legislative consideration.

Minimum wage legislation met formidable resistance in Congress, and it was largely due to United States insistence upon such legislation that Republic Act No. 602 of April 6, 1951, was enacted. The Minimum Wage Law provided for a minimum wage of ₱4 a day, to take effect in Manila in August 1951 and elsewhere one year later, during which time the legal daily minimum was ₱3. For agricultural wage labor (in farm enterprises comprising more than 12 hectares)

[11] David O. Wurfel, "Trade Union Development and Labor Relations Policy in the Philippines," *Industrial and Labor Relations Review*, 12 (July 1959), 604.

[12] Commonwealth Act No. 317 of June 9, 1938, amended Commonwealth Act No. 211 of Nov. 21, 1936, to provide that in the City of Manila the minimum daily wage of such workers should be ₱1.25.

[13] *Bell Mission Report*, p. 4.

the minimum wage was fixed initially at ₱1.75 a day, to be increased to ₱2.50 after two years. The legal minimum wage would apply (beginning July 1, 1952) to all government employees, including members of the armed services.

The act provided for special categories of "learners and apprentices" and for the employment of the physically and mentally handicapped at wages below the legal minimum. Enforcement of the Minimum Wage Law is the direct responsibility of the Wage Administration Service of the Department of Labor, and under the act any court of first instance has jurisdiction to restrain violations. The act includes extensive protection for employees from wage deductions and the abuses of the "company store." It provides that neither workers nor labor organizations can waive rights established by the Act.

The actual wages paid in Manila were generally above the minimum wages established by the law, but the minimum wages were well above current wage rates outside Manila. As a result, opposition to the law has been strong and persistent, and subsequent amendments have resulted in significant breaches in the policy. In the congressional session of 1952, the first session after the Minimum Wage Law had become fully effective, two bills (S.B. Nos. 420 and 516) were introduced into the Senate and seven (H.B. Nos. 2215, 2336, 2649, 2658, 2882, 2921, and 3085) into the House of Representatives which would have weakened, in whole or in part, the Minimum Wage Law. One of the bills (H.B. 3085), which became Republic Act No. 812 of April 6, 1952, amended the Minimum Wage Law to provide: "(d) This Act shall not apply to homeworkers engaged in needle work by hand, farm tenancy, or to domestic servants."

After 1952 the Minimum Wage Law came under increasing attack on the grounds that it was contributing to unemployment.[14] The assault was led by the gold-mining industry, which used the policy as leverage to obtain special concessions and subsidies, and by the

[14] A considerable part of Philippine economic debate since 1950 has been joined over the issue of employment. Unemployment is a major economic problem and industrialization has not been sufficiently rapid to absorb the annual increment to the labor force or even the annual migration to the urban centers. An important political advantage has been derived from conducting economic controversy in terms of unemployment. Inasmuch as there have been no reliable statistics on unemployment until recently, participants in economic disputes could fabricate statistics to suit the argument of the moment.

sugar industry, which was restless in the face of reduced political influence and the overvalued exchange parity.[15] Three bills which would have weakened the Minimum Wage Law were introduced into Congress in 1954, and in the 1955 session forty-two different congressmen sponsored eleven different bills to amend the Minimum Wage Law in a downward direction.[16]

On November 11, 1954, President Magsaysay created a Survey Committee on the Minimum Wage Law.[17] The committee, which included distinguished economists and lawyers, assembled a first-rate staff, held extensive hearings, and produced a reasoned, persuasive report.[18] The report concluded that the Minimum Wage Law should be maintained without changes, that it was economically sound, and that it was capable of enforcement if supported by adequate appropriations. Regarding the relationship between the Minimum Wage Law and employment, the report concluded:

The problem is not solved by reducing wages, but by increasing the rate of capital formation, i.e., the opening of new industries. If we had hosts of men of enterprise, possessing the necessary technical knowledge, if our supply of investment capital could be efficiently mobilized, wages would constitute no real problem. Without these, our unemployment would continue to grow no matter how low we may depress wage levels.

[15] The dominant position of the sugar bloc in the attack on the minimum wage law is illustrated by the bitter intra-administration fight during 1954–1956 between Secretary of Labor Eleuterio Adevoso and Secretary of Agriculture and Natural Resources Salvador Araneta. R.P., President's Committee on Employment and Production, *A Program of Employment and Production* (Manila, 1955), proposed that (a) for a period of three years provincial and municipal councils be allowed to suspend the law, (b) the government not be bound by the minimum wage rate in making development expenditures, and (c) the national statutory minimum be replaced by flexible regional minimum wage rates. The Committee on Employment and Production was chaired by Secretary Araneta and included Oscar Ledesma, Secretary of Commerce and Industry, and Alfredo Montelibano, Secretary of Economic Co-ordination, all faithful representatives of the sugar interests.

[16] R.P., House of Representatives, *Congressional Record*, II:69 (May 11, 1955), p. 2681.

[17] *Manila Times*, Nov. 18, 1954. Members of the committee included Sotero B. Cabahug, Secretary of Defense, chairman; Dr. Jorge Bacobo, former president of the University of the Philippines and chairman of the Code Commission; Amando Dalisay, secretary of the Philippine Council on United States Aid; Gaudencio Garcia; Dr. Pacifico Ortiz, S.J., dean of the Law School, Ateneo de Manila; and Enrique M. Fernando.

[18] R.P., Survey Committee on the Minimum Wage Law, *Report to the President of the Philippines* (Manila, 1955), mimeograph.

The next significant encroachment on minimum wage policy was embodied in the so-called "Moreno rider," which was written into the Public Works Act for fiscal year 1955–56 and which became law without executive approval.[19] The Moreno rider, hidden away on page 570 of a massive pork-barrel appropriations bill, originally would have permitted municipal councils to reduce wages paid on public works to not less than ₱2. The Moreno rider was included in the bill passed by the House but rejected by the Senate. The rider was re-inserted in modified form by a joint Senate-House conference. The law, as enacted, provides in Section 7 that wage rates on public works projects "shall not be less than prescribed by law for agricultural laborers," i.e., ₱2.50 per day.

As with so many aspects of Philippine welfare legislation, enforcement of the Minimum Wage Law has been hampered by lack of congressional financial support. The number of inspectors and field offices of the Wage Administration Service is limited, and enforcement lags, particularly in agricultural industries. Of the 587 violations of the statutory minimum wage uncovered in 1955, 518 involved agricultural enterprises.[20] The first conviction under the Minimum Wage Law did not occur until April 1953, two years after passage of the law.[21] By June 1956 there had been only five more convictions. Not until January 1957 did the first Minimum Wage Law violator go to prison, and he was, not surprisingly, a Chinese.[22]

In the area of tenancy relations it has been Philippine policy to create elaborate legal protection for the rights of the cultivator to the agricultural product. The original tenancy relations law, the Rice Share Tenancy Act (Act No. 4054) was enacted in 1933 toward the end of the colonial period. The law provided for a basic 50-50 sharing of the crop in the absence of a written tenancy agreement. Although it did not touch upon many areas of inequality in traditional tenancy relations, it was not enforced because it provided that it would take effect only in those provinces where a majority of the cacique-dominated municipal councils petitioned the Governor-General for its application.

Subsequent amendments to the Rice Share Tenancy Act provided that, in the absence of a written contract, the testimony of a tenant

[19] Republic Act No. 1411 of Sept. 10, 1955.
[20] Hartendorp, *History*, p. 518.   [21] *Manila Times*, April 22, 1953.
[22] *Ibid.*, Jan. 22, 1957.

should be accepted as prima-facie evidence as to its terms (Commonwealth Act No. 53) and that the act should be applied to tenancy relations in other crops (Commonwealth Act No. 178). More important, Act No. 178 provided that the law could be applied by presidential proclamation. By November 1946 the law had been declared in effect throughout the Philippines.

Commonwealth Act No. 461 of June 9, 1939, provided that tenants were not to be dispossessed without the approval of the Department of Justice and that tenancy disputes were to be adjudicated by the Court of Industrial Relations. Commonwealth Act No. 608 of August 22, 1940, provided that the Department of Justice could issue orders as to the division of crops. Republic Act No. 34 of September 30, 1946, provided for an increase from 50 to 55 per cent in the legal minimum share of the net product accruing to tenants.

Responsibility for enforcement of the amended Rice Share Tenancy Act was assigned to the Department of Justice (Commonwealth Act 608). To enforce the law, the Tenancy Law Enforcement Division (TLED) of the Department of Justice and the Tenancy Division of the Court of Industrial Relations were created in 1939. The period to mid-1954 saw little progress in the implementation of the crop distribution policy in spite of the elaborate structure of legislation. TLED orders were enforced only by bringing criminal contempt proceedings in the appropriate court of first instance or justice of the peace court. The decisions of the latter tended to reflect the interests of the large landowners of the municipality. Contempt proceedings were slow and costly, with both time and money on the side of the landlord. Enforcement agencies were starved of appropriations, and in the absence of adequate personnel docketed cases tended to accumulate, compounding the delay in enforcement. The Tenancy Division of the CIR usually did not have facilities for holding hearings outside Manila, and many tenant complaints were not heard for this reason.[23]

The current Agrarian Relations Act (Republic Act No. 1199 of August 30, 1954) specifies that the basic factors of land and labor shall each be awarded 30 per cent of the net crop on first-class land.

---

[23] On Jan. 1, 1951, Executive Order No. 392 abolished the TLED and transferred responsibility for enforcement of tenancy policy to the Court of Industrial Relations. This change added to the work load of the CIR—including the decision of over 1,000 pending cases—without adding personnel.

The net crop is defined as the crop remaining after the cost of fertilizer, pest and weed control, reaping, and threshing costs are deducted. Five per cent is allocated to the party furnishing the work animal and five per cent to the party who contributes the farm implements. Five per cent of the net crop is allocated to cover the cost of final harrowing and twenty-five per cent to transplanting. Inasmuch as the law provides that the tenant may choose to shoulder any costs that he can, the tenant owning both work animals and implements can, under existing legislation, establish a valid claim to 70 per cent of the net crop.

Congress did not provide for a new agency to implement Republic Act 1199 and did not appropriate any additional funds for enforcement. President Magsaysay was able to give adequate financial support during the first fiscal year of the law by allocating ₱150,000 from his contingency fund while additional support was provided by United States aid counterpart funds.

On September 30, 1954, Magsaysay issued Administrative Order No. 67 creating the Agricultural Tenancy Commission (ATC), and army officers with legal training were detailed to prosecute violations of tenancy laws. The ATC was assigned responsibility "to acquaint the tenants and landholders with their rights and responsibilities" and for "formulating a national enforcement program." During fiscal years 1954–55 and 1955–56 the ATC completed a broad information program and engaged in extensive mediation and legal activities. During the first nine months of operation 596 disputes were brought to the commission and 270 settled amicably. The remaining disputes had either been acted upon and were waiting settlement, were waiting investigation, or had been taken to court. In fiscal year 1955–56 more than twice as many cases were referred to the commission, and the number of those settled amicably increased nearly four times.

Administration proposals for tenancy reform in 1954 included establishment of a "Court of Agrarian Relations," but Republic Act 1199 continued the jurisdiction of the Court of Industrial Relations over tenancy disputes. The Tenancy Division of the Court of Industrial Relations had, since its inception before World War II, been starved for funds and had been relatively ineffective since it sat only in Manila. Tenants rarely had sufficient resources to travel the necessary distance and to maintain themselves in Manila while their cases were being heard.

Creation of the Court of Agrarian Relations (CAR) completed
the establishment of a mobile, flexible judicial agency to give effect to
crop distribution policy of twenty years' standing.[24] In the first year
of the CAR 2,589 cases were newly filed, or slightly more than the
total for the previous three years when such cases were heard by
the Tenancy Division of the Court of Industrial Relations. The court
disposed of nearly 300 more cases than were filed.[25]

The CAR is working hard to break down traditional tenant mis-
trust of all courts. It attempts to accomplish this not only by being
available, but by handling cases rapidly and informally. The court
is freed from many procedural restrictions, and in issuing orders or
decisions it need not "be restricted to the specific relief claimed or
demands made by the parties, but may include . . . any matter . . .
which may be deemed necessary and expedient for the purpose of
settling the dispute or of preventing further disputes, providing that
said matter . . . has been established by competent evidence during
the hearing." The lack of docket fees for litigants and the doctrine
incorporated in Republic Act No. 1199 that grave doubts should be
resolved in favor of the tenant make the CAR an institution which
can contribute materially to the welfare of the landless Filipino peasant.[26]

Two further aspects of welfare policy designed to contribute to
improved living standards for the rural population should be mentioned. First is land reform, which has a long history of legislative
and administrative activity. In spite of its history, land reform still
awaits the Philippines.[27] Second is the Community Development

[24] Republic Act No. 1267 of June 14, 1955, as amended by Republic Act No.
1409 of Sept. 9, 1955.
[25] Implementation of agricultural tenancy policy during the Magsaysay administration benefited from the leadership of Guillermo Santos. Santos, a colonel in
the Judge Advocate General's Office of the Philippine Army, was one of the army
officers detailed, prior to the enactment of Republic Act 1199, to prosecute violations of agricultural tenancy laws. When ATC was created, Colonel Santos became
its chairman and provided forceful, energetic leadership, both in bringing knowledge of the new law to tenant farmers and in mediating disputes in the period
prior to the creation of CAR. When CAR was created, Colonel Santos was appointed executive judge and his leadership contributed very substantially to the
high morale and efficiency of the court in the first months of its existence.
[26] As of Feb. 28, 1958, ATC had settled out of court 5,400 cases involving
65,600 tenants and 3,645 landlords. CAR had decided 4,573 cases involving 27,648
tenants and 8,853 landowners (R.P., NEC, *Joint P.I.–U.S. Econ. Devel. Program*,
p. 19).
[27] See above, pp. 272–277.

Program. As in the case of most agrarian reform measures, congressional attitudes toward the program—first proposed in 1955—ranged from apathy to hostility. Magsaysay, however, initiated community development by appointing a presidential assistant on community development and he allocated discretionary funds at his disposal.

In the face of continued congressional opposition, financial support for the program has devolved upon the United States aid mission. During the three fiscal years ending June 30, 1958, United States aid included $8.6 million of dollar aid plus ₱9.3 million of counterpart funds. Approximately 10 per cent of United States aid expenditures in recent years have been allocated to the Community Development Program.

Although it is too early to assess the impact of the program, continued liberal financial support promises substantial gains. As of mid-1958, over five hundred community development workers had been trained, and 3,445 barrios including 4.5 million people were covered by the program.[28] The Community Development Program will be augmented by the work of the Department of Education and of public school teachers, who traditionally have been active in promoting rural improvement. In addition, Republic Act No. 680 of April 24, 1952, created a Bureau of Agriculture Extension and provided continuing financial support for an extension service. Institutional changes in the last decade should accelerate economic development and modernization of the rural economy at a rewarding rate.

A final aspect of welfare policy which should be described are the systems of social insurance. Retirement systems for government employees were under consideration as early as 1903, and by 1924 systems were in effect for the Philippine Constabulary, for public school teachers, and for Health Service personnel. Commonwealth Act No. 186 of November 14, 1936, created the Government Service Insurance System (GSIS).[29] The law provided for compulsory life insurance financed by equal contributions by the employee and the government of 3 per cent of the pay of the employee. During the Japanese occupation all policies of the GSIS were terminated by executive order. However, in 1945, Commonwealth Acts Nos. 706 and 710 of November 1, appropriated ₱6 million to meet insurance obligations of the GSIS.

[28] R.P., NEC, *Joint P.I.–U.S. Econ. Devel. Program*, p. 96.
[29] Commonwealth Acts Nos. 187, 188, and 189 of Nov. 14, 1936, provided for liquidation of the three departmental systems existing at that time.

More recently, Republic Act No. 660 of June 16, 1951, enlarged the GSIS to provide for compulsory retirement as well as life insurance. Under this law retirement insurance premiums equivalent to 10 per cent of an employee's pay are contributed jointly by the employee and the government. The growth of the GSIS has been very rapid, and at the end of 1958 GSIS resources totaled ₱420 million, including ₱242 million of loans outstanding.

Contributory retirement insurance for employees of private firms is a recent welfare policy. Republic Act No. 532 of June 16, 1950, provided for the creation of a Pension Commission to study problems and make recommendations concerning social security measures. The work of the Pension Commission led ultimately to enactment of the Social Security Act of 1954, Republic Act No. 1161 of June 18, 1954. The act declared it to be policy "to develop, establish gradually, and perfect a social security system which shall be suitable to the needs of the people throughout the Philippines and shall provide protection against the hazards of unemployment, disability, sickness, old age and death" (Section 2). Under the law comprehensive social security was to be established initially in "one or more experimental areas" and subsequently to be extended to "such other areas and industries as experience and conditions" warrant (Section 4). The system was to be operated on an actuarial basis with contributions from both employers and employees to finance the various kinds of insurance.

Toward the end of 1954 the Department of Labor and the Social Security Commission initiated steps to begin the collection of insurance premiums from all firms employing thirty or more employees and the covered employees of such firms. Strong opposition from the affected firms, chambers of commerce, and a number of labor organizations led President Magsaysay to suspend implementation of the act for an unspecified period of time.

The Social Security Act was subsequently amended by Republic Act No. 1792 of June 18, 1957, which reduced the scope of the benefits by eliminating unemployment insurance. The provision for partial and experimental application of the act was eliminated, and coverage was made compulsory for all businesses that have been in operation for at least two years and which employ at least fifty employees. Moreover, after the first year coverage is compulsory for all businesses with six or more employees, agricultural labor and domestic service excluded. The amended law provides for a basic contribution of 3.5 per cent of the employees pay (up to ₱500 per month) by the employer and 2.5 per cent by the employee. Private pension plans are to be integrated into the Social Security System without reduction in benefits.

In June 1957 Rodolfo P. Andal, general manager of the GSIS, was designated chairman of the Social Security Commission and acting administrator of the Social Security System. The Social Security System began operation on September 1, 1957, and growth has been rapid. At the end of 1958, 9,818 firms were covered with 378,534 employees. Of the total firms covered, 1,652 had at least 50 employees, and these firms accounted for 252,000 of the total employees. Monthly income from premiums and investments amounted to approximately ₱3 million by the end of 1958. As might be expected, in the early years of the insurance scheme income was far in excess of benefits, and at the end of fifteen months the system had accumulated investments of ₱28.3 million, including ₱25.3 million in government securities plus a ₱1.0 million time deposit in the Philippine National Bank.[30]

Philippine welfare policy is embodied in an elaborate structure of enlightened legislation. There can be no doubt than an appropriate legal framework exists through which the government can intervene to reduce the inequalities in Philippine income and wealth. Enforcement of the welfare provisions of legislation has generally improved although the intensity of enforcement has varied greatly.

To sum up, a number of generalizations can be made. Laws protecting labor, including workmen's compensation, the labor of women and children, and workmen's safety legislation, are enforced in urban areas and are observed by larger firms. Much remains to be done to extend protection to the more vulnerable workers in small, provincial firms. With respect to efforts on the part of government to influence the economic bargaining power of labor, it seems clear that these have been unimpressive in their economic consequences. The shift in the basic framework of industrial relations from compulsory arbitration to collective bargaining is unlikely to result in relative improvement in the economic position of industrial labor. Rapid urbanization has intensified the competition for the available industrial jobs. Collective

---

[30] Activities of the SSS have been reported in detail in a monthly contribution to the *A.C.C. Journal* by Gonzalo W. Gonzalez, chairman of the Social Security System. Gonzalez succeeded Rodolfo P. Andal.

bargaining works relatively well where large foreign enterprises are involved. Such firms have traditionally paid wages in excess of those paid by Filipino and Chinese firms and they have a strong stake in maintaining good industrial relations in view of the nature of Philippine nationalism.

The available statistical evidence, for what it is worth, supports the conclusion that the relative position of labor has deteriorated in recent years.[31] For example, the index of money wage rates for skilled labor in industrial establishments in Manila and suburbs has actually declined from 102.3 in 1949 to 100 in 1957, while for unskilled labor the index has risen from 94.6 to 101.5. During this same period national income increased from ₱5,464 million to ₱8,799 million and per capita income from ₱280 to ₱390. During the eight years 1949–1957 per capita income increased by 39 per cent as contrasted to an increase of 7 per cent in the index of wage rates of unskilled labor and an actual decline in the index of wage rates for skilled labor.[32] Collective bargaining is probably more effective and the minimum wage law subject to more aggressive enforcement in the Manila area than elsewhere. Therefore, the relative position of wage labor elsewhere in the Philippines has probably not improved relative to such labor in the Manila area.[33]

Welfare measures designed to improve the status of agricultural laborers, whether wage workers or tenants, including the Minimum

[31] Since 1950 the national accounts show an increase in "compensation of non-agricultural employees" of 58 per cent to ₱2.9 billion. Over this same period "non-agricultural entrepreneurial and property income of individuals and corporations" increased by 70 per cent to ₱2.9 billion. See NEC, "An Analysis of the National Income Accounts of the Philippines for the years 1957 and 1958," *Statistical Reporter,* 3 (April 1959), 10.

[32] In 1956 the payroll of all manufacturing establishments with 20 or more employees was ₱273 million. Total employment of these firms was 147,282, and the average annual wage of all employees was ₱1,539. The wage bill for "production and related employees" was ₱174 million, the number of such employees was 116,083, and the average annual wage of such employees was ₱1,498. By either measure the annual wage paid was well in excess of the rate established by the minimum wage law. See R.P., NEC, *1956 Survey of Manufactures, General Statistics for Large Establishments,* vol. I, ser. I, p. 9.

[33] The observer in the Philippines quickly becomes aware that strikes have a persistent tendency to become lockouts of the striking employees as operations are conducted with a new working force. Successful strikes for economic gains are rare. The acquiescence of labor in the face of continuing intervention by the CIR in industrial controversy is indicative of a lack of confidence in labor's bargaining power.

Wage Law and crop distribution laws, have not materially changed the relative position of these depressed elements in the population. Agricultural tenancy policy received vigorous implementation during the Magsaysay administration, and the hopes aroused during this period undoubtedly contributed to the improved stability and security conditions in rural areas. However, the high hopes of 1954–1956 have materialized slowly and the claim of the cultivator to the agricultural product is still largely just that.

The basic limitation on the capacity of the Agricultural Tenancy Commission and the Court of Agrarian Relations to achieve equity in the distribution of the agricultural product is economic. The competition of peasants for the available land and jobs in the densely populated provinces leads to tenant-owner collusion to evade the policy. Philippine tenancy policy is directed at a symptom—the distribution of the agricultural product—and neglects the root causes of poverty and inequality. There are few grounds for concluding that this policy can substitute for more widespread ownership of land and capital.

Not only are agricultural welfare policies poorly conceived in terms of economic realities, but enforcement is sporadic and rarely vigorous. Cacique political power has great capacity to subvert welfare measures by withholding financial support and by personal vendettas against civil servants willing to try to inject minimum equity into economic relations in Philippine agriculture.

Philippine social insurance is a policy which holds great promise. The introduction of social insurance into a society based upon the extended family represents a far-reaching change. Both the GSIS and the SSS schemes are actuarily sound and therefore for some time to come will have premiums and earnings in excess of benefits. Under the circumstances a major consequence of these two institutions will be fiscal, i.e., they will serve to mobilize Philippine savings and channel them to uses appropriate to Philippine economic growth. As of the end of 1957, the assets of these two institutions were in excess of ₱325 million and were increasing at a steady rate. Presently, only about a third of the assets of the two systems are government securities and two-thirds represent private credit.

The Philippines has an enlightened structure of welfare legislation, including protective labor legislation and actuarily sound social security laws. Up to the present time welfare measures designed to redress economic inequality have had little impact on the distribution of wealth and income. This result can and should be deplored on grounds of equity. However, capitalistic economic development has historically postponed the pursuit of welfare objectives until economic development has achieved considerable progress, and the Philippines seems to be following this pattern. The pursuit of welfare goals involves obvious conflict with the pursuit of maximum economic growth. Most regrettable in the Philippine situation are the gross inequalities in the distribution of wealth and income in the agricultural sector. Concentration of agricultural income in rents makes little contribution to social and economic progress in the Philippines.

· XVIII ·

The Summing Up

PHILIPPINE economic growth throughout the postwar period has been rapid by all criteria. The first five postwar years through 1950 were devoted to rehabilitation and reconstruction. The ensuing years have seen rewarding economic growth. National income in the eight years following 1950 increased by 56 per cent, while per capita income is estimated to have increased by about one-third. Inasmuch as prices were relatively stable throughout this period, the increase in per capita income was essentially an increase in real income.

This study of Philippine economic policy has been critical of many aspects. The author is therefore confronted by the need to reconcile his critical appraisal of public policy with the substantial accomplishments of the Philippine economy. The analysis of public policy has been critical for three basic reasons: First, Philippine economic policy is appraised in terms of the main body of theory and speculation regarding the relationships between public policy and economic growth. As was indicated in the introductory chapter, the theory of economic growth is *a priori* and normative and is applicable to a stereotype of an underdeveloped country which has limited resemblance to the Philippines.

Second, the consequences of many Philippine economic policies are

unrelated to their avowed objectives. The Philippine Congress blithely
enacts consumer price controls, personal income taxes, and land reform legislation which it has no intention of seeing enforced. Similarly,
there have been a succession of more-or-less comprehensive economic
plans for accelerated economic growth which have largely been ignored by the policy makers.

Third is the harshness of the emerging economic organization. Income and wealth are concentrated, political power is closely correlated
with wealth, and welfare goals are assigned low priority. The sympathies of the observer go out to the peasantry and growing urban
proletariat who are ill equipped to share in the expanding economy.

This summary chapter is devoted to four questions.

(1) What factors explain postwar economic growth?
(2) What factors will contribute to further economic growth?
(3) What factors will tend to limit further economic growth?
(4) What social problems resist alleviation by economic growth?

What factors explain postwar economic growth? The principal source
of economic growth in the postwar Philippines has been the accelerated
social change in attitudes and values which determine the "will to
economize"—the intensity of economic activity. Internal migration to
the cities and the frontier is both a manifestation of rapid social change
and the source of further change. Similarly, the response of entrepreneurial activity to the incentives demanded by economic nationalism
is both a manifestation of change and productive of further change.
Changing attitudes and values with respect to education in general and
vocational education in particular have improved the quality of economic activity. The standard of living to which the average Filipino
aspires has been subject to rapid change in the postwar period as
awareness of so-called "superior" consumption patterns has spread
through the society. While the "international demonstration effect" may
increase the marginal propensity to consume, in the Philippines this
effect has been more than offset by a contribution to more intense economic activity.

The Philippine economy has many attributes of a fluid "frontier"
economy in which the entrepreneurial class as a competing elite is dis-
placing the heretofore dominant agricultural aristocracy. Entrepreneurship is encouraged by universal approbation and enhanced social
status. Filipino entrepreneurship is distinctively Filipino in its strong

predilection to seek economic advantage through political institutions and processes. It is in the Schumpeterian tradition in that it combines dependence upon credit with close personal control. The resourcefulness of Filipino businessmen has been slowly nourished at the cost of the waste of resources attending haphazard protection and excessive incentives. However, with growing self-confidence, Filipino entrepreneurship is providing leadership in the struggle to reduce the area of discretionary management of the economy.

Merely calling attention to the categories of recent changes without attempting to identify the root causes of accelerated social change begs the crucial question. The growing effectiveness of Filipino participation in the Philippine variety of national enterprise system has roots in factors which have produced intense Philippine identification with the West—an identification manifested in dominant patterns of emulation and therefore adaptation to an institutional environment favorable to the release of the productive powers of individualism. Such identification, I believe, is attributable to two basic factors. First was the success of Spanish missionary efforts, which over three and a half centuries eroded initially weak Filipino ties to a Malayan cultural heritage. Second was the impact of the public school system that flourished after 1900. The public school system, initially staffed by Americans, was not so much an instrument for instruction—this was precluded by the use of English as the language of instruction—as it was a tool for communicating the idea of change to the grass roots of Philippine society. The public school system was instrumental in intensifying the Western identification of Filipinos who had been bypassed by the Spanish cultural impact.

The public school system served to erode the foundations of traditional authority and value patterns. Despite the progressive Filipinization of the teaching staff, the system retained its American orientation in curricula, philosophical attitudes, and many aspects of content. Largely through the public school system there slowly permeated through Philippine society awareness that individual dignity, security, and welfare were dependent upon the efforts of the individual to realize his capacities as well as upon birth and the vagaries of nature.

The contribution of rapid social change to postwar Philippine economic development is illustrated by a minor controversy which took place over economic planning.[1] When the 1957 Plan was under prepa-

---

[1] The controversy is reported in Higgins, *Economic Development*, pp. 648–650.

ration, the Philippine planners—in accordance with accepted planning practice—were seeking for an incremental capital-output ratio on which to base their projections of savings and investment requirements. Analysis of Philippine national accounts indicated that incremental capital-output ratios of less than unity had characterized postwar Philippine economic growth. Philippine planners, hidebound by their education and experience in the Western tradition, rejected the historical evidence of the incremental relationship between investment and income.[2] The explanation of rapid postwar Philippine economic growth is not to be found in the place where economists are prone to look, that is, in the rate of capital formation as sustained by private savings and investment, high levels of government revenues and investment, and/or foreign investment. This is not to say that capital formation—particularly if the concept of capital is broadened to include land colonization and intangible resource accumulation—has not made a major contribution to growth. However, the observer who looks no farther than the incremental-capital output ratio, will ignore the most significant relationship in the Philippine growth process.[3]

Philippine economic expansion in the first five postwar years was primarily a process of rehabilitation characterized by highly productive investment. Since 1950 economic growth has been new growth. The relationship between investment and output during the period of new growth has not been markedly less favorable than during the period of rehabilitation. The explanation for this phenomenon is not to be found by searching for errors in the Philippine statistics but is to

---

[2] R.P., NEC, *The 1957 Plan,* p. 70: "Net investment figures implicit in the available statistics on gross investment and depreciation seem to be highly improbable, if the national income and production statistics are accepted as not too inaccurate."

[3] The confusion over the incremental capital-output ratio was compounded by Philippine planners when they rejected the historical evidence on the grounds that an incremental capital-output ratio of 0.7:1 "implied an average rate of return on new investment of 150 per cent." The incremental capital-output ratio implies little with respect to the productivity of investment, and it is surprising that such an elementary confusion of marginal and incremental concepts should have occurred. The incremental capital-output ratio attributes increments of income to capital accumulation, whereas, in fact, income increments are explained by a wide spectrum of changes including accumulation of intangible economic resources, changes in the will to economize, and changes in demand conditions, as well as the accumulation of capital. The interest rate (marginal efficiency of capital or marginal productivity of capital) is the correct measure of the relationship between investment (capital) and income. Such a concept must be a marginal one in which other variables are held constant.

be understood in terms of the social changes that have produced rapid change in both the quantity and quality of economic activity.

The second principal explanation of rapid postwar economic growth has been the consistency of economic policy. Philippine society, for better or worse, has chosen to rely on an enterprise type of economic organization. The present study of policy has taken this decision as given and has not been concerned with the very important normative aspects of such a decision. At this point it is sufficient to say that such an economic organization has produced rewarding (i.e., accelerated) economic growth in a number of countries. In view of the quality of Philippine politics and the levels of bureaucratic responsibility and integrity, there is a strong case for reliance on private initiative rather than on directly productive government enterprise. Although there have been some prominent exceptions, notably the Philippine National Bank and the National Power Corporation, government enterprises have, by and large, been discredited by waste and inefficiency. Philippine nationalism is distinctive in that there are no "socialists" in the Philippines and "capitalism" is not a bad word.

The reader at this point may react with the query, Are there substantive differences between the incentives of colonial laissez faire and the postindependence national economy? Although the impact of nationalism has been to increase the intensity of economic incentives for Filipinos, the system of incentives has not changed in substantive aspects. Colonial laissez faire was irrelevant so far as Filipinos and other Southeast Asians were concerned because it was premature. Filipinos— ill equipped by economic experiences and culture—generally ignored the incentives of the colonial economy. The productive upsurge in economic activity which has accompanied the emergence of a national enterprise system is explained, for the most part, by the fortuitous conjunction of sovereignty, political maturity, and intensification of the will to economize rather than by changes in incentives to Filipino initiative and enterprise.

Has the role of government been appropriate to the choice of economic organization? Equally important, have appropriate policies been maintained to fruition, or has vacillation in policies limited their effectiveness? It must be admitted that there has been a persistent pattern of policy aberrations of questionable value to the choice of economic organization. Such aberrations include consumer price controls, public investment in ill-conceived manufacturing enterprises, policies directed

at inequalities as symptoms rather than at the root causes of inequalities, and so forth. In the aggregate, these aberrations have been
of minor significance, have in many cases been unenforceable, or have
not been enforced for want of congressional support.

An important source of over-all consistency in economic policy has
been the economic conservatism of Congress. The economic role of
the state has expanded at a moderate rate, while Congress, through its
power to tax and spend, has vetoed a wide range of economic activities
proposed by the executive. The conservatism of Congress is enhanced
by the residual colonial influences in Philippine society. Policy consistency has also resulted from the dominant role of the Monetary
Board under the strong leadership of Governor Cuaderno. The power
of the Monetary Board has grown from the decision to defend the prewar parity of the peso and the intense external disequilibrium arising
out of that decision. Major aspects of economic policy are circumscribed by the availability of foreign exchange, and the Monetary
Board has tended to determine exchange control and exchange rate
policy. Exchange and import controls have created strong vested interests that can be depended upon to support the Monetary Board.
Moreover, strong official support from the United States as well as the
backing of the influential American Chamber of Commerce has contributed to the influence of the Monetary Board.

While monetary and fiscal policies have been essentially conservative, the government has aggressively promoted industrialization by
(a) using foreign exchange allocation to subsidize entrepreneurial
activity, (b) reserving the domestic market to domestic producers, and
(c) giving tax exemptions. A policy which the government has pursued consistently and with considerable success is Filipinization of
the economy. Although the policies of economic nationalism are to be
deplored on many grounds, they have undoubtedly accelerated the
growth of Filipino entrepreneurship and contributed to the accumulation of Filipino capital. Finally, agricultural development through land
colonization has contributed materially to postwar economic growth.
The fact that agricultural production has kept abreast of population
growth since before World War II is largely due to expansion in land
under cultivation.

The third major factor explaining postwar Philippine economic development is the supplement of foreign savings. The deficit on current
account of the balance of payments (excluding United States govern-

ment expenditures) amounted to $1.5 billion during the five years ending 1949 and an additional $1.5 billion in the following eight years.[4] Foreign savings available to the Philippines have accounted for the principal part of Philippine net investment during the postwar period. The unrequited import surplus of goods and services represented a unique opportunity for the Philippines to accelerate economic growth.

The Philippine current account balance prior to World War II consistently showed an export surplus on the trade account and a substantial deficit on the current account which was more than offset by United States government expenditures and an inflow of foreign capital. In the postwar period the trade account has been heavily in deficit, which with a modest deficit on invisible payments explains the large and persistent deficit on current account.

The contribution of foreign savings to Philippine economic development is due to recognition on the part of the United States of a responsibility to participate in the economic development of less-developed countries. In the case of the Philippines, this factor was reinforced by the special relationship between the two countries, which has amplified the flow of United States savings to the Philippines for postwar rehabilitation, aid for economic development, and private foreign investment. United States aid and rehabilitation programs have been imaginative, flexible, and efficiently administered; they have contributed materially to Philippine agricultural and industrial development.[5]

The inflow of foreign savings is also attributable to Philippine exchange rate and exchange control policy. Currency overvaluation has enabled the Philippines to maximize imports subject to the basic restraint of foreign exchange availability as exchange controls have been

[4] The balance of payments on current account used here to some extent overstates the inflow of foreign savings, inasmuch as a part of U.S. government expenditures represents payments for Philippine goods and services. To some extent such goods and services are analogous to exports and to some extent they represent resources which would be unemployed in the absence of U.S. programs in the Philippines.

[5] Contrary to the comforting anthropomorphism of *The Ugly American*, successful outside participation in economic development is a complex, frustrating, difficult, and challenging problem. The relative success with which the United States has participated in Philippine rehabilitation and development has little to do with personalities—Filipino or American. The American contribution reflects the magnitude of our effort and, more important, the favorable economic environment in which we were operating.

applied to limit nontrade payments. Moreover, the precariousness of
the Philippine external balance together with the special United States
stake in the Philippines has given the Philippines access to substantial
amounts of *ad hoc* balance of payments assistance. Economic theory
attributes to exchange control the capacity to force savings by limiting
imports of consumption goods. In the Philippines exchange controls
have made a higher level of foreign savings available to the Philippines
by limiting profit remittances and capital transactions and by maintaining a chronic balance of payments crisis amenable to *ad hoc* United
States assistance.

The fourth major factor explaining postwar Philippine economic
growth has been the stimulus of the internal market. Colonial commercial policy in the Philippines was analogous to a revenue tariff.
Although usually referred to as "reciprocal free trade," the principal
consequence of United States colonial policy was to force the Philippines to resort to a jerry-built structure of internal excises to tax import values. Revenues from taxes using import values as a base have
traditionally accounted for approximately half of the national government revenues. With the imposition of effective exchange and import
controls in 1949, the Philippines was in a position to shift from the
colonial-type policy to a national policy of protection.

Filipinos, with few exceptions, if asked to appraise the factors explaining postwar economic growth, would assign great significance
to the attainment of commercial policy autonomy and establishment
of high levels of protection. This has been a major change. I am inclined
to believe however, that such an interpretation exaggerates the impact
of protection. The fact of protection is not as significant as the timing
of this change, which coincided with the emergence of substantial
numbers of Filipinos prepared to take advantage of the incentives
arising from protection.

In addition to the stimulus of protection, Philippine economic growth
has been in response to factors enlarging the domestic market. Population growth has been rapid. Agricultural colonization has tended to
maintain real income in agriculture while preventing improvements
in the internal terms of trade for agricultural output. Finally, urbanization and industrialization have contributed to rapid growth in the
domestic market.

What factors will contribute to further economic growth? The factors which will contribute to future growth, not surprisingly, are closely related to those factors responsible for past growth.

First is the fact that political institutions and processes suitable for continued and even accelerated social change exist. The Philippines seems definitely over the watershed of democratic political development. Incumbent administrations have been voted out of office in relatively peaceful elections.[6] Obstacles to the appearance of alternative economic leadership are essentially cultural and not legal or political. Economic reaction in the Philippines must be interpreted in terms of the *status quo*—the semifeudal rural Philippines. The growing indigenous entrepreneurial and industrial elites, actively promoting something remotely akin to late-nineteenth-century laissez faire, are not reactionaries in the Philippines but progressives promoting change. Economic reaction in the Philippines has its stronghold in Congress and is on the defensive. Although the political power of the agricultural aristocracy is still dominant, economic development in the postwar period has seen the emergence of a countervailing power center which has successfully challenged the agricultural aristocracy on a number of significant economic issues. The unity of the political elites has been permanently destroyed, and intense competition among the elites portends continued change.

Second is the growing literacy and economic sophistication of Philippine society. The ability of economic interest groups with their politician retainers blandly to identify the national interest with their particular interests is being reduced. The ratio of college students to total population is unmatched in other less-developed countries. While the quality of education leaves much to be desired, Philippine educa-

[6] This is not to contend that Philippine democracy is model, which it very obviously is not. However, traditional political behavior is increasingly circumscribed by the social will to improve Philippine democracy. I have heard Philippine democracy likened to an elastic sac within which political behavior is violent and erratic, with the sac subject to extreme distortion. Although the participants are willing to twist and strain the sac to accommodate narrow interests, there is a strong social consensus that the essential qualities of Philippine democracy must be maintained and strengthened. The depth of Philippine attachment to democratic institutions is indicated by the national indignation aroused when the Philippines is referred to as a "banana republic," with its connotation of military authoritarianism, corruption, and reaction. The maturity of Philippine democracy is deliberately misinterpreted in much of non-Communist Asia out of envy and out of resentment of Philippine failure to identify with Asia.

tion is economically and socially useful. Preoccupation with economic questions is widespread, and improvements in internal communications promise that political controversy in the future will be less dominated by personalities and will reflect issues and ideologies more.

Third is the nascent middle class. Traditional patterns of kin-oriented behavior are eroding with internal migration, urbanization, and economic growth. In Manila political and economic relations are impersonal to a degree unknown two decades ago. Preoccupation with the welfare of the extended family is lessening, and awareness of the community of self-interest and the national interest is increasing. Contributing to the middle class is an intellectual proletariat—the rapidly growing body of college and university graduates—which remains politically passive but highly individualistic. Also contributing to the emerging middle class are the beneficiaries of economic nationalism— Filipino importers, retailers, industrialists, and salaried workers. Vertical mobility in Philippine society is, except at the highest levels, relatively unimpaired and depends upon wealth.

Fourth is the existence of a structure of economic institutions appropriate to accelerated economic growth. Financial institutions have become functionally specialized in advance of the need for such specialization. For example, within the last two years three common stock mutual funds dealing in Philippine securities have been established. At the same time the existence of such institutions will tend to promote economic changes appropriate to accelerated economic growth. Most impressive is the proliferation of institutions which encourage savings—life insurance, social security, government service life insurance, postal savings, rural banks, rural credit co-operatives, and so forth. These institutions may well promote an increase in the rate of savings, while the functional specialization of such institutions will reduce present reliance on commercial bank lending for long-term industrial uses.

Fifth is the continued availability of foreign savings. There is every reason to believe that the United States will continue to recognize her self-interest in seeing that "democratic-capitalism" works in the Philippines and will continue to participate effectively in Philippine economic development. Moreover, private long-term direct foreign investment in production for the domestic Philippine market will continue at modest levels as the profitability of such investment and the forced savings induced by exchange controls offset the effects of economic nationalism. Of somewhat less importance will be the inflow of

Japanese reparations and loans scheduled under the reparations agreement for the next twenty years.

Sixth is the continued "normalization" of Philippine commercial policy.[7] The analysis of exchange rate and commercial policy in this study attaches great importance to the use of protection and subsidization through exchange allocation in explaining the rapid emergence of Filipino entrepreneurship and industrialization. By forgoing its claim to the windfall arising out of import restriction, the government has developed a powerful weapon for promoting private economic activity. The ultimate success of this policy will be measured by the extent to which Philippine industrialization can be weaned from the heavy subsidization incorporated in imports of industrial raw materials and can survive and expand solely on the basis of protection.

At the present time tax concessions under the "new and necessary industries" policy are scheduled for rapid reduction. Moreover, a larger part of the windfall arising out of import restriction should be diverted to the government by collection of Philippine tariffs on imports from the United States and the heavy premium on sales of foreign exchange. These changes will, of course, reduce the rewards for entrepreneurial activity by Filipinos. However, there are few reasons to believe that the emerging Filipino entrepreneurs will not resist loss of function on which their status and welfare depend.

The ultimate success of Philippine industrialization policy depends on the development of internal sources of supply of present imports of industrial raw materials—fibers, plastic raw materials, steel and other metals, fuels, and other items. At present the incentive to establish such industries is minimized by liberal allocations of foreign exchange to import such materials. The development of Philippine sources of supply is a formidable challenge but one in which the likelihood of success must be assessed as favorable. If this problem is tackled with the same imagination that the problem of market industrialization was tackled, its solution seems clearly within Philippine capacities.

Normalization of Philippine commercial policy will also have the effect of diverting large amounts of revenue to the government, which in turn will help support high levels of social investment and other developmental expenditures. Finally, scheduled changes in commercial policy will promote Philippine progress toward a more normal

[7] Where "normalization" refers to diversion to the government of the monopoly windfall arising out of import restriction.

geographic distribution of Philippine foreign trade. Concentration
of trade with the United States has been markedly reduced in recent
years, and this trend should persist.

Seventh is the essential stability of the Philippine economy. The
stereotype of the less-developed economy is analogous to a small
boat in a choppy sea, tossed about by external influences beyond the
control of the occupants. Such a stereotype has little relevance in the
postwar Philippines. Economic expansion has continued without
interruption, and economic fluctuations have been of minor significance. The relative importance of foreign trade in the determination
of employment and income in the Philippine economy has been
rapidly reduced. More important, Philippine policy makers have acquired ten years of experience and have displayed increasing competence in the management of their economy.

Economic management has been, and will be, simplified in the
foreseeable future by the essential conservatism of fiscal policy. Power
in Congress still resides with defenders of the *status quo,* and the
colonial-type policy of minimum government functions is subject to
slow erosion. There has been little tendency for government receipts
and expenditures to increase as a share of aggregate economic activity, and deficit finance has been confined within limits which
have not disturbed the continuing postwar stability. This claim is
made with full awareness of the clamorous crises which have attended
management of the international reserve. The ability of Philippine
policy makers to maintain economic expansion in spite of the external
disequilibrium attests to the fundamental stability of the Philippine
economy and the diminished significance of external economic relations. So long as management of the controlled external disequilibrium is not subject to excessive deficit financing by the government,
maintenance of the stability and progress of the past ten years
should be within Philippine capabilities.

What factors will tend to limit economic growth? In view of the
present structure of economic policy, the principal obstacle to further
economic expansion is the foreign exchange restraint. The importance
of imports to government revenues and consumer incentives as well
as the use of foreign exchange allocations to subsidize emerging
entrepreneurs tends to establish limits within which dominant economic policy objectives are pursued.

Maintenance of the prewar currency parity has denied to the

Philippines participation in the remarkable postwar expansion in international trade. As a result, the Philippines has had to exist on unnecessarily low levels of foreign exchange earnings. The essential poverty of Philippine exchange rate policy is evident in the erosion of the exchange control system and the uncertainty which attends continual controversy over exchange rate policy. It is abundantly clear that there was an optimum time for revision of exchange rate policy, but that time was a number of years past. The tragedy of Philippine exchange rate policy is the failure to recognize that the contribution of currency overvaluation to the pursuit of industrialization is marginal. The important change of the postwar period has been the establishment of Philippine autonomy over commercial policy and the high levels of protection which have been established.

The case for postwar Philippine exchange rate policy is not economic but political. Currency overvaluation has contributed to the growth of independent centers of political power—importers and industrial interests—which have reduced the traditional dominance of exporting interests and their cacique allies. It is, however, increasingly evident that a political and economic stalemate has developed in which exporting interests, through evasion of exchange controls both legally and illegally, will be able to break down the system of exchange controls.[8] It is the opinion of the author that devaluation is a calculated risk that holds considerable promise for the Philippines, particularly if it is combined with an appropriate tax on sugar exports to the United States market. There are, of course, other approaches to the problem of expanding foreign exchange earnings including export drawbacks as well as direct subsidies. These alternatives are inferior to devaluation—in the Philippine case—because of the element of administrative discretion and the probability of bureaucratic corruption. More important, they are inferior because of the element of uncertainty, which cannot help but offset the incentive that such a policy is designed to establish.

The second factor that will operate to limit Philippine economic development is the rapid rate of population growth. Philippine mortality rates have been reduced rapidly under the impact of public health programs, advances in antibiotics and sulfa drugs, and the

---

[8] The free market rate for the peso has declined steadily over the past three years and currently (Jan. 1960) is about four pesos per dollar as compared to the official parity (including exchange premium) of two and a half pesos per dollar.

increase in medical school graduates. On the other hand, there are
few reasons to expect an early decline in fertility rates, which are
among the world's highest. The best available estimates of Philippine
population growth suggest that current growth is taking place at
about 3 per cent annually. This means that the Philippine population
will double in no more than thirty years.

While present ratios of land and other natural resources to population are relatively favorable for economic growth, the pressure of
population on natural resources will undoubtedly increase within a
few decades. Filipinos are in complete agreement that the rapid
industrialization of the postwar period has not absorbed the annual
increment to the labor force, and there is little likelihood that future
expansion will achieve rates that will accomplish such a goal.

The third factor is the low marginal propensity to save. The available statistical evidence indicates little or no increase in the rate of
savings by Filipino society as national and per capita income have
increased. While statistical discrepancies may be substantial, there
can be little question that the rate of net savings by Filipinos is low
—probably as low as 5 to 6 per cent.

Given the rate of population growth and levels of investment, it is
clear that the rapid economic growth sustained over the past decade
and a half is explained primarily by changes in values and attitudes
which have increased the quantity and intensity of economic activity.
Although there are many grounds for expecting such changes productive of output to continue in the near future, it is obvious that
ultimately the rate of change must decelerate. It is not unlikely that
increases in Philippine output will be increasingly dependent upon
the accumulation of capital resources. One would be more encouraged
about the future if there was stronger evidence that saving out of increments of income was greater than the average rate of savings.

Fourth among the factors which are likely to limit Philippine economic growth is the stalemate which has tended to develop in the
political environment of economic policy. Economic interests with
a stake in a change in exchange rate policy have been gathering
strength, and the legislation enacted in the 1959 congressional session
suggests that maintenance of the existing policy structure will become
increasingly difficult. In the bitter controversy over economic policy in
recent years opposing personalities have taken such extreme positions
that a victory for the opponents of existing policy may bring whole-

sale changes, including a revival of the political strength of the sugar bloc. Such a conclusion is reinforced by the fact that Governor Cuaderno is now several years past the official retirement age. His retirement cannot be postponed indefinitely, and there is no successor in sight capable of organizing political support among the heterogeneous interest groups with a stake in the present policy structure.

Cuaderno's role in the evolution of Philippine developmental policy is subject to severe criticism—such as permeates this study—but the success of his tactics and his resolution can only be praised. Whether or not evolved by trial and error and expediency, a consistency which recognized the political realities of the Philippine environment and which contributed to economic expansion runs through the substantive aspects of Philippine economic policy.

It is appropriate at this point to discuss briefly two further factors which are widely recognized as capable of exerting considerable influence on Philippine economic growth. First is the concentration of wealth, which is a dominant characteristic of Philippine society. A recent appraisal of Philippine economic prospects concluded:

The concentration of income and wealth presents social problems, but it can be converted into a source of strength from the standpoint of economic development. It means that high ratios of savings and investment to national income can be achieved without reductions in the standard of living of the masses of the people. In the Philippines, diverting 12 to 15 per cent of national income to public and private investment purposes, which is necessary to launch a sustained economic growth, can be accomplished without imposing hardship on any group, even in the short run.[9]

Such an appraisal is not uncommon but hardly realistic. The present concentration of wealth and income is unlikely to be a source of strength for two reasons. First, there is no evidence that a Congress dominated by agricultural wealth is willing to use wealth and agricultural income as an important tax base. Second, with respect to the contribution of the gentry to private capital accumulation, there is scant evidence that they are capable of shifting out of their traditional role as rent receivers. The security and prestige of agricultural wealth have deep roots in Philippine society, and it will take strong pressures to convert the agricultural rent receivers into entrepreneurs or even into dividend receivers. The influence of the existing

[9] Higgins, *Economic Development*, p. 746.

concentration of wealth on Philippine economic development is likely
to be neutral barring an unforeseen departure from the existing structure of developmental policy.

Finally, it is necessary to appraise the role of the Roman Catholic
Church in Philippine economic development. The role of the church
probably will be, as it has over the past six decades, essentially neutral. Economic development has been "rendered unto Caesar," and
intervention by the church will be limited to special areas of interest,
e.g., educational policy.

The church is a complex organism. It comprises an extensive re-
ligious-administrative machinery for supervising the spiritual affairs
of some 19 million people. It is an important property owner, with
properties ranging from landed estates to stocks in banks and industrial plants. Apart from basic fundamentals of religious doctrine
and morals, it is difficult to speak of a single unified church policy
with regard to the more earthy details of political, social, and economic
life. Strong elements of the church structure are identified with the
status quo and will inhibit the social change essential to material
progress. Other elements represent a potent force for evolutionary
change.[10] In view of the long tradition of nonmaterialism, the church
is likely to perform a passive role in Philippine economic growth.

What social problems resist alleviation by economic growth? Economic growth is an important social solvent capable of submerging
divisions within society. Has Philippine economic development shown
a comparable capacity as a social solvent? First, it should be remarked
that Philippine economic policy contributes to, rather than alleviates,
concentration of wealth and income. To the extent that economic
policy is designed to concentrate increments of income in the capitalist
entrepreneurs in the form of profits, it changes the past pattern of
income distribution, but not in the direction of greater equality.

Postwar Philippine economic development has tended to bypass
the rural and urban proletariat. The rapid expansion of land under
cultivation has not reduced tenancy in the densely populated areas.
Observers consistently comment that the pattern of land colonization
is creating tenancy in the frontier areas rather than diffusing land

[10] The Jesuit order has had remarkable success in attracting to their schools—
the *Ateneos*—the children of elite groups. The training given these students has
developed in this select group a liberal social conscience. As a result, *Ateneo*
graduates have provided a considerable part of the progressive social leadership
necessary to the postwar improvement in political institutions and processes.

ownership. The principal part of the Philippine population is engaged in agriculture, and agricultural output per head of population is no greater than it was twenty years ago. Tenancy is widespread, and the claim of the cultivator to the agricultural product is impaired by debt. The prices of agricultural products consumed domestically have persistently declined, while currency overvaluation has prevented recovery of agricultural production for exportation to prewar levels. The agricultural economy has expanded with the expansion in the domestic market, i.e., population growth, but economic development as measured by increasing per capita real income has largely bypassed the principal part of the Philippine population.

Similarly, the small but growing industrial proletariat has not been able to keep abreast of increases in per capita income. Internal migration to urban centers has increased the industrial labor force more rapidly than jobs have materialized, and labor competition has limited wage increases. Labor organizations are growing, and collective bargaining over economic aspects of employment is increasing. Labor legislation is enlightened, and enforcement is being steadily improved. However, real wages reflecting the realities of factor proportions and population growth have increased slowly.

There is a long history of desperation and violence arising out of the poverty and insecurity of cultivators. Philippine agrarian reform measures have had limited success in redressing the fundamental inequalities in the distribution of the agricultural product. Dissidence has become latent in the face of the promise of agrarian reform held out by the political developments of recent years as well as the success of government military operations against the Huks.

An economic change needed in the Philippines is land reform, i.e., transfer of land ownership to the cultivators. Land reform, preferably with a substantial element of expropriation, is warranted on grounds of equity. Such a change would hold few risks for Philippine economic development; indeed, the dispossessed rent receivers with capital resources would probably become dividend receivers and possibly entrepreneurs. Breaking up large landholdings would have little impact on the organization of production in the short run. Over the longer run, land reform would change the structure of investment incentives in such a way that improvements in labor and land productivity would result. The concentration of wealth in the cacique class presently makes a negligible contribution to Philippine eco-

nomic development, and there is no persuasive case for continuing
the socially disturbing pattern of land tenure that prevails in the
Philippines. After making such an assertion, one must not compound
candor with naïveté. There is little prospect of effective land reform
in the Philippines, although Republic Act No. 1400 purports to be
a land reform law.

The Philippine fiscal system is deplorably regressive and is not
amenable to change through economic growth, although there are
moderate elements of progression in tax legislation. Personal income
tax revenues have declined as a ratio of total income as national
income and per capita income have increased. Revenue from self-
assessed personal income taxes has not only failed to increase with
the expansion of income, but has actually declined. The principal part
of income taxes collected from Filipinos is obtained from withholding taxes on wage and salary employees, including civil servants.
The corporation income tax is an efficient revenue producer, but
this is explained in large part by the income tax discipline of aliens
in the environment of Philippine nationalism.

At least three-quarters of Philippine national government revenues
are derived from excise-type taxes. The Philippine pattern of taxation
is in the historical tradition of capitalism. The Philippines may, however, be forgoing an important opportunity to mobilize productive
resources by neglecting income and wealth as bases of taxation. Even
more pressing than the need to collect self-assessed income taxes from
Filipinos is the need for a realistic tax on real property. Ownership
of land is a reliable index of ability to pay taxes, and large revenues
could be derived from appropriate taxation of land. There is little
likelihood that such changes will be made in the Philippines in the
near future.

Is the economic growth of the past fifteen years due to neglect of
welfare considerations and aggressive concentration of income in
profits and rents? Such a question cannot be answered categorically,
and the observer can offer only his subjective, but more-or-less informed judgment. The traditional concentration of Philippine national
income in rents has made little, if any, contribution to postwar economic growth. The concentration of income in profits is another way
of describing the entrepreneurial incentives which comprise a major
explanation of postwar expansion. Entrepreneurial incentives generally have been excessive and have been maintained too long at the

expense of alternative and possibly more productive policies. Major advances toward desirable welfare goals could have been made without sacrificing growth and, indeed, there are strong reasons to believe that policies which promote the development of human capacities would contribute substantially to further growth.

It might be expected that economic development would serve to temper and submerge economic nationalism. This would be true to the extent that *national* economic development redressed the alien dominance of the nonagricultural economy. A number of beneficial consequences have accrued from economic nationalism. Social change has been accelerated, Filipino entrepreneurship has been nourished, and industrialization has been promoted. At the same time economic nationalism and in particular anti-Chinese emotions continue to serve self-seeking politicians.

Filipinos urgently need to begin to think about a policy structure which will be appropriate to the social and economic assimilation of alien minorities. The economic nationalism of the postwar period, when appraised in terms of economic development, has probably been constructive. There are, however, reasons to believe that a critical point has been reached. The Philippines has the choice of devising policies which will culminate in the assimilation of the Chinese minority or, alternatively, of taking a path of repression, expropriation, and isolation which will maintain a cancerous division in the society. It is clear that Filipino resistance to assimilation of the Chinese minority is as strong as Chinese resistance to such assimilation. It is also clear that the environment in which a solution must be sought has changed in recent years in important respects. Philippine economic nationalism is a complex phenomenon and combines both rational and irrational elements. Unfortunately, emotion will probably not be subordinated to reason in Filipino attitudes toward this problem.

At the end of this prolonged sifting of the Philippine economy some over-all assessment is in order. The writer is quite aware of the inevitable ambivalence which attends an ordering of the pros and cons. Postwar Philippine economic development and developmental policy must be assessed from two points of view. First, economic development has been sustained at a rapid pace throughout the postwar period. The structure of economic policy has been relatively consistent and appropriate to the choice of economic organization which has been made by Philippine society. On the other hand, per capita real income in the

Philippines today is only moderately increased over the levels of twenty years ago. In other words, the progress of the past fifteen years has surmounted the destruction and dislocation of World War II, provided the increase in population with the prewar level of income, and in addition furnished a modest increment of economic development. From this point of view the accomplishments of the postwar economy are somewhat less impressive.

It is possible that the rapid economic growth sustained by the Philippines over the past decade and a half will prove to be a false start. Barring unforeseen external political developments, the prospects for continued growth in the pattern of past growth must be considered favorable. Philippine manufacturing is admittedly high cost and dependent upon excessive incentives, without which continued viability would be precarious. On the other hand, growth has been broadly distributed over the sectors of the economy, with agricultural output after 1945 growing at rates well in excess of population growth.[11]

Probably the most important fact in assessing the future is the inertia of the Philippine economy. Progress currently is rapid, the resource endowment is favorable, extensive investment in the human factor is taking place. Moreover, a number of the major obstacles to further growth—the foreign exchange restraint, the low marginal propensity to save, and the political stalemate in the formulation of economic policy—are amenable to rapid change. The likelihood that changes favorable to further economic growth will take place should be assessed as favorable.

Philippine economic growth in excess of population growth will probably continue with little change in the basic structure of economic policy.[12] Market industrialization will continue as the Philippines

[11] Appraisals of the pursuit of industrialization by less-developed countries tend to be colored by awareness of the structural distortions and misuse of resources which have occurred in such countries as post-1933 Chile and Peron's Argentina. Postwar Philippine development differs from these two cases in at least three important respects. First, as mentioned above, the relatively rapid growth of manufacturing output has been superimposed upon broadly based and rapid economic expansion of the economy. Second, there has been no inflation and monetary and fiscal policies have remained essentially conservative. Third, elements in the society with a strong stake in expansion in governmental functions—urban labor, the bureaucracy, and the peasantry—have limited political power.

[12] Effective devaluation of the peso is inevitable. The author, for obvious reasons, would prefer that this change be delayed until his study is published. See above pp. 138–139.

solves problems in the supply of industrial raw materials from domestic sources. The ultimate outcome of Philippine development is not particularly promising as population growth will ultimately press upon available resources.

One final caveat. This has been a case study, the analysis and conclusions of which apply to the Philippines. There is little in the Philippine experience to serve as a guide to developmental policy in other countries. Critically important to Philippine economic growth has been the fortuitous conjunction of sovereignty, political maturity, and intensification of the will to economize. Such factors contribute to the uniqueness of the postwar Philippines. Unique, too, are all other underdeveloped countries.

Bibliographic Essay

THE prospect of compiling a bibliography—although it signals the completion of an arduous task—is not a happy one. One is appalled by the sense of redundancy which attends such a chore inasmuch as the footnotes are a reasonably comprehensive guide to the principal references. Moreover, a number of bibliographies adequate to introduce both the general reader and the scholar to the accumulated Filipiniaña exist. The fact that bibliographies inevitably list in juxtaposition the reliable and the less reliable, the relevant and irrelevant, adds to the bibliographer's feeling of malaise.

Instead of a bibliography, therefore, the student is offered a Baedeker to research into contemporary economic problems. This guide has been organized to provide two types of research assistance. First is an introduction to the principal source materials and bibliographic aids. It is intended for the economist and provides only rudimentary guidance to reference materials in related fields. Second are bibliographic notes to guide the student to specific references useful to an understanding of Philippine economic policy issues and problems. These notes follow the organization of the study and should be used in conjunction with the footnote references because a conscious effort has been made to minimize reference to sources identified in footnotes.

Study of contemporary Philippine social problems is facilitated by an accumulation of bibliographies both general and topical. The student is strongly advised to consult the Annual Bibliography issue (September) of the *Journal of Asian Studies.* From 1941 to 1956 this journal was called the *Far Eastern Quarterly* and the Annual Bibliography, which first appeared in 1949, was the September issue of the *Quarterly.* This bibliography lists books, periodical articles, monographs, government publications, and other items treating the countries of southern, southeastern, and eastern Asia. In addition, it is valuable as a reference to current bibliographic publications. It has steadily improved in coverage and is a useful research aid for the social scientist investigating current Asian problems.

A widely available general bibliography, topically arranged and annotated, is the *Selected Bibliography of the Philippines,* prepared by the Philippine Studies Program, University of Chicago, preliminary ed. (New Haven, Conn.: Human Relations Area Files, 1956). A useful bibliography of broader coverage than the title suggests is Karl J. Pelzer, *Selected Bibliography on the Geography of Southeast Asia: Part II, The Philippines* (New Haven, Conn.: Yale University Southeast Asia Studies, 1950), mimeograph. A specialized bibliography of economic references is Cecilio Lopez (ed.), *An Annotated Bibliography of Philippine Social Science: Volume I, Economics* (Diliman: University of the Philippines, Social Science Research Center, 1956). This bibliography, a catalog of economic references in the Filipiniana collection of the library of the University of the Philippines, is useful for materials published in the Commonwealth period and in the early postwar years. Also available in the projected series of bibliographies in the social sciences is Cecilio Lopez (ed.), *An Annotated Bibliography of Philippine Social Science: Volume II, Sociology,* pt. 1 (Diliman: U.P., SSRC, 1958).

Among the more specialized bibliographies the student is referred to the publications of the University of the Philippines, Institute of Public Administration, including Andaya Aracelis, *An Annotated Bibliography on Philippine Public Administration* (Manila, 1953), mimeograph; Gregorio A. Francisco, Jr., *Annotated Bibliography on Philippine Civil Service* (Manila, 1953), mimeograph, and Ajit Singh Rye, *A Selected Bibliography on Studies in Government Reorganization* (Manila, 1954), mimeograph.

Graduate studies of the Philippines have accumulated rapidly in recent years. Research has been strongly supported by the Fulbright Program, the Ford Foundation, and other sources of support for scholarly research. While the product has steadily improved in quantity and quality, distribution has not kept pace, and the generally available works only hint at the solid research principally in the form of graduate dissertations deposited in American universities. With few exceptions, these dissertations have resulted from field research and reflect the mature, supervised efforts of strongly motivated, energetic scholars.

Curtis W. Stucki's *American Doctoral Dissertations on Asia, 1933–1958* (Cornell Southeast Asia Program Data Paper No. 37; Ithaca, N.Y., 1959) lists doctoral dissertations in the social sciences and humanities which have been reported in the Association of Research Libraries, *Doctoral Dissertations Accepted by American Universities* and *Index to American Doctoral Dissertations*. Stucki lists 137 doctoral dissertations on Philippine subjects, of which 18 are in economics. Stucki's compilation also includes an appendix listing 164 master's theses on Asia written at Cornell University between 1933 and 1958, of which 28 deal with Philippine problems.

A listing of graduate dissertations prepared in the Philippines is to be found in the University of the Philippines, Institute of Public Administration, *Philippine Journal of Public Administration,* vol. I, nos. 1, 2, and 4 (1957). The initial listing covers all dissertations prepared between 1915 and 1956. In subsequent years the December issue of the *Journal* lists doctoral dissertations and master's theses deposited in the current year.

Copies of Philippine dissertations are to be found in the libraries of the universities granting the degrees and also in the Filipiniaña division of the Bureau of Public Libraries, Manila; in the case of private universities duplicate copies are in the library of the Bureau of Private Schools, Manila. There are many provocative titles among Philippine dissertations, but such items are available only to students engaged in field research. Furthermore, the quality of graduate dissertations in the social sciences is uneven and frequently low.

A second major source of information on current Philippine social and economic developments is the growing volume of Philippine periodical literature of professional and semiprofessional quality. Journals in the various social sciences have appeared at a rapid rate in recent years. This is a commendable phenomenon which in time will contribute to a tradition of research so badly needed in the Philippines. Since journals have appeared in advance of the supply of research results, they are presently filled with speeches and symposia of negligible professional value. The practice of publishing articles several times in various publications is widespread. Until the student becomes aware of this, he will waste time tracking down references to scarce journals only to find that the articles in question have already been consulted. After appearing one or more times in the Philippines, many of the articles on the Philippine economy are republished in the *Far Eastern Economic Review,* which is published in Hong Kong.

In the field of economics a primary reference is the *Statistical Reporter,* a quarterly published by the National Economic Council, Office of Statistical Co-ordination and Standards. The *Statistical Reporter* publishes the economic research results of the staff of the NEC and other specialized government agencies. There is a growing division of labor between the Central Bank and the National Economic Council in the collection and dissemination of economic information, and the *Statistical Reporter* has tended to absorb functions and responsibilities heretofore fulfilled by the *Annual Report* of the Central Bank. A useful department of the publication is "What's Going On in the Philippine Statistical Program," which reports on the statistical and economic research activities of government departments, bureaus, and independent agencies. The *Statistical Reporter* began publication in January 1957.

A second quarterly, the *Philippine Journal of Public Administration,* Institute of Public Administration, University of the Philippines, Manila, began publication in January 1957. Public administration is broadly conceived, and the *Journal* has become a major research aid for the economist and sociologist as well as for the political scientist. Particularly valuable are the bibliographic notes as well as a "News and Notes" section devoted to current developments in public administration and related problems.

A quarterly of considerable interest to economists is the *Philippine Statistician,* published by the Philippine Statistical Association beginning in 1952. The Association is active in improving Philippine statistical standards. Research of major significance is occasionally reported in the *Statistician.*

The quarterly *Economic Research Journal,* published by the Graduate School, University of the East, Manila, began publication in June 1954. Edited by Amando M. Dalisay, the *Journal* has published a number of useful studies. Unfortunately, the quality of contributions has been uneven, and in the absence of research results the *Journal* has been filled out with speeches and symposia by politicians and by articles that have already appeared elsewhere.

Philippine Social Sciences and Humanities Review, a quarterly published by the University of the Philippines, Diliman, Quezon City, began publication in 1929. The first postwar issue is vol. 14, no. 1, March 1949. It is a scholarly journal of high quality. Because of its scope, the number of contributions in economics are limited. Many articles are written by faculty members of the University of the Philippines. Occasionally, outstanding graduate dissertations are published in whole or in part.

Comment, a quarterly published by the Benipayo Press, Manila, began publication in October 1956. This journal is devoted to political and economic analysis as well as to literary criticism. High standards have been maintained, and most issues include one or more articles dealing with economic questions. *Comment* is particularly valuable to an understanding of Philippine nationalism.

Philippine Studies, a quarterly published by the Society of Jesus in the Philippine Islands, 2913 Herran Street, Manila, began publication in June 1953. It offers a broad range of contributions in the social sciences and the humanities, with infrequent economic contributions, though occasionally of high quality. An annual Philippine Bibliographical Survey (March issue) as well as an extensive book review section in each issue is of considerable value in keeping informed regarding books published in the Philippines.

Among other professional journals which have acceptable standards of scholarship and which include occasional economic contributions, the following should be consulted: *Silliman Review*, a quarterly published by Silliman University, Dumaguete, Negros Oriental, beginning in January 1953; *Journal of East Asiatic Studies*, a quarterly published by the University of Manila, 105 Alejandro VI, Sampaloc, Manila, beginning in October 1951; and *Philippine Sociological Review*, a quarterly published by the Philippine Sociological Society, University of the Philippines, Diliman, Quezon City, beginning in August 1953. Mention should be made of publications devoted to research performed by the faculty and graduate students of three of the larger private universities in Manila: *Unitas*, a quarterly published by the University of Santo Tomas, beginning in 1922 with its first postwar issue, vol. 21, no. 1, in January–March 1948; *Graduate and Faculty Studies*, an annual published by Centro Escolar University, beginning in 1951; and *Far Eastern University Faculty Journal*, a quarterly, beginning in 1957.

The student is also referred to two indexes to current Philippine periodicals. The *Index to Philippine Periodicals* is published quarterly by the University of the Philippines, Institute of Public Administration. It began publication in March 1956 and is available also in an annual cumulative issue. In addition, the *Silliman Journal* includes a quarterly periodical index. This index was initiated in the January–March 1956 issue and continued through 1956. It was not published in 1957, but it resumed in 1958 and has continued to the present time. At the end of 1959 twenty-four Philippine periodicals were being indexed.

Special mention should be made of the *American Chamber of Commerce Journal*. The *Journal*, a monthly, began publication in June 1921 and the first postwar issue was vol. 22, no. 1, December 1945. Thanks to the energy and discrimination of the editor, A. V. H. Hartendorp, the *Journal* is a valuable basic reference for postwar Philippine economic development. Significant legislative acts, executive orders, monetary regulations, and judicial decisions are accurately reported and frequently reproduced. Major speeches treating economic issues are reported in detail and frequently reproduced. Similarly, speeches of the President including the State of the Union and budgetary messages are reproduced. A considerable volume of statistical information is published. Although the *Journal's* editorials must inevitably represent a special interest—the American business community—the reporting of economic developments is comprehensive and accurate.

A recent periodical of potential value is *Vital Documents*, a monthly, beginning in September 1959. Major public documents are reproduced.

For further information on Philippine periodical literature, see Donn V. Hart and Quinton A. Eala, *An Annotated Guide to Current Philippine Periodicals,* Yale University Southeast Asia Studies, Bibliography Series, 1957. This publication lists some 312 periodicals under 73 different areas of interest.

A third broad category of economic sources consists of the economic and statistical publications of departments, bureaus, and agencies of the Philippine government. The single most valuable reference for the economist is the *Annual Report* of the Central Bank of the Philippines, Manila, which began publication in 1949. Reproduced as an appendix to the *Annual Report* are the texts of major economic policy measures including laws, executive orders, and administrative orders as well as administrative regulations issued by the Central Bank in executing its policy responsibilities. The *Annual Report* is concise, sophisticated, and informative. The format of the report has remained relatively stable over time, and the successive reports comprise a valuable chronology of postwar economic history. It should be remembered, however, that the Monetary Board and Governor Cuaderno were deeply involved in the major postwar economic controversies, and the *Annual Reports* reflect a partisan position with respect to many issues.

The Central Bank also publishes a quarterly *Statistical Bulletin* (vol. I, no. 1, March 1949) which includes more than one hundred principal statistical series in the areas of money and banking, capital market, foreign trade and payments, public finance, physical production, prices, employment, and wages. Beginning with 1956, the December number (4) of the *Statistical Bulletin* serves as the statistical appendix to the *Annual Report.* The Central Bank also publishes a monthly, *Economic Indicators,* a graphical survey of the Philippine economy, and a weekly, *Central Bank News Digest.* Publication of these two publications also began in 1949.

A reference of major importance is the *Official Gazette* of the Office of the President (Manila: Bureau of Printing). This semimonthly includes an executive diary and texts of laws approved by the President, of executive and administrative orders, and of Supreme Court decisions. The annual publication of the Office of the President, *Laws and Resolutions* (Manila: Bureau of Printing), should also be consulted. Publication commenced with vol. I, which included the texts of laws and resolutions approved during the congressional sessions of 1946.

Each house of the Philippine Congress publishes a record, *Congressional Record—House* and *Congressional Record—Senate.* Publication of the *Congressional Records* has been somewhat irregular and distribution haphazard. Complete files of these publications are impossible to find outside the Philippines. The *Records* are invaluable for texts of laws introduced and of laws passed by Congress and subsequently vetoed as well as for a transcript of congressional debates. Much frustration arises out of the fragmentary nature of the holdings of these important publications.

The annual reports of various executive departments and bureaus as well as independent agencies should be mentioned. The annual publication of the Bureau of Census and Statistics, *Foreign Trade of the Philippines,* is a detailed tabulation of foreign trade by country and commodity. An irregular statistical reference of great value is the Bureau of Census and Statistics, *Yearbook of Philippine Statistics.* Three volumes (1940, 1946, and 1957) have been published in this series. The *Annual Report of the Collector of Internal Revenue* provides detailed information on tax revenues, returns filed, returns taxable, and so forth. The annual *Budget* of the Budget Commission is a huge document of limited usefulness to the student. The *Annual Report of the Philippine National Bank* is a valuable reference, but distribution is limited, and only irregular issues are to be found in most reference libraries. Similarly, the annual reports of the Rehabilitation Finance Corporation and of its successor, the Development Bank of the Philippines, as well as those of the Agricultural Credit and Co-operative Financing Administration include valuable economic information but are difficult to obtain. These reports have been singled out for particular mention here, but all bureaus and departments of the Philippine government as well as independent agencies publish annual reports.

The student is also referred to a limited number of bibliographic guides to government publications. The National Economic Council, Office of Statistical Co-ordination and Standards, *Statistical Services of the Philippine Government* (Manila, 1957), provides detailed information on statistical sources as well as on publications. Another publication which should be consulted is University of the Philippines, Institute of Public Administration, *Union List of Serials of Government Agency Libraries of the Philippines* (Manila, 1955).

The annual *Economic Survey of Asia and the Far East* and the quarterly *Economic Bulletin of Asia and the Far East* published by the United Nations, Economic Commission for Asia and the Far East (ECAFE) should not be overlooked. Periodic surveys as well as special articles are to be found in these publications. The special studies and reports of ECAFE should also be consulted.

Adequate guidance to basic statistical references relevant to study of Philippine economic development and policy is provided by the footnotes to the tables included in the present book.

Law as a profession has always strongly attracted Filipinos, and a disproportionate share of the intellectual resources has been diverted to law.

The legal profession is highly competitive, and relatively high standards are maintained in law journals, legal texts, and reference works. The student of Philippine public policy problems is strongly advised to look into this type of reference work.

A basic reference is *Philippine Annotated Laws,* vols. 1–17 (Manila: The Lawyers' Co-operative Publishing Co., 1956). This is a compilation of the statute law of the Philippines containing all of the Philippine acts, Commonwealth acts, and Republic acts of a general and permanent nature, as well as the Philippine constitution and organic laws of the American colonial period.

A concise guide to the available legal materials is *An Annotated Philippine Legal Bibliography,* by Leticia Pacis-Nebrida and Avelino P. Tendero (Manila: University of the Philippines, Institute of Public Administration, 1954), mimeograph. This item provides guidance to "Acts and Resolutions" of Philippine legislatures beginning with the Philippine Commission (1902), "executive orders, administrative orders, proclamations, etc." of the Philippine executive, "court rules and decisions," and "regular reports and publications" as well as "general references, legal annotations and commentaries." This work is now becoming dated and should be supplemented by more recent bibliographies.

Among the law journals that should be consulted, the outstanding journal is the *Philippine Law Journal,* a bimonthly publication of the College of Law, University of the Philippines, which began publication in 1914. A second journal of high quality is the *Ateneo Law Journal,* quarterly publication of the College of Law, Ateneo de Manila, which began publication in 1951. Other legal journals include the *MLQ Law Quarterly,* published by the Manuel L. Quezon School of Law; the *Law Review,* quarterly publication of the Faculty of Law, University of Santo Tomas; and the *FEU Law Quarterly* of the Institute of Civil Law, Far Eastern University.

Finally, mention should be made of the various aids which can reduce the drudgery of research through files of newspapers. The *American Chamber of Commerce Journal,* especially the executive diary published under the heading "The Government," is of considerable value. Of comparable coverage, but less well edited, is *Commerce,* monthly publication of the Chamber of Commerce of the Philippines since 1928. A useful periodical is the weekly *Philippines Free Press,* a combination news-family magazine which began publication in 1908. The *Free Press* is particularly useful for following political controversy.

Valuable press summaries for economic research are the *Philippine Newsletter* published weekly by the Philippine Association, 507 Madison Avenue, New York, and the *Central Bank News Digest,* a weekly publication of the

Central Bank of the Philippines. The Philippine Association also publishes irregularly during the congressional session a series of *Special Reports* surveying economic legislation introduced in Congress.

The first five chapters of this study comprise an introduction to the more detailed analysis of public policy that follows. The introductory chapters are treated as a unit in the notes that follow.

For an introduction to Philippine society, the reader is referred to *Area Handbook on the Philippines,* vols. I–IV (Subcontractors Monograph HRAF-16, Chicago 5; New Haven, Conn.: Human Relations Area Files, 1956). The *Handbook,* prepared by the staff of the Philippine Studies Program, University of Chicago, is "designed to provide an understanding of the social, political, and economic organization" of the Philippines. While the *Handbook* is uneven and much of it pedestrian, the anthropological and sociological sections treating "The People," "Social Organization," and "Organized Religion" are outstanding. Each chapter of the *Handbook* is followed by a bibliography. The textbook prepared in the Department of Sociology, University of the Philippines, by Chester Hunt *et al., Sociology in the Philippine Setting* (Manila: Alemar's, 1954), and the symposium, "Social Factors in the Economic Development of the Philippines," *Philippine Sociological Review,* 7 (Jan.–April 1959), 2–65, should be consulted.

The nonanthropologist is impatient with the concentration of anthropological studies on the relatively primitive, spatially and economically isolated ethnic groups and the neglect of the less well-integrated politically and economically dominant "lowland Filipinos," who are providing the leadership in culture change and economic growth. This deficiency is slowly being reduced, and our knowledge of the urbanized, mobile Filipino is accumulating. Among the doctoral dissertations that should be consulted for insights into Philippine social organization and cultural change Edward A. Tiryakian, "The Evaluation of Occupations in an Underdeveloped Country: The Philippines," 1956, Sociology, Harvard; Carl H. Lande, "Politics in the Philippines," 1958, Political Science, Harvard; and Thomas R. McHale, "An Econecological Approach to Economic Development: The Philippines," 1959, Political Economy, Harvard, are valuable.[1] For insights into the rural society the dissertations of Agaton P. Pal, "A Philippine Barrio: A Study of Social Organization in Relation to Planned Culture Change," 1956, Rural Sociology, Cornell †; Frances L. Starner, "The Agrarian Impact on Philippine Politics," 1958, Political Science, California (Berkeley); and David R. Sturdevant, "Philippine Social Structure and Its Relation to Agrarian Unrest," 1958, History, Stanford, should be consulted together with the well-

[1] Those dissertations marked with (*) have been published either partially or wholly and can be identified in general bibliographies of Philippine reference materials. Dissertations marked with (†) are available on university microfilm.

known "Rivera-McMillan Reports"—Generoso F. Rivera and Robert T. Mc-Millan, *The Rural Philippines* (Manila: The Philippine Council for United States Aid, 1952), and *An Economic and Social Survey of Rural Households in Central Luzon* (Manila: The Philippine Council for United States Aid, 1954).

Understanding of postwar Philippine social change and development is facilitated by a number of useful historical surveys. An excellent brief survey of the period 1898–1951 is Garel A. Grunder and William Livezey, *The Philippines and the United States* (Norman, Okla.: University of Oklahoma Press, 1951). Of comparable scope is David Bernstein, *The Philippine Story* (New York: Farrar, Straus and Co., 1947). This volume is valuable for its account of the complex, confused transition to Philippine sovereignty in 1945–1946. Useful surveys dealing more specifically with the early postwar period include Shirley Jenkins, "The Philippines," in Lawrence K. Rosinger (ed.), *The State of Asia* (New York: Alfred Knopf, 1951), and Claude A. Buss, "The Philippines," in Lennox A. Mills (ed.), *The New World of Southeast Asia* (Minneapolis: University of Minnesota Press, 1949).

Essential to understanding of postwar Philippine economic development is the Bell Mission *Report to the President of the United States by the Economic Survey Mission to the Philippines* (Washington, D.C., 1950) and the accompanying *Technical Memoranda* (Washington, D.C., 1950). Predecessor to the Bell Mission report and of comparable scope is the *Report and Recommendations of the Joint Philippine-American Finance Commission* (80th Cong., 1st sess., House Doc. No. 390; Washington, D.C., 1947). Of book-length studies of the postwar Philippine economy, the most valuable is A. V. H. Hartendorp, *History of Industry and Trade of the Philippines* (Manila: American Chamber of Commerce of the Philippines, 1958). The Department of Commerce, *Investment in the Philippines* (Washington, D.C., 1955) is a detailed and informative handbook, but it is rapidly becoming dated. A recent handbook is Urbano A. Zafra, *1960 Philippine Economic Handbook* (Silver Springs, Md.: Westland Printing Co., 1960).

Recent dissertations of a more general nature dealing with the Philippine economy include William I. Abraham, "Problems of National Income Measurement in Underdeveloped Countries with Special Reference to the Philippines," 1954, Economics, Columbia °; Amado A. Castro, "The Philippines: A Study in Economic Dependence," 1954, Economics, Harvard; and Leo C. Stine, "The Economic Policies of the Commonwealth Government of the Philippine Islands," 1949, Economics, Illinois.

The major speeches of Philippine Presidents are important source materials, and fortunately these have been collected. See Republic of the Philippines, *Messages of the President*, vols. I–VIII (Manila: Bureau of Printing, 1935–1951). Manuel Roxas, *The Problems of Philippine Rehabilitation and*

Trade Relations (Manila: Bureau of Printing, 1947), contains a number of the major economic addresses of President Roxas. Similarly, Elpidio Quirino's *The Quirino Way* (Manila: Carmelo and Bauermann, 1955) and *The New Philippine Ideology* (Manila: Bureau of Printing, 1949) reproduce a number of economic policy addresses of President Quirino. For major economic policy speeches of Presidents Magsaysay and Garcia it will be necessary to consult current periodicals and newspapers.

Two of the principal antagonists in Philippine economic policy formulation have published collections of writings and speeches which are valuable to understanding the postwar issues. These are Miguel Cuaderno, *Guideposts to Economic Stability and Progress* (Manila: Central Bank of the Philippines, 1955), and the two volumes by Salvador Araneta, *Economic Re-examination* (Manila: Araneta Institute of Agriculture, 1953) and *Christian Democracy in the Philippines* (Malabon, Rizal: Araneta University Press, 1958).

For an understanding of the background of the political environment of economic policy, the best survey of Philippine political development is J. Ralston Hayden, *The Philippines: A Study in National Development* (New York: Macmillan Co., 1942). Of less importance, but useful, is Dapen Liang, *The Development of Philippine Political Parties* (Hong Kong: South China Morning Post, 1939).

Information regarding current political institutions and processes is rapidly accumulating. Particularly valuable are the studies of the University of the Philippines, Institute of Public Administration, including H. B. Jacobini and associates, *Governmental Services in the Philippines* (Manila, 1956), Edwin O. Stene and associates, *Public Administration in the Philippines* (Manila, 1956), John H. Romani and M. Ladd Thomas, *A Survey of Local Government in the Philippines* (Manila, 1954), John H. Romani, *The Office of the Philippine President* (Manila, 1954), and *The Philippine Presidency* (Manila, 1956), and Lloyd M. Short, *The Relationship of Local and National Governments in the Philippines* (Manila, 1955). The footnote references of the first three Institute of Public Administration reports cited above comprise a useful guide for the social scientist undertaking research into contemporary Philippine problems.

Another reference valuable for understanding political institutions and processes is Jorge R. Coquia, *The Philippine Presidential Election of 1953* (Manila: University Publishing Co., 1955). The best account of the 1951 elections is James J. Dalton, "Ins and Outs in the Philippines," *Far Eastern Survey*, 21 (July 30, 1952), 117–123. Lawrence Olson, "After Magsaysay, What?" *American Universities Field Staff Report*, Oct. 1957, and Albert Ravenholt, "The Peso Price of Politics," *ibid.*, May 1958, report on the presidential election of 1957. A recent study is Virginia F. Baterina, "A Study of

Money in Elections in the Philippines," *Philippine Social Sciences and Humanities Review*, 20 (March and June 1955), 39–86, 139–212.

Reliable and informative political reporting of contemporary Philippine developments is to be found in the quarterly *Pacific Affairs* and the monthly *Far Eastern Survey* published by the Institute of Pacific Relations. The irregular reports of the American University Field Staff should also be consulted.

The outstanding study of Philippine geography is Albert Kolb, *Die Philippinen* (Leipzig, 1942). Unfortunately this work is not available in translation. A standard geographical reference is Reginald G. Hainsworth and Raymond T. Moyer, *Agricultural Geography of the Philippine Islands* (Washington: U.S. Department of Agriculture, Office of Foreign Agricultural Relations, 1945). For further information on demographic characteristics of the Philippines, the student should consult Amos Hawley, *Papers on Demography and Public Administration*, rev. ed. (Manila: Institute of Public Administration, 1954). The definitive study of Philippine transportation is Robert O. Shreve and others, *An Economic Analysis of Philippine Domestic Transportation*, vols. I–VII (Menlo Park, Calif.: Stanford Research Institute, 1957).

Chapters VI through VIII treat related aspects of Philippine foreign economic policy—exchange rate, exchange and import control, and commercial policy. Two recent doctoral dissertations provide comprehensive coverage of this dominant policy area, Pedro C. Leaño, "The Postwar Balance of Payments Problem of the Philippine Republic," 1956, Economics, Chicago, and James A. Storer, "Foreign Trade Policies of the Philippine Republic," 1955, Economics, Harvard.

Controversy over the peso exchange rate has dominated all other political issues over the past decade, but economists have made a relatively minor contribution to analysis of this issue. The successive economic plans (see notes to Chapter XIV) provide insight into official analysis. *The Yulo Plan, 1950*, the *1957 Plan* and the *Three Year Plan, FY 1960–1962* are particularly useful. The controversial Schacht report contained in a letter from Dr. Hjalmar Schacht to Mr. Juan Pajo, chairman, Philippine National Bank (Manila, 1959), is republished in *Vital Documents*, 1 (Dec. 1959). Valuable studies include Sixto K. Roxas, *A Multiple Exchange Rate System for the Philippines*, a memorandum submitted to the Senate Committee on Banks, Corporations, and Franchises (Manila, 1957), mimeograph, and A. J. Jison, *The Philippine Situation and the Steps for an Orderly Decontrol of Foreign Exchange*, a memorandum submitted to the House Special Advisory Body on Decontrol (Manila, 1958), mimeograph. An informative, balanced appraisal of issues and problems raised in the controversy over exchange rate policy is contained in Amando M. Dalisay, "The Extremes of Monetary Proposals," *Economic*

Research Journal, 6 (June 1959), 32–39. Two studies which illustrate the problem of sorting out the ramifications of this policy issue are Lorenzo M. Colcol, "The Economics of Devaluation and What It Means to the Philippines," *Economic Research Journal,* 3 (June 1956), 9–17, and the pamphlet by a member of the Department of Economics, University of the Philippines, Anacleto Lacebal, *Why We Should Not Devalue the Peso* (Diliman, Quezon City: University of the Philippines, College of Business Administration, 1958). Still another contribution to the controversy over this policy is Salvador Araneta, *A Proposal for Orderly Adjustments of Exchange Rates* (Manila: Advocate Book Supply Co., 1953). An early study dealing with the issue is Konrad Bekker, and Charles Wolf, Jr., "The Philippine Balance of Payments," *Far Eastern Survey,* 19 (Feb. 22, 1950), 41–43. Finally, the reader is referred to Frank H. Golay, "The Emerging Alternative to Peso Devaluation," *Philippine Studies,* 4 (Sept. 1956), 373–390.

The problem of the relationship between exchange rate and exchange control policies and the supply of foreign exchange has been virtually ignored by economists. Analysis has been fragmentary and contributions on the professional level are, so far as I know, nonexistent.

The colonial commercial policy imposed upon the Philippines has been thoroughly analyzed or, more accurately, belabored. As it required fifteen years of self-rule for the Philippines to assert commercial policy autonomy, analysis of colonial commercial policy accounts for the major share of the postwar accumulation of references in this area. Standard works valuable both for analysis as well as for bibliographic information include Pedro E. Abelarde, *American Tariff Policy towards the Philippines, 1896–1946* (New York: King's Crown Press, 1947), Grayson Kirk, *Philippine Independence, Motives, Problems and Prospects* (New York: Farrar and Rinehart, 1936), and Shirley Jenkins, *American Economic Policy towards the Philippines* (Stanford: Stanford University Press, 1954).

Analyses of the postwar transition to a national commercial policy have accumulated slowly. A reference which reproduces a number of the documents involved in this important policy change is Philippine National Bank, Department of Economics, Research and Statistics, *The New Executive Agreements under the Bell Trade Act* (Trade Information series 1, no. 1; Manila, 1956). The *Annual Reports* of the Central Bank of the Philippines include a section on "Trade and Exchange Policies" which is useful in tracing the development of this policy. Information of a similar nature is available in the International Monetary Fund, *Annual Report on Exchange Restrictions,* which began publication in 1950. Valuable for understanding the Philippine position on revision of the 1946 Trade Agreement with the United States is the discussion and appendixes in the *Fourth Annual Report, 1952* of the Central Bank of the Philippines. Basic information necessary to analysis of the revised tariff code is contained in the *Annual Reports of the Tariff Commission to the Congress of the Philippines*. The first *Report* was made in 1953.

Montaño A. Tejam, chairman of the Tariff Commission and member of the United States–Philippine Trade Agreement Revision Mission, has published a number of articles on commercial policy including "The Story of the 1954 Philippine Economic Mission to the United States," *Economic Research Journal*, 2 (Dec. 1955), 138–148, "Alternative Tariff Policies for the Philippines and the Bell Trade Agreement," *ibid.*, 1 (Sept. 1954), 57–66, and "Implications of the New Tariff Code," *ibid.*, 4 (Dec. 1957), 125–128. The reader is also referred to Frank H. Golay, "Economic Consequences of the Philippine Trade Act," *Pacific Affairs*, 28 (March 1955), 53–70, and *The Revised United States–Philippine Trade Agreement of 1955* (Cornell Southeast Asia Program Data Paper No. 23; Ithaca, N.Y., 1956).

In the area of monetary policy the basic references are, of course, the *Annual Reports* of the Central Bank of the Philippines. By their nature the *Reports* fail to provide the continuity and the perspective necessary to analysis of postwar monetary policy in the large. This has been remedied by the highly competent and perceptive work by the Central Bank Survey Commission, *Final Report and Recommendations (Minority Report)*, (Manila, 1956). Unfortunately the distribution of this report, which was critical of postwar monetary policy, was quite limited.

Governor Cuaderno has ably defended postwar monetary policy and his previously mentioned volume, *Guideposts to Economic Stability and Progress*, should be consulted. In addition, his *Monetary and Fiscal Policies in the Philippines* (Manila: Philippine Council, Institute of Pacific Relations, 1954), prepared for the 12th Conference of the Institute of Public Relations, Kyoto, 1954, is a useful survey.

For monetary policy during the foreign exchange crisis of the last half of 1957 and early 1958, see the critical analysis by Sixto K. Roxas, *Austerity: Why, How Much, and Where* (Philippine National Bank, Economic Items of Vital Interest; Manila, 1958). For another interpretation see Miguel Cuaderno, "Austerity as an Instrument of National Policy," *Economic Research Journal*, 4 (March 1958), 163–167. A recent article of considerable value is Armando Maglague, "Some Aspects of the Role of Monetary Policy in the Philippines," *Statistical Reporter*, 2 (Oct. 1958), 1–7.

In the area of fiscal policy a recent doctoral dissertation is Agustin Kintanar, "An Analysis of the Effects of Certain Modifications in the Tax Structure on the Rate of Economic Development in the Philippines," 1960, Economics, Yale. A valuable reference is Odell Waldby, *Philippine Public Fiscal Administration* (Manila: Institute of Public Administration, 1954). A discriminating selection of articles and documents are collected in this volume, including

Louis E. Shere, "A Tax Program for the Philippines," *National Tax Journal,*
4 (June 1951), 97–115, and summaries of the studies by Melville Monk and
Orville J. McDiarmid, *The Taxation of Real Property in the Philippines*
(Manila: U.S. Foreign Operations Administration, 1953), and Ray E. Davis,
Special Report on Income Tax Collection of the Bureau of Internal Revenue
(Manila: U.S. Mutual Security Administration, 1953). An interesting attempt to identify aggregate government expenditures at all levels and to
reclassify such expenditures into categories meaningful to analysis of eco-
nomic development as Amando M. Dalisay, Angel Q. Yoingco, and Aniceto
Z. Jalbuena, "The Level of Government Spending in the Philippines, 1947–
1957," *Economic Research Journal,* 6 (Dec. 1959), 128–151.

A number of works are available which survey the extent of Philippine
industrialization. An initial survey of manufactures was made in 1956 and
is summarized in National Economic Council, *1956 Annual Survey of Manufacture,* vol. I, series 1 and 2 (Manila: Bureau of Printing, 1958). A survey
that should be consulted is *Industrial Philippines: A Survey of Ten Philippine
Industries* (Manila: Philippine Council for United States Aid, 1953). A more
recent survey is UNESCO National Commission of the Philippines and the
NEC, *A Survey of the Social Implications of Small Scale Industry in the
Philippines* (Manila: National Economic Council, 1959). Still another survey
useful for its summary tables and analysis is Republic of the Philippines, Department of Labor, *Directory of Key Establishments in the Philippines in
Selected Non-agricultural Industries Employing Five or More Workers during 1955* (Manila, 1956).

A concise survey of policy with respect to public corporations is presented
in Leo C. Reithmayer, "Government Corporations," in Edwin O. Stene, and
associates, *Public Administration in the Philippines* (Manila: Institute of
Public Administration, 1956).

For details of various policies and programs to promote industrialization
by private enterprise, see R. N. Shreve, and others, *Industrial Research and
Development in the Philippines* (Manila: National Economic Council,
1956), and Alden Cutshall, "Industrial Program in the Philippines," *Journal
of Geography,* 55 (March 1956), 130–156. For information on Philippine
foreign investment policy, see Harry J. Robinson, *Stimulating Foreign Investment in the Republic of the Philippines* (Menlo Park, Calif.: Stanford
Research Institute, 1955).

As might be expected, the accumulation of research into Philippine agrarian policies and problems is most substantial. A valuable reference is Horst
von Oppenfeld *et al., Farm Management, Land Use, and Tenancy in the
Philippines* (Central Experiment Station Bulletin 1; College, Laguna: University of the Philippines, College of Agriculture, 1957). The findings of this study
derived from a survey of more than 4,000 Philippine farms provide a wel-
come change from the accumulation of subjective and frequently emotional

studies of Philippine rural economy and society. Recent doctoral dissertations include David O. Wurfel, "The Bell Report and After: A Study of the Political Problems of Social Reform Stimulated by Foreign Aid," 1960, Political Science, Cornell †, and Nathaniel B. Tablante, "An Appraisal of Agricultural Problems and Policies in the Philippines," 1956, Agricultural Economics, Purdue.*† Two recent studies by important participants in agricultural policy making are Amando M. Dalisay, *Development of Economic Policy in Philippine Agriculture* (Manila: Phoenix Publishing House, 1959), and Guillermo S. Santos, *The Law on Agricultural Tenancy in the Philippines* (Manila: Phoenix Press, 1957). Still another study by a public administrator actively involved in agricultural programs is Francisco Ortigas, Jr., *Planting Rice Is Never Fun* (Manila: Alemar's, 1953).

For brief, informative surveys, see Malcolm A. Parsons and George A. Peek, Jr., "Land Reform," in H. B. Jacobini and associates, *Governmental Services in the Philippines* (Manila: Institute of Public Administration, 1956), and Jose F. Sionil, "The Philippine Agrarian Problem," *Comment*, 9 (3rd quarter 1959), 85–143. A useful reference is *Public Land Laws of the Philippines*, compiled by the Central Book Supply, Inc.

Official reports and surveys accumulated rapidly in the period following the visit of the Bell Mission. These include *Report of the Special Committee on Land Settlement and Title Issuance and Clearance* (Manila: Office of Economic Co-ordination, 1951), *Report and Recommendations of the Advisory Committee on Landed Estates Problems* (Manila: Offiice of Economic Co-ordination, 1951), *Philippine Land Tenure Reform, Analysis and Recommendations* (Manila: U.S. Mutual Security Administration, 1952), *The Philippine Agricultural Land Tenure Study* (Manila: Foreign Operations Administration, 1954), and James P. Emerson, *Land Reform Progress in the Philippines, 1951–1955* (Manila: International Co-operation Administration, 1956).

Recent articles include Amando M. Dalisay and Aniceto L. Jalbuena, "The Status of Agricultural Financing in the Philippines," *Economic Research Journal*, 4 (Sept. 1957), 58–70, and Frank H. Golay, "Economic Aspects of Philippine Agrarian Reform," *Philippine Sociological Review*, 4 (Jan. 1956), 20–32.

Although foreign aid and reparations questions have been important issues, analytical studies are scarce in this field. Jose S. Alejandrino, "Foreign Assistance Program in the Philippines," *Statistical Reporter*, 3 (Jan. 1959), 1–16, surveys the various programs including ECOSOC, UNTA, and the Colombo Plan. A second article which should be consulted is Timotea Diaz-Suelto, "Japanese Reparations Payments and the Growth of Philippine Industries," *Economic Research Journal*, 6 (June 1959), 40–47.

Information about the economic manifestations of nationalism has accumulated rapidly in the postwar period. Recent doctoral dissertations include

George Weightman, "The Philippine Chinese: A Cultural Study of a Marginal Trading Community," 1960, Sociology, Cornell †; Margaret W. Horsley, "Sangley: The Formation of Anti-Chinese Feeling in the Philippines— A Cultural Study of the Stereotypes of Prejudice," 1950, Sociology, Columbia; and Remigio E. Agpalo, "The Political Process and the Nationalization of the Retail Trade in the Philippines," 1958, Political Science, Indiana.

The nationalist movement in recent years has been dominated by Senator Claro M. Recto, whose position is defined in *A Realistic Economic Policy for the Philippines,* a speech delivered at the Philippine Columbian Association on Sept. 26, 1956 (Manila, 1956), and in *My Crusade* (Manila: P. C. Calica and Carog, 1955). Other useful works dealing with the nature of Philippine nationalism include Jose P. Laurel, *Educational Orientation for Filipinos* (Manila, 1955); Jose A. Lansang, "Nationalism and Our Social and Economic State," *Comment,* 3 (2nd quarter 1957), 15–24; Benito Legarda, Sixto K. Roxas, Salvador Araneta, Amado Castro, and Horacio Lava, "Forum on Economic Nationalism," *Comment,* 6 (2nd quarter, 1958), 3–55; Francis A. Starner, "The Problems of Philippine Nationalism," *Philippine Social Sciences and Humanities Review,* 22 (Sept. 1957), 259–298, and Frank H. Golay, "Commercial Policy and Economic Nationalism," *Quarterly Journal of Economics,* 72 (Nov. 1948), 574–587.

Useful references include Republic of the Philippines, Department of Justice, Anti-Dummy Board, *Handbook on Philippine Nationalization Laws,* 2nd ed. (Manila, 1956), Vicente Espiña, *Immigration and Alien Registration Laws of the Philippines* (Manila: Educational Book Store, 1956), and Republic of the Philippines, Industrial Development Center, *Doing Business in the Philippines,* a résumé of Philippine laws and regulations governing the establishment and operation of a business enterprise revised 1959 (Manila, 1959).

A brief, informative survey of the evolution of economic planning institutions and policy in the Philippines is Amos H. Hawley, Leonardo C. Mariano, and H. B. Jacobini, "National Planning Administration," in Edwin O. Stene and associates, *Public Administration in the Philippines* (Manila: Institute of Public Administration, 1956), 263–288. A major addition to the official planning documents identified in Chapter XV is Benjamin Higgins, *Report to the Government of the Philippines* (New York: U.N. Technical Assistance Administration, 1957). Additional references include: Walter Krause, "Planning for Economic Development," *Philippine Statistician,* 4 (March 1957), 3–22, and Report of Task Committee "A" of the Research Committee, Philippine Statistical Association, "An Inquiry into the Statistics on the National Income of the Philippines," *ibid.,* 6 (Sept. 1957), 129–158.

Basic sources of information are the 53 reports prepared by the Republic of the Philippines, Government Survey and Reorganization Commission.

Particularly useful for understanding Philippine economic planning are the two reports of the Government Survey and Reorganization Commission, *Report on Economic Planning* (Manila: Bureau of Printing, 1955), and *Report on the Presidency* (Manila: Bureau of Printing, 1955). For further information see Louis J. Kroeger, *Final Report on Reorganization of the Philippine Government* (Counterpart Project No. 799 of the NEC and the U.S. Operations Mission to the Philippines; Manila: Bureau of Printing, 1956), and Quirino E. Austria, "The Reorganization Plans of 1955–56," *Philippine Social Sciences and Humanities Review*, 22, 215–257.

Economic studies of Philippine price policies are rare, and information must be pulled together from fragmentary sources. Hartendorp's *History* has an informative chapter surveying consumer price control policies. For a bleak report on the activities of government corporations with price functions, see Malcolm B. Parsons, "Agriculture," in H. B. Jacobini and associates, *Governmental Services in the Philippines* (Manila: Institute of Public Administration, 1956), pp. 290–341.

Research into social welfare policies is facilitated by consultation of various legal works including Emilio Y. Hilado and Juan M. Hagad, *Philippine Labor and Social Legislation*, rev. ed., 1957–1958 (Manila: Philaw Publishing Co., 1958); Antonio M. Castro, *Labor and Social Legislation, Commentaries and Jurisprudence* (Manila: Modern Book Co., 1957); Republic of the Philippines, Department of Labor, *Compilation of Effective Labor Legislation in the Philippines*, a joint project of the U.S. International Cooperation Administration and the Department of Labor (Manila, 1958); Vicente J. Francisco, *The Law Governing Labor Disputes in the Philippines* (Manila: East Publishing Co., 1956); and Leon S. del Rosario, *Agricultural Tenancy Act of the Philippines, Republic Act No. 1199*, with comments and annotations (Manila: Domerte Book Supply Co., 1956).

Useful studies of particular aspects of welfare legislation include recent doctoral dissertations by Jose V. Abueva, "Formulation of the Philippine Community Development Program," 1959, Political Science, Michigan †; Buenaventura M. Villanueva, "A Study of the Competence of the Barrio People to conduct Barrio Government," 1959, Political Science, Southern California. See also David O. Wurfel, "Philippine Agrarian Reform under Magsaysay," *Far Eastern Survey*, 27 (Jan. and Feb. 1958), 7–15, 23–30; Arturo Tanco, Jr., "Our Social Security Act," *Philippine Studies*, 4 (Dec. 1956), 521–534; Buenaventura M. Villanueva, "The Community Development Program of the Philippine Government," *Philippine Journal of Public Administration*, 1 (April 1957), 144–153; and Jose V. Abueva and Buenaventura M. Villaneuva, *Survey Report on the Operation of the Philippine Community Development Program as Administered by the Presidential Assistant on Community Development* (Manila, 1957).

Index